Applied consumer behaviour

Applied consumer behaviour

Martin J. Evans

> Bristol Business School, University of the
> West of England, UK

Luiz Moutinho

> Glasgow Business School, University of
> Glasgow, UK

W. Fred Van Raaij

> Erasmus University, Rotterdam, The Netherlands

ADDISON-WESLEY PUBLISHING COMPANY
Harlow, England • Reading, Massachusetts • Menlo Park, California
New York • Don Mills, Ontario • Amsterdam • Bonn • Sydney • Singapore
Tokyo • Madrid • San Juan • Milan • Mexico City • Seoul • Taipei

Many of the designations used by manufacturers and sellers to distinguish their products are claimed as trademarks. Addison-Wesley has made every attempt to supply trademark information about manufacturers and their products mentioned in this book. A list of the trademark designations and their owners appears on page xviii.

Cover designed by TGC Ltd, London
and printed by The Riverside Printing Co. (Reading) Ltd
Typeset by Pantek Arts, Maidstone, Kent
Printed in Great Britain by TJ Press (Padstow), Cornwall

First printed 1996

ISBN 0–201–56501–3

British Library Cataloguing-in-Publishing Data
A catalogue record for this book is available from the British Library.

Library of Congress Cataloging-in-Publication Data applied for

To my father and Anne *Martin J. Evans*
To my god-daughter, Joana *Luiz Moutinho*
To my wife Gerrie and my children Mark, Bart, Erik and Estia *W. Fred Van Raaij*

Foreword

The analysis of consumer behaviour often takes place at a very high level of abstraction. Of course, the theoretical and conceptual analysis of consumption is central to understanding not only marketing management but also our place as consumers in a complex economic system, and long may it continue. But it is often not what students of marketing, business and society are initially looking for.

Their primary objectives are usually for practical application, sooner rather than later, of what is known, not for speculation about the nature of the system itself. *Applied Consumer Behaviour* by Martin Evans, Luiz Moutinho and Fred Van Raaij is therefore to be welcomed as a manual which bridges the gap between the academic world of theory and the practical world of business.

But the intention to fill this gap is never enough. The self-image of many business academics includes the assumption that what they are doing is automatically of interest and value to the business community. The reality may be different: we hear little of the *Frankfurt Business Review* or the *Tokyo Business School*, but we are well aware of Germany and Japan as economic giants.

The intention must be matched by closeness to managers, gained inter alia through consultancy and post-experience teaching, and based for sure on an intelligent awareness of the needs of the companies, and thus of today's students who will run those companies tomorrow. Such experience and awareness should culminate in an ability to write clearly for these readers, to communicate effectively with them as future managers and to integrate theory and practice in order to produce relevance.

The authors of this book have more than adequately achieved this, and I recommend *Applied Consumer Behaviour* to everyone interested in the future of consumer-oriented marketing.

Professor Gordon Foxall
The University of Birmingham

Preface

Although this text is intended to be a mainstream text on consumer behaviour, its structure does not follow the usual one found in many such texts. Most consumer behaviour books tend to analyse discrete dimensions of behaviour via distinct chapters on 'social class', 'family', 'attitude', and so on. Our approach is deliberately different and is based on the intention to provide a more applied treatment of these areas. Throughout, examples are provided showing how the various points of theory can be applied, via case studies, problems, illustrations of marketing activity and 'clippings' from the marketing press. Such application is drawn mostly from experience throughout Europe.

In the first chapter we set the scene for consumer behaviour very much in a marketing context, in which the basis of customer orientation is laid together with marketing's response in the form of the marketing mix. We also discuss wider issues concerning consumer behaviour, issues arising from changes in the marketing environment, to demonstrate the importance of a wider marketing context for the study and application of consumer behaviour.

From this point the structure continues to follow the marketing paradigm. That is, because marketing is basically concerned with the satisfaction of customer needs, wants, goals and values in order to achieve the goals of the organization, our starting point (after the scene-setting first chapter) in analysing consumer behaviour focuses on needs, wants and values, based on motivation theory from psychology.

In Part 2, consumer response to marketing actions and innovation is discussed, including consumer information processing. We analyse *how* consumers respond to marketing actions. Further behavioural concepts are drawn, again mostly from psychology, to show how consumers 'attend to' and 'perceive' marketing offerings, how they develop 'attitudes' toward them and how they can reassure themselves that they have responded appropriately (in their terms). Along with this coverage of consumers' response to marketing offerings we delve into the area of their response to 'new' and 'repeat' purchasing and discuss consumers' decision-making processes.

In Part 3 we concentrate on analysing and researching markets by showing, initially, that marketing can rarely be all things to all people. Consumers may have similar need and value structures but there will be different needs to the fore at different times amongst different groups of consumers. This major premise of marketing is that there are different market segments that the organization may (or may not) choose to target with distinct marketing mixes. Our coverage of segmentation, targeting and positioning is intended to be fairly extensive and incorporates many behavioural components (such as social stratification, family, lifestyle and self-concept) in this applied manner that are all too often treated as discrete topics not always related to their marketing significance.

Specifically we look at a variety of behavioural topics within this segmentation theme, ranging from the demographic 'class' and 'family' to the psychographic 'lifestyle' and 'self-concept' theory. So, rather than analysing discrete concepts from social psychology or psychology, our approach is to draw from these and to apply what is relevant within a marketing context. More recent approaches to understanding consumer behaviour based on databases and geodemographics are also analysed here.

How to research markets comes next. The techniques for researching many of the aspects discussed in the preceding chapters are provided here: motivation research, attitude research, segmentation and positioning research, for example, as applications of a variety of consumer research approaches which are also provided.

Once the chosen segments have been selected, marketing mixes are created and targeted on these segments. Part 4 of the book examines marketing-mix implications of consumer behaviour: product, pricing, distribution and marketing-communication strategy. We also provide a chapter looking ahead and suggesting some future developments in consumer behaviour.

Throughout we provide European examples of marketing applications of the concepts and approaches discussed and this is further enhanced by short case studies, marketing problems and clippings from the marketing press. These, apart from being a manifestation of our 'applied' and practical approach to consumer behaviour, are also helpful to student and instructor in the senses of:

■ providing a short cut to (but not total substitute for) material found in the marketing press and in other application vehicles,
■ providing seminar/small group exercises and cases,
■ providing course work assignment topics and exercises.

The book has been devised for the semester system which is becoming the norm in many institutions of higher education.

Semesters are having the effect, in many cases, of compressing what previously might have been covered over three terms into 15 weeks. There is also evidence that students, instructors and employers are looking for greater levels of applied theory and practical coverage in courses. Our approach addresses these issues. We provide 13 chapters and it is typical in a 15-week semester for there to be 13 teaching weeks, with the last two weeks of the semester being devoted to personal student revision and examinations.

Seminars, tutorials and course assignments can be built around the clippings from the marketing press, cases and problems in consumer behaviour which are provided at the end of each Part of the book. In many instances these also extend our text-based coverage of the topics concerned.

A possible programme could be as follows:

	Chapter	Seminar work from Clippings, Cases and Exercises
Week 1	1	UK 1994: to have and to have not
Week 2	2	Needs, features, benefits
Week 3	3	Application of motivation theories
Week 4	4	Consumer response to marketing
Week 5	5	Diffusion–adoption case
Week 6	6	Hemispheral lateralization
Week 7	7	Fear of failure
Week 8	8	PRIME Magazine
Week 9	9	Generation X
Week 10	10	Brand switching
Week 11	11	Has the DM medium finally come of age
Week 12	12	Benetton drops its shock tactics
Week 13	13	Targeting the Euro-consumer
Week 14	Revision	
Week 15	Examination	

Two pieces of course work could be set, such as:

(1) Cognitive Dissonance for (say) week 6, and
(2) Self-Concept Case for (say) week 10.

This would leave the following to be used on a rotational basis with the above, or, of course, instead of some of the above:

Actor Slates Advertising

The Deconstruction Industry

Proxemics and Other Behaviours

On a personal note, the authors wish to thank J. P. Peter and J. C. Olson for their work in *Consumer Behaviour: Marketing Strategy Perspectives* (1987. Homewood, IL: Irwin) which provided us with the structure for Part 4.

Martin J. Evans
Luiz Moutinho
W. Fred Van Raaij
November 1995

Contents

Part 4 Consumer behaviour and the marketing mix   247

9 Product strategy and consumer behaviour   249

10 Pricing strategy and consumer behaviour   269

11 Distribution strategy and consumer behaviour   289

Trademark notices

7-Up is a trademark of 7 Up International
ACORN is a registered servicemark of CACI Ltd
Araldite is a trademark of CIBA (A R L) Ltd
Ariel, Ariel Ultra, Liquid Tide, Head and Shoulders, Wash & Go and Crest are trademarks of Procter & Gamble
Barclay's Connect is a trademark of Barclays Bank plc
Beck's Beer is a trademark of Brauerei Beck & Co.
Beefeater Gin is a trademark of James Burrough
BMW 5 Series is a trademark of BMW
Bud Light, Budweiser and Budvar are trademarks of Anheuser-Busch
C5 is a trademark of Sir Clive Sinclair, Co.
Calvin Klein is a trademark of Calvin Klein
Canada Dry is a trademark of Canada Dry Int.
Canon is a trademark of Consolidated Micrographics
Chanel is a trademark of Chanel
Charlie is a trademark of Revlon
Close Up is a trademark of Elida Gibbs Ltd
Coca-Cola is a registered trademark and Diet Coke, Classic Coke and Cherry Coke are trademarks of The Coca-Cola Company
Colgate is a trademark of Colgate Palmolive
Corona Extra and Corona Light are trademarks of Britvic Corona Ltd
Crunchie is a trademark of Cadbury
dBase is a trademark of Borland International Inc.
Del Monte is a trademark of Del Monte Foods
Dunhill is a trademark of Alfred Dunhill Ltd
Duracell is a trademark of Duracell Ltd
Fiat Tempra is a trademark of Fiat Auto Ltd
Gola is a trademark of Gola Sports Ltd
Gold Blend, Nescafé, Smarties and Lean Cuisine are trademarks of Nestlé
Golden Wonder is a trademark of Dalgety Spillers Foods
Haagen Dazs is a trademark of Haagen Dazs (UK) Ltd
Heineken is a trademark of Whitbread
Jaguar is a trademark of Jaguar plc
Johnson's Baby Shampoo is a trademark of Johnson & Johnson
Kaliber is a trademark of Guinness
Kellog is a trademark of The Kellog Co
Kleenex is a trademark of Kimberly Clark Ltd
Landrover and Rover are trademarks of Rover Group
Lee is a trademark of Lee Apparel (UK) Ltd
Levi 501 is a trademark of Levi Strauss (UK) Ltd
Lucozade, Ribena, Aquafresh and Macleans are trademarks of SmithKline Beecham
Mars, Mars Hazelnut and Mars Ice Cream are trademarks of Mars Ltd
Marvel Light is a trademark of Cadbury Foods Ltd
Maxwell House is a trademark of Kraft General Foods
McDonalds is a trademark of McDonald Corporation
Miller High Life and Miller Light are trademarks of Miller Brewing Co.
Newcastle Brown is a trademark of Scottish & Newcastle Breweries
Nissan 300ZX is a trademark of Nissan Motor Co.
Opel is a trademark of General Motors

Pepsi is a registered trademark of Pepsico Inc.
Pernod is a trademark of Pernod
Persil, Lux, Sunlight and Radion are trademarks of Lever Bros
Philishave is a trademark of Philips
Pringle is a trademark of Pringle of Scotland Ltd
Quaker Oats is a trademark of Quaker Oats Ltd
Ray Ban is a trademark of Ray Ban (US)
Ritz [crackers] is a trademark of Jacobs
Sainsbury is a trademark of J S Sainsbury
Seiko is a trademark of John Hornby Skewes Ltd
Skoda is a trademark of Skoda (Great Britain) Ltd
SR is a trademark of Elida Gibbs
Travelodge is a trademark of Forte Group
Twingo and Zoom are trademarks of Renault, SA
Ultra Brite is a trademark of Colgate Palmolive
Vauxhall, Chevette and Astra are trademarks of Vauxhall Motors Ltd
Volkswagen is a trademark of Volkswagen A G
Volvo is a trademark of Volvo A B
Walkman is a trademark of Sony
WeightWatchers is a trademark of Heinz
WordPerfect is a trademark of WordPerfect Corp.
Wrangler's Blue Bell Apparel is a trademark of Wrangler Inc.

The following trademarks are used on the cover with permission:

Club Med is a trademark of Club Mediterranee
Heinz Baked Beans is a trademark of H J Heinz
Levis Batwing Logo is a trademark of Levi Strauss & Co
(trademark reproduced with kind permission of Levi Strauss (UK) Ltd)

Part 1

Identifying and anticipating consumer needs and wants

Consumer behaviour in a marketing environment

Chapter objectives

(1) To place consumer behaviour in a marketing context.
(2) To introduce many aspects of consumer behaviour and marketing in a simple case study.
(3) To introduce a wide range of aspects of the environment in which consumers behave, which marketing should recognize and to which marketing should respond.

1.1   Introduction

In this first chapter the basics of marketing are outlined and the nature and scope of theory, research and application of consumer behaviour is reviewed. We overview the marketing process and demonstrate the position and implications of consumer behaviour within this. The nature of how consumers view products (as providing benefits rather than merely features) is emphasized. Furthermore, the wider marketing environment is discussed because we believe it is important to broaden horizons of perception and look at all sorts of events and trends which might potentially affect consumer and therefore marketing behaviour, as well as to use and apply specific behavioural theories and concepts within a consumer behaviour context. The latter is provided in some of the subsequent chapters.

First, a definition or two. Essentially, marketing is concerned with understanding the needs and requirements of consumers, those who are likely to buy products and services, and providing them with what they need and want in a way that is profitable to the marketer, and at the same time satisfying to the purchaser. To state this more formally, The Chartered Institute of Marketing in the UK defines marketing in this way: 'Marketing is the management process that identifies, anticipates and supplies customer requirements efficiently and profitably.'[1]

Essentially marketing management is concerned with identifying, anticipating and supplying the requirements of consumers and this is the means to the end of achieving the organization's goals. It is a matching exercise: what the market wants matched with what the organization can provide. Note that markets are people; potential and actual customers.

An example will help with the application of this to practice and will also introduce some of the main aspects of marketing and consumer behaviour that the rest of the book covers in greater detail. The example comes from the cosmetics market.

Glamco Ltd

Glamco Ltd is a small manufacturer of specialist cosmetics and toiletries. Recently the company decided that a new product had to be introduced because in recent times no new product line had been added and profits were declining.

The managing director, Samantha Love, contacted her pharmacist, Hugh Pratt, who informed her of the new toothpaste he was working on. He also explained that the clinical tests of the product suggested that it cleaned teeth better than the other brands on the market.

Based on these tests it was decided that this product was what was needed. The company then planned the product launch. They decided on the name 'Sparkles' and a pack design featuring smiling white teeth on a buttercup-yellow background. Sparkles was put into those specialist retail outlets, health and beauty shops and chemists, that Glamco used for their other specialist products.

The final retail price was recommended at about 70% higher than brands like Crest and Colgate because of the up-market positioning of Sparkles, but also because the relatively small company could only manage low levels of production. National commercial TV was used to advertise Sparkles.

However, eight months after the launch it was clear that sales had not reached the minimum targets that were set. Ms Love was naturally concerned about this. Therefore she commissioned some market research to find out what had gone wrong. A quota sample of 250 consumers, being a reasonable representation of the population as a whole in terms of demographic characteristics, were interviewed and the main results are summed up by these quotes:

> 'I don't think I've seen Sparkles at the supermarkets I go to.'
> 'I'm currently using SR. It tastes good and Sparkles doesn't.'
> 'I'm not going to pay those prices for a toothpaste, it can't be that much better than Crest and Colgate.'
> 'Sparkles is for older people. I prefer Ultrabrite.'

If you think about what went wrong here, you might well agree with some of the quotes.

Generally you wouldn't pay over the odds for yet another toothpaste that does not appear to be much different from existing brands.

However, there is more to this example than first meets the eye! First, the company should not necessarily conclude that falling profits were a result of no new product launch. Modifications, deletions or repositioning of existing product lines may well be a solution to the profit problem.

Also, there is clearly a communications barrier within Glamco. It appears to come as a surprise that their own pharmacist has been developing a toothpaste. The fact that the product performed well in clinical tests is not sufficient to declare that it will be what the market requires. This is a classic example of a product as opposed to a market orientation!

The use of market research, then, has been a case of revealing the problems 'after the event' of the launch rather than discovering, during the development stage, whether there are opportunities in the market along the lines of the proposed product. Some of the more obvious errors such as taste could certainly have been avoided, if these dimensions had been checked out prior to the launch of Sparkles.

The components of the marketing mix, the four P's (product, price, place and promotion) are described in the example and there are potential problems with all of them here. Specifically, the *product* is supposedly one aimed at more up-market segments, and appears to have some exclusivity and specialist properties. However, it is given a somewhat glib name in 'Sparkles' and, in being called a toothpaste, doesn't convince people in the marketplace that it is something different from the mainline brands.

In technical terms, the product is a superior cleanser of teeth. This is not an advertising copy headline, but it is scientifically true. In this sense, it might be worth positioning the product quite away from toothpastes, more towards the cosmetics end of the toiletries–cosmetics continuum. There are, after all, toothpowders and tooth polishes that command premium prices and claim superior cleansing properties compared with the basic toothpaste brands.

This last paragraph suggests that people might be less critical of the higher *price* if the product was differently positioned in the market. But other elements of the marketing mix (distribution, promotion) would have to be changed as well. Even if changed, is there really a market for such a product in the first place? Figure 1.1 shows that a way of marketing the product might have been to disassociate it from the toothpaste market altogether. After all, the main benefits were clean teeth, not fresh breath (Figure 1.2) or the prevention of tooth decay.

Sparkles is *distributed* ('place') in a rather exclusive way. This might fit with an up-market product sufficiently differentiated from mainstream toothpastes, and with low production volumes and a high price.

However, it is *promoted* in a 'mass' way, via networked television. The up-market intentions are rather weakened by the 'pop' name Sparkles. Also, the pack, in yellow, is a problem. Pepsodent, another toothpaste brand, was advertised some years ago with a television jingle that included the words 'you'll wonder where the yellow went, when you brush your teeth with Pepsodent'. Although a positive point was being made, even the mention of yellow in the context of teeth creates a negative association between the brand and yellow teeth.

Figure 1.1 'Sparkles' might not be toothpaste. © Innovations (Mail Order) Ltd.

Marketing concept

The brief review of this example draws attention to some of the main dimensions of marketing and consumer behaviour.

The marketing concept is introduced as being the fundamental 'market' or 'consumer' orientation as opposed to 'product' or 'production' orientation. The role of marketing research is also clear in this respect. One obvious way of summarizing the marketing concept is to think in terms of a customer orientation that leads to 'making what we can sell, rather than selling what we can make'. Another aspect of this goes a little further and probes what it is that people do buy. A Revlon cosmetics executive is reported as saying: 'In the factory we make soap; in the market we sell hope.'

The 'branding' of products is an important marketing instrument. In the factory physical products are produced. In the store consumers buy brands such as Revlon or Anais-Anais and it is the branding that guarantees a certain quality and conveys an image. L'Air du Temps is a Nina Ricci brand of perfume for the young adolescent girl expressing her femininity. In the advertising, David Hamilton's misty photography creates an image of veils as a sign of virginity such that L'Air du Temps is clearly about initiation to femininity. Generalizing, brands

Figure 1.2 Toothpaste 'benefits'. © Elida Gibbs, UK.

seem to have a 'soul' and a personality, and through marketing and advertising strategy the product from the factory becomes a brand, a symbol, an expression of values. In a similar way Lacoste shirts and Levi 501 jeans are not just pieces of clothing but symbols and ways for consumers to express a certain lifestyle.[2]

Later chapters will examine the difference between products and brands in greater depth, but at this point it is worth commenting that people are buying *benefits*, both technical and psycho-social benefits, rather than the tangible or chemical attributes or *features* of products.

The Glamco case also overviews the marketing-mix elements of 'product', 'price', 'distribution' and 'promotion'. Later chapters examine the marketing-mix implications of the various aspects of consumer behaviour that are presented through this book. What is probably the hardest task in practice to achieve is not coming up with each 'mix' element in isolation from the other elements, but rather to manage to get all of the marketing-mix elements communicating the same meaning to consumers. In the above case, for instance, the name and advertising approach were communicating a less exclusive image than were the price and distribution channels chosen, so there is a lack of coherence in mix elements – distribution and price suggesting one thing, name and advertising another, and so on.

To combine these points in a simple graphical framework may be helpful at this point. Figure 1.3 also adds other dimensions implied in the original definition of marketing, but not explicitly referred to until now. Understanding what customers require is specified in the Institute of Marketing's definition in two senses. First there is the 'identifying' part. This involves relatively straightforward market research. The second dimension to understanding markets is summed up in the Institute's word 'anticipating'. This introduces another key aspect of marketing, namely the constant monitoring of trends and changes in society, technology, and economic and political influences. These are longer-term macro factors and are not the focus of market research projects, which tend to be concerned with more immediate decision-making issues. Instead, these macro influences are labelled as elements of 'the marketing environment' in Figure 1.3 and their nature and possible future impact on markets and marketing is analysed through 'environmental scanning'.

In Section 1.3, some of the specifics of these environmental influences are discussed. At this stage we have introduced what marketing is, and some of the processes that are involved. The next chapter takes the point about satisfying needs and wants a stage further. Specifically, it distinguishes between a need and a want and shows how marketing draws from a knowledge of customer motivation and motivation theory in general.

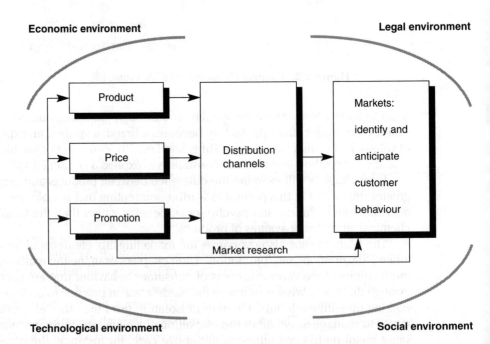

Figure 1.3 The marketing mix and the marketing environment.

1.2 Products, services, causes and ideas

Marketing is not only about physical products, it is also about services and ideas. In modern society, consumer spending on services such as holidays, recreation, hairdressing, car repairs and medical services is increasing. As compared with physical products, services are intangible, produced on the spot, often to the specification of the customer. Services are also produced in cooperation with the customer. The doctor and the dentist cannot produce their services without the cooperation of the customer. The customer needs to trust ('credence') the service provider because the quality of the service cannot be judged before the service is provided.[3]

A service may be the core of a transaction or may be additional. For example, a computer repair service may be part of the 'augmented product' for a consumer buying a personal computer and if so the service is then included in the deal. A service may also be the core business of a computer repair firm, and it is generally realized that many retailers of electrical goods consider the sale of their warranties to be more profitable than the heavily discounted goods themselves.

Many service providers also try to make their service as tangible as possible. Travel insurance companies will send a policy and even luggage stickers to make the service and the feeling of security more tangible. Some service providers like to call their services 'products' – banks talk of their 'products' and airline companies describe their transportation 'products'.

Both products and services deliver benefits to consumers. Consumers may also be asked to contribute to a social cause, for example to give money to a charity such as the Red Cross, AIDS Funds, Foster Parents, Amnesty International, UNICEF, the Third World and other charities. Their marketing policy is to maintain databases of donors, to provide donors with information about their charity and to increase the yield of the campaigns, both in number of donors and in yield per donor. Charities are using direct marketing methods more and more, though there is evidence to suggest that caution should be exercised. In a study of consumer attitudes to such targeting, Evans *et al.*[4] found older women in particular to be greatly upset by being individually targeted by charities – certainly they identified with the cause and wanted to donate but were often not financially able to, creating emotional turmoil. Charities compete with each other to get a larger share of the donations from consumers and companies, and the benefits to donors can be that they contribute to the alleviation of social problems.

A fourth category is 'ideas', either political, religious or other ideological ideas and values. An idea is an opinion or a set of values about a 'better world', superiority of a class of people or a desired state of affairs. This 'better world' can be reached through the promotion of the idea and 'selling' the idea to others. If many people start to accept the idea, change their behaviour accordingly and become promoters of this idea themselves, the idea has a chance to become successful. The idea can be marketed through advertising campaigns for political parties, for churches, for governmental issues, for referenda, for Amnesty International, Greenpeace and other groups.

Marketing is thus not only for tangible products, but more and more also for intangible services, causes and ideas. Some of the people involved in these applications of marketing are reluctant to call their activity 'marketing'; for example, churches will seldom employ the concept of 'marketing' for their work to attract and to keep members of their church. Generally, the application of marketing for charities and ideas could often be much improved.

1.3 Consumer behaviour and the marketing environment

As introduced in Figure 1.3, the marketing environment refers to those conditions and influences impinging or potentially impinging on marketing management. Examples include the effects of government economic policy, changes in technology, and the implications of societal change.

These environmental factors are different for the various European countries, differing both on the north–south dimension of economic development and on the west–east dimension of capitalist versus former communist countries.[5]

The importance of the environment comes from the nature of marketing itself, indeed from standard definitions of marketing management. For example, the one put forward by the Chartered Institute of Marketing, cited earlier, includes the word 'anticipating' in connection with market requirements. This requires a degree of forecasting and projection into the future. To (merely) identify customer requirements usually involves specific market research programmes, but to anticipate requires a broader perspective: continuously monitoring current trends, not all of which are necessarily obviously relevant, in order to plan ahead.

It is the marketing function in an organization which is primarily responsible for looking outwards. Indeed it is generally the case that this function, being at the interface of the organization and its environment, is at least theoretically in a particularly good position to understand what is happening and what might happen in society, in order to initiate appropriate organizational response.[6]

Having said this, it should be added that marketing's environment is not only concerned with things external to the organization, but also with those influences both internal to it and external to the marketing function, such as the organizational position, competencies of the firm, and relative power of the marketing function vis-à-vis other functions, such as production and finance.

Direct and indirect implications for marketing management

Depending on the specific influence, marketing activities might be directly affected by, for instance, new technology providing alternative methods of conducting the same activities, or legislation governing these. Alternatively, market behaviour might change due to changes in the social structure or social attitudes, or perhaps due to changed lifestyles resulting from technological and/or economic change; these factors have indirect implications for marketing response.

It is the indirect influences which probably provide the greatest challenge. This is because the direct influences are generally easier to spot. They are more obviously relevant to the organization's marketing activities because they are concerned with marketing activities themselves. However, those influences which are indirect will often be 'further away' from the immediate focus of the organization, since they are the 'knock-on' effects of environmental change elsewhere, and, in some cases, their eventual impact within the marketplace could be relatively obscure.

A further point is the interaction of influences, the combined impact of economic and technological change. For example, the combined impact might give extra momentum to (say) the home-centred society in certain segments, since in-home entertainment expands with technological development and leisure time expands with high unemployment or increases in high-tech production processes.

Marketing's 'environments'

It is worth pointing to the types of environmental influences concerned. Some have already been briefly mentioned. Figure 1.3 provides a framework for considering these and other influences. This is put forward as merely a picture of a way of thinking of the variety of environmental influences on the marketing process. It should not be analysed much further *per se* because this might misleadingly imply some mutual exclusivity of such influence. 'Lists' of influence are prone to imply this.[7]

The previous example of economic and technological change interacting with each other in a 'Gestalt' or synergistic manner to create societal and market change demonstrates this point.[8] This might not have been foreseen from monitoring and analysing 'discrete' environmental influences.

If the marketing process is thought of in this way, it reinforces the market environment as the focus of marketing activity and, taking its direction from the market, the marketing mix is then the organization's marketing response. The whole process is therefore influenced and affected by changes in economic, technological and societal factors and the changes in levels and types of competition in factory, reseller and consumer markets and so on.

Environmental influence

Space prevents anything more than a cursory coverage under this heading. In order to provide something of a flavour of environmental influence, the following review looks briefly at a few events and considerations in market, social, economic, legal and technological change.

Market and social environments

The most obvious aspect of the market environment is concerned with a fundamental marketing principle: customer orientation. Marketers should think in terms of what customers are buying rather than what the supplier is selling. This is expounded in the question 'What business are we in?'[9] This is a question firms should profoundly explore. Take for instance Hollywood. Hollywood is in the 'entertainment business' rather than in merely 'making films'. In a similar way, railroads are in the transportation business and not the business of running trains. This means that Hollywood could, or even should also produce video movies and television programmes. Railroads should also consider road and ship transportation to provide a more complete and integrated service to their customers.

This is of great importance in understanding the environment. First, it is not only the marketing function that should be so market oriented. It is also important for this philosophy to pervade the entire organization. Thus, the internal environment of the organization should be understood and influenced, if need be. The principles of the Hollywood and railroad examples relate back to our earlier discussions of customers buying benefits rather than features.

Markets are not static and there will be changes in market behaviour which straightforward 'targeted' market research, even continuous research programmes, will not even be attempting to pick up. Such changes might emanate from other environmental influences, for example economic or technological in origin, which may eventually be reflected, indirectly, in new and changed market behaviour. For example, highly focused market research into the cinema market might not, in itself, have identified changes in the broader entertainment market.

Thirdly, Figure 1.3 could include the competitive environment as a component of the market, and a greater understanding of the competitive nature of the market environment is becoming more important.[10] A company must be competitor oriented. It must look for weak points in the positions of its competitors and then launch marketing attacks against these. However, too much competitor orientation may cause it to lose contact with the consumer. Consumer monitoring and research remain necessary to develop and improve products and services that are needed and can be sold.[11] An optimal mix of consumer and competitor orientation is required.

Moving to more specific market and social environmental influence, currently topical trends include changes in the demographic structure and changes in social attitudes. The demographic trends are easily monitored and projected from population statistics such as Social Trends and Regional Trends, and show that the 'age bulge' of 16–24s of the mid-1980s burst in the late 1980s and early 1990s. This was an important trend with more 16–24s than ever before and more than forecast for the foreseeable future. One importance to many marketers of this segment is that the 16–24s, despite high unemployment levels, spend considerable sums on consumer goods and services, and demand more products for themselves than previous generations of 16–24s.[12] Thus the segment(s) with this age characteristic provided significant marketing opportunities and now, of course, it is important as the 26–34s.

The generation behind it, the current 16–24s, is discussed later, in a 'clipping' on 'Generation X' from the marketing press, but has been found to be especially individualistic in nature and at the same time very cynical toward marketing activity,[13] thus creating significant challenges for the marketer. For example, there is difficulty in creating brand loyalty among these young adults. Once achieved, however, brand loyalty can be quite strong in subsequent years. The example of a bank spending large marketing budgets on influencing 18-year-olds, especially prior to going to university or college, demonstrates this point. As implied, a related aspect of this segment is that these young adults are more conservative and at the same time more interested in self-expression than their counterparts in previous generations.[14]

An inference from this is that whereas they may, in general, be less interested in 'newness' *per se*, there are possibly more marketing opportunities because self-expression is manifested as greater societal pluralism. So there may be many more, though smaller, market segments to identify and cater for. The coverage of self-concept theory discusses this aspect in more detail.[15]

Economic environment

In many instances, it is difficult to separate the economic from the political environment, because one is often, to some extent, a manifestation of the other. That is, government philosophy will be reflected in the economic policies adopted.

For example, a dramatic demonstration of this is in the UK where, since the change in government in 1979, there has been a reduction in income tax and an increase in interest rates. The income tax reduction has had different effects on various market segments. The lowest rate has been reduced from 33% to 20%, giving such payers a certain amount of extra disposable income, but the top band has been reduced from 83% to 40%, giving these payers a substantially greater amount of extra disposable income. At the same time, it is generally known that the latter category has a higher marginal propensity to save and the former a higher marginal propensity to consume. Higher interest rates had the effect of eating up more than the extra disposable income of the base rate taxpayers because of higher mortgage and other credit repayments, but those paying higher rates of tax were attracted to the increased dividend returns associated with high interest rates. For 'income segments', it has been shown that only six per cent of the population were better off in 1986 than they were in 1979 as a result of income tax changes.[16]

Increases in unemployment have obvious implications for lower spending power in those segments, but, at the same time, new buying requirements come from changed lifestyles and greater amounts of spare time. This is a simplified example, but it does show that economic policy changes do not affect all market segments in the same way. For example, 94% of all jobs lost since 1979 were lost in 'the North' of the UK,[17] confirming the popular perception of the two-nation concept, important for geographic segmentation in marketing.

Legal environment

This 'environment' concerns legislative changes which may impinge upon the marketing activities of a firm. For example, changes in food labelling and description laws will directly affect packaging and possibly promotion. Different countries' rules will have implications for international marketing. For example, in Belgium margarine must be packed in oblong packs and butter in square packs.

Laws constraining what can be included in advertising will, likewise, directly affect this element of marketing mixes. Again, there will be international differences and the interpretation and imposition of some of these will become more interesting in the future as DBS[18] expands international advertising possibilities.

Consumer protection legislation may fundamentally change what is permissible in terms of product and service features, and, indeed, the whole area of consumerism may become as persuasive a force as it is in the USA.[19]

Market research may be similarly affected by changes in the laws of confidentiality; the Data Protection Act and Freedom of Information Acts are obvious examples. In the second half of the 1990s the UK debates the introduction of identity cards with ever more implications because of the use of smart cards that can hold a vast amount of very personalized information which can, potentially, be seen, stored and used by organizations with smart card 'reading' machines. Issues of marketing databases on consumers will be discussed in more detail in Chapter 6.

Increasingly the European Union in Brussels sets legal boundaries to marketing activities, for example the banning of tobacco advertising, setting restrictions to monopolistic developments in markets and nations, and promoting 'green' (pro-environmental) production, products and consumption.

A continuous monitoring of the press and of the reporting of parliamentary affairs will help spot proposed legislation that might affect marketing operations. In some instances, the organization might, either by itself, if it is particularly powerful or can influence politicians, or, collectively, in an industry group, be able to lobby members of parliament to influence the nature and wording of such bills. This is a topical debate in ethics: whether it is legitimately a part of the democratic process or whether business should not be able to influence lawmaking. This 'influence of the environment' is conducted through the use of PR consultants who carefully select politicians who have a personal, as well as or instead of a professional interest in the area. These will then be targets of (in some cases) quite lavish hospitality and entertainment budgets and possibly even more persuasive incentives! The concept of attempting to influence the environment (not only the legal environment) has been discussed by several authors.[20]

Technological environment

Currently especially topical, of course, is technological change. This affects marketing in three main ways. First, it contributes directly to new product development, because technology itself sometimes provides new products which customers might demand if they are shown to satisfy needs. Secondly, there may be new ways of conducting marketing activities. And thirdly, technology may change lifestyles and therefore market behaviour. Indirectly, therefore, marketing mixes would have to respond.

The Sinclair C5, an innovative electric vehicle developed by Sir Clive Sinclair,[21] is an example of technology providing a new product, but is also an example of a less than convincing market offering in terms of customer satisfaction and acceptance. In May 1985 Sinclair reported sales of over 8,000 vehicles, but in October of the same year debts on the C5 project of £7.75 million were reported. In 1986, the remaining C5s were advertised as 'working collector's items'.

The personal computer is a more obvious example of technological change through smaller and cheaper chips, providing something which customers are prepared to purchase.

Secondly, the dynamic nature of technology has provided, and is projected to continue to provide, new ways of conducting marketing activities. Many of these are not actually new marketing activities, but the methods of conducting some of these activities are affected by new technology. For example, cable and satellite broadcasting provide new ways of advertising. Cable broadcasting helps target in a more focused manner. It is narrowcasting as opposed to broadcasting. Satellite broadcasting has implications for international advertising.

'Cable' has other implications for marketing, such as conducting market research surveys directly into consumers' living-rooms via the cable, TV screen and a key pad. Mail order buying has been given a boost through this as well, and the future is likely to see increased use of cable technology and the Internet in consumer purchasing from home.

The third level of influence of technological change is that, in an indirect way, market behaviour is altered because of the effects on lifestyles which technological developments sometimes bring. The examples here can probably be summarized with references to Columbus, Ohio, where all homes have been wired for cable, not only so that they can receive several TV channels and shop from home, but also so that they may be able to conduct their financial transactions through the cable links to banks, and to be able to work from home in some cases. The 'attendance ethic' at a place of work has been replaced with a sort of ultimate 'flexitime'. The home terminal allows people to do their work whenever they feel like it, and to download results to their employer's computer network.

There are a great many social implications of the tremendous increase in home-centredness that this brings, but, from a marketing perspective, the changes in lifestyles which result will change the product and services requirements of people affected in this way.

In the UK, there have been, for several years now, examples of each of these developments. Prestel was been used for mail order and even for the odd survey conducted by the big catalogue companies, and many employees now work from home through a modem link between home terminals and the firm's computer. Email and the Internet have provided for something of a quantum leap in the use and application of such remote communications – even between the writers of this book. In France, Minitel, an early precursor of the Internet, is used for personal messages as well as direct marketing and mail ordering for Trois Suisses and la Redoute.

What is likely to happen in the future is the kind of synergy exemplified in Columbus, Ohio, with all the consequences for marketing opportunities, but only if the scanning process is capable of not only identifying the trends, but also projecting specific market implications for the organization concerned. Environmental scanning has been described concisely as 'an early warning system for the environmental forces which may impact a company's products and markets in the future'.[22] In this way, scanning enables an organization to act rather than to react to opportunities and/or threats. The focus is not on 'the immediate', but rather has a longer-term perspective which is necessary for being in a position to plan ahead. It may be concluded that the whole effectiveness of organizations is to some extent dependent on their abilities to understand and use this understanding of environmental uncertainty.[23]

One key point is that environmental influence is not static but continuously changing, hence the need for continuous monitoring of various influences, both internal and external. A danger of not thinking in this way might be analogous to Toffler's *Future Shock*. 'The speed and frequency of change is such that managers and management systems often cannot cope. What occurs is a sort of internally generated shock which is rooted in managers' inability to see the strategic impact of possible changes and therefore make the changes necessary to adjust the organization's strategy to its environment.'[24] The speed of change is also increasing.[25]

Another essential consideration in managing the effects of environmental change is that many influences may superficially appear to be constraints on marketing activities, but opportunities should always be sought. Even these supposed constraints, where possible, should be converted into opportunities. To reinforce this point, it has been suggested that marketing should think of positive and negative opportunities rather than merely opportunities and constraints.[26]

1.4   Concluding remarks

This chapter has introduced consumer behaviour in a marketing environment. The nature and importance of customer orientation and the associated roles of market research and environmental scanning have also been demonstrated. Marketing's response via the marketing-mix elements has also been shown to take its direction from the market, seller, buyer and consumer behaviour within it, and changes over time due to environmental dynamics. Chapter 13 returns to this particular theme with some suggestions for consumer trends in the future.

Marketing and consumer behaviour research is not restricted to commercial products and services. Non-profit and governmental services are considered as well. There is a trend now for non-profit, charity, political ideological and governmental services to perform consumer research and apply the results in the marketing strategy.

The following chapter goes back to the very heart of the marketing concept: the meaning of products, services and ideas, the satisfaction of consumer needs, wants and values, and the analysis of consumer motivation.

The pattern of the rest of the book is as follows: Part 2 concentrates on how consumers respond to marketing in terms of individual information processing. This draws significantly from psychology and social psychology, for example from concepts such as perception, learning and attitude. This is also discussed in the context of new and repeat consumer buying processes. The focus, then, in Part 3 is on the grouping of consumers within segments and the approaches needed for targeting and researching markets. This 'grouping' approach draws more from sociology with applications of such concepts as the family and social stratification. Part 4 moves our study of consumer behaviour into implications for the marketing mix and how marketing can respond to these. The book ends with some suggestions for future developments in consumer behaviour.

Also, as mentioned earlier, we provide a range of topical issues in consumer behaviour, at the end of each 'Part', in the form of clippings from the marketing press and some consumer behaviour cases and problems. Apart from extending our text-based coverage, these can be used for seminar, tutorial and course work.

Endnotes

1. Chartered Institute of Marketing, UK.
2. Example from J.N. Kapferer, 1992, p. 78.
3. See Chapter 9, Section 9.5 for an elaborated comparison of products and services.
4. M.J. Evans, L. O'Malley and M. Patterson, 1995.
5. See a series of articles on consumer behaviour in the various nations of the European Union. These articles appeared in the *International Journal of Research in Marketing*. The following nations and authors were involved:
   General overview: P.S.H. Leeflang and W.F. Van Raaij, 1995
   Belgium: E. Gijsbrechts, G. Swinnen and W. van Waterschoot, 1995
   Denmark: O.S. Nilsson and H.S. Solgaard, 1995
   France: M. Filser, 1996
   Germany: K.G. Grunert, S.C. Grunert, W. Galtzen and H. Imkamp, 1995
   Greece: A.G. Kouramenos and G. Avlonitis, 1995
   Ireland: M. Lambkin and M.F. Bradley, 1995
   Italy: R. Varaldo and G. Marbach, 1995
   The Netherlands: P.S.H. Leeflang and W.F. Van Raaij, 1993
   Portugal: M. Farhangmehr and P. Veiga, 1995
   Spain: J.L. Nueño and H. Bennett, 1996
   UK: J. Saunders and J. Saker, 1994.
6. F.E. Webster, Jr, 1992.
7. S. Glaser, 1985.
8. 'Gestalt' or 'whole' is a concept from the German psychologist Kurt Lewin, 1936.
9. T. Levitt, 1964.
10. L. Unger, 1981.
11. D. Wittink and P.S.H. Leeflang, 1994. Inaugural speech of D. Wittink at the University of Groningen, The Netherlands.
12. J. Piper, 1978.
13. M. Ritson, 1995.
14. M.J. Evans, 1981; P.A. Shay, 1978; W. Lazer, 1981.
15. For 'self concept' see Chapter 6.

16. Institute for Fiscal Policy Studies, 1986.
17. Employment Census, 1984.
18. DBS is Direct Broadcasting by Satellite.
19. Consumerism is a social movement to promote the interests and to increase the power of consumers vis-à-vis producers, retailers, and even the government as a producer of services.
20. For example, R.M. Thorpe, 1975, and P. Kotler, 1984. This type of PR is often called 'public affairs'.
21. T.H. Payton, 1988.
22. S.C. Jain, 1981.
23. R.H. Thorpe, 1975.
24. G. Johnson and K. Scholes, 1984.
25. D.W. Cravens, G.E. Hills, and R.B. Woodruff, 1980.
26. A. Book, 1981.

2

Consumer needs, values and product benefits

Chapter objectives

(1) To demonstrate that the role of understanding consumer motivation is at the very heart of the marketing concept.
(2) To distinguish between needs and wants.
(3) To explore various theories of motivation and to show how motives can be considered to be driving forces derived from different levels of depth within the human psyche.
(4) To illustrate the application of consumer motivation within a marketing context with examples and cases.
(5) To provide distinctions between needs, values and goals.

2.1   Introduction

As introduced in the previous chapter, a major cornerstone of marketing management concerns customer satisfaction with products and services. The nature of being market rather than product oriented requires organizations to consider who their customers might be, where they are, how to target them, and with what, in order to satisfy their needs and requirements.

Aspects of defining, segmenting, locating and targeting customers are dealt with in later chapters but the focus of this chapter is to examine customer requirements, their needs, wants and values. Much of this is based on what motivates customers and so we start by exploring consumer motivation theories and applications.

2.2 Consumer motivation

Motivation is a basic concept in human behaviour and also in consumer behaviour. Why do people do what they do? Someone who is eating might be motivated by hunger. Another person might also go out to lunch with a business colleague to discuss an important contract. Motivation thus cannot be inferred from observing behaviour. Some economists may argue that preference may be inferred from consumer choice,[1] but the motivation behind this preference may come from different sources. The same behaviour may be performed for different reasons, for example hunger or a business contract. For instance, observing someone in the supermarket studying product packages does not explain why that person is doing so. It may be that the customer is looking for low prices, or for ingredients he or she likes, dislikes or is not allowed to eat. And there may be many other reasons for studying the packages.

Motivation may be defined as follows. Motivation is an activation, drive and/or reason to engage in a certain behaviour and to maintain that behaviour. Motivation determines the direction and the strength or intensity of behaviour.

Positive and negative motivation may be distinguished: approach and avoidance, respectively. As positive motivation, people are looking for positive situations, positive mood, pleasure, sensory gratification, intellectual stimulation, social approval and comfort; also, things that may enrich their lives and are worthwhile to strive for, and goals that they want to reach.[2] Holidays and entertainment are examples of products and services appealing to a positive motivation. With negative motivation, people are motivated to escape from negative situations, negative mood, pain, illness and discomfort such as a headache. And they want to avoid and remove problems. Pain relievers and amusement parks are examples of products appealing to a negative motivation. Note that entertainment might be sought from a positive or a negative motivation, to enrich your life and to escape a boring situation, respectively.[3]

Motivation is either internal ('from within a person') or external ('from the environment'). Internal motivation is called instinct, need, drive, or emotion. It often has a physiological base, for example hunger, thirst, sexual needs and need for stimulation. External motivation is based on the attractiveness of environmental stimuli such as products and services. Note that external motivation often becomes internal motivation in the form of preference for products, services and situations.

Combining positive and negative motivation with internal and external motivation gives the four types of motivation of Table 2.1.

Table 2.1 Different kinds of motivation.

Motivation	Internal	External
Positive	Pleasure, comfort	Attractive goods and services, attractive situations
Negative	Pain, discomfort	Unattractive goods and services, unattractive situations

Internal motivation

The early approaches to motivation of human behaviour are based on (internal) instincts and drives, mainly innate physiological processes. These drives are 'pushes' rather than 'pulls' in certain directions. This type of motivation is related to the gratification of existence needs of hunger, thirst, protection and sexual drives.[4] This motivation is mainly negative and is essential for survival in cases of danger and deprivation.

The famous Austrian psychiatrist Sigmund Freud developed his psychoanalytic theory and distinguished the Id, Ego and Superego. The Id is the basic instinct, a source of psychic energy. The Id is a 'beast' looking for immediate hedonic gratification (pleasure), self-interest, and a short-term perspective. Freud argued that the libido, sexuality, is the driving force of the Id. According to psychoanalytical theory, the Id is an unconscious drive. The Superego is a conscious drive ('conscience') to control the Id and to serve long-term and collective interests. The Superego represents conscience, norms, morality and other values. The Ego manoeuvres between the hedonic demands of the Id and the moral requirements of the Superego (Figure 2.1).[5]

To the distinction between the conscious and unconscious areas of the mind, a third category is added: the subconscious. The conscious part concerns thinking, deliberation and spontaneous memory, such as recognition and recall. The subconscious part consists of thoughts, ideas and concepts that are not conscious, but may be made conscious with some effort. Depth interviewing, hypnosis, free associations, non-verbal and projective techniques can be used to bring subconscious thoughts into the conscious. Qualitative consumer research is often directed to subconscious elements in consumer perceptions, preferences and decisions.[6] The unconscious part consists of thoughts and ideas that cannot be made conscious. These unconscious elements may nevertheless influence subconscious and conscious elements in consumer thinking. Traumatic experiences from the past may linger in the unconscious and exert influence on conscious and subconscious processes.

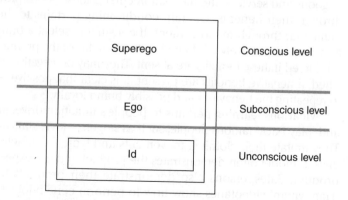

Figure 2.1 Id, Ego and Superego.[7]

Many people believe that consumers may be influenced at the subconscious or even unconscious level with 'subliminal' advertising. Subliminal advertising is supposed to exert influence on behaviour without consumers being aware of it. Examples of subliminal advertising are short flashes such as 'Eat popcorn' or 'Drink Coca-Cola' which were inserted in a movie in New Jersey. These flashes are too short to be consciously observed.[8] Subliminal images may also be inserted in pictures, in a scrambled or hidden way, for example the word SEX to be read in the ice cubes in a glass of whisky.[9] The argument is that these hidden flashes or pictures are being unconsciously observed, processed and, without any cognitive defence or screening by the Superego, transmitted to the minds of consumers. These subliminal messages exert a strong effect on behaviour without people knowing that they are being influenced. Recent research, however, does not support this view. The movie experiment in New Jersey proved to be a fake. It is not very likely that advertisers may influence consumers in this unconscious way, but if subliminal advertising worked, it would bring many ethical questions to the fore regarding whether this type of advertising should be allowed. Subliminal messages encouraging us to buy a particular brand of baked beans might, if it worked, be bad enough, but what about the implications of a subliminal 'vote for me' at election time ?

External motivation

The attraction power of objects is another source of motivation. This is the 'pull' effect. These objects may be products, services, ideas, persons or situations. Consumers want to possess certain goods, experience certain services, reach certain goals, or imitate certain persons and behaviours. The attractiveness of the benefits of these goods, services and behaviours is the motivating force. These benefits may be rewarding. People may feel that they will be happier or more comfortable enjoying these goods and services, and performing these desired behaviours.

Operant conditioning and vicarious learning are based on the attractiveness of goods and services and the reinforcements these goods provide for consumers through their benefits. Operant conditioning pertains to the strengthening of behaviour through reinforcement. If consumers select a brand or product type they may be positively reinforced by the benefits of the product. They may not be reinforced if these benefits are absent. They may be negatively reinforced or 'punished' if negative benefits are present. It is clear that positive reinforcement leads to repeating the behaviour and possibly brand loyalty.

Vicarious learning pertains to people's imitation drive. Many like to imitate and 'play back' famous people, such as singers, movie stars and fashion models. They imitate their clothing, movements and typical characteristics. In commercials, a model often demonstrates the product and the experiences of using the product. Salespersons also demonstrate their products for their prospects. 'Handyman' videotapes show how to perform certain jobs such as fixing bathroom tiles and hanging wallpaper. Vicarious learning or learning by imitation is a conscious process in the case of the handyman jobs. It is often a subconscious process in the case of imitating the behaviour of other people.

Motivation is often not purely internal or external. Often it is a combination of both internal and external factors, push and pull factors. The motivational driving forces are internal (mainly biological factors and/or processes such as an equilibrium and optimization of the state of an individual) or external (attractiveness of objects). Examples of the combination of internal and external factors and processes are the following approaches to motivation.

It might be tempting to assume that a 'need' would be for the necessities of life whereas a 'want' would be for something that is merely desired in, perhaps, a 'luxury' sense. This is *not* the marketing view. Marketing sees 'needs' as being any motivator that encourages some sort of behavioural response. In this way, a need can certainly be for the necessities like food and drink, but can equally be for more social and psychological reasons. Higher-order needs come close to values. Values are enduring beliefs that specific behaviours or goals are personally or socially preferable to other behaviours and goals.[10] Values are thus more cognitive in nature. People try to realize their values through their behaviour, including consumer behaviour.

2.3 Needs

Every individual has needs, but these needs will be to the fore in different individuals at different points in time. Thus, marketing does not create needs, but rather encourages us to 'want' brand X by associating its acquisition with the satisfaction of a latent need. This, to some, will be a strong statement of contentious merit! However, the point is that marketing management may be involved in the researching and identification of relevant and salient needs in the market, reminding consumers that they have these needs and then, of course, suggesting a way in which they might satisfy them. The needs themselves have always been there and, if correctly identified and tapped, there is a greater chance of the consumer responding favourably to the marketing activity.

A well-documented theory is the one proposed by Abraham Maslow.[11] Maslow's proposition is that we are motivated by more than the physiological essentials such as food and drink and that we operate on a sort of 'satisfying' basis for the satisfaction of our needs. Another key element of his theory is that once these needs have been reasonably satisfied, we move on to other and higher-level needs and attempt to satisfy these. It is a sort of ladder of motivation or hierarchy with five levels (Figure 2.2).

Two principles reign in the need hierarchy: deprivation/domination and gratification/activation. If a person is deprived of the satisfaction of a basic need, this need tends to dominate that person's behaviour, but if this need is reasonably gratified, the next higher need is activated and dominates the behaviour.

In the ERG model the five levels are summarized by three levels: existence, relatedness and growth.[12] In empirical research, more support is found for the

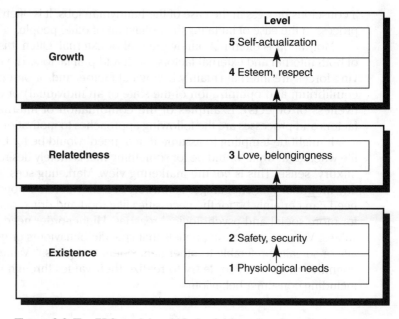

Figure 2.2 The ERG model and Maslow's hierarchy of needs.

ERG model than for the Maslow hierarchy, although the Maslow hierarchy remains popular with many people.[13]

Once the basic physiological needs such as thirst and hunger have been reasonably satisfied we start being aware of the need to be safe and secure. These are the existence needs. Then it becomes important to feel accepted and loved by others, the relatedness or social needs. The need to be respected by others and self-actualization are the growth needs. Maslow's highest level, self-actualization, is a difficult concept because Maslow himself wondered whether many of us would ever reach this level. But it remains a goal to strive for. It could be one of the most significant motivators of all, a kind of personal inner Utopia, being at one with oneself in an almost spiritual sense. In this way it might vary between individuals but it is what we ultimately strive for, along this continuous onwards and upwards path through life.

Hierarchy

The marketing significance of the ERG/Maslow hierarchy is great. First, it clearly demonstrates that a need is more than mere physiological essentials and can be just as powerful as a driving force behind our behaviour if it comes from a concern for our safety, social integration, personal recognition or from the perceived importance of spiritual satisfaction.

The hierarchy can be criticized; for example, Maslow suggested that as societies develop they move further up the hierarchy in terms of their most salient needs. It could be argued here that not everyone will move up the ladder in quite the same way, perhaps missing some levels and perhaps moving back down to lower-level needs. An illustration of this would be in western industrialized countries, where, at the same time as attempting to satisfy social and growth levels of the hierarchy, many will be heavily oriented to, for example, safety and security as a result of fears about criminality and the violent society. Marketing clearly recognizes this, as is evidenced by the plethora of advertisements for personal alarms, life assurance policies and home and car security devices. Chubb locks, for example, use the copy 'Pick your own lock before a burglar does...and lock out unwelcome visitors'. In the context of the discussion of consumer motivation, such criticisms are relatively pedantic. We present Maslow to reinforce the point that consumers can be motivated by more than the 'essentials' of physiology and that there can be changes, over time, to what motivates individuals.

Other needs

The need hierarchy does not cover all the needs that people may have. People may have 'needs for cognition', that is, to know and to understand things, even without a direct purchasing motive.[14] People have 'equilibrium needs', that is, they look for an optimum level of stimulation, a situation or even an environment that is not boring and not stressful either.[15] A holiday may be taken to reduce the level of stimulation and thus stress; also, it may be taken to make life richer and to get new and stimulating experiences. Further, there is a need to reduce cognitive dissonance (discussed in more detail in Chapter 3, Section 3.8). Briefly, there is dissonance in a smoker who knows that smoking is dangerous for his or her health, and the smoker is motivated to reduce the dissonance, perhaps by stopping or reducing the smoking behaviour or by not reading or screening out the messages conveying the dangers of smoking.[16] The need for achievement is related to setting life goals and realizing important values in one's life. In fact the list of needs, motives and values is endless. Motivation is a basic construct in human behaviour and all behaviours may be seen as being motivated by internal or external factors, or a combination of both.

2.4   Values and goals

Relatedness, growth and existence needs such as safety and security are closely related to values. Often, instrumental and terminal values are distinguished. Instrumental values are related to preferred modes of conduct such as honesty, cleanliness and friendliness. Instrumental values are related to competence such as ambition and self-control, or morality such as helpfulness and obedience. People know that by being honest, clean and friendly, they may be accepted by others and have good relations with others. Instrumental values are thus a means of reaching a goal; these values are often not goals by themselves. Products and services may provide benefits that help consumers to realize their values. In advertising, product benefits are then related to customers' important instrumental values.

Terminal values are more related to growth. Wisdom, happiness and freedom are goals themselves for many people. Terminal values are related to self-actualization values such as wisdom, inner harmony and salvation, and to social values such as a world in peace, a world of beauty, freedom, equality and national security. Products and services may also be related to terminal values. Classic Coke and apple pie seem to have strong connections to American values. An American Express card is related to privileges for the members, to independence, security and power.

Values are enduring dispositions. They change only gradually over time. Values are related to norms of acceptable and desirable behaviours. Products and services may be instrumental in realizing values, and have to fit into existing patterns of values and norms. Clairol introduced in the USA a new shampoo 'A Touch of Yoghurt' that 'feeds' the hair with the natural substances from yoghurt. This was not a success, because it was not compatible with existing value patterns. Consumers did not want to put yoghurt in their hair. A brand name such as 'A Touch of Glamour' could have been a success because glamour is part of existing norms and values.

Values are related to *lifestyle*. Lifestyles are sets of coherent activities, opinions, norms and values. Lifestyles are ways of spending time and money, pursuing hobbies, sports and other activities, and having patterns of interests and opinions related to these activities. It is clear that products and services should fit into consumers' lifestyles.[17]

Values are related to goals people want to reach in their lives; for example, some have ambitions to reach a certain position in their career, to own certain products such as a BMW 5 series or a nice house, to see the places they have read about, to have a happy marriage and family life and to earn an income to pay for all this. Recently more research is being done on 'life goals' of people and the way consumption may contribute to reaching these goals.

Goals possess a hierarchy in themselves. Life goals may be reached with possession and usage goals which may in turn be reached with acquisition and information goals. Advertising may be a source of information to satisfy information goals. This hierarchy is given in Figure 2.3. An information goal may be to know more about studying consumer behaviour at a specific university; the next goal is to get enrolled on that programme and then to be a student on the programme; the life goal may be to complete the programme successfully and to find a job as a consumer marketing manager.

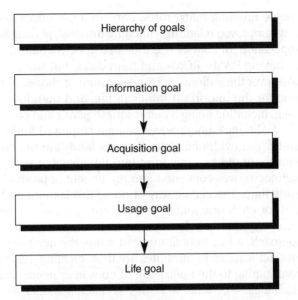

Figure 2.3 Hierarchical goals.

2.5 Product benefits

Another fundamental dimension of marketing management implied in the above discussions of the hierarchy of needs, wants and values is that consumers might be motivated by a variety of needs, but they satisfy some of these through the acquisition of products and services. That is, they are less concerned about *what* products and services *are* than what they can *do* for them. In short, consumers do not buy product and service features *per se*, rather they buy the benefits of these products and services. These benefits should be related to their needs, norms and values. This point is significant and is worth exploring further.

The point can be illustrated in many ways. A quotation often attributed to Charles Revlon of Revlon Cosmetics is: 'In the factory we make soap, in the market we sell hope'. In other words it isn't the physical composition or features that are being purchased, but rather what they can do for consumers and what benefits consumers might derive from their purchase. Another, perhaps glib, illustration is: 'We make 8 mm drill bits, you buy 8 mm holes'.

An advertisement for Canon microcomputers depicted a variety of situations in the life of a man. Each box in the press advertisement showed, variously, the man at the office working on business plans, with employees in a negotiating situation, with clients in a selling situation, on the squash court and at home with his family. This multifaceted way of life fits very well in this post-modern era of people fulfilling many roles. Each of these boxes had captions: forward planning, employee relations, clinching the deal, playing hard, and being a dad. The implication, of course, was that a prospective Canon computer buyer would not be buying RAMs, ROMs and hard disks, but would be buying something that takes over the tedious and time-consuming chores, thus allowing the buyer more time for the important things in life, and therefore being more successful at them, including being a better squash player and parent!

A Minolta camera advertisement employed three categories headed respectively: 'the evidence', 'the features' and 'the benefits'. It demonstrated how features could be converted into benefits. For example, the feature of having 'autofocus' was converted into the benefit of producing perfectly focused shots every time. The classic way of doing this is to identify the needs of the market, and for each one match one or more product or service features that are in some way relevant. Then convert each feature, using a 'which means' or 'why' approach, into a benefit that can satisfy the need or value (Figures 2.4 and 2.5). Product features or attributes are thus 'creating' benefits, and these benefits are contributing to the realization of consumer needs and values. The sequence of 'attributes → benefits → values' is called a 'ladder' or a means–end chain.[18] The research technique to investigate the connections between attributes, benefits and values is called 'laddering'.

Consider for instance the toothpaste market. Brands of fluoride toothpaste may be very similar. These brands will often be targeted at different market segment. Even the brand names used sometimes suggest this, on the basis of varying benefits being sought: Close Up, Aquafresh, Macleans and so on. The

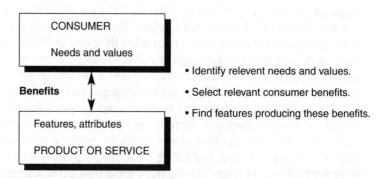

Figure 2.4 Product benefits as related to needs, values and features of consumers.

Needs	Features	Benefits
Identify needs	Select relevant features	Convert features into benefits that satisfy needs

Figure 2.5 Needs, features and benefits.

imagery surrounding the advertising of these brands similarly suggests the difference between 'features' and 'benefits'. Some might show two mothers with their children in a dentist's waiting room. One child has to have several fillings and the other does not. Explicitly there might be references to the brand used by the child who has no cavities, suggesting that this is the brand for you, if you want to prevent tooth decay and hence satisfy a need or value to safeguard yourself (needs at level 2 – see Figure 2.2). Implied, however, is an even stronger benefit that if you don't use this brand as a parent, in some way you are not such a good parent (needs at levels 2, 3 and perhaps 4).

Consider the copy from an old Jaguar advertisement: 'It will reassure you when you need it, it will restore your confidence should it ever desert you, it will soothe and solace you after a hectic day, it will insulate you from the noise and chaos of the outside world, it will rebuild your morale, your ambitions, but most of all it will remind you that your life has not been totally without success.'

This somewhat 'over the top' copy does at least demonstrate that consumers are not buying a set of mechanical features. They derive all sorts of benefits from a car and each one can be related to one or more needs or values – as an exercise try relating this back to our discussion of need and values structures.

A similar but somewhat simplified message appeared for BMW: 'Success is a reality for some and a pleasure for a few.' And for Rover, where in the Rover marque in the middle of the radiator grill in the advertisement the word 'Winner' appeared instead.

Not all cars will tap these higher-level needs. Volvo, for example (see Figure 7.7 in Chapter 7), have depicted a diver in a cage feeling secure from a threatening shark, with the copy: 'cages saves lives'. Subaru's copy 'safest in the class' also clearly targets level 2 of the needs hierarchy (Figure 2.2).

Many of the higher-level needs are actually values. The need for safety and security corresponds to the values of safety and security. The social needs relate to the values of affiliation and acceptance by others. The growth needs relate to social recognition, respect and self-actualization. This means that the higher-level needs may be represented as values. Features are related to benefits that satisfy values. For instance, an economical car appeals to thrifty or pro-environmental people.

2.6   Deeper needs

A somewhat different approach to what motivates consumers is reflected in the following copy for the MGB GT car: 'Psychologists say a saloon car is a wife and a sports car is a mistress.' This piece of copywriting can clearly be criticized as being sexist but it is useful in the current context to demonstrate a deeper way of looking at consumer needs. The copy is based on 'motivation research' and introduces the Freudian approach to motivation.[19]

The MGB advertisement plays on the proposition that consumers are not only buying benefits rather than features, but that the benefits can sometimes

satisfy more deeply seated needs. In this case, the sports car would be consid
ered to be a subconscious symbol.

This is based on Freud's three mental components: Id, Ego and Superego. In
the Id are the basic drives of, for example, sex and violence. These are strong
motivators and at the time Freud was conducting his research society was partic
ularly repressive of personal and primitive drives. The internalization of society's
constraints and taboos is what Freud meant by the Superego and the conflic
between the Id and the Superego could create tremendous internal battles for
the individual.

It is the Ego, according to Freud, that finds some sort of acceptable compro
mise. It manages to put the Id drives in the context of social norms and finds
socially acceptable forms of behavioural outlet for the Id (Figure 2.6). Perhaps
the Id is really only partially satisfied, but the manner of this is within society's
values and the solution is satisfactory all round.

Appeals to the Id can be made in subconscious ways. Pack designs that per
haps spark off a subconscious set of associations might be based on phallic and
other symbolism in the designs, shapes, textures and materials. Other message
might attempt to tap the subconscious Id drives with what superficially would
appear to be rather obscure references. Take for instance the advertisement in
Figure 2.7 in which the woman is about to eat a toffee apple. She wears a
bracelet on her wrist in the form of a snake and the copy reads 'Adam just cured
my fear of snakes!'. The advertisement is actually for gold jewellery, but there i
plenty of Freudian symbolism here! It might go completely over or under the
heads of the target market, at least at the conscious level, but if it reaches the Id
then it might well be doing what was intended. The problem with the subcon
scious, of course, is that it is very difficult to identify and research, even if i
exists. Different psychoanalysts might well interpret research findings in differen
ways and so the whole approach attracts critical attention.

What might happen, though, as shown in Figure 2.8, is that what is seen a
being totally socially acceptable and thus satisfying the Superego (middle) i
also rather boring. It is 'nice'. At the other extreme, what might satisfy the Id i
really rather 'naughty' (left). The Ego's compromise (right) is to come up with
something that is 'naughty but nice'. There have been plenty of examples over
the years of this particular approach. Fresh cream cakes have been advertised
using these three words, Aristoc tights as being 'naughty but very nice', and ever
yoghurt in the sense of 'even a virtuous yoghurt ought to have a wicked taste'.

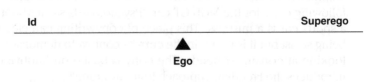

Figure 2.6 Freudian conflicts.

"Adam just cured my fear of snakes!"

When you buy a gift of gold, look
for a jeweller who displays the symbol
of the Jewellery Advisory Centre.
It's your guarantee of personal
service, good value, sound advice
and a very wide choice.
A gift of gold is a
gift of love. Buy it with
confidence.

GOLD IS
FOR LOVERS

Figure 2.7 Freudian motives. © The Jewellery Advisory Service.

A classic piece of market research years ago investigated the reasons for poor sales of the newly introduced instant coffee. The widely quoted study of instant coffee usage illustrates that there can be 'good' and 'real' reasons for behaviour.[20] The indirect questioning approach employed in this project was to ask women what sort of housewife would have compiled the shopping lists shown in Table 2.2. One half of the sample had list 1 which differed only by having instant coffee included. The instant coffee shopping list was seen to have been drawn up by a lazier, less well-organized woman who was described as not being a good housewife. Direct questioning, on the other hand, revealed good reasons for preferring real coffee, which revolved around the product not tasting as good as drip-grind coffee. Respondents were considered to be unwilling or

Id

Superego

Ego

Figure 2.8 'Naughty but nice'.

Table 2.2 Haire's shopping list.[21]

Shopping list 1	Shopping list 2
1½ lb hamburger	1½ lb hamburger
2 loaves Wonderbread	2 loaves Wonderbread
Bunch of carrots	Bunch of carrots
1 can Rumford's baking powder	1 can Rumford's baking powder
1 lb Nescafé instant coffee	1 lb Maxwell House drip-grind coffee
2 cans Del Monte peaches	2 cans Del Monte peaches
5 lb potatoes	5 lb potatoes

unable to reveal their true (real) reasons for not buying instant coffee and the principle of 'good' versus 'real' reasons for behaviour has been a long-held premise in marketing.

Another aspect of this 'deeper' approach to motivation concerns the balance between the Id and the Superego. If a main tenet of the theory is the conflict and ultimate compromise between these components, consider the effects of alcohol. In a classic television anti-drink advertising campaign, the same sense was played twice, through the perceptions of the two main characters. First, a man was drinking more and more and through his eyes becoming more and more sophisticated, suave and attractive to the women around him.

Then the same episode was played through their eyes: a drunk was getting more and more obnoxious. What this nicely demonstrates is the effect alcohol can have on reducing the constraints of the Superego. Indeed, in a series of advertisements for Pernod, the copy, in a variety of different settings, read 'Pernod: Free the spirit'. Apart from being the obvious play on words, it could also be equated with the notion of freeing the Id.

Take the freeing of the Id further, geographically. When on holiday in a foreign country we often don't know of the local norms and some will deliberately ignore them such that there is little perception of social constraints at all! Again the Id can be free and this might explain the misbehaviour of the lager louts in Spanish resorts.

Tapping the Id, but in a way that can ultimately be manifested in a socially acceptable way, is the key to this approach. Consider the following statement: 'Why do people take so much pleasure in immersing themselves in warm water? A psychoanalytical theory is that it awakens distant memories of floating in the comfort of the womb.' This is actually part of the copy for a British Gas advertisement used in the 1990s!

Another possibility concerns the use of subliminal messages to reach the subconscious. The earlier experiments (p. 22) were based on editing in a single frame insert to cinema films.

The approach was pounced on by the media and as a result of general public concern, subliminal advertising was made illegal in many countries. However, other experiments attempting to replicate the results were not entirely conclusive about its effectiveness. Nevertheless there was sufficient concern for the legislation to remain.

A more recent example of this was reported by Reuters in 1994. Red-faced officials at the Walt Disney company were trying to answer the question 'Who undressed Jessica Rabbit?' Apparently three additional frames (depicting Jessica without her underwear) had been inserted into the laser disc version of the film *Who Framed Roger Rabbit?* At the normal 24 frames per second playback this wasn't consciously noticeable but when viewed frame by frame they are!

In one sense this Freudian approach might suggest a role for symbolism as being a way of satisfying the Id, but not directly or fully. If one motivator is the sex drive then what has been described as another sexual revolution might be particularly open to this sort of 'substitution effect' analysis. The sexual revolution of the 1960s might have involved 'the real thing', increased levels of sex with more partners. But since AIDS there might be more value in symbolism than the real thing. In a book, *Rituals of Love*[22], it has been suggested that the relatively instant gratification of earlier eras has been replaced to some extent by fantasy, for example by the dressing up (down) of some club scenes which could be largely explained by our earlier picture of 'naughty but nice' garments.

The research implications of this are that indirect questioning methods may be needed and that the subconscious may be analysed through subtle and specialized techniques.

2.7 Conclusions

Satisfaction of needs and wants is the main emphasis of the marketing concept and these needs and wants are often activated through social interaction, observation, vicarious learning (imitation), advertising and the presence of products. Marketing may make latent needs manifest (through specific wants) but it does not create needs in people. These needs may be ordered in a hierarchy of three or five steps and after satisfying a need in the hierarchy the next higher need will be activated according to the model.

People are not always aware of the 'real' needs determining their behaviour and purchase of products and services and subliminal advertising may appeal to these subconscious and unconscious needs. Although there is no scientific evidence that subliminal advertising has the effects it is supposed to have, in many countries this type of advertising, with subliminal insertions appealing to unconscious needs, is forbidden in advertising codes or even by legislation.

Needs are motivational forces providing direction and intensity of behaviour: both approach and avoidance behaviours. Approach behaviour results from a positive motivation (sensory gratification, intellectual stimulation and social approval). Avoidance behaviour results from a negative motivation (problem avoidance and problem removal).

The higher-order needs are more cognitive; 'values' and related life goals that people strive for. Values, goals and aspired lifestyles are conscious motivating factors for people. Consumption of goods and services may contribute to reaching these life goals and realizing these values.

Before Part 2 of the book, we provide some practical illustrations and examples of some of the points made so far, concerning (a) the wider environment in which consumers behave and because of which their behaviour changes over time and (b) consumer motivation. We provide these via some clippings from the marketing press and exercises which can be used to extend and apply the text material and can also be used for seminar discussion and assignment work.

Part 2 of the book moves into other aspects drawn mostly from psychology and are integrated within the framework of consumer response patterns to marketing activity – for example, how consumers attend to, perceive and learn about marketing offerings, how they act post-purchase, how they can behave towards new products and how their decision-making processes operate.

Endnotes

1. P. Samuelson, 1948, calls this 'revealed preference'.
2. T. Scitovsky, 1976.
3. J.R. Rossiter and L. Percy, 1987, p. 170.
4. A. Maslow, 1954, and C.P. Alderfer, 1972. See Chapter 2.3.
5. See Figure 2.3.
6. See Chapter 8 on consumer research.
7. D. Nye, 1981, p.18.
8. V. Packard, 1957.

9. W. Key, 1973.
10. M. Rokeach, 1973.
11. A. Maslow, 1954.
12. C.P. Alderfer, 1972.
13. M.A. Wahba and L.G. Bridwell, 1976.
14. J.T. Cacioppo and R.E. Petty, 1982.
15. P.S. Raju, 1980.
16. L. Festinger, 1957.
17. See Chapter 6 on psychographics.
18. T.J. Reynolds and J. Gutman, 1984.
19. E. Dichter, 1964.
20. M. Haire, 1950.
21. M. Haire, 1950.
22. E. Polhemus and H. Randall, 1994.

Part 1 Clippings from the marketing press and Exercises

Clipping 1 Consumer behaviour and the marketing environment (see p.38)

Clipping: UK 1994: to have and to have not

Key points

(1)   Impact of economic, political, technological and social environmental change on consumer behaviour

(2)   Need for marketing to identify, anticipate and respond to changes in the marketing environment

(3)   Application of economics, sociology and psychology to understanding changes in consumer behaviour

Questions

(1) What has accounted for what the article described as the widening gap between rich and poor and what are the implications for marketing?

(2) Select two of the product categories mentioned in the article and conduct an environmental scan of these markets, identifying those environmental factors to which marketing should especially respond.

(3) Select two of the product categories mentioned in the article and discuss how various aspects of economics, sociology and psychology contribute to and explain current changes in consumer behaviour in these markets.

(4) This article was based on research conducted in the mid-1990s. How do you see the issues unfolding over the next few years and why?

Clipping 2 The deconstruction industry: What the experts say (see p.40)

Key points

(1) Symbolism via graphic imagery
(2) Possible Freudian approach based on subconscious or unconscious symbols
(3) Changes in sexism in advertising

Questions

(1) To what extent do 'deeper' motivational appeals appear in the advertisement – do you agree with 'what the experts say' and why?
(2) Does the advertisement use a sexist and/or a sex appeal and why?
(3) Provide examples of Freudian symbolism in advertising and packaging.

Marketing 3 February 1994

UK 1994: to have and to have not

Research into UK lifestyles shows the gap between rich and poor is growing and points to greater caution among consumers. Alyson Cook on the implications for marketers

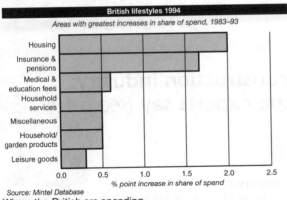

British lifestyles 1994
Areas with greatest increases in share of spend, 1983–93

% point increase in share of spend

Source: Mintel Database

Where the British are spending

"The rich are getting richer, while the poor are getting poorer' is a cliché with huge implications for marketers, but it is now a fact, according to a survey released this week.

The 1994 British Lifestyles report by Mintel shows there is an increased polarisation of wealth in the UK, with two-fifths of the income now being earned by one-fifth of the population.

The implication for marketing is significant. in the past 16 years disposable income has increased by 255%, which is good news for marketers, but which ones? Just as his conventional idea of the typical family was savaged by the General Household Survey late week John Major's ideal of the classless society is now being threatened – the economic divisions between British people are widening. And with the forthcoming tax changes and the impositions of VAT on fuel, families on a tight budget will undoubtedly be hit even harder.

Marketers will have to come to terms with, on the one hand, an increasing demand for luxury goods and greater amounts spent on education fees, and on the other, the 'fact that' a growing proportion of households only have sufficient income for staple products and necessities', says the report.

In contrast to the proportionate decrease in spend on tobacco and clothing over the past decade, the financial services industry has already benefited from this polarisation – and will continue to do so, according to Mintel. The pensions sector in particular will be helped by a big increase in the number of adults between 35–44 and 50–59 years-old by the year 2003, as will gardening products, furnishings and magazines.

Part 1, Clipping 1

"We have seen the opposite of the decrease in consumption which has affected traditional consumption markets, such as cars," says Raoul Pinnell, marketing director for the Prudential.

"People feel less secure in their jobs or in society and they are spending more on providing for the future."

The Government's emphasis on self-sufficiency has given financial marketers "an opportunity. Our customers are saving more. We have about 1.3 million personal pension customers and they are mainly self-employed people. The very nature of their jobs is less certain and more variable and these customers tend to be lower down the social scale."

The flourishing discount market is another significant development. Post-recession UK is ripe for an invasion by US value-for-money, price-led retailers such as the giants Wal-Mart and KMart. Some analysis predict that up to 50 are poised to join Costco and use the UK as a springboard for an attack on European markets.

The impact of these discounted means that the cost of food in ships is continuing to fall as supermarket chains such as Netto, which sell a limited range of cheap groceries, reduce prices further and grow their share of he UK grocery market. Verdict research released this week predicts that food discounting will account for 14.2% of the ottal grocery market by 1997. "We also confirmed a strong link between health and diet among the special consumer groups we devised for the diverging sectors of the population. With the trend towards healthy eating, plus a wider variety of products, the affluent are more likely to eat fresh fruit and vegetables regularly, to have a varied diet, and to say they try to eat healthily, than those on a lower income," says Mintel's head of research, Peter Ayton.

The home is a key factor in the British lifestyle of 1994. In-home food and drinks, along with transport, still made up the second largest proportion of household spend – despite the proportionate decrease in the household spending figure because of the increase in restaurant and pub meals. Entertaining at home is a thriving market too and this will help to grow the brown goods sector, which has suffered at 5% decrease in real terms between 1988 and 1993. "The number of teenagers is set to rise by 2003 there will be more children under 14 in the population – and this will help grow this market," says Ayton. Clothes, snacks, sports goods and soft drinks should also see growth.

At more than £88bn for last year, housing still represents the largest proportion of household expenditure. According to Mintel, we are also spending more on maintaining our homes and their contents, rather than splashing out on new items – for example, shoe, TV and video repairs and vehicles maintenance. Marketing products as durable, long-terms investments could be a key marketing ploy for the 90s.

What every the pattern of consumer spending in the next ten years, one thing is for certain. The consumer spending bonanza may never dawn again and the customary caution of today may be with us for a long while to come.

Observer Sunday, 30 May 1993

The deconstruction industry

What the experts say

We asked Semiotic Solutions to deconstruct the Ajax ad [below] here are their comments:

1. Depersonalised naked torso suggests pornographic image but reflects more generally the current fad for male pin-up images, Chippendales, hen parties etc. The figure is not only an analogy for Ajax power but a fantasy hunk of real male flesh.
2. Mop as phallus although pointing downwards, it is stiff, if not sexually potent, and implications of the hand squeezing out the mop cannot be ignored.
3. Leather belt, heavily stitched, is made the focal centre of the ad, part of the bondage fantasy.
4. Slogan – consistent with having a half-naked slave in the kitchen – puts the female buyer in the dominant role, even if she is still the one who ends up going to the supermarket.

VERDICT: A very knowing ad. Art direction opens up and admits all the ambivalences of meaning that lie along the signifying chain of desire.

The ad says 'forget the drudge' by forgetting the floor – a semiotic invitation to put the cleaning into the background and focus on something much more interesting.

Exercise 1

Using the needs–features–benefits framework

(1) Using the 'needs – features – benefits' framework complete the following:

Needs	**Features**	**Benefits**
(Also, how could Motivation Theories – Maslow/Freud, etc. – be relevant in each case)		
(a) Family including a shift worker, two teenagers who are rock music fans, and their grand-mother who is keen on classical music and on the films of the 1930s and 1940s. The whole family spend two weeks of most summers in their time-shared apartment on the Costa Brava.	This stereo video has remote control and is programmable for 8 programmes over a 2-week period and has a 5-pin auxiliary input–output socket	
(b) Busy career couple both embarking on heavy work commit-ments over the next five years, and have just moved into a flat.	This freezer has 12 cu.ft. capacity and is of the upright type.	

(2) Using your course of study as a product/service context, construct a needs–features–benefits framework and discuss its use in marketing the course.

Exercise 2

Application of motivation theories

Select THREE press advertisements and for each of these:

(a) discuss the likely target market and promotional objectives based on media and message used and your knowledge of the competitive nature of the respective markets;

(b) analyse and evaluate the contribution of the work of Maslow and Freud (using the 'needs–features–benefits' framework) to explain both the message employed and motivational factors in the market targeted.

Part 2

Consumer response to marketing

3

Consumer response to marketing actions

Chapter objectives

(1) To demonstrate how more concepts from psychology can contribute to understanding how consumers behave.

(2) To integrate such application in an hierarchy of effects model of how consumers respond to marketing activity.

(3) To demonstrate the importance of ensuring that what the marketing message offers is in the right place at the right time for the target market to see.

(4) To examine ways of creating conditions for a greater likelihood that consumers will attend to the marketing message/offering and

(5) To apply some of the principles of the psychology of perception to increase the likelihood that consumers will interprete the message/offering in the intended manner.

(6) To apply aspects of the psychology of learning to increase the likelihood of consumers remembering and learning about the marketing message/offering.

(7) To apply aspects of attitude theory to increase the likelihood of consumers developing a favourable predisposition towards the marketing message/offering.

(8) To apply cognitive dissonance theory to help explain how consumers can respond after purchase.

3.1 Introduction

This chapter is concerned with aspects of how consumers respond to marketing activity. One view is based on what are often termed 'sequential models' of behaviour or hierarchy of effects model. There are several sequential models, such as

AIDA (attention, interest, desire, action) and the stages leading from awareness to adoption, discussed in Chapter 4 on innovation and the product life cycle.[1]

The basic framework of this chapter is the hierarchy or sequence of communication effects: exposure, attention, perception, retention, conviction, action, and post-purchase (Figure 3.1). This is not necessarily a sequence that consumers follow in all situations, but it is a logical manner in which to discuss consumer responses to marketing actions.

Not all consumers expose themselves to all marketing activities, advertising, media and distribution channels, so there are significant implications for media and distribution channel selection, the point being to get the marketing offering in a position to be at least potentially noticed by the target market of consumers.

Even if the marketing offering is in the right place, there is no guarantee that the target group will see it, so in this stage the marketer's concern is to attract attention. There are particular techniques that can be employed here, such as colour and movement in marketing messages.

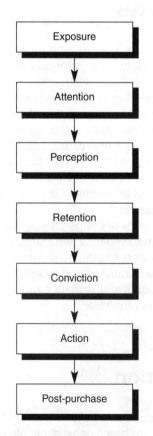

Figure 3.1 Hierarchy of effects.

Once noticed, the message or offering should be understood in the intended way. This stage draws on the psychology of perception.

Retention is the remembering of the message in the intended way. This stage is characterized by applications from the psychology of learning. Although the intended meaning of the message might be understood and remembered, this is not the same as a development of a favourable predisposition. The conviction stage is therefore concerned with attitude theory.

The previous stages determine whether action will take place and what kind of action (purchase, usage, asking for more information). Once a purchase has been made, this is not the end of the process as far as marketing is concerned. One transaction only is not the purpose of marketing which is concerned with regular and mutually satisfactory transactions. Satisfaction with the purchase is a good starting point for a relationship, loyalty, repeat purchases, the spreading of goodwill, and the study of cognitive dissonance can be of benefit in this regard.

3.2   Exposure

Exposure is ensuring that the marketing offering is in the right place for the target market to have access to it, at least potentially. There is a similarity here with the 'accessibility' criterion of market segmentation. There are implications for promotional media selection and for distribution channel selection, both with the objective of reaching the target groups of consumers.

An example of how this did not work out too well a few years ago concerns the launch of the Sunday colour supplement of the newspaper *News of the World*. A typical pattern at the time was for Sunday colour supplements to be packed with 'off the page selling' advertisements (direct-response advertising). These provide a picture of the product or other descriptions together with a coupon to post in order to place an order. This was fine for those with cheque accounts or credit cards but the profile at the time of these owners and of the readership of the paper shows something of a mismatch (Table 3.1).

Table 3.1 Bank accounts and readership related to social class.[2]

Social class	Bank account (%)	Readership of News of the World
A	88	7
B	81	10
C1	69	22
C2	45	38
D	29	43
E	15	28

Exposure to advertising is a basic requirement for reaching an advertising effect in terms of changing consumer knowledge, attitudes or behaviour. Advertisers often pay advertising rates to media related to exposure, such as GRPs (gross rating points) for television advertising and media reach for print media. Media reach and GRPs are measured as the percentage or number of people that are reached at least once through the medium or a combination of media. Only one confrontation is often not enough for consumers to understand or to accept the message. In many media plans, the reach and a minimum or average number of confrontations is the objective. (Note that the reach of a newspaper or magazine is different from the number of copies sold. Many copies are read by more than one reader, thus the reach of a newspaper is usually larger than the number of copies sold.)

Reach of the medium is different from the reach of a part of the medium. Not all readers see all pages of a newspaper and thus miss several advertisements. TV viewers do not see all programmes and commercials. Advertising reach is thus generally lower than medium reach.

An interesting example of advertising reach concerns the audio tape producers Maxell. Rather than selecting media according to the traditional television ratings approach, they asked tape users directly what their favourite programmes were. The result was a six-week TV campaign leading up to Christmas with many slots at slightly unconventional times such as 2 a.m. The campaign cost £330,000 which is very inexpensive for a six-week television campaign of the intensity employed.

Media selection can also be manifested in a very detailed manner. Some years ago when the film *Jaws* was being reshown on television and the relevant page in the *TV Times* also had a piece on the making of the film, Guinness placed a full-page advertisement on the adjacent page depicting a watery scene with a shark's fin breaking the surface (in the Guinness colours of the time) and the copy saying 'you could probably do with a Guinness tonight'. It is a nice example of attention to detail with respect to media selection and the satisfaction of the exposure stage.

3.3   Attention

Even if the marketing offering is in the right place, there is no guarantee that the market will see it. Consumers often scan the media to see whether there is something interesting on TV or in the newspaper. If so, they focus on this relevant 'news' to see whether it is really important. If so, they continue to focus their attention on this message, be it editorial or commercial news (initial attention). If the 'news' is not really important to them they continue scanning for other news in the medium (persistent attention). See Figure 3.2. Whether a message will be attended to or not it thus depends largely on the consumer.

It has been estimated that every American consumer is exposed to at least 1,500 promotional messages a day but that they notice less than five per cent. So

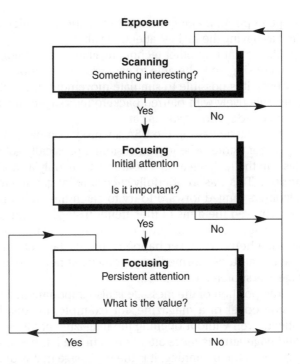

Figure 3.2 Scanning and focusing.[3]

there is a clear implication that once the marketing offering is in the right place for customers to potentially see, this next stage is concerned with ensuring that it is noticed. So in the attention stage advertisers are concerned with attracting attention and there are particular techniques that can be employed here, such as using colour and movement in marketing messages.

Four aspects of attention may be distinguished:

(1) gaining attention, especially in the overload of commercial messages;
(2) holding attention: once the attention has been gained, with a gimmick or otherwise, the attention should be hold for the actual message;
(3) leading attention towards the message and not to peripheral elements in the advertisement or situation;
(4) distracting attention is usually ineffective, unless the arguments of the message are weak. Distraction might then prevent consumers discovering the weakness of the arguments. However, distraction as a way to convince people is an unethical way to get the message across.

There are a variety of techniques for gaining attention, including the use of colour. Generally, colour rather than black and white gains more attention and indeed different colours have different attention values. The warm colours (orange and red) advance toward us in our perception, having the effect of making whatever it is appear larger, whereas the cooler colours (blue) recede in our perception, making the message appear smaller. On this basis red is often cited as having the highest attention value.

Movement is another technique. Film, in television or cinema advertising, is often considered to be able to gain greater attention than static press messages. However, it is possible to simulate movement in a still picture and this is often done effectively with blurred backgrounds suggesting a moving foreground, for instance the speeding sports car.

In a classic case in the USA a whisky company supplied display racks to a department store. Whenever a customer physically got close to the rack, a mechanism in the rack released a bottle so it fell, only a short way, to be held again by the rack. This was wonderfully successful at gaining attention, as nearly all the customers lunged forward to try to catch the falling bottle. However, although this achieved the aims of the attention stage, it had negative effects on subsequent stages, being thought of as a rather 'sneaky' trick. There is an important message here. Whatever happens in one stage can affect other stages. In this case the attitudes formed were somewhat negative, even though the attention stage was supremely achieved.

The position of the message is also important in gaining attention. The back outside cover of a magazine, for example, means that the message can be noticed even without opening the magazine at all. Some believe that the right-hand page attracts more attention than the left because as we leaf through the pages from the beginning, it is the right page that is uncovered first. Those, however, who start with the sports page at the rear of a newspaper may well disagree and argue that the left-hand page is the one that is usually noticed first! If a double-page spread is there are no competing messages and so attention could be more likely because of this. Some artists divide their canvas/page with two equidistant horizontal and two equidistant vertical lines and consider that the eye does this automatically anyway. They consider the four points of intersection to be where the eye is taken naturally and therefore position key images to be noticed at these points. Perhaps marketers could do the same.

The size of the message has also been the focus of marketing discussion. This is not, however, a straightforward matter. Doubling the size of a message is unlikely to double attention. A suggestion is that attention increases as the square root of the message size.[4]

Another approach to gaining attention uses what might be described as known conditioned responses. We attend, almost automatically, to the sound of a telephone ringing and this approach is used to good effect in radio advertising. Other examples include introducing a radio advertisement with a statement such as 'Here is a news flash'. The Avon advertisement, using a ringing doorbell and the 'Avon calling' slogan, is another well-known example.

If a message is in some way different then because of this contrast it can stand out and attract more attention. Novelty messages such as upside-down ones in print media or something that is unusual fit into this category. The use of technology is another example. The use of moving placards at sports venues was once considered new and different and attracted attention for these reasons. The problem, of course, is that novelty only lasts a short time so the employment of this approach must be especially dynamic in order to maintain the novelty element.

One poster advertisement for Levi jeans actually had a pair of 501s glued to the poster itself. The result was that many people clearly noticed the message because many of them tried to get the jeans, but of course they were positioned too high on the poster for this to be an easy matter. Another version of this also involved a poster. A Ford car was glued to the poster, which was advertising Araldite, not Ford! A later version of this series actually saw two cars glued to each other on the poster.

It is not only important to attract consumers' attention but also to hold their attention and get the message across. Attention-getting devices are many, but if this attention is attracted by methods that do not fit with the message or the situation, the attention is readily lost. Irritation might even result from these artificial attention-getting devices, as in the whisky bottle example. The ad with the word SEX may attract attention, but if the message has nothing to do with sex, irritation and a negative connotation may result.

Attention may be held through 'participation'. These messages might be ambiguous or incomplete and for this reason the audience (sometimes through a 'double take') will attend to the message more than would otherwise be the case, in order to 'complete' the message and to make sense of it. There will be more of this approach in later stages (perception and learning in particular) but a couple of examples might help at this point.[5]

The well-known Benson and Hedges advertisements depicted something ambiguous, a packet of B&H in a parrot cage with the shadow of the parrot being projected onto the wall behind the cage. Or, the depiction of one of the stones at Stonehenge as a packet of cigarettes. These provide a sort of game. Hunt the pack, where will it be this time? A pyramid in the dessert? In any case, some participation in the approach on the part of the receiver of the message is needed and this means more effective attention-getting and attention-holding.

3.4 Perception

Once noticed, the message/offering should be perceived and understood in the intended way. For this stage we draw information from the psychology of perception. Try interpreting the pictures in Figure 3.3. What sort of product or brand would have logotypes like each of the four variants of 'KAZON'?

These pictures were used to demonstrate the importance of *how* messages are presented.[6] These versions of a hypothetical brand were developed and respondents were asked what sort of product category they belonged to. Version 1 produced no uniform reply and nothing very spontaneous was forthcoming. It was seen by different people as being a range of very different categories. Version 2, however, started to produce more rapid replies and ones which were a bit more focused: on a brand stamped on a car tyre or tea chest, presumably because of the stencilled style. Version 3 was stronger again. Most people readily thought of a comic or a powerful cleaner. Version 4 also produced fairly spontaneous and similar responses: a travel company of some kind, such as a ferry operator or airline.

Figure 3.3 KAZON.
Source: Bernstein (1974).

The point of this experiment was to convey the important message for marketers that the way in which something is presented can affect perception of it. That is, perception is not confined to the substantive element of a message. Clearly there are important implications here for logo and pack design.

Have a look at the picture in Figure 3.4(a) and you probably won't have any difficulty in seeing two messages: either a glass or two faces in profile, looking at each other. This demonstrates another principle of the psychology of perception, the use of 'figure-ground' relationships.

This was used to great effect in some 1930s advertising campaigns by Shell. The classic images were interpreted differently depending on which was taken as the figure or ground.

Figure 3.4 demonstrates yet more principles, and ones which are currently very popular in their application. Figure 3.4(b) is a picture of a couple dancing together. Although it is an incomplete picture it takes the mind only a fraction of a second to fill in the gaps and complete the incomplete and meaningless picture. This is an illustration of the 'law of closure' and it is discussed in more detail in Section 3.5. As with the attention stage it is considered to be an effective approach, because not only does an incomplete message attract attention because of its ambiguity, but it can also be effective in the perception stage because the audience often spends more time interpreting the message. Even if this extra time is only a fraction of a second, it can lead to a more effective interpretation.

Figure 3.4(c) is another well-known picture and the reader is probably ahead of us at this point. Yes, the two lines are supposed to be the same length but we are supposed to perceive the bottom one to be longer because its 'wings' extend our perception outwards whereas the top line's more inwardly directed wings

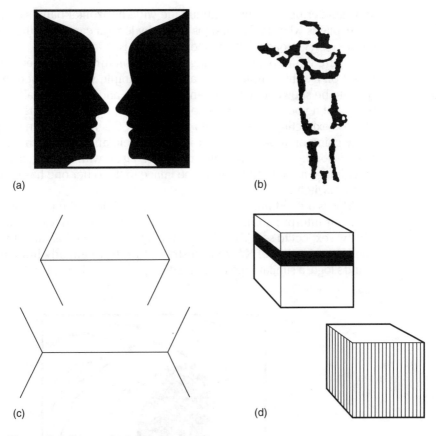

Figure 3.4 Some principles of perception.
(a) Figure-ground relationships
(b) Law of closure
(c) Visual illusion based on law of continuity
(d) Visual illusion based on law of continuity

take our interpretation to a more contracted shorter length. This is an example of the 'law of continuity', also discussed more in the 'retention' stage. Actually we have 'tweaked' this story a little here – if measured very precisely, you will find the top line slightly longer! This might make the point even more strongly.

In Figure 3.4(d) there is another variation on this process of our minds 'extending' lines. The boxes are the same size and shape but the bottom one might appear taller and thinner due to our minds continuing the thin vertical lines upwards. This is used in fashion design, where, for example, pin stripe suits are supposed to make the wearer appear taller and thinner. There is a cautionary note here, because the approach does not necessarily produce a 'slimming' effect. Where there are extra curves/bulges, the thin lines are sometimes seen to waver, thus accentuating the problems! Larger swirling patterns might be better at disguising such shapes. Conversely, the top 'pack' might appear to be wider and squatter because we continue the wide horizontal band sideways. Perhaps this explains why similar designs on rugby jerseys can make the wearer appear thicker (sorry, broader!) than he or she really is.

Figure 3.5 depicts two images in one picture. The experiment here was based on a split sample. One half of the sample was informed that they were going to be shown a picture of an old woman and the other half of the sample a picture of a young woman. Although it did not work with all respondents, most of those expecting to see the old woman saw this image first in the picture, with many going on to see the other image as well, and most of those expecting to see the young woman saw this image first, again with many going on to see the other image as well. To go from one image to the other one has to turn a kind of 'mental switch'.

This is a good illustration of another principle of the psychology of perception. Our interpretation of a message is often based on 'expectations'. We see what we expect to see. This is perhaps related to something already in our minds. The interpretation of KAZON illustrates this. If we already hold an image of a brand's logo, a similar logo might be thought to be a similar product category.

Figure 3.5 The old and the young lady.[7]

Sensory thresholds

A further consideration is that our perceptual senses have limits. These are called sensory thresholds. The point here is that although a message might exist, our senses are not capable of picking up all sensory inputs. Our hearing or sight is not as acute as that of some members of the animal kingdom. One implication of this has already been discussed in a different context, that of subliminal messages. If a message is below our sensory threshold it is just possible that although the message is not perceived consciously it might be subconsciously. 'Veteran' readers may remember the track of the (first pressing only) of The Beatles *Sergeant Pepper* album. If played with a dog in the room, this can produce strange behaviour from the animal because although unheard by the human listener, the police dog whistle on this track was clearly heard by the dog!

A marketing application of the sensory threshold concept is the use of an audio message as part of supermarket musak that says something to the effect of 'I must not steal'. The message might be below the sensory threshold to be consciously heard but perhaps it reaches the mind subconsciously and if so, by definition, the receiver is not consciously aware of the message so does not put up emotional barriers to the message and may therefore react as intended. This would, of course, be further support for the existence of the subconscious and the power of being able to reach it.

It was discovered that beers were perceived as tasting differently due to the type of music being played in the background. Apparently the (same) beers tasted stronger when the music harmonized and weak or watery when the music was harsher.[8] A similar result was obtained in an experiment in which the preference for a ball-point pen was greater when shown with attractive music than with unattractive music.[9]

A variation on this sensory threshold point concerns sensory discrimination. That is, something might be perceived, but can differences between similar messages be perceived? The marketing application here is reflected in the many taste tests that are regularly conducted. A recent group of students, for example, during a market research course in which a taste test was part of the teaching programme, claimed they liked chocolate, that they preferred one particular brand and that they would be able to identify that brand in a blind test (in which all brand identification is removed). This, of course, was the challenge. Chocolate obviously became the focus of the test and the results were probably equally predictable. Respondents stated which sample of chocolate they preferred and which brand they generally preferred and thought that the preferred sample was that brand, mostly incorrectly! This sort of experiment demonstrates the importance of branding, advertising imagery, packaging and so on, in affecting consumers' perception of a marketing offering.

In a similar experiment, regular and brand-loyal smokers tasted cigarettes, their own brand and other brands, but without brand names. They could not identify their own brand, but when asked which cigarette they liked most, they significantly chose their own brand. Although at a cognitive level they were unable to identify their own brand, they could do so at an affective level when asked for the cigarette that tasted best.[10]

Colour

Under the attention stage we discussed the use of colour in attracting attention. In this perception stage, we return briefly to the use of colour. Different colours can transmit different meanings and emotions. Most colours have both positive and negative meanings and of course different colours are more or less fashionable at different times. Furthermore, different colours can mean different things in different countries, thus making any generalizations almost impossible.

However, in western cultures, red is often seen as being a fiery, passionate colour; white as being pure and virginal; black as being mysterious, perhaps wicked but sometimes smart. Yellow might be seen as being cheerful but also sometimes as connected with deceit and cowardice. In other cultures mistakes can easily, but foolishly, be made.

Packaging garden products in green might not be controversial but in Malaysian markets this can mean jungle and disease. The funeral colour of black, in the UK, has no major taboo attached to it, but the funeral colour of other countries is not always black and sometimes should not be used outside the funeral context.

Selective perception

A final point on perception is that perception is selective. That is, different individuals might perceive the same message differently, or selectively. This might lead to the conclusion that the above discussion is totally irrelevant, that there is nothing we can do to affect perception. This is very far from the truth because the more we understand about the perceptual process, both generally and of the target market concerned, the more we can ensure that intended receivers of the message will interpret our message in the intended way. The regions in Figure 3.6 are the fields of experience of the sender and the receiver. Region C is the common frame of reference for the message between sender and receiver. If the sender of the message understands the experience and general frame of reference of the receiver and puts the message in terms that mean the same to both sender and receiver, there is a greater chance of effective communication. The receiver will then perceive and understand the message in the intended way.

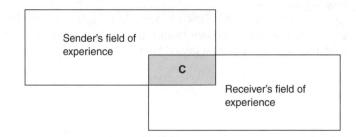

Figure 3.6 Schramm's model of communication.[11]

3.5   Retention

Assuming the marketing offering is interpreted appropriately, retention is concerned with ensuring it is remembered in the intended way. Marketing communication may be considered to be concerned with teaching consumers about various marketing offerings. If this is the case, marketing itself can benefit from a knowledge of how consumers learn about things.

Two approaches to 'teaching' customers to 'learn' and remember are outlined here. First, associationist learning theory which is summarized in Figure 3.7.

Associationist learning

Associationist learning is based on the early work of the Russian physiologist Ivan Pavlov, who considered learning to be essentially concerned with stimulus–response relationships. His experiments included observation of dogs' response to various stimuli. For example, when presented with food, dogs often salivate. There was nothing exceptional about this. It is a natural and even automatic response to that stimulus. Pavlov went on to present various other stimuli at the same time as presenting the food. Again the dogs salivated. When this process of 'paired stimuli' presentation had been repeated very often, he then presented 'the other' stimulus (the sound of a tuning fork, light bulb being flashed, and so on) by itself and the dogs salivated to that other stimulus even though no food was present. What he argued was that an unnatural response to the light or sound had been conditioned into the animals. This type of learning became known as 'classical conditioning'.

Marketing might not operate precisely at the level of Pavlov's experiments but the principles are used every day. If marketing understands what the

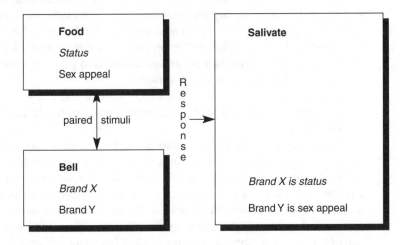

Figure 3.7 Associationist learning.

intended market segment is interested in, for example status appeals or sex appeals, it can present the relevant appeal and the market is likely to respond favourably to that appeal. What also happens, of course, is that the brand is presented at the same time and, with plenty of repetition of this paired stimuli approach, the market may well learn to associate the brand with that particular benefit. The associations attached to a large number of well-advertised brands can be explained by this process.

Chapter 2 discussed how marketing does not create needs, but rather encourages a want for a specific product because it associates its acquisition with the satisfaction of a need. This is the basis of the associationist learning approach.

Insightful learning

Another school of thought with respect to how we learn is the 'Gestalt' school. Gestalt theory is based on Kohler and his ape Sultan who displayed insight by being able to put the components of a problem together to form a (greater) whole, or solution. These experiments were conducted around the same time as Pavlov's but Kohler thought there was more to human learning than mere stimulus–response relationships. Kohler presented apes with a variety of puzzles. One such puzzle involved an ape in an almost bare cage, with a bunch of bananas hanging from the roof, but not directly accessible, and with a table in the corner of the cage.

The aim of the apes was to get the bananas but they were left to solve the problem on their own. Nothing much happened for some time until one ape, Sultan, eventually moved the table underneath the bananas, stood on it and managed to reach the fruit. Kohler described this as an extra element of mental processing that was needed to solve the problem and the learning process therefore includes a degree of 'insight'.

The 'law of closure' and the 'law of continuity' have already been discussed and it is from Gestalt theory that they originate. The marketing implication is that by encouraging participation, because the 'problem' is not solved at the immediate superficial level, marketers are tapping into this process of insight. Indeed, because of this the approach is often considered to be more effective in helping with the learning of a marketing message.

A useful summary of the Gestalt process is that 'the whole is greater than the sum of the parts' and there are plenty of examples of this in practice, especially in recent times.

Figure 3.8 demonstrates a simple example. The poster for Welsh Bitter plays on the main generic copy of the time, 'never forget your Welsh', but the message receiver has to participate in making sense of the poster by mentally moving letters around. This is an example of the law of closure. Another, which is not perhaps so effective, was for Newcastle Brown. Here there was a series of advertisements depicting initially ambiguous messages. One, for example, pictured a can of the beer with the ring pull having just been opened and the spray forming

Figure 3.8 Welsh Bitter. © Whitbread Beer Co.

a speech balloon in which the word 'woof' appeared. Another pictured an irate, arched-back cat confronting a bottle of the beer. Clearly some extra degree of mental processing is needed to make sense of these messages and perhaps any 'Geordies' of Tyneside who might be reading this will already have added the one missing piece of information. The latter example appeared as a poster campaign in the Cardiff area in Wales and out of several hundred students only a couple were able to 'make the whole mean more than the sum of the parts'. Once it is known that Newcastle Brown is colloquially known as 'the dog' then all fits into place! But, the pieces of the jigsaw must be available to receivers and in the latter instance in Cardiff this was not the case; Cardiff being in a different region in the UK (see Figure 3.9).

A wonderful illustration of the law of closure and the encouragement of receiver participation is demonstrated by a series of Beck's Bier advertisements in the style magazines of the early to mid-1990s. These advertisements were superficially very surreal and ambiguous, with strange and 'off the wall' mixed-up images. The reader, however, was shown how to make sense of the message by folding the page along dotted lines. When folded the message was simplified and the words 'just buy Beck's' were produced. It is a superb example of participation (even physical participation) (see Figure 3.10)!

There have equally been a large number of recent examples of the law of continuity. Take a 1987 campaign which presented ambiguous messages over a series of months, each time revealing just a little more. The basic approach was to present a brown paper bag and a cat about to be let out. The 'letting out' date was given and this was reinforced on television, in the press and on posters. The time of the all-revealing TV commercial was given and when the appointed time arrived the cat was indeed let out of the bag in the form of the unveiling of Barclays Connect card. The 'continuity' element concerns a staged presentation

Figure 3.9 Newcastle Brown. © Scottish & Newcastle plc.

over time encouraging participation in the story. A classic example of this, of course, is the 'soap opera' style of episodic advertising employed by Nescafé with their Gold Blend brand.

A somewhat more dubious example comes from France and concerns a poster campaign. The first poster showed a bikini-clad woman and the copy to the effect that in two days' time she would remove her top half. Two days later another poster appeared with the woman topless and the copy promising the bottom half would be removed in another two days. Sure enough on the appointed day another version appeared, with the woman now naked but with her back shown! The copy this time merely stated that the company keeps its promises.[12] The objective here was to show potential advertisers (the poster was run by the poster owners themselves) that the poster could be more responsive than many clients thought by being able to be turned around within days rather than the previously perceived months. A poster campaign on the London Underground in the mid-1990s also used this approach. Consecutive posters depicted a man in increasing states of undress. The advertisement was for a beer! The approach demonstrates the law of continuity in that people not only noticed the messages but waited for the next instalment in the sequence to appear.

Perhaps the main cautionary note to make was hinted at in the description of the Newcastle Brown poster series. It is that as long as the receiver of the message possesses the extra pieces of information needed to 'fill in the gaps' then this can be highly effective, but as soon as the messages get so ambiguous as to be meaningless, much effort and expenditure can be wasted.

Figure 3.10 Beck's Bier. © Scottish Courage Ltd.

In the same way that we discussed selective perception earlier, there can be an equivalent at this stage as well – selective retention. Indeed the selective processes affect all stages so far – selective exposure, selective attention, selective perception and selective retention. The techniques and theory on which to base marketing approaches, however, provide potential means for ensuring a reasonable degree of uniformity of response even though there is equally the potential for individualistic responses.

3.6   Conviction

This next stage aims to develop favourable beliefs, attitudes, and intentions towards the marketing offering. These are components of the structure of attitude and the attitude–behaviour relationship. Attitude (A) consists of a set of beliefs multiplied by their evaluations. In a similar manner, the social norm (SN) consists of a set of normative beliefs multiplied by the motivation to comply with these norms. Normative beliefs are convictions about what is socially acceptable, that is how reference persons (the notorious mother-in-law) might evaluate the behaviour. The motivation to comply is the degree to which one accepts the evaluations of the reference persons. Behavioural intention is a weighted sum of attitude and social norm. Behavioural intention is a good predictor of behaviour. This is represented in the formula below and in Figure 3.11.[13]

$$B \approx BI = w_1 \times A + w_2 \times SN = w_1 (\Sigma_i B_i \times E_i) + w_2 (\Sigma_j NB_j \times MC_j)$$

Note that the cognitive elements are represented in the product and normative beliefs. The affective (emotional) elements are represented in the evaluations of the beliefs. The conative (behavioural) elements are represented in the behavioural intention of the model of Figure 3.4.

Such a structure helps define promotional objectives, creates messages and evaluates campaigns. Objectives can be defined by discovering the nature of perception, and indeed misconception, over the marketing offering together with reasons for 'like' as opposed to 'dislike' and whether 'intend to buy' is the stage the segment generally is at. Messages could be determined directly from this exercise because the precise point of misconception, for example, can be the message headline. Campaigns can be evaluated by re-measuring the same dimensions to see if the campaign has progressed the segment along the attitude continuum from basic knowledge about the offering, through favourable attitudes towards it, to the intention to act.

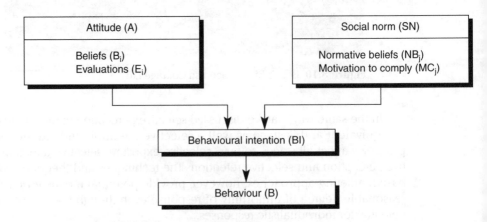

Figure 3.11 Attitude–behaviour structure.

The conclusion of the conviction stage is, hopefully, that the segment will have been moved significantly towards 'intention' to act, for example to buy.

3.7 Action

The whole rationale behind this model is that there is no simple checklist of marketing activities that result in instant action by consumers. The previous stages of response move potential customers through pre-purchase events so that there is a better chance of the conversion of 'intend to buy' into 'buy'.

There are several kinds of consumer behaviour that may be the target for marketing policy:

■ Information behaviour: Consumers asking for more information about the offerings, for example travel guides.
■ Store traffic: Consumers visiting the store, attracted by marketing activities.
■ Purchase behaviour, actual transactions and purchases.
■ Usage behaviour: Marketing communication might be directed towards stimulating or diminishing the usage of a product, for example governmental campaigns to reduce the use of private cars. A mail order company may advertise to stimulate the use of the catalogue.
■ Disposition behaviour: Discarding, scrapping or recycling products at the end of their lifetime.

What actually is action or consumer behaviour? Consumer behaviour is a meaningful activity for people. Marketing offerings and their communication have to fit into the goals and interests of consumers. Only then can consumers be persuaded to accept the marketing offering. Consumer behaviour is an ongoing stream of meaningful and goal-directed activities, through which people try to get and to maintain control over their lives, relationships and environment. Marketing activities influence the 'wanting' and the 'doing'. These processes are closely connected. Consumer goals and plans are generally much more influential on their behaviour than marketing stimuli. Furthermore, it is the total marketing mix that influencies consumers, not only marketing communication.

Even the gimmicks aimed at impulse buying are to some extent dependent upon some level of prior understanding and interest in the product or service. For example, the point of sale promotions will themselves be building upon the above sequence of events. The process may operate rapidly and some stages are worked through less thoroughly than others, as might be the case in some product markets.

3.8 Post-purchase

Purchase is not the end of the process. Marketing is concerned with satisfied customers, good relationships with customers, repeat purchasing and/or the spreading of goodwill. Especially in the case of fast-moving consumer goods, advertising is important to keep customers loyal.

Post-purchase advertising and other product information on packages and labels is important for consumers to structure their product experience. Consumers who bought a bottle of Moldavian wine like to learn about the country of origin of this wine, the type of grapes and other information. The wine may taste better for knowing this information. The same is true for Scottish single-malt whiskies. Background information helps to structure the experiences with the product and to appreciate the product.

Cognitive dissonance

This stage can be better understood with reference to cognitive dissonance theory. Cognitive dissonance is a kind of psychological tension due to perceived inconsistencies in cognitions.[14] An example will help here. A car has just been purchased after a fairly extensive pre-purchase search amongst alternatives and evaluation of these. The final choice is probably a bit of a compromise because no car is completely tailored to the requirements of each individual customer. Having said this, the final choice is seen as being highly satisfactory by the purchaser. There may be, though, some design features of the dashboard of one of the rejected alternatives that are still seen as being superior or more appealing. These slightly contradictory 'cognitions' can produce dissonance. 'Have I done the right thing?' buyers might ask themselves.

The level of dissonance is a function of the importance of the cognitions to the individual. So, if the point about the dashboard is very minor, the level of dissonance might be negligible. If, however, you drive your new car home and the next door neighbour, who you see as being especially knowledgeable about cars, says 'Why on earth did you buy that, that model has a terrible repair record?', your level of dissonance could be very substantial indeed.

The individual tries to reduce cognitive dissonance. It is, therefore, a motivator, as mentioned in Chapter 2. In the above example, a high level of dissonance over the car might lead the buyer to seek supporting evidence for his or her decision, to provide reassurance that he or she has 'done the right thing'.

Indeed, much advertising is aimed at people who have already bought, in order to help them overcome dissonance, reassure them of their purchase decision and therefore to ease the way for a repeat purchase or at least to spread positive messages to others.[15]

It is worth emphasizing that if a purchase is clearly unsuitable, if we are dissatisfied with it, this cognition is clearly at odds with how we felt about it before purchase and therefore there is a high level of dissonance. That is, if we are dissatisfied with a purchase we experience dissonance. However, we can be basically satisfied, but still have a few doubts along the lines reported above and can experience dissonance in this way. Thus, dissonance is not the same as dissatisfaction. Dissatisfaction produces dissonance, yes, but a generally satisfying purchase may also produce cognitive dissonance if some of the cognitions over it are slightly inconsistent with each other.

Another example of dissonance comes from the cigarette-smoking market and this provides us with something of a framework for overcoming dissonance or avoiding it in the first instance. This last point is also an important one; although we are discussing dissonance in this post-purchase stage, because it applies particularly well here, it can occur in the pre-purchase phase as well. Wherever there are alternatives we can perceive positive and negative cognitions of all alternatives, so the mental processing of these pros and cons can obviously lead to levels of confusion and doubt over the best choice.

Back to the smoking example: smoking cigarettes is initially a positive and rewarding activity. There is initially no dissonance. However, receiving messages about health risks and negative societal reactions to smoking poses a problem and leads to the psychological tension of dissonance. Table 3.2 shows four generalized ways of overcoming dissonance.

The first method looks simpler than it really is. Changing our behaviour by stopping altogether (apart from being easier to say than to achieve) might reduce the dissonance resulting from the health and social warnings. All the positives (the nicotine, and so on) have gone, and dissonance can arise over not smoking! Ex-smokers might turn to eating more, especially mints, and this might lead to dissonance over gaining weight or tooth problems! Less dramatic changes in behaviour such as switching to smoking cigars or a pipe might enable smokers to reassure themselves that the health risk might be less and that although dissonance still exists, it is not at the same level and therefore it might be manageable. Once cigar smokers realize, however, that by smoking cigars in the same way that they smoked cigarettes (inhaling) the result can be even more damaging, dissonance would clearly rocket again!

The second method is to refuse to accept that there is a strong or proven link between cigarette smoking and health problems. It has been found that some smokers rationalize their behaviour in this way. They say there might be a correlation but not necessarily a causal link. The point here is that if dissonance is based on the balance between positive and negative cognitions, then by reducing the perceived level of the negative ones, dissonance can be reduced to a tolerable level.

The third strategy reduces the importance of all of the cognitions. By convincing ourselves that the issue is relatively insignificant in our lives we might still experience dissonance over it, but at a much reduced and acceptable level. We might, of course, increase dissonance over car driving, especially if we drive and smoke at the same time!

Table 3.2 Dissonance-reducing strategies in smoking.

Generalized strategies	Example in smoking
(1) Change one's behaviour	Stop smoking
	Change to smoking cigar or pipe
(2) Distort the dissonant information	Refuse to accept cancer connection
(3) Minimize the importance of the issue	Say there is more chance of death in a car crash
(4) Ignore dissonant information and seek consonant information	Seek social support

The fourth approach is a variation on the second. Rather than distorting that which is dissonant, we might seek more of that which is consonant. The argument that our friends are fit and healthy – and smoke – serves to accentuate the positive cognitions to an extent that they outweigh the dissonant cognitions. Early cigarette advertising actually used this approach and depicted young, fit and energetic smokers with the implication that 'you too can be like this if you smoke this brand'! Even sporting heroes were used in such smoking advertisements. In the Russia of the mid-1990s some of these old advertisements have been used on TV.

Based on the above we can transfer the general strategies into workable approaches in marketing. It might appear obvious to suggest that we emphasize the consistent cognitions (positive aspects of the product) and indeed this is based on the balancing act between the consonant and the dissonant aspects. However, there are occasions when a slightly negative set of points can be made as well. The use of two-sided arguments has been suggested as being effective for more educated audiences. An example is in a Volkswagen advertisement in which the VW is shown to be slower than a competitor. The small print, however, goes on to point out the extra safety and other features that the Volkswagen possesses.

This also takes us to the implication that there are dissonant elements of competing products. This is again based on the balance between the consonant and dissonant. We perhaps try to increase dissonance over competing products. Comparative advertising, although banned in some countries, is used extensively in others. In the UK for instance, it is not uncommon for advertisements for model X car to show the market leader as well and to emphasize, selectively, only a few features, such as the smaller boot that the competitor has. The other car might be the market leader but 'ours' is so much less expensive and still comes with many similar features.

Another good illustration of this was an advertisement for new homes. The two-column message listed the advantages of buying a new home in one column, such as a ten-year guarantee, the latest fittings, new electrical systems and energy-saving heating. In the other column, the negatives associated with buying a 20-year-old house were given, for example the need to spend money on a new kitchen, rewiring the electricity and replacing windows. The advertisement in figure 3.12 demonstrates this approach by trying to create dissonance over travelling by road rather than rail, based on traffic congestion and cones.

Another approach, based on the smoking strategies, is the equivalent of seeking social support and building up the consonant cognitions. For example, we can emphasize how many other (satisfied) customers there are. In the mid-1990s a satellite broadcaster, in advertising its dishes, used the copy headline 'half a million people can't be wrong'.

The approach is also to be seen in the music industry where the record companies strive to get their records into the charts, not only because this means they sell more at that stage and get more airplay, but also because once they can be promoted as 'a hit' it appears to give them additional credibility and reduce potential dissonance by the buyer thinking that if he or she is silly to buy then millions of others are as well, and that is unlikely! The same applies to the book

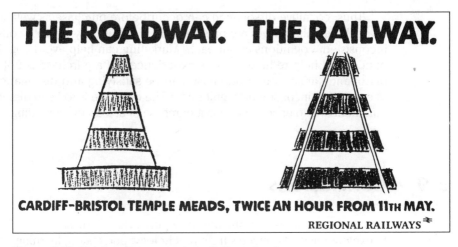

THE ROADWAY. THE RAILWAY.

CARDIFF–BRISTOL TEMPLE MEADS, TWICE AN HOUR FROM 11TH MAY.

REGIONAL RAILWAYS

Figure 3.12 Creating dissonance out of 'alternatives'.

market. Faced with rows of novels, the one with 'million seller' on the cover can attract the buyer in the same way.

Related to this is offering reassurance through after-sales service and warranties. This is again very prominent in the car market and reflects the pragmatic view that cars are complicated pieces of machinery and that no car is tailor-made for each individual customer, so there are bound to be both consonant and dissonant cognitions. However, by emphasizing that if anything goes wrong, there is really nothing to worry about because the company will look after the purchaser, there is less basis for dissonance.[16] Mitsubishi in the mid-1990s used the copy headline 'They would cost us a fortune if they were not so reliable'.

Another approach based on a 'smoking' strategy is to help reduce the importance of the issue. How many of us have bought a garment in a sale, and even though our dissonance over how it fits or its colour is so great that it comes from dissatisfaction, not just inconsistent cognitions, we are able to reduce this dissonance to a tolerable level. We even go back and buy something else from the sales, because we rationalize it as 'a bargain' and that for this reason it doesn't matter so much!

A final approach is perhaps the most dubious. If, as we have said, individuals interpret messages in their own individualistic ways, that is, there is degree of selective perception, then if we do not provide many cognitions at all, there is less chance of cognitions being seen as dissonant ones. An example of this was the Vauxhall Chevette which, when launched, pictured a young family in the car in one quadrant of the advertisement, two nuns driving it in another, a more sporty scene in another and a different driver in the fourth. The copy read 'Vauxhall Chevette. It's whatever you want it to be'. The dubiousness is based on a possible lack of commitment over what the car is or who it is aimed at, trying to be all things to all people and ending up being nothing very strong for any particular group. More recently Vauxhall have employed a similar approach with the Astra: 'Every car you'll ever need'. The magazine *Bella* was advertised with the copy 'Bella: It has got whatever you want'.

Thus, cognitive dissonance can occur before purchase as well as after purchase. When alternatives are presented there will usually be both consistent and inconsistent cognitions about each. Marketing can help avoid cognitive dissonance, and help reduce it if it is experienced. If a purchase is not satisfying, dissonance arises, but a purchase can be satisfying and dissonance can still occur due to inconsistent cognitions.[17] The objective is to keep dissonance to a minimum and to encourage repeat purchase or at least the spreading of goodwill.

3.9   Conclusions

This is but one model of pre- and post-purchase buying stages but it does serve to explore relevant concepts from psychology: perception, learning, attitude and cognitive dissonance. Another model is described briefly in the next chapter as being the stages leading to the full-scale adoption or brand-loyal buying of a product. The intention of that chapter is to introduce another set of valuable concepts that marketing can apply: consumers' response to new products and their repeat buying responses as the product life cycle progresses.

Endnotes

1. The following is based on Delozier's (1976) model.
2. Mintel Banking (1982).
3. R.G.M. Pieters and W.F. Van Raaij, 1992, p. 103.
4. This is the 'square-root law' developed by H.J. Rudolph, 1947.
5. This is called the Zeigarnik effect. B. Zeigarnik, 1927.
6. D. Bernstein, 1975.
7. E.G. Boring (1930).
8. K. Holt-Hansen, 1978, p. 1023.
9. G.J. Gorn, 1982. These are examples of associationist learning.
10. R.A. Littman and H.M. Manning, 1954.
11. W. Schramm and D. Roberts (eds), 1971.
12. D. Ogilvie, 1983.
13 M. Fishbein and I. Ajzen, 1975.
14. R.G.M. Pieters and B. Verplanken, 1991.
15. L. Festinger, 1957.
16. D. Ehrlich, L. Guttman, P. Schonbach, and J. Mills, 1957.
17. See T. Roselius, 1971, for ways to reduce perceived risk with the purchase.

4

Innovation and the product life cycle

Chapter objectives

(1) To take the principle of 'stages' of consumer response to marketing activity in a logical but different direction, namely that different consumers go through this sort of sequence more quickly than others and are therefore more innovative than others.
(2) To examine the concept of innovativeness in the context of the buyer and marketing of new products and services.
(3) To explore different adopter categories and show how a knowledge of their buying behaviour can be used in marketing new products.
(4) To apply the ideas of multi-step communications flows to the buying and selling of new products.
(5) To extend the concepts of adoption processes and repeat purchase into models of new product-buying predictions.

4.1 Introduction

What is proposed in this chapter is that over the product life cycle, different marketing management approaches are required to persuade consumers to buy the product or service. One reason is because there is generally a trend towards increased competition over time such that marketing needs to be competitively responsive as the product life cycle proceeds.

The other main reason why marketing changes through the life cycle stages is because customers themselves change. Early on, those who 'adopt' a new product or service tend to be more interested in newness and might even be termed 'innovators', whereas those who do not adopt until it has been on the market for quite some time are less innovative and could sometimes be called the 'late majority' in this respect.

This chapter discusses different adopter categories and the marketing approaches required to reach and to influence them.

4.2 Diffusion and adoption

First, a brief look at the theory. Diffusion refers to how the innovation is communicated and distributed through society over time. An innovation is anything perceived as being new in the market-place. An innovation may be completely new: a discontinuous innovation, such as the first television set or the first PC. An innovation may be an improvement of an existing product: a continuous innovation, such as the detergent Ariel Future compared with standard Ariel.

Communications approaches can draw from direct and deliberate personal forms or from less formal, indirect ones that perhaps allow some of the natural opinion leadership flows of information to take their usual course. This can be of crucial importance. Often a local opinion leader will be more persuasive than a paid-for expensive advertising campaign. But how to influence the influencers is the inevitable question here.

The adoption process is really the other side of the same coin. It refers to the acceptance of innovation by individuals in terms of how they progress through the stages of awareness, interest, evaluation, trial, and adoption. Specifically, the more innovative consumers go through this sequence at a speedy rate.

The same elements as there are for diffusion exist here. For example, we are concerned with the progression through these stages over time due to individuals' innovativeness, which in turn can be related to their position in society and how they influence others and/or are influenced by others and the communications sources they seek and are influenced by.

A major focus of consumer research has been to identify the characteristics of the more innovative consumers and their differences from other consumers. A review of this research found that innovators tend to be more highly educated and younger, and to have greater social mobility, more favourable attitudes towards risk (more venturesome), greater social participation and higher opinion leadership than other consumers.[1]

Innovators also tend to be heavy users of other products within a product class. Innovators may have better developed knowledge structures for particular product categories. This may enable them to understand and evaluate new products more rapidly and thus adopt earlier than other consumers.[2]

Finally, it should be noted that the five adopter categories and the percentages in Figure 4.1 are somewhat arbitrary. Their validity has not been fully supported in consumer research, particularly not for low-involvement products.[3]

However, the idea that different types of consumers purchase products in different stages of the product's life cycle does have important implications for

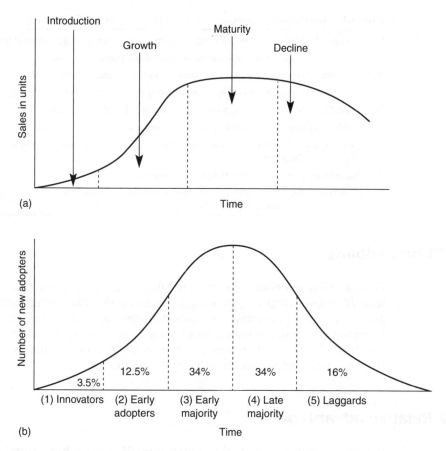

Figure 4.1 (a) Product life cycle and (b) adopter categories.

product strategy. Namely, product strategy (and other elements of marketing strategy) must change across time to appeal to different types of consumers.

4.3 Characteristics of innovations

In analysing consumer/product relationships, it is also important to consider the product characteristics listed in Table 4.1. A number of these characteristics have been found to influence the success of new products and brands.[4] There is no absolute demarcation. But some of the dimensions are more directly involved with facilitating trial, while others both facilitate trial and encourage brand loyalty. Each of these characteristics will be discussed below: compatibility, relative advantage, trialability, observability, speed, simplicity, perceived risk, product symbolism, and the role of marketing strategy in this regard.

Table 4.1 Some important questions in analysing consumer/product relationships.

(1) *Compatibility.* How well does this product fit consumers' current cognitions and behaviours?

(2) *Relative advantage.* Which attribute makes this product better than competitive products?

(3) *Trialability.* Can consumers try the product on a limited basis with little risk?

(4) *Observability.* Do consumers frequently see or otherwise sense this product?

(5) *Speed.* How soon do consumers experience the benefits of the product?

(6) *Simplicity.* How easy is it for consumers to understand and use the product?

(7) *Perceived risk.* What type of risks and which amount of risk do consumers perceive in the new product?

(8) *Product symbolism.* What does this product mean to consumers?

(9) *Marketing strategy.* What is the role of other marketing-mix elements in creating a functional or image-related advantage?

1 Compatibility

Compatibility refers to the degree to which a product is consistent with consumers' current values, cognitions and behaviours. Other things being equal, a product that does not require an important change in consumer values, beliefs, purchase, or use behaviours is more likely to be tried by consumers. For example, Wash 'N' Go, a shampoo and conditioner in one bottle, required little change on the part of consumers to try the product.

2 Relative advantage

Relative advantage refers to the degree to which an item has a sustainable, competitive differential advantage over other product classes, product forms and brands. There is no question that relative advantage is a most important product characteristic not only for obtaining trial, but also for continued purchase and the development of brand loyalty.

In some cases, a relative advantage may be obtained through technological developments. For example, at the product class level, Philips and Sony introduced HDTV (high definition television), an improvement over the traditional television picture quality.

At the brand level, however, it is often difficult to maintain a technological relative advantage. This is because new or improved technology is quickly copied by competitors. Competitors simply copy the technology and, by saving money on R&D, can sell at a lower price.

Relative advantage is a most important element of successful product strategies. However, such an advantage can seldom be sustained through technology or modifications of product attributes alone. One of the most important sources of sustainable relative advantage is product symbolism.

3 Trialability

Trialability refers to the degree to which a product can be tried on a limited basis or divided into small quantities for an inexpensive trial. Other things being equal, a product that facilitates a non-purchase trial or limited-purchase trial is more likely to influence the consumer to try the product. Test driving a car, trying on a sweater, tasting bite-sized pieces of a new frozen pizza, accepting a free trial of a new encyclopaedia, or buying a sample-sized bottle of a new shampoo are ways that consumers can try products on a limited basis and reduced risk.

4 Observability

Observability refers to the degree to which products or their effects can be sensed by other consumers. New products that are public and frequently discussed are more likely to be adopted rapidly. For example, many clothing styles become popular after consumers see film and recording stars wearing them. Satellite dishes are also highly observable, and this feature is likely to influence their purchase.

5 Speed

Speed refers to how fast the benefits of the product are experienced by the consumer. Because many consumers are oriented towards immediate rather than delayed gratification, products that can deliver benefits sooner rather than later have a higher probability of at least being tried. For example, diets that promise results within the first week are more likely to attract consumers than those that promise results in six months.

6 Simplicity

Simplicity refers to the degree to which a product is easy for a consumer to understand and use. Other things being equal, a product that does not require complicated assembly and extensive training for the consumer to use it has a higher chance of trial. For example, many computer products are promoted as being 'user friendly' to encourage purchase.

7 Perceived risk

If the perceived (physical, financial or social) risk of the new product is low, it is more likely to be adopted. Products with a high level of perceived risk, such as drugs and dangerous sports, will generally have a lower adoption rate.

8 Product symbolism

Product symbolism refers to what the product or brand means to the consumer and what the consumer experiences in purchasing and using it. Consumer researchers recognize that some products possess symbolic features, and that consumption of them may depend more on their social and psychological meaning than on their functional utility.[5] For example, the blue-jean market is dominated by major brands such as Levi's, Wrangler's, and Lee's, and it is difficult to explain differences in market shares, given the similarity among brands. It seems clear that jeans brand names have meanings and symbolize different values for consumers. For example, teenagers make up a large portion of the market for Levi's '501' jeans. These consumers may be seeking to present an identity different from that of wearers of traditional brands, such as their parents.

It is also likely that appropriate images can be far more important than technological superiority. For example, the IBM personal computer is not the fastest, most technologically advanced PC on the market. In fact, many users even criticize its keyboard layout. IBM was not the first in the PC market and had little experience in consumer goods marketing. However, IBM dominates the PC market, perhaps because of its superior company image as a computer manufacturer; that is, IBM means computers to many people.

4.4 Adopter categories

As has already been indicated, there is a relation here between the product life cycle and categories of adopter (seen in Figure 4.1).

A useful summary of the characteristics of adopter categories is reproduced below.[6]

(1) *Innovators* are eager to try new ideas. They do not need much persuasion. They are fairly well off and are willing to take risks. They tend to be younger and to have higher status and education. Their reading goes beyond 'local' and mass media communications. They have the closest contact with scientific and specialist sources of information and in general rely on impersonal sources. They seek social relationships outside their local peer circle. They are extrovert in a 'jet set' sense. They have a broad range of interests and are socially mobile.

(2) *Early adopters* tend to have the greatest contact with salespeople and local people and are often leaders in local clubs and organizations. They exhibit the greatest opinion leadership and are highly 'localite'. They have a high status and are fairly well off. They are highly respected in local society and are often asked for their opinions and advice.

(3) *Early majority* have contact with mass media, salespeople, but also with early adopters. They do not exhibit so much opinion leadership and deliberate over adoption decisions.

(4) *Late majority* tend to be sceptical and need much pressure from peers before they adopt. They are below average in terms of income, status and education, and so on. They adopt when they perceive it as little risk, perhaps when they see others like themselves using it.

(5) *Laggards* are bound in tradition and often use other laggards as sources of information. The past is their frame of reference. Some are semi-isolates. They do not use the mass media or salespeople as information sources. They tend to be older and from lower socio-economic groups and are less wealthy. They might become adopters when innovators are adopting the next innovation. 'Laggards' is however a misnomer for consumers who are actively against the usage of a product, for instance anti- or non-smokers, vegetarians, or people that do not possess a car for pro-environmental reasons. In such circumstances there may be innovators/early adopters in terms of these social values.

It becomes clear, on reading through this description of the various adopters, how there can be a sort of segmentation over time, because each category is quite different from the others in both innovativeness and demographic profile.

4.5   Opinion leadership

As can be deduced from the above, a major factor in speeding up the diffusion process is the use of opinion leadership. Indeed, when people want to set up their own business, one marketing approach that is usually recommended is to consider targeting various opinion leaders. For instance, small businesses have scarce resources and cannot really afford to compete with the large advertising budgets of some of their powerful competitors. So, rather than booking expensive television advertising campaigns to target the final consumer, it is often recommended that they consider targeting business correspondents of their local newspapers and magazines so that they might achieve some editorial coverage of their new ranges or other aspects of their business.

These correspondents are read as if they possess a degree of knowledge of and credibility in the subject matter and can act like opinion leaders, sometimes in a far more persuasive way than a paid-for advertising campaign. On a larger scale, this is why, for example, the top fashion designers are keen to 'show' at the major fashion shows in order to get editorial coverage in the leading fashion and women's magazines and in national newspapers. The 'saleability' of their collections is often only secondary to achieving 'exposure'.

Using real opinion leaders

To demonstrate the power of opinion leadership an experiment was set up.[7] A pop record was produced, but not distributed widely. In some university towns, sociometric research was done (Figure 4.2). This entailed asking each student,

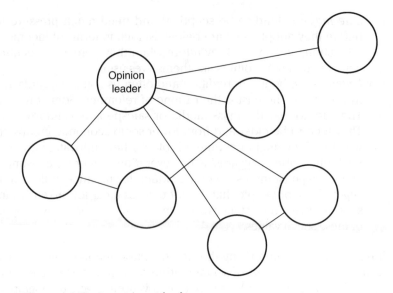

Figure 4.2 Sociometric methods.

in isolation from the rest of the group, which other members of the class that student would most like to listen to when it comes to music and buying records. This produced a sort of network of communication between students in the class, some being mentioned by many other students in this respect, some being perhaps more isolated in terms of music and records. If students are mentioned by many others, this implies that they possess a degree of credibility in terms of music and records. These students were considered to be more likely to be higher in opinion leadership than others. A copy of the record was mailed to these opinion leaders as a token of appreciation.

As a 'control group', a copy of the record was mailed to other students in other universities. In this case, though, some student names were selected at random from class lists. Some may have been opinion leaders, but this would really only be a coincidence and fewer of these would be opinion leaders than those selected in the other universities through sociometric research. Distribution of the record was recognized in the university towns that were used as both experimental and control groups.

In those towns where the 'real' opinion leaders were selected, the record actually moved into the charts, but in the control towns, where few opinion leaders were targeted, the record was nothing of a 'hit'.

This research demonstrates the potential power of targeting opinion leaders. It also demonstrates the complexity that is often encountered when attempting to identify real opinion leaders by name and address.

In medical markets this approach is frequently used. An example was described by Michael Rawlins in *The Lancet* in somewhat critical terms.[8] He described how medics are targeted by the pharmaceutical industry and are classified as either conservatives or risk takers. The more innovative are identified by sales representatives who discuss doctors' prescribing habits with local pharmacists. This information can be used to target the more innovative when a new drug is being launched. The opinion leaders are then invited to various 'events', seminars, lunches and so on and often go back and start prescribing the new drug. Their behaviour is observed by the less innovative and emulated, thus demonstrating the two-step flow of communication.[9] The first step is reaching opinion leaders and the second step being the social communication from opinion leaders to opinion followers.

Rawlins is critical of the industry for the approach but also lays a charge of potential corruption at the door of some medics. They expect such rewards in return for sometimes needless prescribing habits.

To take this further, some time ago the drug 'Flosint' was launched. It treated rheumatoid arthritis and the launch was based on selected medics (opinion leaders) being taken to Switzerland for a weekend conference with plenty of food and drink and an all expenses paid trip on the Orient Express. Many went back to prescribe Flosint and were copied by the opinion followers. The approach can clearly be effective in speeding up the diffusion rate. The final twist to this particular story was that within a few months of its launch Flosint was associated with several deaths and it was banned.

Marketing-PR

Similar methods are employed in other industries, in agricultural markets for the introduction of new practices, in machinery and fertilizers, and also in the car market. Most car manufacturers employ advertising agents to devise promotional campaigns but many also have PR consultants. These work on new product launches in various ways; for example, they possess databases of motoring correspondents and categorize these in terms of credibility with the consumer. Selected journalists will be taken to (for example) Spain where they can road-test the new car, enjoy the sunshine, food and hospitality and be given a 'press release'. Now, this is not merely a list of technical specifications but will usually be full of favourable adjectives.

The journalists will not plagiarize these releases but some of the adjectives may well reappear in their road report as published in the motoring press. The consumer will read these road reports as if from some totally objective and independent source. An editor of one such magazine has admitted that there is pressure on editors to do this, from the advertisers. If particularly discreditable reports are published, he says, there have been occasions when the advertiser has informed the editor that they will advertise elsewhere for a while.

This goes even further: a PR consultant confessed that they regularly check the daily press and estimate that two-thirds to three-quarters of the news/editorial (that is ignoring all advertising content) originates from a PR source. Small businesses are often advised that they would not be able to afford much mass media advertising, but if they wine and dine their local business correspondent and provide him or her with an interesting story about the development of the business or product, they can achieve perhaps half a page of (almost) free publicity. This type of publicity isn't advertising, it comes from an (objective) business journalist, so again the cognitive defences on the part of the readership are not raised.

Fashion journalists are similarly targeted on this 'opinion-leading' basis. In this way there is a multi-step flow of communications: designers to opinion-leading journalists to those who are more 'followers' and to buyers of chain stores and their designers to opinion-leading consumers to 'the majority' in the market-place.

Political lobbying is also based on this. PR companies maintain computerised databases of all members of parliament and their political and non-political interests. When the small print of proposed legislation is scrutinized by these companies on behalf of their clients and something is discovered that might affect the client, the PR agents set to work on opinion-leading politicians. Often it will not be members of the Cabinet who are targeted but those known to have an interest in and credibility over the issue. These members of parliament will be dined and will receive a presentation in favour of the PR consultant's client. If they go back to the parliament and set up 'working committees', they will probably be more influential because they are seen to have additional credibility over other members of parliament in the issue concerned. Is this a good example of democracy at work, or is it buying access to the legislators? There is a strong argument here for considering the ethics of such approaches – if anyone has concerns over advertising on the grounds of its being manipulative then the approaches described here must surely raise far more ethical issues.

It has been found that opinion leaders are rarely opinion leaders in many product markets. Opinion leadership is mainly product class or domain specific. Fashion opinion leaders, for instance, do not necessarily possess this kind of credibility in electronics or car markets.

It can be prohibitively costly in time and money to conduct research to identify actual opinion leaders. There are ways around this problem, though, and the next section discusses one approach.

Simulating opinion leaders

As was seen in Figure 4.1, those in the early adopter category are more likely to be higher in opinion leadership, and they possess certain demographic characteristics. This means that with some further research into specific markets, it is usually possible to identify the sort of people who are opinion leaders. These characteristics can then be depicted in promotional campaigns.

Sometimes, specific well-known personalities can be used to simulate the opinion leadership that is desired. Although not necessarily an example targeted at the readers of this book, research has shown that the use of Lulu to promote the Freemans Mail Order Catalogue, and Lorraine Chase and the Great Universal Catalogue, were extremely effective for the respective target markets.

Something to guard against in these circumstances is that consumers remember the personality but not your product or brand! A long-running campaign using Joan Collins and Lennard Rossiter for a brand of vermouth was well remembered for the personalities but the actual brand being promoted was not always correctly remembered.

Product placement

Many films and television programmes are subject to 'product placement', where brands are shown or mentioned in the film. Viewers do not put up their cognitive defence to the same extent as they might if the same products appeared in commercials. The suppliers pay for the privilege, of course.

A classic example concerns the James Bond series. Many products are mentioned or shown, often just once, and part of the idea is that James Bond is some sort of aspirational reference point for some of the audience, an opinion leader in effect, and if he wears a Seiko watch, shaves with a Philishave and drinks Bollinger champagne then followers should do so as well! This is a classic example of a simulated opinion leader.

Another example is yet another mythical character, Roy of the Rovers. The comic of this name was bought by Gola the sportswear company and whereas there was little advertising in the publication, the sporting hero, Roy, was always wearing Gola kit.

Some years ago the brewing industry wanted to change the image of lager as being a feminine drink. The approach was to advertise more macho images of men drinking lager and to associate lager, through sponsorship, with energetic and aggressive sports. All of this probably contributed to the 'lager lout' image but certainly demonstrated effective campaigns. The simulated opinion leadership approach was prohibited in that anything vaguely communicating a lager lout stereotype could not be used. One company took the simulation even further and introduced a bear character who was only a stone's throw away from being a lager lout himself, but even this approach was banned, serving to reinforce its potential effectiveness.

The overall implication is to communicate with the opinion leaders first (by formal marketing activities) and then through a two-step or even multi-step flow of communication and influence, the 'followers' are persuaded. There is indeed a body of research that has tended to confirm this as a general process, the study of nylon and dacron for example.[10]

Diffusion patterns

In some markets, for example fashion markets, it is typical for marketing to use multi-step flows of communications, in this instance from designers to fashion shows, to fashion editors and journalists, to retail buyers, to consumer fashion opinion leaders, to fashion followers, in early and late 'majority' categories (see Figure 4.1). Again in this instance, fashion opinion leaders are characterized as young, gregarious and high in status.[11] However, fashion opinion leaders can be found at both the top and bottom of the socio-economic scale.[12] If they are so spread for a single fashion then there can be difficulties in maintaining consistent marketing communications. Other researchers have come up with theories of 'trickle down' (from designers to the general public), 'trickle across' (spreading within social strata) and even 'trickle up' (for example, the mini skirt and punk fashions).

Up-down-sideways theories are likely to disenchant practitioners; if not, then there is also a 'parallel diffusion' process which suggests that boutiques adopt a fashion line before multiples, who in turn adopt before independents or department stores.[13] Elements of reality can be seen in all of these approaches, but which one does the practitioner choose?

What is evident, however, is that there is a reasonably logical 'cascading' sequence from innovators through to early majority consumers. The 'big divide' is between early and late majority. For the latter, the 'newness' appeal is precisely why these people are not already adopters. So it means the appeals should change to being less based on newness, even turning this around to state a degree of longevity in the market, 'tried and tested' and so on. It might also mean prices falling a little, to appeal to the late majority. If so, then the whole character of the brand is being changed, perhaps too much for the earlier adopters?

Another feature to emerge from this discussion of the adoption process is that it provides a sort of segmentation over time, because each category is quite different from the others, in both innovativeness and demographic profile. Indeed it can be deduced from the above that a major factor in speeding up the diffusion process is the use of opinion leaders. It was mentioned earlier that Levi's employed different advertising campaigns for the 15–19-year-olds in the style press in order to 'reach the key opinion formers in that age group'.[14]

The concepts of new and then repeat purchase, as introduced by the notion of the adoption process, also provides us with a useful basis for evaluating new products. Specifically it allows first time and subsequent repeat buying to be measured and on this basis to predict the likely brand share of a new product before it is actually launched (through the use of consumer panel data).

4.6   Parfitt–Collins model

For the Parfitt–Collins model, consumer panel data provide the consumption patterns of each household that reports, so it is possible to identify when an individual household buys a product for the first time, and when they buy the product again.[15] The Parfitt–Collins model utilizes such data to calculate the penetration of the market and the repeat purchasing rate in order to estimate eventual brand share. It is thus a predictive model.

Figure 4.3(a) shows how panel households bought different brands (T, R and S) in the same product category, from the time (week 1) that new brand (T) was launched. In week 1, two households purchased this brand for the first time, so this is the cumulative number of new buyers for week 1. In the second week, households 3 and 4 buy T for the first time, bringing the cumulative number of

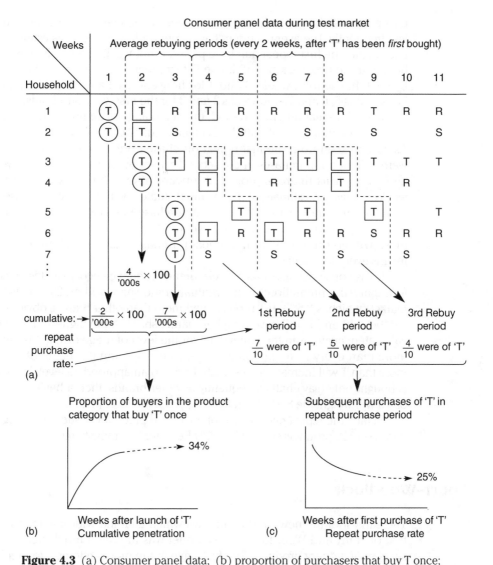

Figure 4.3 (a) Consumer panel data; (b) proportion of purchasers that buy T once; (c) subsequent purchases of T in repeat purchase period.[16] © American Marketing Association.

new buyers to four in week 2, and so on. When expressed as a percentage of those buying in the product category, this provides the market penetration rate. In Figure 4.3(b) the cumulative number of buyers for the first few weeks was projected forward as an estimate of what the eventual penetration percentage would be. In this case, it was estimated that 34% of those buying in the product category would have tried T once (Figure 4.3(b)). Figure 4.3(a) shows only seven households from a panel that might have comprised several thousands. From the entire panel an average period for repurchase is calculated. Some buyers in this category will buy every week, some every two weeks, and others less frequently. The average repurchasing period in this case was estimated to be a fortnight. The first repeat purchase period is not weeks 2 and 3 for every household, but the two-week period immediately preceding the time of first purchase by each household: weeks 3 and 4 for households 3 and 4, weeks 4 and 5 for households 5, 6 and 7, and weeks 2 and 3 for the first two households.

In each repeat purchase period, the percentage of all purchases in the product category that were of brand T is calculated. This is the repeat purchase rate. As can be seen from the first repeat purchase period, of ten purchases, seven were of T; of ten purchases in the second repeat purchase period, five were of T and so on. This figure is projected forward after calculating it for just a few weeks, to give an estimate of the eventual stable level of repeat purchase. In this case the prediction is for a 25% repeat purchase rate (Figure 4.3(c)). Thus, 34% of the market will (it is estimated) eventually have bought T once, and 25% of these will go on to buy it on a repeat purchase basis (which in this instance means every fortnight).

If T is consumed at average levels for the product category (that is, once every fortnight), the prediction for its eventual brand share will be 25% of 34% of the market (which is 8.5%). If T is consumed more than other brands, obviously more will be sold and it will have a higher market share. A buying level index can be calculated, again from the panel data, for the level of usage of T. If it is purchased more than every fortnight, on average, a corresponding 'weight' of something more than 1 will increase the estimated 8.5% to an appropriate level. Likewise, if T is bought only (say) half as frequently as other brands, then a buying level index of 0.5 will weight the 8.5% down to the appropriate level (4.25%).

In fact, the repeat rate alone is often a good predictor of success, as Figure 4.4, based on 120 products studied by 'NPD Research', demonstrates.

Fourt–Woodlock

The earliest of the new product models which attained widespread interest was that of Fourt and Woodlock.[17] This model was intended to predict the market success of grocery products. The first stage in the model attempts to predict penetration (eventual level of trial). It assumes that there is an eventual penetration level and that each period some percentage of the non-buyers who eventually will buy the product buy it. The second stage in this model focuses on the repeat ratios, the portion of initial buyers who repeat purchase once, the portion of first repeat purchasers who purchase a second time, and so forth. This stage is used for forecasting sales in the next period as the sum of new buyers plus first repeaters plus second repeaters, and so forth. This model has proved to be somewhat cumbersome in application. It also assumes that the market is constant in terms of advertising, distribution, pricing, and so forth. This is a very troublesome albeit useful assumption.

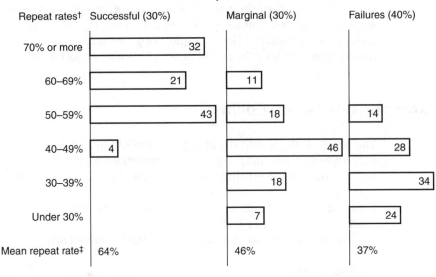

Product performance

Repeat rates[†]	Successful (30%)	Marginal (30%)	Failures (40%)
70% or more	32		
60–69%	21	11	
50–59%	43	18	14
40–49%	4	46	28
30–39%		18	34
Under 30%		7	24
Mean repeat rate[‡]	64%	46%	37%

† Based upon 120 new products
‡ Per cent of triers who will never repeat

Figure 4.4 Use of repeat rate as predictor of new product success.[18]

Ayer

Both the Fourt–Woodlock and Parfitt–Collins approaches are based on observing repeat purchasing from panel data. The Ayer model, on the other hand, is based on the notion that the adoption of a product follows a series of stages.[19] More specifically, three main stages are used: awareness, initial/trial purchase, and repeat purchase/loyalty. Using data from several product introductions, this model estimated the relationship between marketing variables and these three variables. This was done by means of three regressions:

Awareness = a1 + b11 (product positioning) + b12 (media impressions; copy execution) + b13 (ad message containing consumer promotions) + b14 (category interest) + e1

Initial purchase = a2 + b21 (estimated awareness) + b22 (distribution; packaging) + b23 (if a family brand) + b24 (consumer promotion) + b25 (satisfaction with product samples) + b26 (category usage) + e2

Repeat purchase = f (initial purchase, relative price, product satisfaction, purchase, frequency)

By inputting data to the estimated model, sales projections can be derived. Notice that many of the variables are marketing variables, which is in some sense an improvement over the previous models. Notice also, however, that many of these variables (for example, copy execution) must be subjectively estimated, hence making the results potentially more subject to researcher bias.[20]

Extensions of Parfitt–Collins

The News Model is advertising agency BBDO's model for predicting sales of a new consumer product.[21] As such, it competes with the Tracker model, used by the Leo Burnett advertising agency.[22] These models use consumer survey data and explicitly include the impact of controllable marketing variables, mainly focusing on advertising as it impacts awareness and trial. As such, they are extensions of the Parfitt–Collins approach.

The awareness and trial stages of the Tracker model are:

Awareness

$$\ln \left(\frac{1 - A_T}{1 - A_{T-1}} \right) = a - bG_T$$

where

A_T = cumulative awareness in period T
G_T = gross rating points in period T

Trial

$$T_T - T_{T-1} = \alpha(A_T - A_{T-1}) + \beta(A_{T-1} - T_{T-1})$$

where:

T_T = cumulative trial in period T.

The News Model awareness stage breaks apart awareness due to advertising and promotion. Similarly, the trial model is also different from Tracker. Experience with the model has been quite good, with predicted share within 1% of actual share, when test market data are used as input, and within 2%, when only pretest market data are used.[23]

4.7   Conclusions

This chapter has shown that some consumers progress through the unawareness to repurchase continuum more quickly than others. It also clear that there are several different categories of adopter and that this helps greatly in understanding how consumers behave towards new products. The concept of two- or multi-step flows of communication from more innovative opinion leaders to the followers is especially helpful in speeding up the diffusion rates for new products and services. There are also, however, some ethical concerns over some uses of this knowledge and it is probably not generally realized how much of the editorial and news content of our media is derived from publicity sources based on their understanding of the multi-step flow of communications approach and their knowledge and exploitation of specific opinion leaders.

The concepts of the adoption process and repeat purchasing leads logically into a discussion of models that analyse and even predict this process and we have shown the basics of some such models, all based on the original work by Parfitt and Collins.

From this point we turn to other issues of how consumers process information and present another model of the process.

Endnotes

1. H. Gatignon and T.S. Robertson, 1985.
2. E.C. Hirschman, 1980.
3. H. Gatignon and T.S. Robertson, 1985.
4. E. Rogers, 1983.
5. M.R. Solomon, 1983; M.B. Holbrook and E.C. Hirschman, 1982; M.B. Holbrook, R.B. Chestnut, T.A. Oliva and E.A. Greenleaf, 1984.
6. E.J. McCarthy, 1977.
7. J.R. Mancuso, 1969.
8. M. Rawlins (1984), *The Lancet.*
9. P.F. Lazarsfeld, 1955.
10. G. Beal and E. Rogers, 1951.
11. E. Katz and P.F. Lazarsfeld, 1955.
12. D. Midgely and G. Wills, 1979.
13. D. Midgely and G. Wills, 1979.
14. R. Edmonson, 1993.
15. J.H. Parfitt and B.J.K. Collins, 1968.
16. J.H. Parfitt and B.J.K. Collins, 1968.
17. L.A. Fourt and J.W. Woodlock, 1960.
18. NPD Research, 'We make the answers to your marketing question perfectly clear', New York: NPD Research, 1982.
19. N.W. Ayer, 1900.
20. H. Claycamp and L. Liddy, 1969.
21. L.G. Pringle, R.D. Wilson and E. Brody, 1982.
22. R. Blattberg and J. Golanty, 1978.
23. L.G. Pringle, R.D. Wilson and E. Brody, 1982.

5

Consumer information processing and choice

Chapter objectives

(1) To explore how various information processing theory elements can explain how consumers process information about products and services.
(2) To present, analyse and discuss the applications of a model of consumer information processing.
(3) To explore aspects of consumer decision making again in an applied marketing context.

5.1 Relevance of consumer information processing

In the chapters on consumers' responses to marketing activity, new and repeat buying responses, the application to marketing activities of the firm in influencing consumer behaviour was the central focus. In those chapters various aspects of consumer information processing were discussed, for example exposure, attention, perception, retention, conviction, action and dissonance. In this chapter, more of a consumer perspective is taken, although still within the marketing management framework of this book. How do consumers process information about products and services? How are they influenced by advertising and other sources of product information such as word-of-mouth communication with their fellow consumers? And how do consumers make decisions about their purchases under conditions of high and low involvement? Marketers should be aware which information consumers need and use in their decisions and how consumers trade off attributes, features and benefits of the set of products and services from which they have to make a selection. Marketers should know which product features are important for consumers and how consumers use the information that marketers provide to make their choices.

Information processing and decision making is often a recurrent behaviour of consumers, comparing alternative options or alternatives, and making a decision about which alternative to select under several kinds of constraints such as the financial and time budget. In other cases such as purchasing a house it is a decision that may be made only once in one's life. Consumers may expect that a 'best' alternative can be found that leads to reaching a desired goal or avoiding an undesirable situation (positive and negative motivation, respectively, as introduced in Chapter 2).

Motivation is therefore an important part of decision making. Consumers try to accomplish their goals and to reach desired situations. Information about the attributes of the available alternatives is often instrumental in the decision-making process as a step towards reaching the goal.

For some choices, the information stored in memory, for example internal information and habits, may be sufficient. Choice may then be based on earlier decision-making processes, for example brand loyalty or habit formation, or known characteristics of the alternatives. This is often called routine or limited problem solving.[1] If the information stored in memory is insufficient, additional information may be actively sought (external search). This is called extensive problem solving. Especially for choices involving high perceived risk of possible negative consequences, uncertainty about outcomes, and thus a level of high involvement, information may be functional in reducing the risk and the uncertainty.

The first topic to be discussed in this chapter are the functions of information in decision making and choice (Section 5.2). Then a model of information processing is described (Section 5.3), followed by a description of levels of processing and internal representation of information (Section 5.4) and an overview of decision rules (Section 5.5). In Section 5.6 the limitations to information search and processing are described. Section 5.7 concludes with some issues and trends in the present consumer decision-making research.

5.2 Functions of information

What is information? Information is often described as relevant data about choice alternatives, for example the attributes and prices of the alternatives, the stores or other distribution channels through which the alternatives are available, comparative product tests of consumer organizations and the experiences of other consumers. Data become information if the data are relevant for consumers in their decision-making process. Information may be in a spoken or written, verbal or pictorial format, and may originate from marketing sources such as advertising and product packages, personal sources such as fellow consumers, or neutral sources such as the government or consumer organizations.

Information may serve consumers in several ways:

(1) Consumers may expect to take a better decision after information acquisition, processing, and retrieval from memory.
(2) Information may reduce the perceived risk of the choice.
(3) Consumers may feel more confident after using information, although their decision may not necessarily be better.
(4) Information is needed to trade off the present costs and expected future benefits of information processing. This is a kind of information processing about information processing!
(5) Information processing may be useful in finding desirable alternatives or ruling out undesirable ones.
(6) Information may be used in an ego-defensive way to justify one's behaviour once the actual decision has been made.

The consumer decision may be on a generic level (for example 'whether to go on vacation or not'), a modal level ('which type of vacation'), or a specific level ('which destination or which travel agency') (Figure 5.1). A generic decision is largely based on the time, financial budget and general benefits of the product or service. Alternatives are not easily comparable in a generic choice situation, often only at an abstract or experiential level.[2] Advertising at the generic level is mainly advertising for category need, that is, making consumers aware of a product category and making latent needs manifest. An example is a collective advertising campaign to make consumers aware that they should be well insured, both life and indemnity insurance. Modal and specific decisions generally require more specific information on the attributes of the alternatives. At the specific level, advertising is mainly brand advertising, that is, advertising to increase the prominence and attractiveness of a brand or specific product in relation to competing brands.

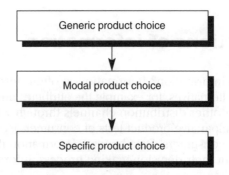

Figure 5.1 Generic, modal and specific product choice.

Internal and external search of information should be distinguished. Internal search of information, stored in memory, employs information from previous learning and experience that may be suitable for similar decisions. Search of information from external sources employs information obtained from the mass media (advertising and neutral sources), shopping and retailers, conversations with others, and from one's own observations. External search for information is larger with high product involvement but low product class knowledge, with positive attitudes towards shopping, and with ample available time.[3] Apart from active search for internal and external information, people may be confronted with information they did not search for, and learn consciously or unconsciously from it. This is called incidental learning.[4] Some advertisers strive for omnipresence of their brand names to stimulate incidental learning from unsought confrontations.

A better decision outcome

Consumers may expect to make a 'better' decision after information acquisition and processing, due to a cultural norm that all decisions should be based on reason and documentation. Consumer decisions are, however, often based on normative and affective factors, for example on the brands one likes or is accustomed to.[5] Compliance with the cultural norm of rationality will generally be stronger for 'important' decisions, involving a major financial outlay or affecting others. Impulsive behaviour is often not appreciated, except maybe for minor choices or 'spontaneous' gifts.

In this chapter, the emphasis is on the description of consumer decision processes, not so much on the normative and prescriptive approaches of helping people to make better decisions. However, descriptive knowledge of how consumers make decisions may be helpful in designing 'better ways' of information presentation. In this way we can help consumers to make better decisions and marketers can influence the outcomes of consumer decision processes.

Reduction of perceived risk

Consumers may perceive risk in their decisions, either financial, social or other types of risk.[6] Reduction of uncertainty is not the same as reducing risk. Better knowledge of probabilities reduces the uncertainty or ambiguity around risk, although it does not reduce the risk itself. Information may reduce some uncertainty about the alternatives by stating the risk in a more precise way, for instance knowing better the side-effects of a drug or the mortality rate of a risky operation.

Risk perception may create internal conflicts for the decision maker. The degree of conflict is related to four factors: the number of competing alternatives, the perceived equality of the alternatives, the importance, and the incompatibility of the alternatives.[7] More uncertainty will be experienced if many alternatives are available, if these alternatives look very similar but may differ in their consequences, and if a large financial outlay is required.

Consumer decisions are often characterized by a financial, temporal and/or behavioural effort risk. For some decisions, a physical risk becomes relevant, for instance car driving, some types of sports, food, and drugs. There are many risk reduction methods for consumers. Retailers, for instance in the mail order business, may use these risk reduction methods to convince people to buy without risk.[8] Consumers perceive mail order buying as risky because they cannot see, feel or try the product before purchasing.

(1) More precise and valid information for consumers about the choice of products and services, for example better catalogues and travel guides.
(2) Consumers may become brand and store loyal after having a positive experience. The store may pre-select an assortment that appeals to a specific target group.
(3) Consumers may rely on recommendations of others with a positive experience. Stores could reinforce their customers to act as 'ambassadors' for the store with favourable word-of-mouth information. In direct marketing 'member-get-member' actions stimulate word-of-mouth and are an efficient way to increase the customer database.
(4) Sellers may offer a money-back guarantee if there is a problem or dissatisfaction with the product, for instance for mail order purchases.

The first three risk-reduction methods pertain to the probability component (information, brand and store loyalty, recommendation, and reputation), thus reducing the probability of buying a bad bargain or a 'lemon'. The money-back guarantee reduces the negative outcomes or effects of a risky decision, regardless of the probability of the risk. Mail order companies always offer a money-back guarantee to get consumers over this threshold.

Confidence

Many decision makers feel more confident after acquiring information, even if they have not really processed and used this information to reach a decision.[9] Consumers may feel confident with nutrition information on the product packs, although they may not fully understand this information. They may use a peripheral type for processing this information.[10] People may feel confident having access to documentation, but often do not fully understand and use this information in their choice process.

Increasing confidence with the outcome may create the 'illusion of knowledge'. It was found that consumers use only a small part of the available product information but that they are more confident with their decision if a lot of information is available to them.[11] The quality of the decision may even decrease under conditions of information overload, due to the fact that irrelevant information obscures the access to relevant information. Owing to all the trees one fails to see the forest!

On the one hand, consumers have the 'right' to have access to relevant information for their decisions, especially their important decisions such as buying a house. Information overload may, however, have a dysfunctional effect. This is due to the human limitations in decoding, storing and retrieving this information, to the human limitations in information processing, and to the fact that relevant information is often confounded with irrelevant information. Advertising clutter and overload may thus be dysfunctional for optimal information processing. Consumers may 'zap' and thus avoid advertising that is irrelevant and overloading by switching channels or, if it's a video, fast forwarding through the advertisements.

Information about costs/benefits of information processing

Information processing is often costly. Information acquisition and processing involve behavioural, and sometimes even financial costs for consumers. Financial costs include travel and telephone costs. Behavioural costs include the cognitive activity, time and effort spent to obtain the information. These financial and behavioural costs are often traded off against the expected gain of information and the expected future benefits of a better decision. In shopping behaviour, not only the price of a product, but also travel time, costs and effort should be considered in comparing shopping trips.

Consumers often process information on the costs and benefits of information processing. In this 'thinking about thinking' decision makers assess whether it is worthwhile to acquire and to process information, and how much information to process. The 'cost of thinking'[12] is related to the similarity and complexity of the alternatives. However, it is not always necessary to process all information that is available. 'Heuristics' and simple decision rules may facilitate the decision task, although it is not certain in this case that the 'optimal' alternative will be obtained.

In many choice situations it is almost impossible to select the 'optimal' alternative. This is the case if the information comes sequentially, that is, not all information about the choice alternatives is available simultaneously. Consumer decision processes for sequential information are a neglected area of research. The available studies show that a satisficing notion is appropriate here.[13] Maximizing utility is almost impossible in a condition of sequential information, because the new information may change the attractiveness of former choice alternatives. The consumer may set a certain level (threshold), above which an alternative is satisficing. This level depends on the person's expectations of what kind of alternatives will occur and on his or her own needs and values. The threshold level is adapted based on the apparent alternatives at a certain point in time.

At the same time as product information is processed, consumers decide whether to search for further behavioural alternatives or not. This depends on whether the best of the accessible alternatives exceeds a certain level of aspiration or not. In such a situation satisficing behaviour is likely to occur. The costs of finding the optimal alternative are sometimes higher than the expected benefits. If product differences are small, the information processing costs of finding the better alternative may be high in comparison with the benefits of selecting a slightly better alternative.

Desirable and undesirable alternatives

Consumers do not necessarily derive utility from products as such, but from product attributes or features. As we have seen, products are bundles of features. Information may be instrumental in making a better 'matching' of the product benefits and one's needs and values. It is assumed that consumers have more or less detailed specifications of the products and services they want, subject to budget restrictions, and try to match these specifications with actual product characteristics. The product with the optimal matching will then be selected. Product specifications may include price and size intervals, desired product features, acceptable levels of operating costs, and the values that are associated with the product or the brand. The specifications may have minimum and maximum values, or optimum values.

Considering minimum values only, consumers could use a conjunctive decision rule. This means that only alternatives with attribute values above a minimum cut-off value are acceptable. Considering minimum and maximum values, alternatives are acceptable with attribute values between the minimum and maximum. Considering maximum values only, the conjunctive rule could be used as well. Only alternatives with attribute values below the maximum, for instance the maximum price consumers are willing to pay, are acceptable and considered for purchase.

Applying the conjunctive rule for minima and maxima provides a region of acceptable alternatives. However, it does not tell which alternative in the acceptability region will or should be selected. This may be the first alternative found with acceptable attribute values: 'satisficing' behaviour. Or the consumer may proceed and search for the 'best' alternative within the acceptability region. The conjunctive rule is applied to discriminate between acceptable and unacceptable alternatives. A more complex rule, for example a linear-compensatory one, could then be applied to select an alternative from the remaining acceptable alternatives.

In this approach, it is assumed that consumers have correct insights into their needs, desires, time and budget constraints. It is further assumed that these needs and desires remain constant over time. This is not always true because consumers learn from the interaction with products, and through the interaction with alternatives they may change their requirements, desires and acceptability levels. The available alternatives shape or change requirements and desires such that this interaction should be included in a dynamic model.

Justification

An often neglected function of information is the justification of the decision afterwards. In many instances, one has to justify to oneself and to others after a decision has been made, why one has bought the product or service. For this defence, a consumer could effectively use information from advertising or other sources to obtain arguments favouring the decision. On the one hand, it is an ego-defensive mechanism to reduce post-purchase cognitive dissonance and to keep oneself happy with the choice. On the other hand, information serves to produce arguments to defend oneself against the possible critical remarks of others. The important functions of advertising are not only:[14]

(1) to induce product trial and
(2) to keep the brand in the consumer's evoked set, but thus also:
(3) to reinforce the decision that has been made, and to reassure that the choice was right.

Information serves not only before a decision, but also after a decision, to keep or make a person satisfied with the selected product or service. Through information people justify their decision and structure their experience with the product or service. In early consumer research it was found that recent purchasers of a car had long deliberated about which brand to choose and tended to read more advertisements of the selected brand than of not-selected brands.[15] It has become more and more important for marketers to keep their customers. Winning new customers is much more costly than keeping present customers. Advertising might help to retain customers and to keep them loyal to the brand ('retention marketing').

5.3 An information processing model

In most information processing models it is assumed that information acquisition, perception and processing ('cognition') precedes the evaluation ('affect') of the available alternatives. The hierarchy of effect is thus: cognition → affect → conation (behavioural intention). This model complies with the model of rational economic man. It does not explain why consumers attend to some advertisements and not to others, and why we like some products and brands and dislike others at a first impression. Psychological research provides evidence that an affective reaction precedes cognition.[16] A primary affective reaction is needed before a consumer pays attention to an advertisement.[17] In information processing as well, the triggering mechanism may be an affective or emotional one. At an early stage, a consumer develops a liking (affect) towards a certain advertisement, product or brand. A certain level of liking and arousal is needed to be motivated to engage in information processing. The primary affect may serve as a selection mechanism to find acceptable and attractive alternatives (cf. conjunctive rule). A third function of the primary affective reaction is to make quick selections from a large number of alternatives ('affect referral'[18]) based on an affective reaction towards familiar and attractive alternatives, including 'impulse buying'.

The primary affective reaction is a quick and almost automatic decoding process.[19] The object or person has to be perceived and is evaluated at a glance. There is a discussion whether this should be called an affective or a simple cognitive process. Some state that cognition precedes affect,[20] whereas others state the primacy of affective processes.[21] In any case, whether cognition or emotion, this primary reaction may guide the remainder of the information processing.

The consumer information processing model of this chapter is given in Figure 5.2. There are essentially two ways by which choice alternatives enter the system. First, consumers may recognize a consumption problem, for instance a defective car or a need for food, and search for ways to solve the problem. Alternatives may be obtained from memory and/or from external search, not only by active search (intentional learning), but also by incidental learning, if a consumer is unexpectedly confronted with an alternative. Such an unexpected confrontation might even create problem recognition, for instance the presence of food triggering a hunger signal. Or, being aware of a problem, this might increase the number of incidental learning occasions. Hungry people tend to see more food items in their environment.

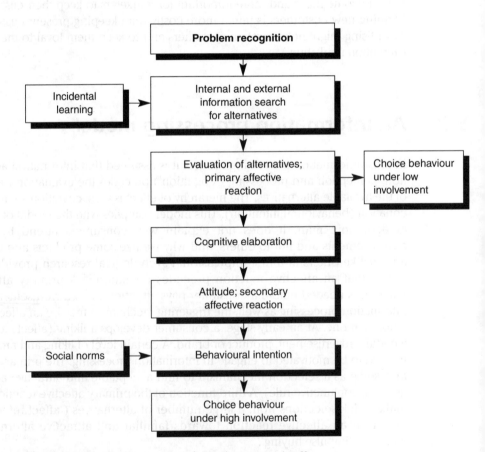

Figure 5.2 Model of consumer information processing.[22]

The primary affective reaction may lead to a direct action, as in the case of impulse buying. Especially for products with low levels of risk and involvement, such as confectionery bars and soft drinks, consumers tend to try the products and perform some cognitive elaboration and evaluation after the purchase, in order to make the same or a better decision next time (trial and repeat buying).

The primary affective reaction may also lead to a process of extensive cognitive elaboration, that is, the collection and processing of detailed information about the alternatives. After the cognitive elaboration process, a more detailed evaluation (secondary affective reaction or attitude) may be formed or revised. The attitude towards the act consists of beliefs about acting towards the alternative (cognitive elements) and evaluations of beliefs in terms of favourableness.[23] Behavioural intention is a function of attitude and social norms, such as in the Fishbein and Ajzen attitude model.

Cognitive elaboration

Cognitive elaboration is more detailed information processing about the alternatives obtained from internal and external search (intentional learning) and from incidental learning. Cognitive elaboration can be considered as an argumentation process with the following elements.[24]

1 Support argumentation

Information from one source is supported by information from other source(s), for instance own experience (internal search), advertising, and product tests. When information elements from different sources support each other, it is the consistency criterion of attribution theory that is being satisfied.

2 Counter argumentation

Information from one source is not supported by information from other sources, for instance from own experience. Then, the person tends to refute the information from the external source, especially if this external source is biased or unreliable, for example advertising. A moderate form of counter-argumentation is curious disbelief; this disbelief is normally changed into a positive interest by processing the information.[25]

3 Source derogation

Source derogation is a means of solving the problem of inconsistency of information sources. It is the derogation of the expertness and/or trustworthiness of the information source, with the consequence not to believe the information. Information sources, such as advertising or salespersons, may be easily derogated, because of the one-sidedness of their arguments and their persuasive intentions.

4 Thoughts about the medium and form/layout of the message

Thoughts about the medium and the form and layout of the message may inhibit or reinforce the information acquisition and understanding. The way information is presented has a strong effect on the persuasiveness of the message. Media effects may operate as well, for example print media (newspaper, magazine) allow the readers to process the information at their own speed, read the texts twice, and skip parts of the message if they wish (this is internal pacing). With audio visual media (television, radio) the speed of information transmission is controlled by the sender and not by the receiver (this is external pacing). Externally paced media do not allow for much cognitive elaboration, if the speed of information transmission is high.[26]

5.4 Information processing

Levels of information processing

The level of information processing is relevant in order to assess the impact that information may have on the formation and change of knowledge about the choice alternatives. Levels of information processing will be approached from two perspectives: central vs peripheral route, and depth of processing.

Under conditions of high involvement information processing is thought to occur via the central route.[27] This means that product attributes will be thoroughly scrutinized and information will be processed at a deep level (extensive problem solving).[28] In contrast, if involvement is low, consumers tend to base their judgement mainly on context and peripheral message cues, such as the style or the credibility of the communicator. Product information is then often ignored or processed at an undeep (shallow) level. In most information processing research it is assumed that consumers follow the central route and are willing and able to process information on the attribute values of the alternatives. It is, however, more likely that consumers follow the peripheral route in many instances.

A low level of information processing implies that only the surface level of information has been processed. Information that is processed at a shallow level is stored in memory in an isolated and episodic manner.[29] No or limited connections with existing information will be established if there is little cognitive elaboration. If no time or opportunity is available, information processing will normally be at a shallow level, because cognitive elaboration takes too much time and effort.

A deep level of information processing implies that the consumer spends more time and effort on information processing. With some degree of cognitive elaboration, the content and meaning of the information could be understood. Cognitive elaboration consists of support and counter-argumentation, and comparison of new information with existing knowledge. Information processed at a deep level is stored in memory in an integrated manner (breadth of information storage), embedded in a meaningful structure of concepts and relations between concepts. A deep level of information processing is a prerequisite to memorize the information, and to understand the meaning. The major differences between shallow and deep levels of information processing are given in Table 5.1.

A shallow level of information processing is instrumental in memorizing information for a brief period, for example a telephone number before dialling. For products that evoke only a low level of involvement (low physical, financial or social risk), a deep level of information processing is unlikely. For prospective buyers that are very much involved in a product, for instance prospective buyers of durables, a deep level of information processing could be expected.

Table 5.1 Shallow and deep levels of information processing.[30]

Shallow level	Deep level
Physical, sensory coding	Semantic coding
Emphasis on form and layout	Emphasis on content and meaning
Little or no elaboration	Much elaboration
Low involvement	High involvement
Episodic, isolated storage of information	Integrated storage of information
Low level of generation of cognitive responses	High level of generation of cognitive responses

Internal representation

As noted before, about the primary affective reaction, impression formation is important for subsequent information processing. People form first impressions of another person based on discrete and often limited amounts of information. If the adjectives warm and cold are varied in person descriptions, large differences are found in the evaluation of the persons.[31] Haire's shopping list is another example.[32] First impressions ('primary affective reaction') and previous information tend to change the information processing, in the sense that with a favourable first impression, the cognitive elaboration tends to focus on positive attributes. With an unfavourable first impression, the focus is on negative attributes.

Attributes are often implicitly combined. Price may become an indicator of quality, if no other information is readily available.[33] The brand name may stand for quality and service. In fact, product attributes may be hierarchically ordered with 'chunking' attributes at the top, standing for a number of detailed or unknown attributes. Products may be categorized according to some top attributes (price, quality, brand name). Within a category, minor attributes may play a role in the discrimination between the products/brands.

Categorization

Another approach starts from the multitude of objects around us and the ways people classify and categorize these objects.[34] It is a perceptual process, if the objects are present to immediate perception, or a conceptual process, if the objects are at an abstract level.

Categorization is instrumental for at least five reasons. It reduces the complexity of the environment; a multitude of individual objects is reduced to classes and categories. It also reduces the necessity of constant learning because objects in a class are similar, and permits ordering and relating classes of (competing) objects and events, for example the positioning of products or brands in a category.

A brand name may reduce the necessity of constant inquiry about product attributes. The brand name may function as a 'chunk', that is, it may stand for other attributes. A well-known brand name may be a chunk for a good quality of the product. Package information ('poisonous', X-rated) is further instrumental in avoiding or seeking the use of a product.

In consumer research, product categorization is important for advertising and market segmentation. How do consumers perceive the products, and which products are competing or not? Examples are that yoghurt may be categorized by flavour or by brand, and deodorants categorized by type of package (spray vs non-spray) and by applicator (aerosol, pump, roll-on, sticks, and powder).[35] Each of these categorizations requires another advertising and competition strategy, and another product display in stores. This type of categorization is called 'market partitioning', and the examples are brand-based and flavour-based partitioning. Inference making and product categorization are relevant with regard to comparative advertising.[36] Comparative advertising generates different inferences than non-comparative advertising, and thus affects product categorization.

5.5   Decision rules

Consumers are subject to limitations in their ability and willingness to process information. This means that detailed and complex calculations (a kind of 'mental algebra') or comparisons are the exception rather than the rule. Information processing by attribute or by alternative are examples of decision rules. A decision rule specifies the process by which an alternative is evaluated, that is, assigning a value (evaluation) to an alternative. A decision rule should also specify the choice criterion, that is, the alternative(s) to be chosen.[37] Thirdly, a decision rule should specify the form of processing, such as processing by attribute or by alternative.

A number of decision rules may be distinguished.[38] In order to reach a decision, that is, a choice among the alternatives, one decision rule or a sequence of decision rules may be employed.

1 Affect referral rule

Affect referral is a simple decision rule. No attributes are examined, a simple affective reaction determines which alternative is selected: the alternative you like best or the brand you are loyal to. In fact, little or no cognitive elaboration takes place.[39] Affect referral or liking will often be used at impulse and repeat buying.

2 Linear-compensatory rule

Linear-compensatory decision rules are complex. Alternatives are described as having many attributes. Each attribute is weighed according to its importance or its probability. The decision rule is linear, because the weighted attributes are added in a linear fashion. It is compensatory, because 'poor' attributes may be compensated by 'strong' ones. Most utility and attitude models are of a linear-compensatory nature.[40] The attitude model of Fishbein and Ajzen is an example.[41]

3 Conjunctive rule

Conjunctive decision rules were discussed in Section 5.2. Minimum cut-offs are assumed for each attribute. It was found that cut-offs are used that maximally discriminate between retained and rejected alternatives.[42] If an attribute does not pass the minimum cut-off, it will be rejected. Alternatives are thus categorized as acceptable vs unacceptable. If two or more alternatives are retained as acceptable, another decision rule, for instance a linear-compensatory one, could be used to choose between them. Conjunctive decision rules are useful in the first stage of a selection process to eliminate unacceptable alternatives. This is related to the 'satisficing' concept, in the sense that the first satisfactory alternative is selected.[43]

4 Disjunctive rule

Disjunctive decision rules are based on positive or even extremely positive values on one attribute. An alternative is selected based on at least one superior attribute value, disregarding other attributes. Just like the conjunctive decision rule, the disjunctive decision rule is non-compensatory.

5 Lexicographic rule

Lexicographic decision rules start from an ordering of the attributes in terms of importance. Alternatives are first compared on the most important attribute. If one alternative is superior to all others (disjunctive decision rule), that alternative is selected. If two or more form a tie, they are compared on a second attribute, and so on. The lexicographic decision rule assumes information processing by attribute and is non-compensatory. Advertising sometimes suggests the use of a lexicographic rule. A Fiat advertisement started with the question: 'You want to have a car priced under £15,000?' There are 30 cars available. 'You want to have an engine of at least 1200 cc?' Only 22 cars remain. 'You want to have five doors?' Only 15 cars remain. Etcetera, until only one Fiat remains.

6   Sequential elimination rule

Sequential elimination is conjunctive in the sense that minimum cut-offs are stated for each attribute. Alternatives are eliminated, considering one attribute at a time. There is no rule for the order of the attributes. Information processing by attribute is assumed. A variant of sequential elimination is elimination by aspects.[44] An attribute (aspect) is selected with a probability proportional to its weight. All alternatives with unsatisfactory values are eliminated.

Some decision rules mentioned above assume information processing by alternative, for instance the linear-compensatory rule. With these rules each alternative gets a composite score, and these overall scores are compared. Other decision rules assume information processing by attribute, for instance the conjunctive, disjunctive, lexicographic and sequential elimination rules. With these rules alternatives are compared on one attribute or a subset of attributes.

As mentioned before, decision rules are often used in sequence (phased strategies). Conjunctive decision rules are frequently used in a first predilection stage of the decision process to select acceptable alternatives.[45] Information processing by attribute in a first stage or as the total process does not necessarily lead to attitude formation or change. Attitude formation is more likely with information processing by alternative. However, alternatives may be accepted or rejected based on affect referral.[46] For the final alternative(s), a secondary, more elaborated, affective reaction (attitude) may be formed, based on information processing by alternative. In a second stage, the 'best' alternative is selected from the set of acceptable alternatives.

Decision rules may be stored in memory to be used in actual choice situations, or they may be constructed during the decision process. In the latter case, decision rules will be built up rather than recalled as units. The way the information is presented has a strong effect on the decision rule constructed for the decision process. The use of rules stored in memory can be seen as the result of decision processes in the past. Three types of behaviour may be distinguished:[47]

(1) Routinized response behaviour, in which a stored decision rule is used, for example affect referral or brand loyalty. The regular purchases of a brand of coffee may be routinized for many consumers.

(2) Limited problem solving, in which there is some simple construction or cut-off, for example conjunctive rules. Less regular major purchases belong to this type, for example the purchase of simple tools and kitchen appliances.

(3) Extensive problem solving, in which a decision rule is constructed or used after information search, for example compensatory rules. This type of

behaviour takes place under conditions of high involvement such as the purchase of a house or car.

The use of decision rules

The more time and opportunity for cognitive elaboration and information processing, the more important the decision, and the more involved the decision maker, the more complex the decision rule normally will be. Under constraints of time pressure, distraction, competing activities, social pressure and risk perception, certain decision rules may be preferred to others. Under stressful conditions, elimination of alternatives based on negative evidence may occur, because there is no opportunity for the use of compensatory decision rules.[48] If only small differences are perceived and/or limited risk is involved, a conjunctive decision rule may be used to select the first acceptable alternative ('satisficing').

It may be argued that the information processing models are primarily models of the task structure.[49] Understanding the task requirements (contingency) yields an understanding of the subject who performs more or less adequately in the given situation. Instead of considering individual differences, the research direction should then be to the information structure, format, and the environmental factors determining consumer choice behaviour.

5.6 Limitations to information search and processing

Humans have limited capacities and are not always motivated to maximize utility. It may even be asserted that 'rationality' is rather the exception than the rule in human behaviour, because 'rationality' involves costs of information acquisition, cognitive elaboration, information processing, selection of an alternative, and the implementation of the choice.[50] Habits, such as brand loyalty, involve almost no costs and will thus be preferred, unless the habitual choice is no longer attractive (or available).

The limitation to information search and processing may be classified under the headings: information environment, situational environment, information stored in memory, and individual differences.

Information environment

The structure and format of the available information is an important determinant of information search and processing.

Structure

Information structure pertains to structuring of information:[51]

(1) Structuring by alternatives, such as in advertising: information about each alternative product or brand is given separately.
(2) Structuring by matrix (table), such as in comparative product testing by consumer organizations.
(3) Non-simultaneous structuring, for example sequential availability of information.

Structuring by alternatives facilitates processing by alternatives. Structuring by matrix facilitates processing by attributes, although processing by alternatives is still feasible. Non-simultaneous structuring, in which the alternatives are not available at the same time, facilitates 'satisficing' and the use of conjunctive decision rules.

Format

The format of the information pertains to the type and unit of information. Examples of formats are:

- ratio-scale numbers, such as weight and price;
- ordinal numbers, such as hotel classifications with stars;
- binary form, such as the presence or absence of an attribute;
- pictorial format, such as pictures, logos or pictograms, for instance eco-labelling or recyclability of products.

Information may be given quantitatively (as 'facts') or qualitatively (as 'evaluations'), for example a price in pounds and the evaluation 'low price', respectively. A quantitative item will not necessarily be processed as such via the central route, but is often transformed into a qualitative evaluation and processed via the peripheral route.[52] This will happen if the consumer is unwilling or unable to process the quantitative information.

Studying the information processing of pictures in print advertising, it may be concluded that information processing depends on the 'framing' of the pictures, that is an unframed picture does not refer to the accompanying text and distracts the attention away from the text, while a framed picture supports the information processing of the text.[53, 54]

Framing

The way information is presented influences information processing in other ways as well. This is also called 'framing'. Framing of the information is important, in this case, stressing positive or negative consequences.[55] This affects the preference for and choice of alternatives. An example is: 'Which of the following would you prefer? Fifty per cent chance to win £100 or £45 for sure?' Most people will select the sure option. If asked: 'Which of the following would you prefer? Fifty per cent chance of losing £100 or a sure loss of £45?' Here, most people will select the chance option. This means that for gains people are risk-averse and select the sure gain. For losses, however, people are risk-seeking and do not want to select the sure loss; they rather take their chance to avoid the loss.

People tend to reformulate ('edit' or 'frame') risky decisions into 'prospects', and then select the prospect with the highest gain or the lowest loss.[56] In the domain of gains people are risk-averse and prefer a sure gain over a chance to gain. In the domain of losses people are risk-seeking and prefer a chance not to lose over a sure loss. People use reference points for comparing choice alternatives.[57] A choice alternative with a value below the reference value is perceived ('framed') as a loss, whereas a choice alternative with a value above the reference value is perceived as a gain.

Some other heuristics, for example representativeness and availability, also depend on the way in which the information is presented to the decision-maker.[58]

Amount of information

The amount of information available may constitute a situation of information overload. Overload means that (too) many alternatives with (too) many attributes compete for attention; cf. the advertising environment in the media and in stores. Although a certain amount of information is needed to make a good decision, too much information may lower the quality of the decision. This may be due to irrelevant information obscuring relevant facts, or due to human capacity constraints to process that much information. Another explanation is that with ample information a consumer feels overconfident and takes a worse decision than with less information.[59] Additional information may not always increase the quality of the decision. Too many alternatives is more detrimental to choice quality than too many attributes.[60] Both too many attributes and too many alternatives decrease choice accuracy.[61] Information quantity decreases information effectiveness, while information quality keeping the quantity constant improves decision effectiveness, although too high levels of quality may be detrimental to the evaluations.[62]

Integration of information

The understandability and usability of information plays an important role. New information should be easily integrated in to the existing knowledge in memory. If the new information is hard to categorize in existing categories, for instance new attributes, it is likely that the information cannot be used in an easy way. The person has to spend time and effort (cognitive work and strain) to obtain the integration of new and existing information in to the nodes and links of the brain network.

Consumers may use stores and catalogues as external memories. Instead of searching information from several sources (active search or need formulation), they may be influenced by the products available in the store or in the catalogue (passive search or need recognition). Instead of preparing a shopping list, consumers may walk through the supermarket to recognize the products that are needed. In-store information processing (Is the product needed or not?: conjunctive decision rule) replaces out-store information processing. It is likely that a 'passive' shopper is more easily persuaded by an attractive product presentation than an 'active' shopper, armed with a shopping list. In many cases, shopping behaviour is a mixture of active and passive search.

In the case of complete information use of decision rules is facilitated, whereas in the case of incomplete information the problem has to be 'framed' and a decision rule often has to be constructed.[63] In the case of complete information, attributes that are common to all or most choice alternatives are used more frequently than attributes that are not common. Common attributes are necessary for a lexicographic decision rule to compare alternatives. Product differences are more difficult to assess with uncommon or unique attributes. In the case of incomplete information but common attributes, consumers tend to make inferences about the missing attributes. Attribute information about a partly described alternative has greater influence than that of a fully described one. Consumers do not always ignore the attributes for which no information is available. They make inferences about missing information. Alternatives with much missing information obtain a less favourable evaluation.[64] Consumers complete the information by a same-alternative strategy,[65] that is, they use the available information about an alternative to infer the missing information ('halo effect'). To a much lesser degree they use information of other alternatives to infer missing information.

Situational environment

The store environment with the presentation of products is an example of a situational environment with a lot of product information. The same is true for the mass media with advertisements and commercials. Information search and processing also takes place in social conversation with friends and relatives.

Under high time pressure and distraction conditions consumers will overweight negative evidence in order to eliminate unsatisfactory alternatives (without compensation).[66] Distraction may be created by crowding in a store or by concurrent or joint activities, for instance watching television while eating and talking. Time pressure increases the reliance on negative evidence; distraction showed a tendency towards this effect. Time horizons have an impact on information processing.[67] Negative evidence is more heavily weighted for outcomes that are expected to come sooner. Store atmospherics may change the mood of the shoppers and thus induce them to use other decision rules.

Information stored in memory

It seems to be reasonable to expect that external information search is complementary to internal information search.[68] Consumers who know less of a product class should spend more time and effort to compensate for this lack of knowledge. However, one may state the opposite hypothesis. Consumers who know more of a product class are better equipped to process new information, because they already know the basic categories to judge the alternatives. They are probably also more interested in new information, or they want to check the validity of the information they possess. The latter hypotheses are not in favour of the complementarity hypothesis.

Not only information in memory, but also memory for rules, heuristics and operations plays an important role in information processing. Knowledge of facts is useful, but knowing how to obtain and how to evaluate information may be just as important.

Information in memory may direct the type of information sought and the interpretation of this information. Prior knowledge may lead to less information search, due either to the information already stored in memory or to a more efficient information search.[69] On the other hand, prior knowledge may lead to more information search, because information search and interpretation is facilitated by the categories and attributes one already knows.[70] The manner of coding and storage of product information in memory may also determine the additional information one searches. It may be concluded that prior knowledge and external search for information have an inverted U-shaped relationship. Consumers with an intermediate level of knowledge search more than consumers with either limited or elaborate knowledge.

Choice tasks that require both internal and external information simultaneously are more difficult than tasks that require only internal or only external search for information.[71] Differences in the accessibility of prior information in memory affect brand choice outcomes.

Prior knowledge facilitates the acquisition of new information and increases search efficiency.[72] The categories one employs may create an open mind for products fitting the categories, and probably a closed mind for products that do not fit the categories. In this study it is assumed that prior knowledge in memory gives direction to the external search. Many search patterns for external information may be distinguished among purchasers of a new automobile, including low, moderate, high search, and, interestingly, purchase-pal assisted search, that is, shopping with the assistance of a more experienced friend.[73]

Individual differences

A certain level of arousal is needed for information processing. Individuals differ in the level of arousal they already have, or the level of arousal that is activated by advertising or the product presentation. The optimal level of arousal potential in the environment is ideal for information processing.[74] Too low levels of arousal potential stimulate the desire to increase stimulation (and to search for more information). Too high levels of arousal potential lead to avoidance of stimulation (and to stop searching for more information). Individuals with a higher education level and/or living in urban environments generally have a higher optimal level of arousal potential. One may expect that these individuals are able and willing to process more information, experience less information overload, and use more complex decision rules.

Among housewives more information processing by alternatives was found as compared with students.[75] In an information display board (matrix) task design, students process more information by attribute. Processing by alternative is probably stimulated by the experience of information presentation by alternatives in daily life (advertising, packages). The rather abstract matrix task contains a two-dimensional presentation in a table, more easily employed by students.

Individual differences between students and housewives, young people and elderly people,[76] and consumers with high and low levels of cognitive skill limit the generalization of the results of laboratory experiments.[77] Individual differences may affect a number of aspects of the decision process. The following may be mentioned:[78]

(1) Particular decision rules known by the individual.
(2) Processing abilities, for example cognitive skills, intelligence, or speed of processing.
(3) Level of involvement: with high involvement more complex decision rules may be used.[79]
(4) Perceptions of the degree of difficulty and the potential of various decision rules for leading to good choices.
(5) Amount and organization of product-related information in memory. Elderly people have more retrieval problems.
(6) Degree to which various methods are used for implementing choice, for instance recall versus recognition, prior versus in-store information processing, and stored rules versus construction of rules.

5.7 Issues and trends in research on information processing and decision making

The cognitive approach to economic behaviour tends to emphasize the rational and reasoned aspects of behaviour, assuming that information processing precedes decision making. In many instances, the degree of information processing before a decision is low or even non-existent. In many low-involvement choice situations, habits and brand loyalty influence the decision without much information processing. Information processing will then take place after the purchase and is relevant for repeat purchase behaviour.

A second issue is the role of affective factors in decision making. A primary affective preference for one of the alternatives may influence the information processing in the direction of that alternative. Information, thus, is not so much a priori processed to come to a better choice, but is an a posteriori justification of the preference. Thus, affective factors not only play a role in the (detailed) evaluation of choice alternatives after cognitive elaboration (attitude), but also before cognitive elaboration choice alternatives are (globally) evaluated. The emphasis in information processing research relies heavily on the choice between specific choice alternatives. In a broader context, budget allocation, the generic choice between expenditure categories and store patronage often precede the specific choice.[80] For low-income households especially, the budget allocation decision may take more time and effort than the specific decision between brands.

A fourth and neglected issue is group decision making. Households, as a small group, take many decisions together. Dominance of one partner, bargaining, coalition formation and conflict resolution are part of the group decision process. Due to a fuzzy attribution of responsibility, households may take a riskier option than anyone in the family would have taken individually. This is called the 'risky shift or polarization' effect. Little is known of these group decision processes, especially over time.[81]

5.8 Conclusions

This chapter has provided a thorough review of the issues involved in consumer information processing and has provided a model that integrates some of the main factors. Consumer states and their decision-making processes have also been analysed. The approach builds naturally and cumulatively on the preceding chapters on consumer responses to marketing activity and provides an additional level of depth of treatment of some of the recent theories and research projects in this area.

This concludes our coverage in this part of the book of the more individual aspects of consumer response to marketing and in the next part we turn to more 'group' aspects, which we integrate within the applied framework of market segmentation. Following this, the related topics of targeting and positioning are discussed, together with ways of researching markets. The overall theme for this next part is 'market analysis'.

Endnotes

1. J. Howard and J.N. Sheth, 1969.
2. E. Johnson and J.E. Russo, 1984; M. Holbrook and E. Hirschman, 1982; W.F. Van Raaij and K. Wandwossen, 1978.
3. S.E. Beatty and S.M. Smith, 1987.
4. J. Bettman, 1979.
5. A. Etzioni, 1988.
6. D.F. Cox, 1967.
7. F. Hansen (1972) proposed a conflict model, based on Berlyne's (1963) arousal theory.

8. T. Roselius, 1971.
9. S. Oskamp, 1965.
10. R.E. Petty and J.T. Cacioppo, 1986.
11. J. Jacoby, D.E. Speller, and C.A. Kohn, 1974a, 1974b; W.F Van Raaij, 1977.
12. S.M. Shugan, 1980.
13. H. Simon, 1900.
14. H. Murray, 1979.
15. D. Ehrlich, L. Guttman, P. Schonbach and J. Mills. 1957.
16. D.E. Broadbent, 1977.
17. W.F. Van Raaij, 1989.
18. P. Wright, 1975.
19. J.R. Rossiter and L. Percy, 1983.
20. M.H. Birnbaum, 1983; R.S. Lazarus, 1984.
21. R. Zajonc, 1984.
22. W.F. Van Raaij, 1988, p. 84.
23. M. Fishbein and I. Ajzen, 1975.
24. P. Wright, 1980; R.E. Petty, T.C. Brock and T.M. Ostrom, 1981.
25. J.C. Maloney, 1962.
26. W.F. Van Raaij, 1989.
27. R.E. Petty and J.T. Cacioppo, 1986.
28. J. Howard and J.N. Sheth, 1969.
29. F.I.M. Craik and E. Tulving, 1975.
30. F.I.M. Craik and E. Tulving, 1975.
31. S.E. Asch, 1946; G.A. Kelly, 1955.
32. M. Haire, 1950.
33. A. Gabor and C.W.J. Granger, 1966.
34. J.S. Bruner, J.J. Goodnow and G.A. Austin (1956) describe the processes of categorization.
35. J. R. Rossiter and L. Percy, 1987 pp 47–50.
36. M. Sujan and C. Dekleva, 1987.
37. P. Wright, 1975.
38. J.R. Bettman, 1979.
39. P. Wright, 1975.
40. G. Antonides, 1989.
41. M. Fishbein and I. Ajzen, 1975.
42. N.M. Klein and S.W. Bither, 1987.
43. H. Simon, 1955.
44. A. Tversky, 1972.
45. B. Pras and J. Summers, 1975.
46. P. Wright, 1975; W.F. Van Raaij, 1989.
47. J. Howard and J.N. Sheth, 1969.
48. P. Wright, 1974.
49. R.M. Dawes, 1975.
50. A. Etzioni, 1986, 1988.
51. W.F. Van Raaij, 1977.
52. R.E. Petty and J.T. Cacioppo, 1986; R.F. Yalch and R. Elmore-Yalch, 1984.
53. J.A. Edell and R. Staelin, 1983.
54. See J.R. Rossiter and L. Percy (1983) for more details on the processing of visual information.
55. D. Kahneman and A. Tversky, 1979.
56. D. Kahneman and A. Tversky, 1979, 1984.

57. C.P. Puto, 1987.
58. A. Tversky and D. Kahneman, 1974.
59. S. Oskamp, 1965.
60. J. Jacoby, D.E. Speller and C.A. Kohn, 1974a, 1974b.
61. N. Malhotra, 1982.
62. K.L. Keller and R. Staelin, 1987.
63. J.R. Bettman and M. Sujan, 1987.
64. R.D. Johnson and I.P. Levin, 1985.
65. G.T. Ford and R.A. Smith, 1987.
66. P. Wright, 1974.
67. P. Wright and B. Weitz, 1977.
68. J.R. Bettman, 1979.
69. G. Katona and E. Mueller, 1955; W.L. Moore and D.R. Lehman, 1980.
70. E. Johnson and J.E. Russo, 1984.
71. G. Biehal and D. Chakravarti, 1983, 1986.
72. M. Brucks, 1985.
73. D.H. Furse, G.N. Punj and D.W. Stewart, 1984.
74. D.E. Berlyne, 1963.
75. W.F. Van Raaij, 1977.
76. J.D. Roedder and C.A. Cole, 1986.
77. N. Capon and R. Davis, 1984.
78. J.R. Bettman, 1979, p. 223.
79. D.H. Gensch and R.G. Javalgi, 1987.
80. K. Gredal, 1966; R.W. Olshavsky and D.H. Granbois, 1979.
81. J. Rudd and F.J. Kohout, 1983.

Part 2 Exercises and Cases

Exercise 1

Consumer response to marketing activity

(1) select some more press advertisments that are good illustrations of the use of any of the following concepts:

Perception,
Associationist learning,
Gestalt pychology,
Cognitive dissonance.

(2) Explain how theory might be being applied in each advertisement and comment on the likely effectiveness.

Exercise 2

Cognitive dissonance

(1) What is post-purchase dissonance?

(2) Provide some examples of this from your own experiences. Did you go on to buy the same product/service/brand again and what did you tell others about it?

(3) How did you overcome this dissonance and what else could you have done?

(4) What could marketers do to avoid/reduce dissonance? Give examples of good/poor practice in this respect.

(5) What sort of dimensions should be built in the questionnaire to measure levels of dissonance and consumers' reactions to dissonance?

Exercise 3

Adoption–diffusion of innovation case

Using 'diffusion–adoption of innovation' theory to introduce new products Tec Shoes is a specialist manufacturer of high quality athletic footwear. The company has been manu-facturing scientifically designed specialist shoes for top runners, racket-sports players and other athletes for several years.

Now the company feels that most people interested in sport could benefit from wearing this footwear because of the increased care and protection of the feet they can provide due to the contribution that the medical profession as well as experienced footwear and fashion designers make to the creation of the products.

Tec Shoes has been concerned only with top sportspeople on a personal basis and is unsure about how to reach a wider target market. One company executive suggests that different promotional approaches be used to reach different adopter categories over the products' life cycle.

Question

(1) What promotional mixes (Advertising, Publicity, Sales Promotion, Personal Selling) should be used to reach these market segments which adopt in different ways over time?

Case 1 Hemispheral lateralization

Introductory Comments

The right and left hemispheres of the brain perform specialized functions which are triggered by the level of mental concentration of the individual. The right hemisphere of the human brain specializes in non-verbal and pictoral information. The left side of the brain analyses information and is considered the logical side. It is used for mathematics and for developing reasoning. The right hemisphere is regarded as the 'conscious' part of the brain. The right side of the brain retrieves and saves the information. It is considered as the creative side of the brain and is used for music reception or creation.

The level of consumer involvement may determine whether the right or left side of the brain dominates in the areas of information processing and consumer decision making. When the right side of the brain dominates attention and information processing, recall rather than recognition is more likely. When the left side of the brain dominates attention and information processing, higher levels of advertising copy recognition can be achieved. Only advertisements that receive high levels of attention can affect consumer information processing.

A whole-brain approach to advertising

Our understanding of the left and right brains is as recent as the past two decades. Science has shown us that the left brain is our logical, rational side. It works with information – numbers, letters and words – in a sequential way. On the other hand, the right brain deals with intuition and emotion. It works with images, concepts and ideas.

The truth is, intuitive thought (the right brain) actually existed in humans first, millions of years ago. But then a remarkable thing happened – the human brain began to develop the ability to reason. The left brain rose to power. As a result, each of us literally has two different kinds of brains. Although we all have elements of both brains, most of us are dominated more by one than the other. We all know people who are essentially 'scientists' or essentially 'artists', which brings us to advertising.

Like the human personality, most advertising is essentially left-brained or right-brained. Like most humans, advertising usually leans too far to one side or the other. The real trick to understanding how to create truly effective advertising is to strike a balance between the left and right: a whole-brained approach.

A classic example of right-brained advertising is the perennial girl in a bikini, usually for a product such as auto parts that has nothing to do with either girls or bikinis. This kind of advertising garners attention, but fails the relevance test miserably.

On the other hand, advertising that is relevant may be terribly boring. This is left-brained advertising: logical and factual. Most advertisers err on this side, believing that product features motivate prospects to pick one product over another. But with just a little brainpower, they will come to see that we hardly ever buy for rational reasons. Otherwise, no-one would drive a Porsche or shop at Tiffany.

This is not to say that we do not have logical reasons for making purchases. Once the emotional decision has been made, a Porsche owner can defend his purchase with convincing reasons, but these may not be the real reasons.

More proof? How about paying 30% more for a brand of premium-priced bottled water? Now there is a rational decision. In more categories than any of us suspect, consumers make purchases based on how they feel about the brand, not what they think. As products become more similar, emotion plays a bigger role in the purchase decision.

If you look at truly inspiring advertising, you will find that it integrates elements from both the left and the right brain. Advertisements that combine rational and emotional benefits are almost always more effective than those with only rational benefits. 'This detergent gets clothes clean and white' becomes much more meaningful with the promise, 'And your mother-in-law will think more of you'.

Left-brained advertising is the easiest because Western society places more value on left-brained thinking. So we create headlines, illustrations and copy packed full of rational reasons why people should buy a product. This is advertising that states the obvious – or more likely, overstates it.

The problem with this approach, besides being incredibly mundane, is that it is a completely inside-out approach to advertising. It is advertising that is manufacturer-driven rather than consumer-driven.

Even when armed with marketing research that shows the features prospects are looking for in a product category, this left-brained approach still makes the assumption that people buy for rational reasons. So part of discovering prospects' wants and needs is getting inside their heads to determine the emotional or sensory benefits of your product, not just the rational ones.

To uncover these benefits, you have to add the missing dimension – the right brain – to a traditional advertising strategy. The result? A whole-brained advertising strategy that can be a blueprint for creating advertising that speaks to both sides of the brain.

For example, traditional left-brained advertising strategy might describe prospects as housewives, age 35, with three children, living in the suburbs. Right-brained advertising goes a step further to paint a three-dimensional portrait of this person that describes what she thinks, her values, her interests, and how she spends her spare time.

Anyone can put words and pictures on a page and call it an advertisement. But that is a little like calling a canvas with some paint on it a painting. It is the artistry of the right brain that makes advertising engaging, unique and memorable. It takes advertising beyond a mere recitation of product features – all presumed to be immensely important – and addresses the real reason people buy (Williams, 1995).

Reference

Williams, Tim J. (1995). A whole-brain approach to advertising. *Marketing News*, **29**(9) (April 24):4.

Problem

Corona Extra, losing some of its appeal among yuppies, is moving into the Japanese market with an advertising campaign that compares drinking Corona to a rhythm that stimulates the right side of the brain.

Corona, which is also introducing a light beer, is emphasizing the brew's tropical Mexican roots and its popularity with seasoned surfers. 'The US market is flat because of lifestyle changes', said Michael J Mazzoli, executive vice president and general manager of Chicago-based Barton Beers Ltd which imports Corona to the western US, 'there's a new emphasis on fitness, and sales are flat with the yuppies', whose purchases almost enabled Corona to displace Heineken as the No.1 import.

Americans drank less beer in 1988, on a per capita basis, than they did in 1981. At 2.4 billion cases, the US market grew negligibly over 1987, while imports rose just 0.4% after two years of sustained growth.

Corona's share of the US import market peaked in 1987 at nearly 25 million cases, or 19.1%. In 1988, the brew sold just over 20 million cases and its share of US imports shrank to 16.2%.

Corona's hold on the No 2 spot is secure, and sales still are far above those of previous years, when it sold just over 1.5 million cases in the US but the stalled growth has provoked concern.

'We've really been clobbered over the past year', Mazzoli said. 'We need some excitement.' Its brewer, Cervecerias Modelo, hopes to stir something up by introducing what hardened beer drinkers may consider an anomaly of sorts: Corona light. 'It's the formal evolution in light', said Thomas A. McNichols, Barton's marketing director.

While total US beer consumption has topped off, light brews are becoming more popular. For the first time, three of the five top brands are lights, and the trend has carried over into imports.

Modelo shipped its first case of Corona light northward in April 1989 and began test-marketing in Los Angeles, San Francisco, San Diego, Phoenix and Chicago. Eventually, a new plant in Guadalajara will produce up to 400,000 cases of Corona light a month.

'There are people who say Corona's already light. But I can't tell you how many times I've heard people say, wrongly, they're worried about its calorie content', said Mazzoli, adding that Corona averages 400 calories a bottle. 'It will have the same long-neck, painted bottle with colour changes. This is the first real chance we've had to come in with a new package', said Roberto S. Viejo, President of Procermex Inc., of San Antonio, Texas.

Modelo and its US distributors, Barton and Cambrinis importing Co. Inc. of San Antonio, plan to duplicate marketing tactics used to promote Corona Light's heavier cousin: rely at first on word-of-mouth advertising by introducing the brand in trendy restaurants and bars. Modelo's successful, and voiceless, TV ads, filmed in such tropical resorts as Ixtapa, were also used to tout Corona Light.

Modelo also is trying to counter its slippage in the US market by reaching out to others, such as the Japanese.

'We're going after young adults, the opinion leaders, and what we call the 'sensitive trend leaders', said John R. Hamaguchi, import marketing director for

Hiroya Co. Ltd. of Tokyo, Japan's oldest liquor merchant. 'There's the opinion leader: the one always with the latest news, fashions, and hairstyles and who drinks Corona because it's a new thing', Hanaguchi said, 'then there's the sensitive trend leaders. Corona's a very sophisticated item in Japan, especially in Tokyo night-clubs', he said, "that's where the sensitive trend leaders go."

Since it introduced Corona to Japan in July 1987, Horoya sold 130,000 cases of Corona through 1988, making the beer the No 5 import and 10th overall. 'We want one million cases five years from now', Hamaguchi said.

The Japanese advertising campaign, like many there, is not wordless but is highly emotive, with a man singing about what he likes and how Corona fits his lifestyle:

'I like two-branch roads in the middle of the city;
A rhythm that stimulates the right side of my brain;
A melody that has lost the code begins to be heard;
If I take the right road, it'll lead me to the end of the sea ...;
In my left hand I've got a lime;
In my right hand, I've got a Corona ...;
At this moment, I'm in the bottle of paradise'

Hamaguchi denied that by pricing Corona at up to $7.40 a bottle in Tokyo bars and emphasizing the beer's trendiness, Hiroya risks portraying the Mexican brew as a passing fad. 'Our target market is the mass market. Corona's a beer, not a champagne', Hamaguchi said.

In Canada, where beer drinkers as a whole quaff less than one-tenth what their American neighbours do, Corona has displaced Heineken as the leading import in three provinces, said Antony von Mandl, president and CEO of the Mark Antony Group Inc., of Vancouver.

Von Mandl's company, one of two Canadian importers, has accomplished that despite pricing Corona a $7.54 a six-pack, or 65c more than Heineken. Canadian sales totalled 110,000 cases in 1987, 355,000 cases in 1988, and well over half a million cases in 1989, even though Canadians, like Americans, are drinking a lot less, and despite what is called a discriminatory distribution system dominated by outlets owned by Canadian brewers and government-run liquor shops that mark up imports.

'Corona has done immense good for Mexico,' von Mandl said. 'It has produced a major psychological change among consumers abroad towards Mexican products.'

Questions

(1) What are the particular specialized functions of both left and right sides of the brain?

(2) Explain how the level of consumer involvement may determine whether the right or left side of the brain dominates in the areas of information processing and consumer decision-making.

(3) Comment on and explain the whole-brain approach to advertising.

Case 2 Proxemics, kinesic behaviour, paralanguage, atmospherics, aromatics and consumers' information processing flows

PINK LADY stores

Until early this summer, the PINK LADY women's clothing stores could have been more appropriately named the UPS & DOWNS stores. Financially, the stores were faltering. Physically, they lacked direction. Some of the outlets had a high-tech feel. Some were projecting a trendy image. Others simply had no character whatsoever. The clothing presentations were muddled and failed to emit an aura of fashion awareness. Separates (shirts, shorts, skirts, trousers, accessories and so on) were clumped together. Havoc ruled. Such an arrangement would proba-bly turn off just about any modern shopper, but it especially failed to suit the tastes of PINK LADY stores' customers.

The chain, based in Newport, Wales, caters to a young clientele, with most of the customers between the ages of 16 and 20. They are active and aestheti-cally oriented. They want stores that are visually pleasing, where they can manipulate the displays.

A store that satisfies these needs is now located in Cardiff's Queen Shopping Centre, Wales, and is setting the standard for all the chain's outlets. The shop was developed by Robert P. Jones Associates Ltd, a London industrial design com-pany. Since its unveiling it has experienced an 80% sales increase.

Jones Associates developed kinetically controlled display racks, unusual high-tech mannequins, murals for the store's walls, and a lighting scheme that makes the store seem more vibrant. These techniques add a modern feel to the PINK LADY prototype store. The murals in the background help to build on its new image. The elements have combined to make a store that is 'responsive to the customer's interests and appetites', according to Robert P. Jones, Managing Director of the design company.

The exterior of the shop has four vertically rectangular glass columns with a bright sign featuring the store's new, rounded logo between the two centre cases. Within the columns are mannequins wearing some of the latest fashions. This fully transparent, open storefront draws customers in as they see what is inside the shop, Jones said. And the really neat stuff is inside. Internally lit kinetic cloth-ing carousels revolve with a light touch from the customer's hand, Jones said. These racks mostly hold seasonal clothing and promotional items. 'The easily moving racks help the customer choose by allowing her to see more items than on a stationary rack', he said 'and clothes shopping becomes fun, because she gets to move the racks around. She is lively and, as part of her normal life, she likes things that move.'

Atop these carousels are lilac-coloured mannequins that spin with the racks, which have rails of the same hue. By matching the dummies with the rails, the store projects a more unified image, Jones said. 'The mannequins are definitely not naturalistic', he added. Their surreal appearance was one reason they were chosen. Young people today like such images. In a semicircle around the wheels and dummies are additional clothing racks and shelves for folded items. This adds to the neat appearance of the store. Besides these racks, there is the PINK LADY feature fixture in the centre of the store, which is designed to make a major 'merchandise statement', Jones said. Because the fixture also is run by kinetics, the customer can vertically rotate one of the three merchandise bays to move the hanging or folded merchandise into reach. The up and down motion was chosen because it acts as a metaphor for the store. Besides the kinetically run racks, the shop also has sales racks. These low fixtures hold hanging merchandise on rails and folded merchandise on low shelf units on casters. These units also fit into the seasonal fixture. Racks are not the only places where customers find clothes. Two entire walls are devoted to specific clothing images. A bright 'fashion wall' draws customers into the store, Jones said. On this wall, high-fashion pieces are displayed in bays created by translucent fins that support lighting tubes. The tubes light the merchandise and the 'fashion-in-action' photo murals above, he said. The large wall graphics are taken from black-and-white photographs of models wearing PINK LADY clothing, and serve as background images of young people actively enjoying the clothing available in the store.

'These images are repeated on shopping bags and boxes, projecting and expanding an integrated image of the store', Jones said. Bowing outwards, the wall accommodates fitting rooms behind it. There is also a 'constant wall'. It is opposite the fashion wall both in terms of its location and purpose. It holds basic separates that are almost always in style, and features a tower of sliding trays for folded clothing separates and double-tiered, revolving carousels for hanging merchandise. In addition, the back wall has a custom wall-covering based on a photograph of a softly folded fabric in grey and white.

Backing all these ingredients are colour-coded signs, Jones said. Each colour represents different seasons, whether the item is on sale, and so on. The idea is that regular customers will eventually know where to look simply by noting the colour of the sign.

'You want the customer to be invited back, both subtly and directly', he said. 'By colour coding the signs we made the customers feel more like it was their store because they would have more direction when choosing their items'.

The next PINK LADY that will try to create an enduring image will be in Tenby, and five others are planned though definite opening dates are not available.

Questions

PINK LADY stores were faltering. Physically, they lacked direction. Some of the outlets had a high-tech feel. Some were projecting a trendy image. Others simply had no character whatsoever. The chain caters for a young clientele, with most of the customers between the ages of 16 and 20. The company's turnaround strategy focused on the use of atmospherics and kinetics to help build a new image and major 'merchandise statements' were developed.

(1) In a sales interaction, there are silent messages that are given by the buyer and seller that affect the likelihood of a transaction. Three types of silent messages that are important are proxemics, kinesic behaviour and paralanguage. Comment on these three types of silent messages.

(2) Comment on the general use of atmospherics in marketing.

(3) Discuss the use of aromatics in marketing in general and in a retail environment in particular.

(4) Analyse the consumer's information processing flow with regard to PINK LADY's atmospherics strategy.

Part 3

Market analysis: Segmentation, targeting and research

6

Market segmentation

Chapter objectives

(1) To build on our earlier discussions which have been more 'individual' based, to show that marketing traditionally tries to group individuals together as far as possible within relatively homogeneous segments. This is one of the major cornerstones of both understanding consumer behaviour and marketing itself.

(2) To examine this important topic in some detail, demonstrating the importance of understanding consumer behaviour within segments.

(3) To integrate various contributions from sociology and social psychology within the contextual framework of market segmentation.

(4) Specifically, to examine relevant dimensions of social stratification, lifestyle, self-concept theory and family influence not as discrete behavioural concepts but more as they apply within a marketing context via an understanding of how markets can be segmented.

(5) To examine some of the more recent approaches to segmentation such as geodemographics, which in many ways take us back to the focus of the earlier chapters, namely the individual, because we are witnessing moves towards individualized marketing.

6.1   Introduction

The very essence of the marketing concept itself leads to an inevitable consideration of market segmentation. If marketing is to do with satisfying consumer needs and wants as a means to achieving the goals of the organization, it should be recognized that whereas the human condition might mean that we all may have a similar need structure, not everyone will have the same needs to the fore at the same point in time.

The notion of varying salient needs and values (or other buying factors) in different individuals (or in organizations) provides the rationale for market segmentation. Those with similar salient needs and values may be grouped together to form a market segment if their buying behaviour is seen to be sufficiently homogeneous and at the same time different from those of other groups. Indeed if, for whatever reason, not only with respect to motivation, buying behaviour within a group is homogeneous, a potential market segment exists. Marketing would then have the task of deciding which segments to target with distinct marketing mixes.

A useful illustration of segmentation is the toothpaste market in terms of the benefits shown in Table 6.1.[1] The example is also useful at this stage in that it provides an early preview of some other segmenting bases that will be discussed in greater depth in this chapter, namely segmentation at the general level (demographic and psychographic approaches), domain-specific level (benefit segmentation) and specific level (customer segmentation).

Many of us might think 'toothpaste is toothpaste' and that we all use it in similar quantities for similar reasons. What is shown is that even in such a 'samey' market, there are different consumer segments that buy in different ways for a variety of reasons and on this basis can be targeted with different marketing mixes. This is a fundamental rationale for market segmentation.

Benefit segmentation is the middle level in the three-level segmentation approach:[3]

- At the general level, the segmentation is based on more or less permanent consumer characteristics such as gender, age, income, social class, occupation, family composition and lifestyle. These characteristics are the same for different products, services and usage situations.
- Domain-specific level: If different product classes and consumption domains, such as taking breakfast, washing clothes, or commuting, are taken into account, the segmentation is domain-specific. The toothpaste benefit seg-

Table 6.1 Toothpaste consumer benefit segments.[2]

	Sensory segment	Sociable segment	Worrier segment	Independent segment
Main benefit	Flavour, appearance	Bright teeth	Decay prevention	Price
Demographic factors	Children, young people	Teens, families	Large	Men
Lifestyle factors	Hedonistic	Active	Conservative	Concerned with value
Brands	Colgate, Stripe	Ultra Brite, Macleans	Crest	Cheapest own label brands on sale

mentation is an example of the domain-specific approach. We will briefly return to benefit segmentation towards the end this chapter to discuss how the 'use'-based approach has been extended to more of a 'situation' (or occasion of use) base.

■ Specific level: If customers are segmented into, for instance, heavy and light users of specific brands, Classic Coke and Cherry Coke drinkers, this is called segmentation at the specific level. Segmentation of present customers is also at the specific level.

Segmentation variables may be objective or subjective. An objective variable may be measured unambiguously, for example age and gender, or may taken from registrations of transactions, for example checkout scanning data. Subjective variables need to be measured with the respondents themselves and are often 'mental constructs' such as attitudes and intentions.

Combining the three levels of segmentation and the distinction of objective and subjective variables, Table 6.2 can be formed. All segmentation variables can be classified in this table.

The aim of this chapter is to provide both the conventional and the unconventional with respect to its coverage of segmentation. The conventional concerns itself with the development of segmentation criteria for segmenting markets and a discussion of typical segmentation variables. The unconventional is based on a greater analysis of trends in segmentation than is usually found in chapters on the topic. Specifically, and put simply, it will be proposed that there is an increasing trend towards identifying and targeting smaller segments. Through application of information technology and databases there are clear moves towards targeting individuals, as in direct marketing. Ethical issues are involved with this, such as the correct use of detailed and extensive information databases on most of us as individuals, not just as groups.

In terms of structure, this chapter has three main components. First, we look at the progression from mass production through product differentiation to

Table 6.2 Classification of segmentation variables.

	Objective	*Subjective*
General level (consumption)	Income Age Education level Geographic area	Lifestyle General values Personality
Domain-specific level (product class)	Usage frequency Substitution Complementarity	Perception Attitude, preference Interests, opinions Domain-specific values
Specific level (brand)	Brand loyalty (behaviour) Usage frequency	Brand loyalty (attitude) Brand preference Purchase intention

market segmentation, together with a variety of research and planning issues involved with segmentation strategies.

Next, a currently relevant segmentation theme is analysed and illustrated, namely the trend towards increasing targeting. This is based on the relative decline of demographic segmentation variables, partly due to their lack of explanatory depth and their relatively broad targeting capabilities. The rise of psychographics and geodemographics will be shown to have added to demographics' decline because of their potential abilities to understand target customers in great detail, even individually, and to be able to target them equally specifically (see Figure 6.1).

Figure 6.1 shows that product differentiation is the answer to market segmentation and targeting. Product differentiation depends on the competences of the firm to produce these products and to have access to marketing channels to reach the targeted consumers.

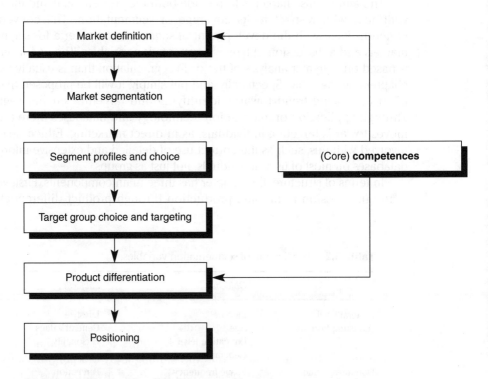

Figure 6.1 From market definition to positioning.

6.2   Development of segmentation

The toothpaste example (p. 122) demonstrates an application of targeting different customer groups with different marketing mixes. However, it has not always been like this. The famous saying in the car industry by Henry Ford, concerning the Model T, that customers could have any colour as long as it was black, was a reflection of the mass marketing of the time. Great economies of scale were achieved through the long production runs of mass producing standardized products for an apparently homogeneous market. In a classic paper by Wendell Smith, who was one of the originators of segmentation thinking, the development of segmentation is explored.[4] As mass production and consumption continued, many organizations attempted to gain some competitive advantage and developed the strategy of product differentiation. As Smith stated: 'Product differentiation is concerned with the bending of demand to the will of supply.' Product differentiation also offers a variety to buyers rather than to appeal to different segments.[5]

This is the key to product differentiation because, although the result might in some cases look very similar to segmentation, differences in product, image, distribution and/or promotion are offered to the market. Perhaps such differences do indeed appeal to different groups within the overall market, but if they do it is mainly due to coincidence. True segmentation starts with identifying the requirements and behaviour of segments and varying marketing mixes accordingly in order to more deliberately match marketing offerings with customer behaviour.

Product differentiation clearly represents a product-oriented approach in that it is an 'inside out' management attitude to marketing planning. A more market orientation starts with market understanding and the identification of market needs and behaviour and thus is an 'outside in' planning approach. This is the segmentation approach and declares that marketing offerings cannot generally hope to be all things to all people and that differences between groups and similarities within groups may be analysed for marketing planning purposes.

The result of market segmentation appears to be a dividing of the market into smaller groups but rather than seeing the process as divisive, it is more helpful and appropriate to consider it as one of aggregating. In this way segmentation groups customers together as far as it is meaningful for them to be targeted with distinct marketing mixes.

However, the extent of such grouping, the extent to which differences in the marketplace can and should be analysed and reflected in segmentation, is part of an ongoing debate. Market 'fragmentation' or 'over-segmenting' may create too small and unprofitable segments and becomes thus less efficient.[6] British Rail's plethora of price segments and the baffling array of shampoos are examples. There are other critics of segmenting, or segmenting too far. Closely positioned and substitutable grocery brands are examples. For this category the basic segmentation philosophy may be questioned. For example, it is found that 'different brands do not necessarily appeal to different types of consumers ... there can be product differentiation without segmentation'. They further pose the fundamental question of whether 'it is better for your brand to appeal to your segment of buyers all the time or to all segments some of the time'.[7] Product differentiation may thus also serve to offer variety to consumers. Frozen dinners are not only differentiated to appeal to different segments but also to appeal to variety-seeking consumers who want to eat different dinners over time.

6.3 Segmentation planning issues

Segmentation involves dividing the market into segments with homogeneous buying behaviour within a segment, but heterogeneous buying behaviour between segments. For a potential segment to be considered as a target for a distinct marketing mix, it should satisfy a number of criteria.

Segmentation criteria

A number of criteria have to be met in developing feasible segments for marketing policy. The following criteria are mentioned in the literature.[8] These criteria are related to typifying the segments, homogeneity, usefulness, and strategic use in marketing management. The four main and nine subcriteria are:[9]

(1) Typifying the segments
   (a) Identification: Differentiation of segment from other segments.
   (b) Measurability: Identification of segments in terms of differences in individual and household characteristics or other 'measurable' characteristics should be possible.
(2) Homogeneity
   (a) Variation: Heterogeneity between segments in terms of behavioural response.[10]
   (b) Stability: The segments should be relatively stable over time. Also, switching of consumers from one segment to another should not be frequent. There should be stability at the individual level.
   (c) Congruity: Homogeneity within segments in terms of behavioural responses.
(3) Usefulness
   (a) Accessibility: Segments should be accessible in terms of the use of media and distribution outlets. Segments are being reached in a 'communicative and distributive' manner. Segments should react consistently to communicative, promotional, distributional and product-related stimuli. This means that it must be possible to reach the segment, for example selecting appropriate advertising media that match the segment's media profile or selecting appropriate distribution channels, again through a matching of market profile with the profile of those most likely to frequent different types of retail outlets. These factors have tradi-

tionally been in demographic terms, but increasingly since around the start of the 1980s other more sophisticated market profiling and targeting dimensions have been explored and used.

(b) Substantiality: Segments should be of sufficient size to enable specific marketing actions. This does not mean that segments need to be especially large, but profitable enough to have distinct marketing mixes aimed at them.

(4) Strategic criteria

(a) Potentiality: The segments should have enough potential for marketing objectives, for example profitability.

(b) Attractiveness: Segments should be structurally attractive to the producer, for example create a competitive advantage for the company.[11]

These criteria can be met using a proper segmentation methodology including a retest study to investigate the stability of the segments. The discriminative power of the segmentation can be assessed by comparing the segments on specific criteria in the market such as brand choice, brand evaluations and brand attribute importance ratings. This provides the researcher with an independent criterion for the validity of the obtained segments.

It is not always the case that for each segment a different product must be developed. It might be this, but equally there might be different prices charged in different segments for the same product or service, for example gas, electricity and train travel, or it could be differences in promotion. Levi's advertise on televison for a fairly wide market but the same product lines are also promoted with quite different images and themes in the 'style' press (for example *The Face*) targeted at the 15–19-year-old fashion opinion leaders.[12] There again, there are examples of where distribution might be the main mix difference between segments. A women's clothing manufacturer might produce a range of dresses but have alternate batches go into department stores and more down-market multiple retailers. There would probably be branding and price differences here as well but the primary difference would be based on retail outlet and hence segment targeted.

The above criteria are also of great significance in researching potential segments. The measurability criterion gives research direction in identifying primary or active segmentation variables. The substantiality criterion indicates market size, potential and share as dimensions to research. Accessibility suggests the importance of secondary or passive characteristics.

Note the distinction between active and passive variables; active variables are the variables that are used in forming the segments, whereas passive variables are used afterwards to characterize the formed segments more completely.

Another practical point is that research methods may determine segmentation. If some variables of market behaviour are difficult, time consuming, or costly to research, sometimes the market will be segmented according to those dimensions that are more conveniently analysed, such as age, gender and socio-economic variables.

Forward and backward segmentation

Forward segmentation may be contrasted with backward segmentation.[13] An example of forward segmentation would be where it has been decided to segment according to the level of usage (active variable) and then to conduct research to determine the (say) demographic characteristics (passive variables) of the heavy users, light users, and so on.

Backward segmentation, however, is where segments are for instance formed on lifestyle variables or on the basis of similar attitudes, interests and opinions (active variables). Then the formed segments are described in terms of their buying behaviour (passive variable).

There may be good reasons at marketing strategy level for deciding to target medium and light users. The forward approach, although it does not sound as market oriented as backward segmentation, can be legitimized. Backward segmentation on the other hand probably, in practice, requires some predetermined hypotheses as to which base to research, so there may not be much pure backward segmentation in the real world. The risk of backward segmentation is that segments prove not to be relevant or different in their buying behaviour after all.

In Table 6.3 forward and backward segmentation are compared. In forward segmentation segments are formed based on their buying behaviour. These segments are afterwards described with person variables such as attitudes, perceptions and lifestyle. In backward segmentation the segments are formed based on person variables. Afterwards the buying behaviour of these segments is investigated.

Table 6.3 Forward and backward segmentation.

Segmentation	Active variables	Passive variables
Forward	Buying behaviour	Person variables
Backward	Person variables	Buying behaviour

Planning segmentation

The market segmentation planning process for backward segmentation can be divided into five stages:

(1) The identification of active variables that might be used for segmenting its markets.
(2) The development of market segment profiles.
(3) The organization needs to forecast the total market potential (buying behaviour) for each segment. Within this stage, an analysis of competitive forces operating within each segment should be carried out as well as the definition of the marketing mix designed to serve each market segment.

(4) The application of forecasting procedures in order to calculate the company's market share for each segment. During this stage, the company should also estimate the trade-off between allocated costs and delivered benefits for each market segment.

(5) The assessment of delivered benefits from each segment in relation to corporate goals, which will provide the rationale and justification for further development of each market segment. This market segmentation decision process cycle is completed when the company decides on the selection of market target segments.

Targeting

The company has to decide on how many segments to cover and how to identify the best segments. There are four alternatives to cover a market:

(1) Undifferentiated targeting, where the organization decides to ignore market segment differences and targets the whole market with one market offering. It focuses on what is common in the needs of consumers rather than on what is different and relies on mass distribution and mass advertising.

(2) Differentiated targeting, where several segments are identified and targeted.

(3) Concentrated targeting, where one segment is targeted exclusively.

(4) Custom targeting, where the market is so pluralistic that each customer is targeted with a different mix (direct marketing). This is something we are likely to see more of and as already mentioned will be discussed later in more detail.

Implementing segmentation plans

The discussion of segmentation planning may be extended by considering the more practical aspects of implementing segmentation strategies, not so much in the marketplace but more in an organizational context.[14]

There is not a single correct way of segmenting a market. It depends heavily on what the organization is trying to achieve and on such factors as its access to, and interest in, various techniques and resources to research and implement what conventional segmentation might recommend. There may be a gap between the findings of segmentation research in markets and the management and implementation of segmentation strategies. An illustration is given with respect to applying segmentation criteria. At a more strategic level it might be more important to evaluate on the basis of the extent to which a segmentation approach can create and/or sustain competitive advantage, or its congruence with corporate competences, values and culture. A useful framework is proposed for addressing some of these issues and this is shown in Figure 6.2.

After the review of the origins of segmentation and some of its research and planning implications, the possible active segmentation variables are now discussed. That is, on what bases can customers be grouped together for targeting

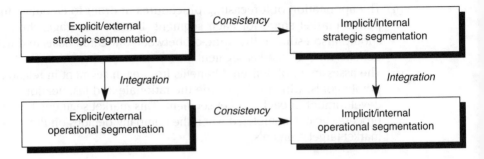

Figure 6.2 Consistency and integration in segmentation implementation.[15]

purposes. The next sections discuss demographics, psychographics and geodemographics but also propose, through the review of these approaches, that segmentation has become more focused in its explanatory and targeting abilities and will continue in this vein through the 1990s. The focus is likely to be on smaller and smaller segments, analysed in greater detail and targeted, sometimes down to the individual. A significant change from the days of Henry Ford.

6.4   Demographic segmentation

This section discusses bases for segmenting markets but at the same time traces the trend of increased focusing of segmentation and targeting from general demographic groups through better understood psychographic and domain-specific segments to more specific individualized targeting via marketing databases and direct marketing.

It is not long since about the only market profiling that organizations relied on was in general demographic terms, and some still rely on little more. It became the norm for markets to be profiled as in Table 6.4, which shows that the most established approaches to segmentation are based on demographic characteristics such as age, gender, social grade, family composition and ethnicity. Many of these demographic variables have been used by marketers over several decades, although as will be seen shortly, there is not only much criticism of some of these variables but other non-demographic approaches are now in widespread use.

It is perhaps no geat surprise that demographic variables have been favoured for so long. First, they are generally easy to study. A market research interviewer needs only to ask respondents to point to their appropriate age category on a showcard, to note the gender of the respondent and to ask the respondent to give the occupation of the chief income earner in their household. Such simple research, together with the geographic area in which the research is conducted, will provide the basic profile with which marketers are so familiar: age, gender, social grade and geographic location profile.

Table 6.4 Typical demographic profile of the drinks market.[16]

	Weekly alcohol drinkers		
	Beer (%)	Wine (%)	Whisky (%)
Age			
18–24	58	23	7
25–34	50	29	8
35–49	45	28	14
50+	30	15	17
Social grade			
AB	39	40	17
C1	40	30	14
C2	48	20	13
DE	38	9	10
Gender			
Male	65	22	19
Female	21	22	8

Age

Age is still a valid base for many markets. 'Young adult' and 'teenage' segments have become important spenders, for example, demanding their own products and searching for their own identity.[17] Their numbers have of course declined through what was called in the UK the 'demographic timebomb' of the mid to late 1980s (Figure 6.3). The phrase was coined because it reflected a dramatic change in the number of people in this age group and that the change held all sorts of implications for marketers and social planners alike. Although the 16–24s of the mid–1980s have moved on in age terms themselves, they are still important as the now older group because they are still, of course, a very sizeable group. As for the 16–24s of today, there may not be so many of them but it is important to target them, either in their own right or as opinion leaders, as mentioned earlier with respect to Levi Strauss. A complicating factor is that this group has been found to be especially individualistic and sceptical of marketing activity. This doesn't make them difficult to reach, but it is proving harder to influence them. They have been labelled as 'Generation X' and Ritson has profiled them very effectively.[18] The issue of individualism is discussed further under consumer psychographics in Section 6.5.

At the other end of the age spectrum, it is noticeable that the size of older age segments have been increasing as society ages. The 1960s generation is likely to become more powerful and influential as they reach more responsible positions and also because they will inherit more substantially from their parents than predecessor generations have from theirs.[19]

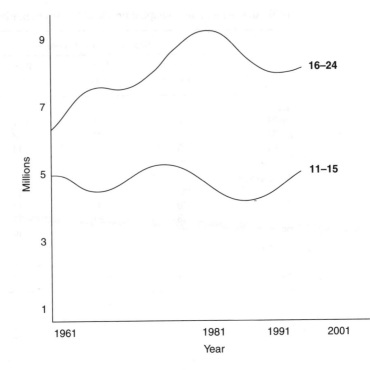

Figure 6.3 The demographic timebomb.

Gender

Gender too has been a long-established segmentation variable, not only in the sense of there being products for men and for women, but rather that tradition-ally most consumer goods were bought by women. Women would be the purchasers for the household; they might not have been the deciders or the final users of everything they bought, but at least they did most of the buying. As a consequence, much marketing activity was directed towards women, with a few changes of approach over the years. Female stereotyping has been the focus of much criticism over the past couple of decades. In the mid-1970s there was a general reliance on either the 'mother' or 'mistress' images of women in advertis-ing. Towards the end of that decade criticisms centred on these approaches becoming less and less realistic.[20] During the 1980s we had the emerging 'career woman' stereotype, but even this was limited and not always appropriately implemented.

Gender is still relevant in segmentation terms. One important trend for the 1990s is the continued change in respect of the 'Feminal Consumer'.[21] Increases in the divorce rate and the 'singles' market have added to the more general changes in sex roles, with women becoming more individualistic through their own careers rather than being housewives *per se*. Marketing to women, however, may still be in need of updating.[22]

The concept of the 'new man' emerged towards the end of the 1980s and we saw the manifestation of this in the advertising of cars, for example. Audi's 'caring-sharing' man who holds the baby was quite different from the aggressive and selfish boy racers of earlier periods. Whether the 1990s really see a significant shift towards the caring and sharing new man is debatable. What is clear is that, as female roles change, so inevitably do male roles. The increase in the divorce rate affects both sexes and produces sizeable singles markets, some male, some female, but all requiring greater independence in buying terms.

Social grade

Marketers have, especially in the past, adhered to the basic principle of social stratification but have long avoided researching possible segments on the basis of social class in any true sociological sense. This would involve rather complicated assessment of income, wealth, power and skill. So instead in the UK and many other European countries social grade is used, determined, in the UK, by the occupation of the 'chief income earner' in the household. A sixfold classification results: A, B, C1, C2, D, E. Many commercial market research programmes have found significant differences in buying behaviour between respondents in the various social grades. Table 6.5 summarizes the occupational basis for social grade in the UK.

The traditional justification for the continued use of social grade is basically twofold. It is simple to research. All that is required is for data to be analysed according to the occupation of the 'chief income earner in the household'. This is recently redefined from 'the occupation of the head of the household'.[24] Secondly, social grade appears to have been a reasonably good discriminator of buying behaviour. Table 6.6 shows a few typical examples of the discriminatory power of social grade and Table 6.7 suggests that it is reasonably stable for political preferences.

Table 6.5 Social grade in the UK.[23]

Social grade	Social status	Head of household's occupation	Percentage
A	Upper middle class	High managerial, administrative or professional	2.7
B	Middle class	Intermediate managerial, administrative or professional	15.2
C1	Lower middle class	Supervisory, clerical, junior managerial or administrative	24.1
C2	Skilled working class	Skilled manual workers	27.1
D	Working class	Semi and unskilled manual workers	17.8
E	Lowest levels of subsistence	State pensioners, widows, casual or lowest-grade workers	13.0

Table 6.6 The discriminatory power of social grade.[25]

	Indices of usage (national average = 100)		
	Toothpaste	Tea	Baked beans
A,B	140	78	89
C1	119	90	95
C2	123	108	128
D,E	52	103	40

Table 6.7 Social grade stability over time.[26]

	UK electorate in 1983, 1987 and 1992%								
	Conservatives			Labour			Liberal/Democrats		
	'83	'87	'92	'83	'87	'92	'83	'87	'92
A,B	60	57	56	10	14	20	28	26	22
C1	51	51	52	20	21	25	28	26	19
C2	40	40	38	32	36	41	26	22	17
D,E	33	30	30	41	48	50	24	20	15

However, during the 1980s in particular, a number of significant criticisms of social grade were made. There are inevitable anomalies in its use, for example nearly a third of those earning over £21,000 are C2DE and half those earning £15,000 – £21,000 are C2DE. Thus, the traditional strong correlations between social grade and income have been destroyed. Some in C2, such as highly skilled manual workers, will be earning more than some middle managers in grade B.

It was shown that of 400 respondents to earlier surveys who were re-interviewed to confirm their social grade, 41% had been allocated to the wrong group and this is an indication of the instability of the system.[27]

However, if we integrate the above demographic variables and perhaps discover that those most interested in our product or service are predominately, say, 'AB male, 45–54' we have a combination of some of the most used segmentation variables of recent decades. Inferring activities, interests and opinions, and indeed buying behaviour, of segments like this, or of others such as 'C1 female 18–24' or 'C2 male 25–34' is quite simple. If you try this you will find it probably can be done easily in a couple of minutes, showing the power of stereotypes but also revealing the probable inaccuracies of inference alone.

Family life cycle

However, one framework that to some extent combines age and gender variables is based on the family life-cycle concept and shows how the family unit's interests and buying behaviour are changing over time due to the progression from the single bachelor stage, to newly married, married with children, married with children who no longer live in the parental home ('empty nest'), and finally to the solitary survivor stage.

It has been found that some product categories, like life assurance, are predominantly chosen by the husband, while other categories, like food and children's clothing, are 'wife dominated', and yet others, such as choice of holiday and housing, are based on joint decision making, including the children to some extent.[28] Buying needs, values and behaviour differ for the various stages.[29] An updated life-cycle model for the UK is shown in Table 6.8.[30]

Table 6.8 UK modernized family life cycle.[31]

Life-cycle stage	Percentages of households
Bachelor	1.7
Newly married couples	3.8
Full nest 1 (with pre-school children)	14.6
Full nest 1 (lone parent)	1.5
Middle age, no children (aged 35–44)	1.5
Full nest 2 (school-aged children)	2.1
Full nest 2 (lone parents)	2.4
Launching families (with non-dependent children)	7.8
Launching families (lone parent)	1.8
Empty nest 1 (childless aged 45–60)	11.6
Empty nest 2 (retired)	11.7
Solitary survivor (under 65)	3.3
Solitary survivor (retired)	17.4
Total	100

A recent promotional campaign by Barclays Bank depicted the life stages through which their customers go, by picturing a young single man, then a couple with a family and an older couple whose childen had left home, and suggesting that the Bank has financial service products to suit not just each stage 'now' but each individual as they progress through these stages of the life cycle. Another example is afforded by Midland Bank in its advertising of financial services for the 'empty nesters'. In this case, the image depicted the broken shakles of unlocked chains attached to balls displaying the legends 'children' and 'mortgage'.

The concepts here have been extended and applied within practical market analysis programmes such as SAGACITY, given in Table 6.9.[32] SAGACITY combines an abbreviated family life cycle with income and occupation. The result is a series of twelve categories based on life stage, whether both partners are working or not, and on 'blue collar' or 'white collar' occupations.

It is perhaps a significant indicator of the end of marketing's love affair with social grade that from 1988 Granada TV replaced social grade as one of the profiling characteristics in its audience research with family life cycle (they call it life stage).[34]

Table 6.9 Twelve SAGACITY categories.[33]

1	Dependent			1.1	White collar
				1.2	Blue collar
2	Pre-family			2.1	White collar
				2.2	Blue collar
3	Family	3.1	Better off	3.11	White collar
				3.12	Blue collar
		3.2	Worse off	3.21	White collar
				3.22	Blue collar
4	Empty nest	4.1	Better off	4.11	White collar
				4.12	Blue collar
		4.2	Worse off	4.21	White collar
				4.22	Blue collar

Race

Another demographic base that marketing has not been especially strong in using is race.[35] Ethnic segments are now being targeted more clearly, although there is perhaps still a long way to go. Ethnic segments have their own culture, language, religion and distinct requirements. It is not always appropriate for them to be targeted with more general products and services by merely changing advertisements for them. Different coloured skin, for example, has different moisture content and the formulation of cosmetics should be different, not merely suggesting how people of different colours can select from existing ranges to arrive at appropriate colour combinations.

There are, now, market research agencies that offer specialized services to research ethnic segments, so the argument of a decade or so ago that they are difficult to research is not as strong as it once was. Also, with the developing ethnic media it is equally possible to reach ethnic segments with marketing messages.

A sensitive issue is whether targeting at ethnic segments is in some way racist. The argument is that if ethnic segments differ in their needs and values, they should be treated differently. This does not mean that they are discriminated against.

Geographics

There always have been significant differences in buying patterns in the various regions of the UK for some products and services.[36] 'Northerners devour 33% more potatoes and 43% more flour than their peers in the south east but guzzle 43% less fresh fruit. And they spend far more on alcoholic drink, most of it on beer. Londoners and Scots on the other hand prefer wine.'

Broadening the discussion on geographics, there is now much debate about 'global marketing' or at least pan-European marketing due to the single market and the technology, for example satellite broadcasting, that allows organizations to reach other countries more easily. However, there is evidence to suggest that

Table 6.10 International attitudinal differences.[37]

Percentages agreeing with various statements:

	US	GB	WG	F	I	JP
Freedom being more important than equality	72	69	37	54	43	37
Equality being more important than freedom	20	23	39	32	45	32
Very proud to be (American/French, etc.)	80	55	21	33	41	30
Confidence in major institutions in your country:						
Press	49	29	33	31	46	52
Education	65	60	43	55	56	51
Civil service	55	48	35	50	28	31
Having 'great' pride in the work you do	84	79	15	13	29	37
Relevance of the ten commandments in today's society: does each of the following 'Thou shalts' still apply today:						
Not steal	93	87	81	69	93	66
Not kill	93	90	88	80	96	65
Not commit adultery	87	78	64	48	62	47

Key	US	United States
	GB	Great Britain
	WG	West Germany
	F	France
	I	Italy
	JP	Japan

for many products and services geographic market segments will stay and even become more heterogeneous at regional and even local level.[38] Table 6.10 reflects some attitudinal differences between nations according to an international Gallup survey.[39] Again it is partly this pluralism in the marketplace that is fuelling a trend towards greater targeting and focusing of marketing activity towards smaller niche markets.

6.5 Consumer psychographics

Although not new in concept, or even in practice, a variety of 'psychographic' approaches emerged during the 1980s. Lifestyle is based typically on the presentation to respondents of a series of statements. Table 6.11 reproduces a short selection of the (246) lifestyle statements used in the Target Group Index annual research programme.[40]

An example will demonstrate the approach. In the 1980s Levi Strauss in the USA went through a new product development programme concerning a range of up-market men's suits. The market research programme that was involved revolved around an attempt to discover 'lifestyles'. This is concerned with investigating activities, interests and opinions, sometimes referred to as AIO analysis.

As with this Levi example, the lifestyle approach usually involves presenting a series of statements to respondents, asking for agreement with each (Likert scales). Such lifestyle data is then cluster-analysed to produce groupings of respondents which are relatively homogeneous within each group but heterogeneous between clusters in terms of their activities, interests and opinions. Each cluster would then be allocated a somewhat glib title. In a lifestyle research programme in the US, for example, Levi Strauss used this type of research to identify the main clothing segments, namely the 'classic independent', the 'mainstream traditionalist', the 'price shopper', the 'trendy casual' and so on.[41] This sort of profile will help determine appropriate product/service features, and will help to arrive at an advertising message which is congruent with the segment's lifestyle.

Table 6.11 Examples of lifestyle statements.[42]

I buy clothes for comfort, not for style
Once I find a brand I like, I tend to stick to it
I always buy Dutch (British, Portuguese) whenever I can
I dress to please myself
My family rarely sits down to meal together at home
I enjoy eating foreign food
I like to do a lot when I am on holiday

All items with a 5-point Likert scale: definitely agree / tend to agree / neither agree nor disagree / tend to disagree / definitely disagree / not applicable

A UK lifestyle typology was named Taylor Nelson's Applied Futures.[43] Table 6.12 shows some extracts from this version.

Table 6.12 Taylor Nelson's Applied Futures.[44]

Lifestyle category	Characterized by	Percentage of population
Belonger	Place great store by home, family, country, the establishment, etc	19
Survivor	Disposed towards identification with groups and accepting of authority. Self-expression and creativity are irrelevant	16
Experimentalist	Attracted to all that is new and different, always looking for new ideas, items and experiences	12
Conspicuous consumer	Energy is directed towards the consumer dream via material possessions, take their cues from reference groups, not critical of advertisers, followers of fashion	18
Social resister	Seeks to maintain the status quo, controlling self, family, society, suppressing self in favour of duty and moral obligation	15
Self-explorer	Self-aware and self-concerned people, self-expression important	14
Aimless	Uninvolved and alienated, aggressive towards the system, resentful of its failure to provide employment	6

Personality variables

A superficially attractive variable for segmenting markets is personality. The logic would be that we buy products and services that in some way reflect or extend our personality traits. A classic study in the US revealed Ford owners to be more independent and go-getting than their Chevrolet counterparts.[45] Unfortunately, personality has had a mixed reception in research programmes. Even replications of this study produced conflicting results, so personality appears to be a less reliable segmentation variable than other variables.

However, some personality variables do offer the marketer much scope for segmentation and these are: innovativeness, self-monitoring, and inner versus outer directedness and the self-concept.[46] Innovativeness was discussed in Chapter 4 on new and repeat buying and the self-concept is discussed in the next section here.

Self-monitoring is the degree to which persons adapt themselves to their social environment.[47] Persons high in self-monitoring behave chameleon-like and are always trying to make good impressions on others. It is important for them to be accepted by others. They tend to buy products and brands that contribute to making favourable impressions on their reference group. Persons low in self-monitoring behave more according to their own beliefs and attitudes and are less influenced by the perceived or actual approval of their social environment.

Inner and outer directedness looks similar to self-monitoring, but is somewhat different. Inner directed people are concerned with their own thoughts and problems. Outer directed people are more social and looking for contacts with other people.

Perhaps one of the problems with personality as a segmentation variable is that an objective personality test might reveal our true personality but we might not know that this is how we are or we may not agree with it. And secondly, we might want to disguise our true personality and therefore buy brands that in some way extend those traits we want to portray, and perhaps different traits at different times in different social circumstances. This leads us to a consideration of how we might want to be and how we think we are, rather than how we actually are, according to some externally determined tests and criteria. This is the self-concept theory.

Self-concept

This variation on the personality theme in psychographic segmentation is based not on what sort of personality traits consumers possess, as identified through administering standardized personality inventory tests, but on how consumers perceive themselves. Indeed, it has been suggested that 'of all the personality concepts which have been applied to marketing, self-concept has probably provided the most consistent results and the greatest promise of application to the needs of business firms'.[48]

Self-concept is indeed an alternative, worthy of consideration. It is based on the premise that as consumers we buy those brands which extend the personality characteristics that we think we possess, or that we would like to possess or that we want others to think we have. This could be more valid than the personality approach, because the self-perception of one's personality might not be the same as that emerging from standard and more objective personality inventory tests.

The self-concept approach might be based on semantic differential scales showing series of bipolar adjectives, for which respondents may be asked to position how they see various brands, and/or themselves and/or their ideal self-concept. The brand preferred would then be the one closest to (greatest degree of congruence with) the segment's self-image or ideal-self image. With distance scores this degree of congruence is calculated and this helps to identify appropriate brand images to create and project.

The variants of 'self' are based on the actual self and the more aspirational ideal self and also on whether consumption is private or more conspicuous with social connotations (Table 6.13).

More support for this approach comes from a change in social attitudes. There has been a trend towards individualism and self-expression which could be manifested in the purchasing of products and services which more closely match brand image and self-image.

The usual methodology involves semantic differential scales and the positioning of respondents by how they perceive themselves (or appropriate variations such as how they would like others to perceive them), and how they position different brands on the same dimensions, in order to calculate distance scores, as shown in Table 6.14. The smaller the distance score, the greater the degree of congruence between brand and self images. Brand preferences can be predicted on the basis of such congruence.

Although self-concept theory has been well established in the behavioural sciences, it has only been since the late 1960s that it has been employed to explain buyer behaviour. For instance, the semantic differential methodology is used to compare self-image with car images.[49] Generally congruence is found, although not at the lower end of the socio-economic scale due to financial con-

Table 6.13 Actual and ideal self in a private and social context.

	Actual self	*Ideal self*
Private context	How I see myself now[†]	How I would like to see myself
Social context	How I think others see me	How I would like others to see me[†]

[†]Perhaps the most appropriate variants of 'self' for the respective buying contexts are the actual self in the private context and the ideal self in the social context.

Table 6.14 Self-concept distance scores (7-point scale).

	1	*2*	*3*	*4*	*5*	*6*	*7*	
Sophisticated	A	B	S					Plain
Appealing	S	B				A		Reserved
Daring		S	B			A		Cautious
Sensitive	A	B		S				Insensitive

S = self image
A = brand image of A
B = brand image of B
DA = distance between S and A
DB = distance bewteen S and B

$$DA = \sqrt{\{(3-1)^2 + (6-1)^2 + (6-2)^2 + (4-1)^2\}} = 7.3$$
$$DB = \sqrt{\{(3-2)^2 + (2-1)^2 + (3-2)^2 + (4-2)^2\}} = 2.6$$

straints. The matching of self-image with car image is even greater after purchase, perhaps as a way of reinforcing the purchase choice.[50]

As an expression of self-perception, this approach could be of further significance because of the evidence to suggest that people are becoming more orientated to self-expression and 'inner direction' as opposed to following mass social movements. There appears to be greater pluralism in the market today.[51] The concept of post-modernism also includes a greater individualism, pluralism and even fragmentation.[52] Indeed this has been a theme throughout this middle section of this chapter.

Research reported by Publicis[53] suggests that from 1973 to 1989 there has been a shift in 'motivators' from functional and rational factors (40% to 27% of the population) and 'outer directedness' (static at 35%) to more 'inner directedness' (25% to 38% of the population). A specific example revolves around some group discussions conducted for Levi Strauss in the mid-1980s which revealed general praise for Levi's advertising in which rock music soundtracks were used. Many in the groups, however, expressed their own personal music tastes to be oriented towards different specific music styles of the time. The result was a poster (Figure 6.4) campaign that showed twelve head shots of different young people who clearly had different fashion tastes, many of them music based. The copy headline of 'we cut our jeans the way you cut your hair: blue jeans cut twelve ways' was the result. The manifestation of such pluralism in society can easily be seen in shopping centres where there is greater diversity in styling than was the case 15 years ago.

Figure 6.4 Levi individualism poster. © Levi Strauss (UK) Ltd.

6.6   Geodemographics

The study of local 'catchment' areas is useful to determine where and how to target community and social facilities. Catchment areas can be analysed with the local census data with the national census being used for commercial purposes. ACORN, A Classification of Residential Neighbourhoods, was developed for this. In the UK, in 1979 Richard Webber moved out of the Centre for Environmental Studies where he found that in order to analyse 'catchment' areas in detail he could analyse the local census data. The study of catchment areas was useful to determine where and how to target community and social facilities. On a grander scale, he was the prime mover in the development of a system of analysing the national census data for commercial purposes. This he achieved by joining CACI, an American-based marketing agency, and developing ACORN, A Classification of Residential Neighbourhoods. From the 1981 UK Census, some 40 variables are cluster-analysed and the emerging clusters of households led to the creation of 39 neighbourhood types (54 types from the 1991 Census).

Table 6.15 provides some examples of what these geodemographic systems are claiming for themselves, which is that they can be more discriminating than

Table 6.15 Discriminatory power of geodemographics.[54]

ACORN group (1981 Census)	Guardian readership	Dishwasher ownership
A	96	259
B	122	92
C	75	59
D	50	8
E	57	37
F	34	23
G	32	7
H	163	7
I	271	136
J	141	241
K	150	148

Dishwasher index for social grade 'ABs' = 322
Social grade 'ABs' in ACORN 'A' = 129
Social grade 'ABs' in ACORN 'B' = 135
NB: Dishwasher ownership is high amongst social grade ABs. Based on social grade alone, it would be expected that those areas with a high incidence of social grade AB people would be high in dishwasher onwnership. In this case that would point to ACORN group B. However, this area actually has less than the national average ownership of dishwashers. ACORN A on the other hand has a lower incidence of social grade ABs but more than two and half times the national average ownership of dishwashers. This is the sort of discriminatory power claimed for geodemographics and which, it is also claimed, is disguised by demographics.

traditional demographics. This table shows that whereas we might expect those groups high in social grade AB to be more interested in some products than groups low in social grade AB, it can in fact be a very different picture. ACORN groups can perhaps uncover anomalies that demographics disguise. This example is based on 1981 Census originated ACORN data.

The significance of this is that the research is based on the census, not on sample surveys. Marketers now have information on all households. Admittedly, names and addresses cannot be revealed from the census, but the statistics for enumeration districts can be. These are groupings of around 170 households. Such data can be linked with the postal code database (there is one postcode for approximately 15 households) and with the electoral register (another database) and ultimately it may be possible to identify individual households and their characteristics.

There are 'me-toos' of the original ACORN system. Richard Webber himself set up one of the newer competitors after he left CACI to join another similar agency, CCN,[55] and developed MOSAIC which analyses the census data together with credit company records and even a database on county court bad debt cases. PINPOINT and SUPERPROFILES are similar systems. These all come under the heading of one of the more recent types of market analysis and segmentation: geodemographics.[56] Such systems are also being used to analyse catchment areas, analogous to Webber's original local government task.[57]

Because there has been a full ACORN analysis of the Target Group Index (this is an annual report in 34 volumes of buyer profiles in most product markets and based on samples of over 20,000) it is easy to determine each ACORN category's interest in the product concerned. In fact the TGI sample design is now based on ACORN categories. In addition, the National Readership Survey is similarly analysed by ACORN and this can provide readership profiles for media selection purposes.

In addition to straight geodemographics we now have something of a merger taking place, between geodemographic and psychographic databases. 'ACORN Lifestyle' includes psychographic data. The TGI as already mentioned now contains a number of lifestyle questions and these can be analysed by traditional geodemographic clusters to enrich the original geodemographics. There is now one lifestyle company, NDL (National Demographics Limited) Direct Marketing, with over 12 million consumers in its files with information on their age, gender, occupation, hobbies, interests and financial status.[58] Several geodemographic companies now operate throughout many European countries, such as MOSAIC (Table 6.16).

This makes it possible to segment at the specific level: customer segmentation. It is likely that the resulting direct marketing will be one of the fastest growing sectors of marketing in the 1990s. There are indications of this already. In the European Union it is already a $75 billion industry[59]. In the US 65 per cent of advertising revenue is now in direct marketing.[60] Table 6.17 shows the growth through the 1980s in various countries and hints at scope for significantly further growth in many, over future years, based on the relative differences currently observed.

Table 6.16 Geodemographics around the world.[61]

	Vendor	Turnover band[†]	Data sources
USA			
Prizm	Claritas	3	Cencus
Microvision	Equifax	3	Census
Cluster plus	Donnelly	2	Census
Niches	Polk	2	
Acorn	CACI	1	
Canada			
Cluster	Compusearch	3	Census
UK			
MOSAIC	CCN	3	Census & others
Acorn	CACI	3	Census
Super-profiles	CDMS	1	Census
Define	Infolink	1	Census & others
Neighbours & Prospects	EuroDirect	1	Census
Ireland			
MOSAIC	CCN	1	Census
Spain			
Regio	Bertlesmann	1	Various
MOSAIC	CCN/PDM	1	Various
Belgium			
MOSIAC	Sopres	1	Various
Netherlands			
MOSAIC	CCN	2	PTT, CARS, Surveys
GEO	Geomarktprofiel	1	Various
Finland			
Acorn	Gallup/Post Office	1	Census
Sweden			
MOSAIC	MarknadsAnalys	1	Personal Registers

[†] Turnover band; 1 < £1m p.a.; 2 £1m–£5m p.a.; 3 > £5m p.a.

Table 6.17 Direct mail per head of population.[62]

Country	1983	1991
Switzerland	82	106
Belgium	42	80
Sweden	49	77
Germany	49	72
France	29	55
Norway	29	50
Denmark	27	49
Finland	36	49
The Netherlands	31	43
UK	19	40
Spain	13	24
Portugal	6	5
Ireland	2	14

Table 6.18 Updated ACORN profiles based on 1991 Census.[63]

CATEGORIES	%POP.	GROUPS		%POP.
A Thriving	19.7	1	Wealthy Achievers, Suburban Areas	15.0
		2	Affluent Greys, Rural Communities	2.3
		3	Prosperous Pensioners, Retirement Areas	2.4
B Expanding	11.6	4	Affluent Executives, Family Areas	3.8
		5	Well-off Workers, Family Areas	7.8
C Rising	7.5	6	Affluent Urbanites Town & City Areas	2.3
		7	Prosperous Professionals, Metropolitan Areas	2.1
		8	Better-Off Executives, Inner City Areas	3.4
D Settling	24.1	9	Comfortable Middle Agers, Mature Home Owning Areas	13.4
		10	Skilled Workers, Home Owning Areas	10.7
E Aspiring	13.7	11	New Home Owners, Mature Communities	9.7
		12	White Collar Workers, Better-Off Multi-Ethnic Areas	4.0
F Striving	22.7	13	Older People, Less Prosperous Areas	3.6
		14	Council Estate Residents, Better-Off Homes	11.5
		15	Council Estate Residents, High Unemployment	2.7
		16	Council Estate Resident, Greatest Hardship	2.8
		17	People in Multi-Ethnic, Low-Income Areas	2.1
	0.5			0.5
Unclassified				

The 1991 Census provided updated versions of ACORN, now with 54 neighbourhood types (see Table 6.18). With the general expansion of databases in marketing and with the linking of these, the biggest growth sector in marketing in the 1990s is based on these approaches.

It is interesting to note, however, that specific and individualized segmentation programmes may be possible and are used if the degree of direct marketing activity is a reflection of this. But at the same time there is perhaps not the sophistication that there could be. In research based on a survey of retailers concerning the extent of personal data held in their databases, surprisingly low levels were found.[64] The findings suggested that synergy is perhaps the needed catalyst between marketing, operations, information technology and database literacy before the power of such systems will be unleashed in practice. In a follow-up study a clear message emerges, namely a call for organizations to 'move away from using technology to do things to and for customers, to doing things with customers by giving the customers a voice in the process of building relationships'.[65]

Greater focusing in segmentation

It is clear that markets are being analysed in ever more sophisticated and detailed ways and this is leading to the identification and targeting of smaller but better defined segments. Markets themselves are fragmenting, not least because of a trend towards individualism which in turn provides support for smaller but more individualistic segments. Technology is facilitating this segmentation and targeting, via cable TV and the various other forms of direct marketing. Already traditional television advertising is losing ground to those techniques that can focus attention on those who are more likely to be interested in specific products or services. It is even possible to target an individualized TV message, analogous to personalized mailing, to a unique address via fibre optic cable.[66]

What all of this relies on, and is getting, is specific information down to household level, and in such detail that household characteristics, possessions and buying patterns are known. Box 6.1 reviews the situation in various countries in the mid-1990s and from this it is evident that a vast array of databases and lists is available to the industry and that direct marketing is thriving in many industrialized countries. What is happening to these lists and databases is that they are being linked to provide the consecutive overlaying of information (Figure 6.5).

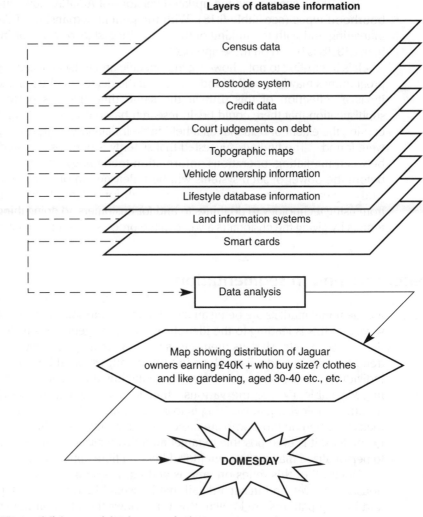

Figure 6.5 Layers of database marketing

Box 6.1 Examples of lists in selected countries.[67]

Direct marketing in the USA and Japan

USA

A study on Database Marketing in the USA conducted by the University of Texas showed that 63% of the respondents reported that their company used database marketing. About one-quarter of those that do not use database marketing indicated that they had cost considerations or that their company was too small.

The types of data being kept in the databases include product owners; inquiries and sales leads, as well as trade show and seminar attendees.

Fujisankei Communications International (FCI) began marketing a 3.5-million-name direct response database in the US in January 1995. The database was culled from the six-to-eight-million names the Fuji TV network collected from its home-shopping operations. The names are active response buyers while the other names came from inquiries. FCI is one of the few Japanese companies to rent lists to outsiders. Not all groups' lists are available. The Fujisankei Living Service Inc. (FLS) does not rent its 3-million-name lists, nor are they traded within the group.

Japan

Direct marketing services are available in Japan but it is a mixed bag. Good mailing lists are still hard to find, even though their quantity has improved over the last couple of years. Most Japanese list owners rent reluctantly, fearing their lists will be copied.

Independent list brokers lack an overview of the market and tend to promote only their in-house lists. Lists are pricey, ranging from $200 to $400 per thousand.

Examples of lists available in selected European countries

Belgium

Direct mail represents approx. 20% of the advertising budget.

Consumer lists

- all kinds of lists, e.g. subscribers to magazines, mail order buyers, prospects lists, clients of luxury shops, etc. available
- approx. 250 lists available for rental
- average size: between 20,000 and 150,000 addresses
- rental price: betveen 4 and 9 BEF per address
- public domain lists

    RTT list (telephone subscribers)
    OCR list (people and companies who registered a car)
    CONSUDATA (cross-file of the 2 files above)

Business-to-Business lists

- approx. 25 buiness lists available
- there are four types of lists

  nomative lists: companies vith name of managing director, decision maker, etc.
  compiled lists: e.g. doctors, lawyers, dentists
  subscribers lists, e.g. Trends
  controlled circulation lists, e.g. Intermediair, Belgian, Business

- the price varies between 2 and 5 BEF per nomative address.

France

Direct mail represents between 10% to 15 % of the advertising budget in France.

Consumer lists

- two types of lists available: mail order buyers and subscription lists
- prices: 600 to 2500 FF per thousand addresses
- number of lists available for rental: 1,000-1,200

Business-to-Business lists

- response lists: approx. 300 lists are available, prices from 300 to 1,700FF per thousand.
- subscriber/controlled circulation lists: 500 lists available, 850–4,500 FF per thousand.
- compiled lists: 50 lists available for rental

Germany

Approx. 13% of the advertising budget in Germany is spent on direct mail.

Consumer lists

(a) Response lists

- typical size: 10,000 to 2.5 million addresses
- rental prices: 200 to 350 DM per 1,000 addresses
- number of lists available: approx. 1,000

(b) Public domain lists

- telephone subscribers
- geographic overlays available

(c) Others:

- lifestyle databases exist, e.g. 'regio', a microgeographic segmentation list

(a) Response lists

- typical prices: 180 to 350 DM per 1,000 addresses
- number of lists available for rental: approx. 1,000

(b) Subscriber/controlled circulation lists

- all descriptions mentioned above are valid

(c) Compiled lists

- selections by NACE code are available
- typical prices: 120 to 1,500 DM
- number of lists available: approx. 7,000

Spain

Direct marketing has grown dramatically over the past years. Today direct marketing accounts for 20% of the overall advertising expenditure and is the fastest growing marketing technique.

Consumer lists

- most reliable sources: mailing houses ('la agencia de publicidad directa') and the Spanish telephone company

(a) Demographic lists

- several large compiled lists, each of them containing a few million files
- variables such as sex, age, educational level, MOSAIC-typology can be selected

(b) Response lists

- size: 500,000 to 2 million names
- many list owners willing to 'swap' their lists
- prices: 1 to 5 pts per name, plus selection costs

(c) Public domain lists

- telephone directory list available, not including geodemographic overlays which have to be ordered with a service company

United Kingdom

There are 1,200 lists available in the UK.

Consumer lists

(a) Response lists

- types of lists are mail order, questionnaire/lifestyle lists, magazine lists, book-buyers, cultural attendees
- typical list universes/minimums range from 40,000 to over 1 million
- rental prices: between £65 and £100 per 1,000 names
- number of lists available: approx. 450

(b) Public domain lists

- geodemographic overlays are Acorn, MOSAIC, Superprofiles

(c) Other

- lifestyle databases are rented by CMT, NDL, ICD

Business-to-Business lists

(a) Response lists

- number available for rental: approx. 150

(b) Subscriber/controlled circulation lists

- number available for rental: approx. 250

(c) Compiled lists

- selections available are job function, trade (SIC codes), size of company, financial information, geographic, telephone numbers
- number available for rental: approx. 20

There is a clear analogy here with the Domesday Book in England in medieval times, in which the monarch of the time collected personal information (though rather more brutally than the database industry of today does!) about each of his subjects. In this sense we have seen the birth of what might be termed 'Domesday Marketing' (not in any 'doom and gloom' sense, but in the analogical sense of the Domesday Book).[68] It also raises a variety of ethical issues concerning the acquisition and use of personal data.

6.7 Domain-specific and specific segmentation

At the beginning of this chapter a three-level distinction was made between segmentation at the general, domain-specific and specific level. We now turn to more examples of segmentation at the domain-specific and specific levels. At the domain-specific level, benefit segmentation, situation-based segmentation, problem segmentation and person-situation segmentation are described. At the specific level, segmentations based on buying intensity and brand loyalty are discussed.

Occasions of use or for purchase

Earlier, an analysis of the toothpaste market in benefit terms was provided (Table 6.1).[69] This approach is a good example of domain-specific segmentation and is essentially user-based. A variant of this is situation-based segmentation.[70] It has not gained much ground, mainly because of lack of empirical data or case histories on its use and effectiveness, and for confidentiality reasons.[71]

The development of situation-based segmentation goes back to Coca-Cola's discovery in 1973 that consumers were seeking different benefits based on different consumption occasions during the day. A study of the US wine market concluded that different clusters emerged between user- and situation-based analysis and that the latter proved effective as a segmentation variable in this instance. Another example is the purchase of popular magazines. These magazines are often bought for specific occasions such as a long train ride, airline flight or a rainy Sunday afternoon at home.[72]

Problem segmentation

Problem segmentation may be especially used in financial markets.[73] With respect to banking, segments are identified as consisting of 'the harmonious', who have no area of frustration about banks, 'the access deprived', who are annoyed by the difficulty of having their transactions processed easily and quickly, 'the personally inconvenienced', who are frustrated by the behaviour of bank staff, 'the exploited', who see banks as only using them to make as much money as possible, and 'the pragmatists', who are annoyed by the two factors that directly affect their net return from a relationship with a bank: loss of time or difficulty in accessing the bank, and financial net return. 'Problem segmentation gives a market segmentation basis which is determinant, appropriate for managerial application and is associated with adverse consumer behaviour.'[74] These problems may be connected to specific persons, as shown by the segments above, or to specific occasions, for example the financial problems and mortgages that are connected to buying a house.

Person-situation segmentation

Person-situation segmentation is based on the interaction of consumer characteristics, product benefits and occasions of use.[75] Persons with specific characteristics may want to use products with specific benefits in specific situations. Table 6.19 provides an example with respect to the suntan lotion market with four situations and four target groups. Note that person and situation benefits are critical in product differentiation in this market. In principle, four times four products may be designed. Taking skin colour and skin factors into account even more different product formulas may be marketed.

Table 6.19 Person-situation segmentation.[76]

Situations	Young children	Teenagers	Adult women	Adult men	Situation benefits
Beach/boat sunbathing	Combined insect repellent		Summer perfume		● Windburn protection ● Product can stand heat ● Container floats
Home-poolside sunbathing			Combined moisturizer		● Large pump dispenser ● Won't stain wood, etc.
Sunlamp bathing			Combined moisturizer and massage oil		● Designed for type of lamp ● Artificial tanning
Snow skiing			Winter perfume		● Protection from rays ● Anti-freeze formula
Person benefits	● Special protection ● Nonpoisonous	● Fits in jean pocket ● Used by opinion leaders	● Female perfume	● Male perfume	

Buying intensity

Buying intensity is based on consumers' levels of buying activity. Often markets may be divided into heavy, medium and light users of a product or a brand. If it is about beer drinking in general, it is an example of domain-specific segmentation. If it is about a specific brand of beer, it is an example of segmentation at the specific (brand) level. For instance, the 20% heavy beer drinkers may be buying 80% of the beer of a particular brand. This is the 20/80 rule of many markets.[77] It is important for producers to know the characteristics of the heavy and medium buyers.

Brand usage and loyalty

With regard to brand usage and loyalty, a number of segments may be distinguished: brand-loyal users, brand switchers, new users and non-users.[78] This will be developed further in Section 9.6.

1 Brand-loyal users

Some consumers use only one brand; this is called undivided brand loyalty. The main marketing effort for this segment is to keep these customers loyal. This is called 'shepherd' or retention marketing.

2 Brand switchers

Some consumers may use two or more brands, depending on the situation, the price ('price-buyers') or consumers who are searching and have not yet found their preferred brand. These switches may be occasional, with the consumer returning to the original brand. It may also be divided brand loyalty, using two or more brands almost with the same frequency. Marketing efforts are directed to convert these 'partially loyal' customers to undivided loyal customers. Why these customers do not prefer the one brand all the time should be studied. It is easier to convert brand switchers to one brand than to convert consumers who are loyal to another brand.

Several reasons may exist for brand-switching behaviour. Some consumers may not yet have found their preferred brand and switch brands to try several before becoming loyal to one. Other consumers are price-buyers and buy brands that are 'on sale' (sales promotion). Still other consumers buy different brands for different occasions, for example one brand of beer for their own use and another for parties.

3 New users

New users are consumers who are entering the market, for instance young people starting to live on their own, or people immigrating into the country. This is an attractive target group for marketing because these consumers might become loyal to the brand for a long period. In some countries, 'congratulation services' give free samples of different brands of products (coffee, tea, newspaper, magazine, and so on) and discounts to local stores to newly marrieds or people who moved to another home. These 'life transitions' are often accompanied by changes in brand and store loyalty.

4 Non-users

Non-users are consumers who decided not to use the product at all, for instance non-smokers or non-drinkers, or people who, because of the Second World War, will never buy a German or Japanese car. These are unattractive target groups for marketers, because these people are determined not to use the product or the brand. It is even unethical to try to persuade an adolescent non-smoker to start smoking.

6.8   Conclusions

To conclude this chapter, two main trends in market segmentation may be distinguished. First, a trend towards smaller segments, individualization and direct marketing. Related to this is customer segmentation, marketers having personal and purchase characteristics of customers in their database and using this information for personalized propositions.

The second trend is the use of domain-specific segmentation. Product benefits, consumer problems and usage situations are the relevant variables in the various product and usage domains. Rather than general characteristics such as age, social grade and gender, domain-specific characteristics are directly relevant for the consumer and the main reason for buying the product or the brand.

Endnotes

1. R.I. Haley, 1968.
2. R.I. Haley, 1968.
3. W.F. Van Raaij and T.M.M. Verhallen, 1994.
4. W. Smith, 1956.
5. P. Kotler, 1984.
6. H. Davidson, 1975.
7. K. Hammond, A. Ehrenberg and G. Goodhart, 1993.
8. R.E. Frank, W.F. Massy and Y. Wind, 1972.
9. W.F. Van Raaij and T.M.M. Verhallen, 1994.
10. J.F. Engel, H.F. Fiorillo and M.A. Cayley, 1972.
11. M.E. Porter, 1979.
12. R. Edmonson, 1993.
13. Y. Wind, 1978; W.F. Van Raaij and T.M.M. Verhallen, 1994.
14. N. Piercy and N. Morgan, 1993.
15. N. Piercy and N. Morgan, 1993.
16. Mintel, 1990.
17. J. Piper, 1978.
18. M. Ritson, 1995.
19. Henley Centre for Forecasting, 1992.
20. R. Scott, 1978; Women in Media, 1981; and R. Hamilton, B. Haworth and N. Sadar, 1981.
21. Henley Centre for Forecasting, 1992.
22. Advertising Standards Authority, 1990.
23. JICNARS, 1991.
24. Market Research Society, 1981.
25. Market Research Society, 1981.
26. *Sunday Times*, 12 April 1992.
27. S. O'Brien and R. Ford, 1988, of Granada TV.
28. One of the earliest applications of this concept in marketing was proposed by W.D. Wells and G. Gubar, 1966.
29. H. Davis and B. Rigaux, 1974; and R.W. Lawson, 1988.
30. R.W. Lawson, 1988.

31. R.W. Lawson, 1988, p. 28.
32. Developed by Research Services Ltd.
33. Research Services Ltd, 1980.
34. S. O'Brien and R. Ford, 1988.
35. J. Piper, 1978.
36. As Mitchell reports on the 1988 Regional Lifestyle Report (MINTEL, 1988).
37. Gallup, 1982. At this time Germany was still divided.
38. Henley Centre for Forecasting, 1992.
39. Gallup, 1982.
40. British Market Research Bureau, 1988.
41. BBC, 1984.
42. British Market Research Bureau, 1988.
43. Christine and Ralph McNulty of Taylor Nelson, 1987.
44. McNulty of Taylor Nelson, 1987.
45. B. Evans, 1959.
46 Innovativeness is discussed in Chapter 5 on new and repeat buying.
47. M. Snyder and K.G. DeBono, 1985.
48. G. Foxall, 1980.
49. A. Birdwell, 1968.
50. H.H. Kassarjian, 1971.
51. Henley Centre for Forecasting, 1978, 1992; P. Shay, 1978; MINTEL, 1981; M.J. Evans, 1981, 1989.
52. W.F. Van Raaij, 1993.
53. R. Block, 1992.
54. CACI Ltd, 1995, OPCS and GRO(S) © Crown Copyright 1991. All rights reserved.
55. Consumer Credit Nottingham.
56. Market Research Society, 1989.
57. There is further coverage of catchment area analysis in Chapter 12, on distribution strategy and consumer behaviour.
58. A. Massey, 1992.
59. D. Bird, 1992.
60. A. Fraser, 1989.
61. R. Webber, 1995, p. 362.
62. Source: PDMS, reported in *Marketing*, 22 April 1993.
63. CACI Ltd, 1995, OPCS and GRO(S) © Crown Copyright 1991. All rights reserved.
64. G. Long, S. Angold and M. Hogg, 1992.
65. M. Hogg, G. Long, M. Hartley and S. Angold, 1993.
66. Channel 4, 1990.
67. FEDIM, 1995
68. M. Evans, 1994.
69. R.I. Haley, 1968.
70. J. Dublow, 1992.
71. R. Stout, R. Guk, M. Greenberg and J. Dublow, 1977.
72. VNU Research in The Netherlands, 1990.
73. J. Martin, 1988.
74. J. Martin, 1988.
75. P.R. Dickson, 1982.
76. P.R. Dickson, 1982.
77. D.W. Twedt, 1964.
78. J.M.G. Floor and W.F. Van Raaij, 1993, p. 164.

7

Market targeting and product positioning

Chapter objectives

(1) To provide an understanding of the most important issues related to market targeting and product positioning.
(2) To introduce key targeting and positioning strategies, options and their underlying rationale.
(3) To discuss the major implications derived from consumer behaviour analysis and their impact on targeting and positioning.

7.1 Market targeting

From a marketing strategy point of view, selection of the appropriate target market is paramount to developing successful marketing programmes. Market targeting is the evaluation and selection of one or more market segments to enter. The process of market segmentation and selecting a target market begins with identifying or targeting a generic market. A company must decide what business it is in and thus the generic need it hopes to fill. By identifying a generic market, the company will be focusing on a larger market than it can hope to reach. Furthermore, by beginning the search for a suitable target market at this broad level, it will avoid the possibility of overlooking significant and attractive market segments that may be worth pursuing. A helpful tool in this regard is the TARGET model, which is a six-step process used to select a target market:[1]

(1) Target a generic market.
(2) Analyse benefits desired in the generic market.

(3) Remove qualifying benefits. The removal of qualifying benefits deals with the benefits that all potential customers desire. A marketer could not productively segment the market based on these desired benefits.
(4) Group remaining benefits into segments.
(5) Enumerate consumer characteristics of segments. This enumeration gives the marketer a profile of the consumers in each segment.
(6) Target a market segment for cultivation. A market is cultivated by developing a marketing mix specifically tailored to the wants, needs and values of the target market.

Selecting target markets involves more than using a market opportunity analysis (MOA) to describe potential customers. Targeting is a strategic decision that guides marketing objectives and marketing programme decisions.

When a company decides to enter all or at least most segments, full-coverage market segmentation is used. Full-coverage market segmentation is the targeting by a company of all or most of the market segments in a product market, using a specific marketing mix for each segment. For example, Holiday Inn uses the same facilities to appeal to business travellers, families on vacation and local residents. However, advertising, promotion, price and amenities are differentiated for these segments. The hotel chain also allocates certain floors to executive guests at some of its properties.

When only one or a few segments are covered, limited-coverage market segmentation is used. Limited-coverage market segmentation is the targeting of only one or a few of the market segments in a product market, using a specific marketing mix for each segment. Tailoring a marketing offer to the unique needs of selected segments should lead to greater penetration and market share. Limited- and full-coverage market segmentation strategies represent the opposite ends of a strategy continuum.

The company has to decide on how many segments to cover and how to identify the best segments. There are four market-coverage alternatives (Figure 7.1):

(1) Undifferentiated marketing
(2) Differentiated marketing
(3) Concentrated marketing
(4) Custom marketing

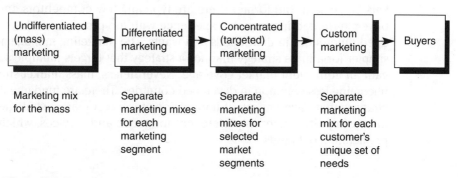

Figure 7.1 Targeting options.

Undifferentiated marketing

The company decides to ignore market segment differences and go after the whole market with one market offer. It focuses on what is common in the needs of consumers rather than on what is different. It designs a product or service and a marketing programme that will appeal to the broadest number of buyers. It relies on mass distribution and mass advertising.

A mass strategy has a built-in cost efficiency that is very attractive to management. Undifferentiated marketing is defended on the grounds of cost economies. It is seen as 'the marketing counterpart to standardization and mass production in manufacturing'. The narrow product line keeps down production, inventory and transportation costs. The undifferentiated advertising campaign also keeps costs down. A company using this approach typically develops a product aimed at the largest segments in the market ... but the larger segments may be less profitable because they attract disproportionately heavy competition. This is called the 'majority fallacy'.

Companies that take the total market approach frequently attempt to use promotional efforts to differentiate their own products from competitors' products. They hope to establish in consumers' minds that their products are superior and preferable to competing brands. This strategy is called product differentiation. Unleaded petrol for example, has a broad appeal. Millions of consumers need and use it. Yet most unleaded petrols are not much different physically from other unleaded petrols. Therefore, oil companies differentiate their unleaded petrols from competing brands by promoting greater mileage, additives or economy.

Undifferentiated marketing is similar to a mass market strategy, but this name can be misleading. The size of the product market is not the real issue. The distinguishing characteristic of the mass market strategy is that no attempt is made to concentrate on any differences among customers. A mass market strategy consists of targeting the entire market. A profile is first developed to describe the typical or average customer within a product market. Then, the marketing mix for a particular brand is aimed at this typical customer. Mass marketing should lead to the lowest costs and prices as well as create the largest potential market.

Mass strategies are often more popular in new markets than in mature markets because in the former there are typically few competitors and because buyers have had inadequate experience with the product and have not developed differences in their needs and wants. The marketing management task is simpler for a mass strategy than for a strategy that targets multiple segments to gain an equivalent market coverage. Nevertheless, mass market strategies are becoming less common in developed countries. There are fundamental societal changes that have important implications for target market strategies, such as increasing differences in preferences for goods and services, which lead to a proliferation of brands.

Differentiated marketing

In the case of differentiated marketing, the company decides to operate in several segments of the market and designs separate offers to each of the segments. By offering product and marketing variations, the company hopes to attain higher sales and a deeper position within each market segment. It also hopes for greater repeat purchasing because the firm's offering matches the customer's desires. A growing number of companies have adopted differentiated marketing. This approach creates a higher level of total sales than undifferentiated marketing but also increases costs: product modification costs, R&D costs, production costs, administrative costs, inventory costs, promotion costs, and so on. For example, promotion costs will increase due to trying to reach different segments with different advertising appeals and USPs (unique selling propositions). This leads to a lower usage rate of individual media and the loss of quantity discounts. Since each market segment may require separate creative advertising planning, this causes promotion costs to increase.

Since differentiated marketing leads to higher sales and costs, the analysis of the profitability of this strategy should be monitored very closely. There is also the danger of oversegmentation of the market by offering too many brands. Such diversification of the product line leads to some diseconomies:

■ Production costs will increase because of shorter production runs.
■ There will be higher set-up (fixed) costs which must be spread over fewer units.
■ Selling costs will increase because sufficient selling and promotional efforts have to be allocated to a variety of offerings and more advertising may be required to get the message across to the various target segments.
■ Inventory costs will also increase since more goods have to be carried to prevent out-of-stock situations, more records and controls are required as well as greater supervision of inventory handling.

Some companies use a counter-movement. They prefer to manage fewer brands, with each appealing to a broader customer group. This strategy is called counter-segmentation or the 'broadening the base' approach and seeks a larger volume for each brand. Also, within the differentiated marketing approach, a company may use either a selective strategy or an all-inclusive strategy of market coverage.

A firm using a multiple segmentation approach focuses on several distinct segments and develops a separate marketing mix for each of the market segments it wishes to reach. The marketing mixes used for a multisegment strategy may vary in terms of product differences, distribution methods, promotion methods and prices. When a business uses the multisegment approach, the costs of planning, organizing, implementing and controlling marketing activities increase, while attaining a deeper position within each market segment. There is also greater repeat purchasing because the company's offer better matches consumers' need. Differentiated marketing is usually used by a company which is financially strong, well established in the product category and facing strong competition. An equally important incentive for using multiple segmentation strategies comes from competitors' use of a segmentation strategy to build differential advantages in targeted niches.

Sometimes, firms use both mass marketing and segmentation in their multiple-segmentation strategy. They have one, two or more major brands aimed at the mass market, a wide range of consumers, and secondary brands geared towards specific market segments.

As a market is segmented using more characteristics, the company achieves finer precision, but at the price of multiplying the number of segments and thinning out the populations in the segments (this is called over-segmentation). To reverse this dangerous situation, companies can engage in a counter-segmentation approach. This means broadening the segmentation base. For example, Beecham launched Aquafresh toothpaste to attract two benefit segments, those seeking fresh breath and those seeking cavity protection.

Concentrated marketing

Concentrated marketing is usually applied when the company's resources are limited. Instead of going after a small share of a large market, the company goes after a large share of one or a few sub-markets. The company achieves a strong market position in the segments it serves, owing to its greater knowledge of the segments' needs and the special reputation it acquires. It enjoys many operating economies because of specialization in production, distribution and promotion. If the segments are chosen correctly, the company can earn a high rate of return on its investment. But, this strategy involves higher than normal risks. The particular segments can turn sour ... or a competitor may decide to enter the same segments. For these reasons, many firms prefer to diversify in several market segments.

The major advantage of concentrated segmentation is that the company can control costs by advertising and distributing only to the market it wishes to attract. In addition, concentrating on a single segment allows a company with restricted resources to compete with much larger organizations. However, if a company's sales depend on a single segment and that segment's demand for the product declines then the company's financial strength also declines. Moreover, when a company penetrates one segment and becomes well entrenched, its popularity may keep it from moving into other segments.

7.2　Niches

Many companies today have attempted to pursue a strategy of segmentation called 'niche-picking'. These firms position their products as true specialities with significant competitive advantages built in. Management must somehow identify possible niches and then, for each niche of interest, determine which marketing programme positioning strategy will obtain the most favourable profit contribution net of marketing costs.

Once niches are formed, each one of interest to the company should be evaluated to accomplish three purposes:

(1) Since there is often more than one promising marketing programme positioning strategy that can be used for a given niche, a selection of the best alternative is necessary for each niche candidate.
(2) After evaluation is completed, those niches which still look attractive as target market candidates should be ranked as to their attractiveness.
(3) Finally, management must decide if a niche strategy is better than a mass target market approach.

Assuming that niches can be identified in a product market, management has the option of selecting one or more niches as a target market.[2] An undoubted attraction of many niche markets is the scope they offer for premium pricing and above-average profit margins. In addition, an effective niche strategy has for many companies provided a convenient jumping-off point for entry into the larger market.

There is, however, a hidden danger in looking at what appear to be niche markets. Many strategists with small brands often deceive themselves by believing they have a niche product. The reality may in fact be very different with the product being a vulnerable number-four or number-five brand in a mass market. To clarify whether a brand is a true market nicher, three questions may be posed:[3]

(1) Is the niche or segment recognized by consumer and distributors, or is it just a figment of marketing imagination?
(2) Is your niche product distinctive, and does it appeal strongly to a particular group of consumers?
(3) Is your product premium-priced, with above-average profit margin?

Unless the answer to all three of the questions is 'yes', it is unlikely that the brand is a true nicher, but is instead a poor performer in a far larger market segment.

In sum, the characteristics of the ideal niche are:

(1) It is of sufficient size to be potentially profitable.
(2) It offers scope for an organization to exercise its distinctive competences.
(3) It has the potential for growth.

Other characteristics that favour niching would be patents, a degree of distribution channel control and the existence of customer goodwill. Niching should not, however, be seen as a strategy limited just to small organizations. One of the most skilful exponents of niche marketing, Reckitt & Colman, is a major company. Among other large companies to have recognized the benefits of niching is 3M, which has long pursued a highly effective niching strategy by finding sectors of the market that have either been missed or ignored by others. The starting point for this involves examining each segment's size and potential for growth. Obviously, the question of what is the 'right size' of a segment will vary greatly from one organization to another. The magazine *Cigar Aficionado*, for example, has chosen to concentrate on a very small and specialized segment of the smokers' market.

In so far as it is possible to develop broad guidelines, we can say that large companies concentrate on segments with large existing or potential sales volumes and quite deliberately overlook or ignore small segments simply because they are rarely worth bothering with. Small companies, by contrast, often avoid large segments partly because of the level of resources needed to operate effectively, and partly because of the problems of having to cope with a far larger competitor.

7.3   Attractiveness of segments

With regard to the question of each segment's structural attractiveness, the marketing manager's primary concern is profitability. It may be the case that a segment is both large and growing but that, because of the intensity of competition, the scope for profit is low. Several models for measuring segment attractiveness exist, although arguably the most useful is Porter's 5-force model.[4] This model suggests that segment profitability is affected by five principal factors (Figure 7.2):

(1) Industry competitors and the threat of segment rivalry.
(2) Potential entrants to the market and the threat of mobility.
(3) The threat of substitute products.
(4) Buyers and their relative power.
(5) Suppliers and their relative power.

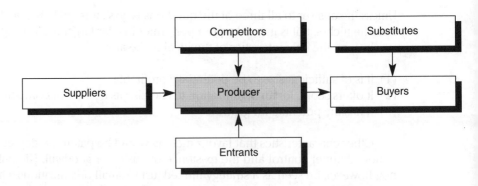

Figure 7.2 Porters 5-force model.[5]

Having measured the size, growth rate and structural attractiveness of each segment, the marketing manager needs to examine each one in turn against the background of the organization's objectives and resources. In doing this, the marketing manager is looking for the degree of compatibility between the segment and the long-term goals of the organization. It is often the case, for example, that a seemingly attractive segment can be dismissed either because it would not move the organization significantly forward towards its goals, or because it would divert organizational energy. Even where there does appear to be a match, consideration needs to be given to whether the organization has the necessary skills, competences, resources and commitment needed to operate effectively. Without these, segment entry is likely to be of little strategic value.

The final segmentation decision faced by the marketing manager is concerned with which and how many market segments to enter. In essence, five patterns of market coverage exist.

(1) Single segment concentration in which the organization focuses on just one segment. Although a potentially high-risk strategy in that the company is vulnerable to sudden changes in taste or preference, or the entry of a larger competitor, concentrated marketing along these lines has often proved to be attractive to small companies with limited funds. Left to itself, an organization which opts to concentrate upon a single segment can develop a strong market position, a specialist reputation and above-average returns for the industry as a whole. An example is Badedas Foam bath.

(2) Selective specialization. As an alternative to concentrating upon just one segment, the company may decide to spread the risk by covering several market segments. These segments need not necessarily be related, although each should be compatible with the organization's objectives and resources. An example is Häagen-Dazs ice cream.

(3) Product specialization in which the organization concentrates on marketing a particular product type to a variety of target markets. An example is Prince tennis racquets.

(4) Market specialization. Here the organization concentrates on satisfying the range of needs of a particular target group. An example is Saga Holidays, which targets the senior travel market.

(5) Full market coverage. By far the most costly of the five patterns of market coverage, a strategy of full market coverage involves serving all customer groups with the full range of products needed. An example is Renault, which has a product mix ranging from trucks to the Twingo and a new electric car named Zoom.

It is assumed that individual segments or combinations of segments could be independently chosen, but this assumption ignores synergies that might exist between various market segments. For example, a market consisting of twelve segments can lead to the development of five super segments that will help a company attain a better efficiency level in terms of its allocation of marketing resources. In Figure 7.3 these twelve identified segments are synergetically redesigned into five super segments, based on certain synergies such as the use of raw materials, manufacturing facilities and distribution channels. For instance, segments 6 and 12 form a new supersegment.

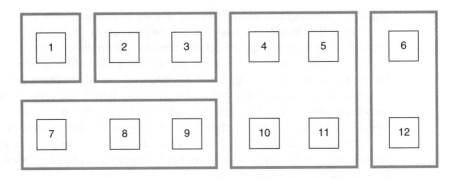

Figure 7.3 Converting segments into supersegments.[6]

In choosing one of these five market coverage strategies, the company must consider the following factors: company resources, product homogeneity, stage in the product life cycle, market homogeneity and competitive marketing strategies.

Some firms combine product-market or 'segments/benefits sought' alternatives in a matrix in order to better define target markets. When using a product-market grid to help decide which segments to target, a company needs to collect data on the market segments, which are represented by each cell in the matrix of analysis. These data to be collected relate to variables such as size, current sales, projected sales, growth potential and rates, estimated profitability, competitive intensity, resource requirements and channel requirements. After the company has identified the more objectively attractive segments, it must ask which segments fit its business strengths best. The company should have a distinctive competence relevant to those segments. Thus, the company seeks not only a segment(s) that is attractive in itself, but also one for which it has the necessary business strengths to succeed.

As shown in Figure 7.4, convergent and divergent strategies result in different degrees of segmentation. With a convergent strategy the company offers few products and tries to appeal to a broad segment of the total market; that is, different market segments converge on the limited offering. With a divergent strategy, however, the company develops a broad variety of products and aims each at specific target markets. An important difference between these two strategies is that a convergent approach works best when a product is first introduced, when demand is such that consumers are satisfied simply by getting the product, regardless of concerns about special features. A convergent strategy works well whenever buyers seek substantially the same product.

Segment profitability analysis becomes complex as more than two or three criteria are used for partitioning and as additional criteria are considered for different classes of marketing decisions. Given responsible means of partitioning market segments, major elements of the marketing mix may be segregated for analysis using the contribution approach to cost accounting. Costing by market segments promises improvement in marketing efficiency by way of better plan-

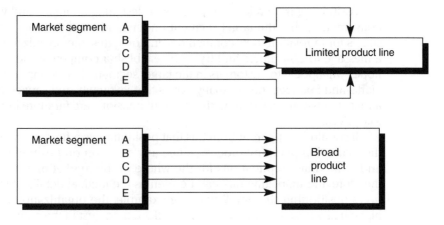

Figure 7.4 Convergent and divergent segmentation strategies.

ning of expenditures and control of costs. Cost accounting by market segments can control marketing costs in relation to profit potentials. Marketing segment profitability analysis is a key component of a marketing information system.

7.4   Custom marketing

Custom marketing is applied when a market is so diverse that the company attempts to satisfy each customer's unique set of needs with a separate marketing mix. The marketing response to the increasing individualism is extreme market segmentation, or even market fragmentation. The important trend toward individualism was discussed in Chapter 6.

7.5   Product positioning

The third strand of what is referred to as STP (segmentation, targeting and positioning), marketing involves deciding on the position within the market that the product or service is to occupy. In doing this, the company is stating to customers what the product or service means and how it differs from current and potential competing products or services. Minolta, for example, is positioned in the copies market with a differential advantage based on high-volume, low-cost performance and reliability. British Midland is positioned in the business executive segment of the air travel market with a differential advantage based on perceived value-pricing and better in-flight service.

Positioning is therefore the process of designing an image and value so that consumers within the target segment understand what the company or brand stands for in relation to its competitors. In doing this, the organization is sending a message to consumers and trying to establish a competitive advantage that it hopes will appeal to customers in the target segment. For example, in the case of Marks and Spencer, the company hopes that its quality and service position will appeal to customers to whom these two dimensions are far more important than low prices.

It should be apparent from this that positioning is a fundamental element of the marketing planning process, since any decision on positioning has direct and immediate implications for the whole of the marketing mix. In essence, therefore, the marketing mix can be seen as the tactical details of the organization's positioning strategy. Where, for example, the organization is pursuing a high-quality position, this needs to be reflected not just in the quality of the product or service, but in every element of the mix including price, the pattern of distribution, the style of advertising and the after-sales service. Without this consistency, the believability of the positioning strategy reduces dramatically.

For some organizations the choice of a positioning strategy proves to be straightforward. Where, for example, a particular positioning strategy and image has already been established in a related market, there are likely to be synergistic benefits by adopting the same approach in a new market or with a new product. For other organizations, however, the choice of position proves to be more difficult or less clear and the company ends up pursuing the same position as several other competitors in the market. Where this happens the degree and costs of competition increase substantially. There is a strong case therefore for the marketing manager to decide in detail on the basis of differentiation. In other words, the organization must identify and build a collection of competitive advantages or benefits that will appeal to the target market and then communicate these benefits effectively.

In the light of these comments, it is apparent that the process of positioning involves three steps, summarized in the IDU model:[7]

(1) Identification of the organization's or brand's possible competitive advantages or benefits.
(2) Delivery: deciding on the benefits to be emphasized and that can be delivered.
(3) Uniqueness of the benefits (unique selling proposition) and implementing the positioning concept.

Having identified the relevant benefit or competitive advantage that appears to offer the greatest potential for development, the final step in the process involves communicating this to the market. In this step the product benefit is related to consumers' needs and values.

Positioning starts with the product or brand benefit and relates this benefit to product attributes or values (Figure 7.5):

(1) This benefit may be 'proven' by referring to the attribute or a profile of attributes that 'cause' the benefit. This rather technical type of positioning is called informational positioning.

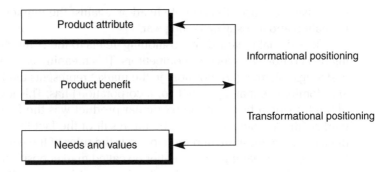

Figure 7.5 Means–end chain for positioning.

(2) In communication campaigns the benefit may also be related to consumer needs and values. This is related to imagery, symbolism and lifestyle, and is called transformational positioning.[8]
(3) If both informational and transformational arguments are used in an advertising campaign, this is called two-sided positioning.

Positioning is first and foremost a communication strategy and any failure to recognize this will undermine the whole of the marketing mix.[9] Too often, however, and despite having identified potentially valuable competitive advantages, organizations fail to signal these advantages sufficiently strongly. This then leads to one of three errors:

(1) Confused positioning where buyers are unsure of what the organization stands for.
(2) Over-positioning where consumers perceive the organization's products or services as being expensive and fail to recognize the full breath of the range.
(3) Under-positioning where the message is simply too vague and consumers have little real idea of what the organization stands for.

In order to select the most effective market position, the marketing manager needs to begin by identifying the structure of the market and the positions currently held by competitors. In electing for a repositioning strategy, the strategist needs to feel confident that, first, one will be able to reach the new market position one is aiming for, and second, that one will be able to operate and compete effectively and profitably in this new position. Among those companies that have succeeded in repositioning their brands are Amstrad and Lucozade.

It should be recognized that very different positioning strategies need to be followed, depending upon whether the company is a market leader, follower or challenger, and that as a general rule market followers should try to avoid positioning themselves too closely or directly against the market leader. The reasoning behind this is straightforward, since a smaller company is most likely to succeed if it can establish its own position within the market and develop its own customer base. To compete head-on against the market leader is to invite retaliation and a costly marketing war.

The original meaning of 'positioning' refers to the competitive market standing of a company vis-à-vis its competitors. This meaning is being used frequently in strategic planning. A 'position' in the market represents the level of leadership and dominance that a product (or a corporation) has. This level can be a result of the historical fact that the particular product was the first to appear in the market (the 'pioneer') or it can be the result of the fact that the product holds the largest market share and therefore sets the rules of the game that others have to follow. This meaning will hereafter be called market position.

The other meaning of the 'position' concept is the one that is related to the product and its attributes. This meaning is based on the observation that a product is a complex concept with many different attributes, and these attributes can be combined to create various 'profiles' of the product. According to this latter meaning, a 'position' of a product represents the profile of its attributes, in comparison to other products or to the consumer's needs. This 'informational' meaning is therefore called product position.

7.6   Where to position?

Another distinction of the meaning of 'positioning' has to do with the type of the battleground in which the marketing war is being fought. There are two different battlegrounds: the marketplace and the consumer's mind. The real economic result of the marketing effort is determined in the marketplace where exchange transactions take place, but a crucial preliminary condition for such results is the state of the consumer's mind.

There are thus two different types of 'positions', market and product, and two different territories in which the positions are being observed or measured: the marketplace and the consumer's mind.

The distinction between the two meanings of the 'positioning' concept helps in the process of planning a marketing strategy, since it is important to determine the market position first, and decide on the best strategy related to that position, and only then to determine and decide on the product position. It is also important to understand the difference between the two types of 'battlegrounds' on which the position is being located.

Not only are the marketplace and the consumer's mind important for the marketing war, but they are interdependent and the 'position' of a product or a company in one 'territory' affects significantly the position in the other. A cross-tabulation and its strategic consequences is presented in Table 7.1.

Table 7.1 Positions in different 'battlegrounds'.[10]

Consumers' mind	Marketplace	
	Positive (desirable)	Negative (undesirable)
Positive (desirable)	Reinforce and continue	Push strategy Change distribution, price or sales policy
Negative (undesirable)	Pull strategy Change image and attitude via promotion and advertising strategic change	Make significant

In addition to the market position and the related strategy that each competitor has to choose, there is also the choice of competitive direction, which will significantly affect the competitive position.

The more common meaning of the 'position' concept is the one related to the product itself and its attributes. In developing a product, the product planner needs to design a profile of attributes, which will best appeal to a target segment in the market. The positioning of the product consists of two stages. First, designing the product itself and its tangible and non-tangible attributes. Second, placing it in the consumer's mind. Consumer perceptions may be represented in a perceptual map, which consists of several dimensions, each one representing an attribute or a specific aspect of the product. The 'location' of the product on the perceptual map is its 'position'. To summarize, the 'position' concept in marketing is multifaceted and has several different meanings which have to be well understood before it can be applied effectively.

Brand ranking

To cope with advertising's complexity, people have learned to rank products and brands in the mind. Perhaps this can best be visualized by imagining a series of ladders in the mind. On each step is a brand name. And each different ladder represents a different product category. Some ladders have many steps (seven is many). Others have few, if any. For advertisers to increase their brand preference, they must move up the ladder. This can be difficult if the brands above have a strong foothold and no leverage or positioning strategy is applied against them.

For advertisers to introduce a new product category, they must carry in a new ladder. In the positioning era, 'strategy' is king. Profits are hard to come by and that 'brilliant' advertising campaign, even if it comes, does not ever seem to turn the brand around. The noise level in the marketplace today is far too high.

Not only the volume of advertising, but also the volume of products and brands. In category after category, prospects already know the benefits of using the product. To climb on their product ladder, the brand must be related to the brands already there.

In order to position your own brand, it is sometimes necessary to reposition the competitor's. Your brand can be on top of one ladder and nowhere on another ladder. And the further apart the products are conceptually, the greater the difficulty of making the jump.

Because of the noise level, a 'well-known' company has tremendous difficulty trying to establish a position in a different field than the one in which it built its reputation. There are just too many 'me-too' companies vying for the mind of the prospect. Getting noticed is getting tougher.

Confusion is the enemy of successful positioning. To cope with change, it is important to take a long-range point of view. Positioning is a concept that is cumulative, and that takes advantage of advertising's long-range nature.

The 'brander' must have a vision. There is no sense building a position based on a technology that is too narrow, or a product that is becoming obsolete. Successful marketing strategy usually consists of keeping your eyes open to possibilities and then striking before the product ladder in the mind of the consumer is firmly fixed.

In the positioning era, the choice of a brand name is probably a company's single, most important marketing decision. Successful companies get their information from the marketplace. That is the place where the marketing programme has to succeed.

A big obstacle to successful positioning is attempting to achieve the impossible. It takes money and resources to build a share of mind. It takes money and resources to establish a position. It takes money and resources to hold a position once you have established it.

Critical attributes and perceptual maps

The product attributes and benefits that are important to consumers provide a way to describe the structure of a market. These characteristics relate to the benefits sought by the buyers and the needs served by the sellers. Competing products or brands have positions within the market structure that are based on the degree of each important characteristic that buyers perceive these brands to possess. Each consumer has a location in the market structure that corresponds to the characteristics of the buyer's ideal product.

Although a given product possesses many characteristics, only a few will be important in the consumer's decision-making process. These critical attributes are used to differentiate among the competitive offerings. The remaining characteristics/attributes are often related to basic product performance and are presumed to be equal among all brands.

Every consumer respondent in a survey can be placed in multidimensional space denoting a position on each scale. That space becomes a kind of perceptual map. By identifying consumer characteristics, marketers can learn what kind of product they have. For the strategic planner, the empty space may represent a marketing opportunity. These perceptual gaps in the market, can only be pursued if the segments have a substantial number of potential consumers and if they represent profitable holes in the market. Psychological maps can help strategic planners locate markets that are not being serviced, or where two brands are competing for the same segment.

Every market has a structure that can be expressed in terms of these critical attributes. Within this structure, the locations of products/brands are determined by the strengths of the attributes they are perceived to possess. The closer products/brands are in this space, the greater the likelihood that consumers will perceive them as similar. These multidimensional configurations are called perceptual maps.

Multidimensional scaling and correspondence analysis can be used to build perceptual maps.[11] These procedures involve algorithms that start with measures of similarity between pairs of products and try to find a geometric representation of the brands in the product category. These techniques position products that are perceived as similar and close to one another, and locate dissimilar products far apart. Dimensions of perceptual maps are not named by the multidimensional scaling programmes. Researchers have to interpret the dimensions themselves based on the geometric representation. Additional information may be gathered from consumers to name the dimensions. The attributes that are the most important in consumers' perceptions of a product category can be determined from survey research.

Perceptual maps can also be used to identify new product opportunities. New products can be positioned in gaps that appear in the markets. However, a new product will not succeed just because it is unique. Gaps in the perceptual space are meaningless unless the ideal points of potential consumers are to be found in them.

The consumers' preference space needs to be superimposed on their similarities space to get a joint space of perceptions and preferences (Figure 7.6). Each consumer is represented in this space by a point representing that individual's ideal product (or ideal vector). Ideal points are person points and represent consumer's preferred product attributes that consumers would like products to possess. Variation in the location of person points over this joint space indicates where there are sufficient prospects to justify current and new products. The consumers' ideal point can be derived using preference data.

Product segments can be interpreted in two ways. When consumers do not have the same perceptual map, a market segment can be defined as a group of consumers who use the same perceptual map. When consumers possess the same map, however, they can be formed into homogeneous preference groups. This is done by cluster analysis, using information on the distances between brands and individual ideal points. In general, consumers' preference decreases as the distance from the ideal point increases.

Knowledge of consumer perceptions and preferences allows companies to identify new product opportunities. In addition, information on perceptions and preferences shows when existing brands need repositioning. Sometimes one

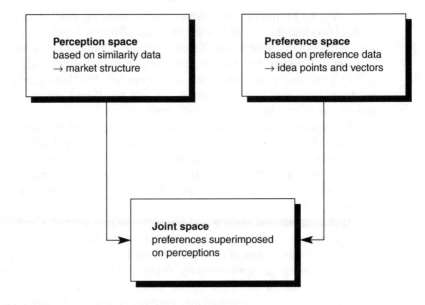

Figure 7.6 Simple and joint perceptual maps.

brand in a firm's product line may be perceived as close to another, causing an unacceptable level of cannibalization. In some cases, companies can exploit regional differences in perceptual maps for several product categories in order to reposition brands through selective advertising change. Positioning is really a state of mind. The key objective of positioning strategy is to form a particular brand image in the consumers' mind. This is accomplished by developing a coherent strategy that may involve all of the marketing-mix elements.

The positioning does not have to be tangible in the sense of a product being really unique. Advertising and promotional efforts can achieve an intangible positioning or product image. Thus there are two broad types of positioning: product positioning and promotional positioning. The best strategy is to have a combination of the two.

A product's positioning is not in the product or even in the advertising. It is in the mind of the consumer. Two identical products may be perceived as different. On the other hand, two quite dissimilar products may be perceived as substitutes if their dissimilarities are not perceived as being significant. A desired positioning is one that clearly distinguishes a product from its competition on attributes considered important by the relevant market segment.

Positioning and the competitive set

A product's competition includes a primary set of other products that are similar and a secondary set of other products that are not similar but may be used as substitutes. The definition of competitive sets is, once again, in the consumer's mind. Some product positioning is easy to imitate, and will be if the position and target market are seen as attractive by competitors.

Positioning has no value in itself, only in its effect on the target market segment. There are a number of approaches to strategically position a product, all starting with consumer benefits:

(1) Relating benefits to attributes. This is strongly related to positioning on product features. It is the informational approach.
(2) Relating benefits to values. This is related to positioning on lifestyle. It is the transformational approach.
(3) Specific usage or applications. It is related to informational positioning.
(4) User category, including lifestyle groups. The latter is related to the transformational approach.
(5) Comparative positioning against another product. This strategy ranges from implicit to explicit comparison. Explicit comparison can take two major forms. First, we can use a comparison with a direct competitor aimed at attracting consumers from the compared product, which is usually the product category leader. The second type of explicit comparison does not attempt to attract the consumers of the compared product, but rather to use the comparison as a reference point.
(6) Hybrid or two-way positioning.
(7) Product-class dissociation. This type of positioning is somewhat less common; it is particularly effective when used to introduce a new product that differs from the typical products in an established product category.

Informational positioning

Probably the most frequently used positioning strategy is associating a product with an attribute, a product feature or a customer benefit. For example, Volvo has stressed safety and durability, showing commercials of crash tests and citing statistics on the average long life of their cars (Figure 7.7). Fiat, in contrast, has made a distinct effort to position itself as a European car with European craftsmanship. BMW has emphasized handling and engineering efficiency, using the tag line 'the ultimate driving machine' and showing BMW performance capabilities at a race track.

A new product can also be positioned with respect to an attribute that competitors have ignored. Sometimes a product can be positioned in terms of two or more attributes simultaneously. In the toothpaste market, Crest became a dominant brand with positioning as a cavity fighter, a claim supported by a dentist's endorsement. However, more recently, Aquafresh was introduced by Beecham as a gel paste that offers both cavity-fighting and breath-freshening benefits.

The price/quality attribute dimension is commonly used for positioning products as well as stores. In many product categories, some brands offer more in terms of service, features or performance, and a higher price is one signal to the customer of this higher quality. Some brands emphasize low price and good quality. The Lada and Yugo cars, for example, are so positioned.

Figure 7.7 Positioning by safety attributes. © Volvo Car UK Ltd.

Transformational positioning

The Volvo, Fiat and BMW examples are not only examples of informational positioning, but also of transformational positioning. These brands are related to values and lifestyle aspects such as safety, durability, craftmanship and 'toys for gentlemen'. Cosmetics are often positioned with regard to values such as beauty, self-respect, affiliation and lifestyle. The difference between Coca-Cola and Pepsi-Cola is more a matter of lifestyle than of taste. The protests against the formula change of Coca-Cola and the subsequent introduction of 'Classic Coke' show that fundamental American values were at stake.

Positioning by use or application

Another positioning strategy is to associate the product with use or application. Campbell's soup for many years was positioned for use at meal time. Now, many Campbell's soups are positioned for use in sauces and dips, or as an ingredient in main dishes. Products can, of course, have multiple positioning strategies, although increasing the number involves difficulties and risks. Often a positioning-by-use strategy represents a second or third position designed to expand the market. Thus, Quaker Oats attempted to position a breakfast food as a natural whole-grain ingredient for recipes.

Positioning by product class

Some critical positioning decisions involve product-class associations. For example, some margarines are positioned with respect to butter. A maker of dried milk introduced an instant breakfast drink positioned as a breakfast substitute and a virtually identical product positioned as a meal substitute for those on diets. Caress, a soap made by Unilever, was positioned as a bath-oil product rather than a soap. The 7-Up 'uncola' campaign is also a classic example of positioning by product-class dissociation that was very successful. This positioning approach is a kind of comparative positioning and can be based on the analysis of product categories.

Positioning by product user

Another positioning approach is to associate a product with a user or class of users. Revlon's Charlie cosmetic line has been positioned by associating it with a specific lifestyle profile. Johnson & Johnson increased its market share when repositioning their shampoo from a product used for babies to one used by adults who wash their hair frequently and therefore need a mild shampoo. A similar repositioning was achieved by Zwitsal shampoo in The Netherlands.

Positioning by competition

In most positioning strategies, an explicit or implicit frame of reference is the competition. Often, the major purpose of this type of positioning is to persuade consumers that a brand is better than the market leader (or other well-accepted brand) on important attributes. Positioning with respect to a competitor is commonly done in advertisements in which a competitor is named and compared. A classic example of this type of positioning was the Avis 'We're # 2, so we try harder' advertising campaign.

Marketing managers can never position their brand in isolation. By definition, all positioning is in reference to competitive brands. This is made explicit in positioning strategies emphasizing lower price but same quality as the market leader, for example IBM. And premium/prestige image, for example Mercedes-Benz in cars.

Hybrid positioning

A hybrid positioning strategy combines two or more of these approaches. The hybrid positioning strategy typically requires multiple branding strategies and it incorporates elements from several bases. Two-way positioning with informational and transformational elements is an example of hybrid positioning.

Figure 7.8 shows an example of product positioning of jeans, combining attributes, competitors and classes of product users. A company can position a product or service to compete head-on with another brand or to avoid competition. Head-on positioning may be appropriate even when the price is higher and if the product's performance characteristics are superior. Conversely, positioning

Figure 7.8 Brand positioning of jeans.

to avoid competition may be best when the product's performance characteristics are not significantly different from competing brands.

Old products, new products

There are a number of basic strategies for change in positioning:

(1) The product may be repositioned to appeal to a new segment. This may involve changing the product, or perhaps just changing the way it is marketed.

(2) The marketer may attempt to add a new target segment, while trying to hold on to the old segment. This is normally done by introducing a new product to appeal to the new segment. Sometimes, however, it is possible for one product to appeal to several market segments.

(3) The size of the existing target segment may be increased (market penetration). This is a difficult task because consumers must change their minds: people in other segments must adopt beliefs that will move them to the target segment.

(4) The structure of the market itself may be changed. If a new product is really new, the universe of potential consumers for the product category may change, and possibly grow. The perceived relationships among products in the market will change, new attributes will become important, and the relevant characteristics defining target segments will also change.

(5) There is actually a fifth strategy: no change. Often this is the best course. After all, a product may be repositioned away from its existing target segment and then never reach its proposed new target segment. Or a new product may simply take over an existing product's segment, without enlarging the market. The organization has then spent a lot of money to stand still. Clearly positioning can be crucial to a company's survival in a market.

7.7 Positioning strategy

Positioning strategy consists of an integrated combination of product or service, distribution, price and promotion strategies. In competitive positioning, the company attempts to determine the difference between competing products and determine an ideal marketing mix to exploit differences. Efforts to position or reposition a product or service should be part of the current-assessment and future-assessment stages of strategic planning. Several elements of strategic positioning should be considered:

(1) Developing a competitive position means recognizing the element of limitation. It sets parameters around creating a marketing mix for a specific target market.
(2) The position determines the correct competitive environment. The product category should have been correctly defined in terms of those products that consumers feel are close substitutes for each other.
(3) A position policy determines relationships with customers. Do we want to bring in new users to the product category, to increase existing customers' frequency of use or to attract specified users of competitive brands?

The pressure of rival companies creates the need for competitive positioning to maintain and increase market share. Competitive positioning requires a systematic analysis of competitors.

In most positioning strategies, an explicit or implicit frame of reference is the competition. In other words, a well-established competitor's image can be exploited to help communicate another image referenced to it. Second, by doing so, customers are made to believe that the company using this strategy is better than or as good as a named competitor. Positioning explicitly with respect to a competitor can be an excellent way to create a position with respect to an attribute, especially price/quality. Products that are difficult to evaluate are often compared with those of an established competitor to help the positioning task. The selection of a positioning strategy involves identifying competitors, relevant attributes, competitor positions and market segments. Research-based approaches can help in identifying the above. The positioning decision is often the crucial strategic decision for a company or brand because the position can be central to the customer's perception and choice decisions.[12]

These strategies are alternative or viable approaches for dealing with the competition. A firm that does not have a competitive strategy usually becomes ineffective and almost always has low earnings on investment.[13]

The success of positioning strategies depends on how the target segments react to the marketing strategies directed to them.[14] The key to success is based not only on identifying a coherent strategy but also on ensuring that such a strategy differentiates the company from its rivals.

A clearly identified and sustainable competitive advantage and a well-conceived and properly implemented strategy of segmentation, targeting and positioning (STP) can contribute to a truly effective marketing programme.

The clarity of a company's positioning has a number of facets. The concept's chosen image must be clear to the consumer. For example, Woolworth's decision to 'focus' on a limited number of key merchandise areas is a move towards clarity and simplification. Coherence is needed as is compatibility between department, store and chain images.[15] Most important of all, employees must be informed of the company's positioning strategy.

Image and profitability

From a manager's perspective perhaps the only valid way to examine image is to assess its effect on company profitability. There are apparent links between market positioning and a number of measures of marketing performance, ranging from gross margins to return on capital employed. The rate of growth in sales volume is sometimes perceived as being the most likely financial measure to be affected by a change in relative image or positioning. Let's take the example of the retailing sector and analyse the way in which a retail image affects the company's financial performance. A better image will mean greater customer flow, fewer walkouts and therefore more customers spending more each time they visit the store. The first major marketing indicator to be affected will, therefore, be sales volume, explaining why sales volume growth seem to be closely linked to an improvement in relative image. Assuming costs do not rise as fast as sales volume, the next indicator to show an improvement will be net margin (the difference between turnover and the total costs involved in achieving that turnover). It is also likely that a better image will allow the sale of higher margin lines or allow the retailer to increase margin, thus increasing profitability. The ultimate measure of marketing performance, the profit or return made as a percentage of the investment in the business (ROCE), will also rise as long as the company does not need to increase assets in order to achieve the desired change in image.

Changing image can be expensive in terms of capital and operating costs. Logically its effect on return on capital employed may not be as noticeable as the effect on sales volume growth. Regular measures of comparable performance on a battery of factors, with the emphasis on assessing positive differentiation, are vital elements in the image management process.

Determining a product's position

The general approach to determining a product's position includes the following steps:

(1) Construct a 'joint map' of the product's perceptual space by comparing its salient features and benefits with consumers' evaluations of how existing brands relate to the ideal point. This process is called perceptual mapping.
(2) Plot the positions of existing brands.

(3) Isolate or identify company brands for which there are no preference points and preference points for which there are no company brands. These indicate possible untapped product opportunities.

(4) If product opportunities exist, use marketing research, R&D, advertising, and other marketing-mix variables to develop new products and brands or to reposition existing ones.

(5) Monitor the position of the brands.

The ideal brand would possess the proper amount of each attribute for each buyer. The plotting of consumers with similar ideal preferences will indicate whether subgroups will form. Marketing managers then need to interpret the results in terms of target market and product-positioning strategies. For example, some car manufacturers prepare brand preference maps about three times each year and use them to analyse the positioning of existing brands, to identify promising market segments, and to spot new trends in consumer preferences for automobiles. Information regarding consumer demand is incorporated into the map to show strong areas of demand. By comparing segment groupings and brand positions, market opportunities, intensity of competition and gaps in market coverage can be identified. The maps are useful in planning strategy and in evaluating strategies that have been implemented. Figure 7.9 shows an automobile brand positioning map.

Given these competitor positions, what position should the company seek? It has two major choices:

(1) To position its brands next to one of the existing competitors and fight for market share by having a superior product or because the market is large enough for two competitors; or because the company has more resources than the competitor; or because this position is the most consistent one with the company's business strengths.

(2) To develop a new product that is not currently being offered to this market since competitors are not offering it. The new product must be technically and economically feasible at the planned price level so that a sufficient number of buyers are going to prefer it. If these answers are all positive, the company has discovered a 'hole' in the market and should move in to fill it.

There are different market-preference patterns such as clustered, diffused and homogeneous preferences. In some cases, the basic market-preference pattern shows distinct preference clusters, called the natural market segment. A company in this market has three options:

(1) Position itself in the centre hoping to appeal to all the groups (undifferentiated marketing).

(2) Position itself in the largest market segment (concentrated marketing).

(3) It might develop several brands, each positioned in a different segment (differentiated marketing).

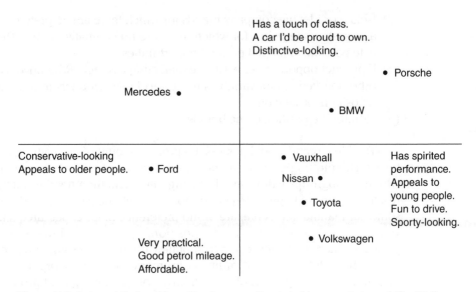

Figure 7.9 Automobile brand positioning map. Reprinted by permission of *The Wall Street Journal* © 1984 Dow Jones & Company, Inc. All rights reserved.

In a diffused preference market, a company faces three options:

(1) Tap preferences of one of the corners: a single-niche strategy, which is useful for small companies.
(2) Two or more products can be introduced to capture two or more parts of the market: a multiple-niche strategy.
(3) Tap the middle of the market: a mass-market strategy.

A product located in the centre minimizes the sum of the distances of existing preferences from the actual product. It will minimize total dissatisfaction.

If a company enters into a market containing a large entrenched competitor, instead of entering with a me-too product, or with a single-segment product, it can introduce a succession of products aimed at different segments, providing the company has the necessary resources. Each product entry will create a loyal following and take some business away from the major competitor. The company should try to find market gaps where there is more profit potential and less risk.

Benetton, the Italian clothing manufacturer and retail franchiser, is attempting to shift its male/female sales ratio from 70% female to a 50/50 mix. A new multi-million dollar advertising campaign is being employed in this repositioning effort. Advertising plays a major role in the positioning of any product.

After the choice of segments, a detailed positioning strategy has to be formulated to seek differential advantages. Ideally, the positioning strategy should be sustainable and not easily matched by competitors. A product's market share can be increased by repositioning:

(1) closer to ideal points of sizeable segments of the market;
(2) farther from other products with which it must compete;
(3) on dimensions weighted heavily in consumers' preferences.

Perceptual map analysis can be improved further by preparing a separate perceptual map for each market segment, instead of one map for the total market. When developing repositioning strategies, marketers should bear in mind that costs also increase as the distance in the perceptual map increases.

Implementation

Following decisions on targeting markets and positioning strategy in these segments comes implementation in terms of the detailed marketing mix. Consistent decisions on product specifications and design, service, technical support, channels, distribution, promotion and pricing must be made. Marketing-mix policies have to be consistent with each product's positioning statement.

Figure 7.10 shows the sequence of stages included in the process of positioning. Through market analysis and competitive analysis, a company is able to define a segmentation policy and the 'differential advantages' of its product mix, respectively. The internal corporate analysis is going to directly influence the target market selection and the decision on the selection of the package of benefits. The next step is the definition of the positioning strategy, which has strong implications for the development of a marketing strategy and the implementation of marketing-mix programmes of product, price, distribution and communication.

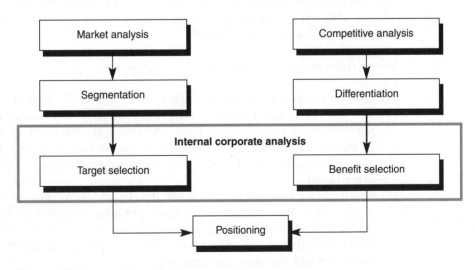

Figure 7.10 Process of positioning.

Selecting the target market and designing the marketing-mix go hand in hand, and thus many marketing-mix decisions should have already been carefully considered. Product positioning also has many implications for selecting appropriate promotions and channels. Thus, many marketing-mix decisions are made in conjunction with (rather than after) target-market selection.

7.8 Brand extension

About 15 years ago, Al Ries and Jack Trout influenced a generation of marketers with their attack on brand extensions, that is, marketing new products under an existing brand name.[16] When should you extend your brand? 'If your competitors are foolish. If your volume is small. If you don't expect to build a position in the prospect's mind. If you don't do any advertising.' Ries and Trout saw marketing as a battle for the consumer's mind, and the more single-minded you were, the better the chance of victory. In these kinder, gentler times, tough single-mindedness has given way to a more sophisticated and, certainly, a sounder view of the marketplace.

It all started when three big marketers, each number 1 in their category, grew tired of ignoring today's realities. And after Bud Light, Diet Coke and Liquid Tide, no one can doubt the wisdom of leveraging or extending the brand name any longer.

How do you go about leveraging your brand? Instead of asking yourself what does your brand name mean, perhaps a better question would be, what can your brand mean? Brands are in transition. So, welcome to the age of unpositioning, where you have a chance to actually stretch your brand's image and extend it in exciting new directions.[17]

Several types of brand names exist:

(1) Umbrella brands, such as IBM, Philips, Shell, and retailer brands such as St Michael. All products of these companies are marketed under the brand name of the parent company. The brand image is generalized over several product classes and becomes weaker as a specialist producer. New products are easier to introduce, because they profit from the image and reputation of the brand.
(2) Specific brands are brands specifically developed for one product or a small product line, for example Ariel, Mars, Sunlight. Procter & Gamble and Unilever market almost all products under different brand names. The advantage is that incompatible products such as detergents and food are not associated with the same brand name.
(3) Endorsement brands: General Motors is an endorsement brand of Opel and Vauxhall. Volkswagen has acquired a majority share in the Czech automo-

bile producer Skoda. In advertisements the name 'Skoda by Volkswagen' is used. Volkswagen is an endorsement brand of Skoda.

The brand name has several functions, to name a few:

■ Trade mark of producer
■ Umbrella for a range of products
■ Protection against counterfeiting
■ Recognition sign for consumers
■ Information chunk for consumers
■ Indicator of quality and other characteristics

The brand name may be extended to new products, marketed under the same brand name. For a successful brand extension, there should be a relationship between the existing products and the new product. This relationship may exist at the three levels of the meaning structure (Figure 7.5):[18]

(1) Extension to technically similar products. This is called a 'line extension'. Examples are Cherry Coke, Mars Hazelnut and Ariel Ultra.
(2) Extension based on the similarity of benefits and complementarity of benefits. A healthy food line such as Lean Cuisine or Weight Watchers consists of several low-fat food products such as cheese, margarine, jam, and even meat products. More products are sold to the same target group which is concerned with health and slimness.
(3) Extension based on values and lifestyle, for example Dunhill jewellery and Ray Ban skis. Although the products are unrelated, this is also the same upscale target group.

Brand extension has not always been successful. Cadillac introduced a small car under the name Cadillac. The small Cadillac benefited from this name, but the larger Cadillacs lost their exclusive image by this extension. The same was true for Miller beer: the introduction of Miller Light beer damaged the reputation of Miller High Life beer. Tuborg tonic may damage the reputation of Tuborg beer. Heineken refused to market a light beer under the Heineken brand. Instead, Amstel Light was introduced to avoid damage to the Heineken brand. Note that Amstel is another brand of the Heineken brewery.

Mars and Raider are 'energy' candy bars, mainly sold in winter. Mars introduced a summer product, Mars Ice Cream, to have more sales in the summer, and to keep the Mars users loyal in all seasons. Brand extension may thus be used to spread the sales more evenly over the seasons.

The conditions for a successful brand extension are the following:

(1) Positive associations should exist with the original brand name.
(2) Extend the brand name only if based on similarity of attributes, benefits or lifestyle. The brand should have a clear and positive positioning on benefits or lifestyle to make this type of extension possible.
(3) A forward image carry-over process to the new product leads to a generalization of the brand name, making the brand name less specific.

(4) Be careful to avoid a negative backward carry-over process to the original brand. The reputation of the existing products should not be damaged, cf. Cadillac.

In some cases a brand may be extended to strengthen the original brand. The Marriott Business Program is a set of office services for business people staying in a Marriott hotel. The Marriott Business Program is a sub-brand (a so-called 'silver bullet') that increases the reputation and strengthens the position of Marriott hotels. In the same way Drum Origins, a brand of high-quality tobacco, strengthens the original Drum brand of tobacco. The endorsement of Drum tobacco is by the Dutch company Douwe Egberts.

Ries and Trout warnings should be well taken. Brand extension is not a cheap alternative for advertising and positioning. But in a number of cases, brand extension may be used for new products, and sometimes even to strengthen the image and reputation of existing products.

7.9 Conclusions

The purpose of this chapter was to provide an overview of market targeting and product positioning. There are four market-coverage alternatives: undifferentiated marketing, differentiated marketing, concentrated marketing and custom marketing. With a convergent strategy, the company offers few products and tries to appeal to a broad segment of the total market, whereas with a divergent strategy, the company develops a broad variety of products and aims each at specific target markets.

Marketing positioning is set into motion by the marketing mix that is developed and implemented to meet the needs and values of a target segment. It is determined by buyers' perceptions of the company's brand relative to the brands of its key competitors. There are several approaches to strategically positioning a product: positioning by product attributes, by benefits, by product usage or application, by user category, by competitor, by product class, by hybrid positioning, or by product class dissociation.

The positioning of a brand may be extended to other products. The marketer should however be careful to extend only to products that are similar in attributes, benefits or lifestyle, and not to damage the existing products with this extension.

A Market Selection System (MSS) is an important tool for evaluating the current status of a multiple end-use product or service in each of the markets a company services and for planning the future market portfolio that meets business objectives. A company's marketing information system can play an important contributing role in the development of a segmentation strategy and its strategic positioning.

Endnotes

1. J. Evans and B. Berman, 1985.
2. D.W. Cravens, 1982.
3. H. Davidson, 1987.
4. M. Porter, 1979.
5. M. Porter, 1979.
6. P. Kotler, 1991a.
7. J.R. Rossiter and L. Percy, 1987.
8. R.G.M. Pieters and W.F. Van Raaij, 1992, chapter 5.
9. A. Ries and J. Trout, 1982.
10. M. Perry, 1988.
11. See Section 8.15 on Multivariate analyses.
12. D.A. Aaker and J.G. Shansdy, 1982.
13. D.J. Luck and O.C. Ferrell, 1985.
14. H. Assael, 1987.
15. G.J. Davies and J.M. Brooks, 1989.
16. A. Ries and J. Trout, 1986.
17. G. Schoenfeld, 1990.
18. W.F. Van Raaij and W.M. Schoonderbeck, 1993.

8

Consumer research

Chapter objectives

(1) To provide for an understanding of the basics of researching consumer markets.
(2) To extend the earlier discussion of motivation, attitudes and segmentation, targeting and positioning with a demonstration of how these areas can be researched.
(3) To examine a variety of secondary and primary data approaches to researching consumers and markets.
(4) To provide a non 'numbers' overview of some data analysis techniques that otherwise can frighten away the reader!

This chapter provides an overview of how to research consumer behaviour. It covers the basics of market research through the main stages of the research process to a discussion of secondary and primary sources of data. Some specific application of the techniques is provided in the areas of motivation, attitude, segmentation and targeting research.

8.1   The marketing research process

'Marketing Research involves the diagnosis of information and the selection of relevant interrelated variables about which valid and reliable information is gathered, recorded and analysed'.[1]

From this, marketing research is both 'systematic' and 'formalized' – Zaltman and Burger's definition introduces a sequence of research events, from diagnosing marketing information requirements through data collection to data analysis. This leads to the structuring of research programmes around a series of stages in the research process as shown in Table 8.1. Such stages can be of great help both in the planning of research programmes and in the control and evaluation of them.

Table 8.1 The marketing research process.

Stage 1 Defining and clarifying the marketing problem and determining what information this requires
Stage 2 Determining cost effective sources of information
Stage 3 Determining techniques for collecting information
Stage 4 Data collection
Stage 5 Data processing
Stage 6 Communicating results

8.2 Stage 1: Defining and clarifying the marketing problem

It is suggested here that of all the stages in the total process it is often this one at the beginning of a research programme that in practice can be riddled with error and bias.

A research programme is manifested in its final research report and it is usually possible to be able to evaluate other stages of the process to some extent. For example, any questionnaire used should usually appear in an appendix which the reader can scrutinize. As will be seen later it is relatively easy to criticize a questionnaire, its wording, structure, sequence and so on, but is not so simple to construct one. Also, the sample design and size should be explained and again the reader is given the opportunity to evaluate this. The manner in which the data has been analysed and reported can also be studied in the report, but although the project objectives may appear reasonable to a reader who is not the person responsible for making decisions on the basis of this report, they may be wholly inadequate for the actual decision area concerned.

The point, then, is that although error and bias can occur at any stage of the process, if the first stage is not fully explored and agreed between decision maker and researcher, the entire programme can waste time and money.

To illustrate this we refer to an advertising research programme which was commissioned by Vaux Breweries to evaluate a poster advertising campaign for a new beer. Levels of awareness were evaluated and attitudes measured using a questionnaire and street interviewing and the results were gratefully received by the brand manager concerned. However, later feedback from the organization revealed that the decision maker resided in general marketing management and while the research results were relevant and useful, they had their limitations. The problem materialized as poor communication: while the brand manager briefed the researchers in line with his perception of the problem, the marketing manager wanted to use the information to decide whether to launch a new lager using, predominately, a poster campaign. The point is that the initial research problem was broader than evaluation of one campaign.

Other instances of wasted marketing research as a result of faults in problem analysis and the briefing of researchers are provided by England[2] and the dangers are generalized by Millward, the joint managing director of the Millward Brown Agency:

> The utility of any research project is critically dependent upon the quality of the original brief ... too often research is neither communicated effectively to the decision takers nor relevant to their decisions... make sure that the real decision makers attend key presentations... the best briefing session is a two-way discussion which both crystallises and challenges current management thinking.[3]

The 'problem definition' stage should lead naturally to the listing of appropriate informational requirements (the 'data list') in the context of the decision areas concerned.

Exploratory vs conclusive research

Developing a clear formulation of the scope and nature of a research problem may be referred to an exploratory research which explores the parameters of the problem, in order to identify what should be measured and how best to undertake a study.

Exploratory techniques are usually relatively unstructured, sometimes merely discussions of the problem with knowledgeable people or the study of case histories of similar projects which could suggest a methodology.

Group discussions with consumers are popular, as they are not constrained by highly structured questionnaires and enable the problem to be seen from a 'market' perspective. Indeed in the practical setting exploratory research may provide enough information for the decision maker's needs (or perhaps all he or she can afford). Certainly, there have been increases in the use of qualitative research, such as the employment of group discussions with small samples without any large-scale follow-up.[4]

In contrast, conclusive research is conducted through the main research design and is aimed at measurement of the variables identified from the exploratory exercises. It provides the information, specified on the data list, which management requires.

8.3   Stage 2: Determine cost-effective sources of information

The list of specific informational requirements (the data list) should have been built up in problem definition and it is necessary to determine where the data can be found. There is a popular misconception that marketing research is no more than an interviewer in the street with a questionnaire and clip-board. While this image is appropriate to some research programmes, there are others where the interviewing is conducted in a hall, or someone's home; others that require no interviewer at all (for example, postal surveys) and some that involve no questioning (such as observation studies); and yet others that rely exclusively on existing reports or other documentation (that is, secondary data sources).

Secondary vs Primary Data Sources

The range of data sources can be broadly categorized under the headings of secondary and primary. Secondary sources involve information that already exists, such as company records or previous reports, government statistics, newspaper and journal articles and commercial market research agency reports.

Box 8.1 lists some examples of the wealth of information that exists and this point serves to demonstrate that it is always worth exploring the possibilities of using secondary sources – as a FIRST resort – before commissioning what would usually be a more expensive and time consuming programme of collecting 'new' information using 'primary' research methods.

In fact, the major area of search which precedes buying agency research or starting an in-company research project involves secondary data and because of the heavy use of such sources, there is a need to adopt a critical perspective in using them. First, the researcher evaluates secondary sources for impartiality to be reasonably sure that there is no slant or bias in the information resulting from the provider or compiler attempting to make a case for or against something; secondly, that sources are valid, that is, whether the information is what the researcher wants to know; thirdly, that sources are reliable, that is, whether the information is representative of the group it purports to describe (for instance, a sample of twelve consumers is unlikely to reflect all consumers in a national population); and fourthly, that sources provide information with internal homogeneity, that is, the consistency of, for example, a set of figures.

So great is the amount and variety of secondary sources that quite large books are published which do nothing other than list possible sources of information to do with certain topics and areas of concern. Indeed, the Government's Statistical Service annually publishes its booklet *Government Statistics: A brief Guide to Sources* together with another guide, *Profit from Figures* which illustrates some of the main uses of government statistics.

Box 8.1 Secondary data sources

Many of these are FREE (either because they are to be found in most public libraries or because they are available free from Government Departments). Even some of the expensive commercial reports can be found in some libraries.

KOMPASS – gives names and addresses of companies (that is, possible competitors) by country and by product category.

Kelly's Guide – lists industrial, commercial and professional organizations in the UK, giving a description of their main activities and providing their addresses. Listings are alphabetical according to trade description and also according to company name.

Key British Enterprises – a register of 25,000 top UK companies which provides company name and address and also some basic financial data such as sales, number of employees, and the Standard Industrial Code (SIC).

UK Trade Names – lists trade names and the parent company.

Who Owns Whom – lists firms and their parent organization.

Business Monitor – gives statistics for different products – for example numbers of manufacturers, industry sales and import levels.

Family Expenditure Survey – gives average weekly expenditure on many products and services according to: different regions, size of household, age of head of household, household income levels. Useful for estimating market size and potential sales levels.

Regional Trends plots population size and structure trends through the regions, together with more on regional income and expenditure.

Henley Centre for Forecasting – projects future social attitudes, lifestyles, income and expenditure.

Market Intelligence (MINTEL) – monthly reports on profile of different markets (both customers and competitors).

Retail Business – monthly reports on profile of different retailing markets (both customers and competitors).

The Retail Directory – gives details of Retail trade Associations and lists retail companies according to type (co-op, Multiple, Department Store and so on) and according to geography (for example, the retail outlets within many towns are listed).

Target Group Index (TGI) – annual profile of most product-markets in terms of who buys what, 34 volumes each year.

National Readership Survey – profile of readers of newspapers and magazines (for advertising media selection); that is, when matched with profile of target market.

BRAD (British Rate and Data) – gives costs of advertising in press, radio, poster, cinema, TV and all other mass media.

MEAL (Media Expenditure Analysis) – provides information on competitors' advertising expenditure on specific brands per month. Also gives advertising agency concerned.

Trade Associations – usually have information on numbers of competitors, and size of market.

Local Chambers of Trade – have statistics on companies in their trading area and information on trading conditions.

Electoral Register – can be used to help define the catchment areas of retail outlets and the number of potential customers. Also used to draw samples for market research.

On-line databases – general-purpose on-line databases including some market and company information. Others are more specialized, for example TEXTLINE provides a 'key word' search of many newspapers and journals for information and articles on the topic concerned. CD-ROM-based sources are also popular, such as ABI INFORM and LOTUS ONE SOURCE.

Primary sources, on the other hand, involve collecting new information, first hand, for the particular research programme.

ad hoc vs continuous research

Another distinction worth making within primary data collection methods is between ad hoc and continuous research. When the same respondents are observed or interviewed repeatedly over a period, this is referred to as continuous research as opposed to an ad hoc study that collects data on one occasion only from given respondents.

An example of this is the consumer panel (not to be confused with a group discussion). Here, respondents – often in the form of 'households' – agree to report on their buying behaviour media habits over a period of time, perhaps completing a type of diary every week or so and posting this to the research agency concerned.

Observation techniques in market research

Structured or unstructured

In a formalized research programme, observation may be used in an unstructured form to record, for example, general purchasing behaviour, as opposed to the more structured observation of such factors as the sex of purchasers of a specific brand of toothpaste. Indeed, a fairly unstructured observational approach may serve as exploratory research in attempting to explore and clarify the focus that is needed in conclusive research.

Natural or contrived

It is usually more realistic to observe in actual or real conditions, such as recording the number of people who look at a poster, although this is not always possible. For instance, when evaluating new store layouts, customer flows can be observed using a hall as a simulated store to test alternative designs without disrupting the real stores.

Disguised or undisguised

Perhaps the greatest potential problem of observation is that of modified behaviour – people who know they are being watched may not act as they otherwise would. For example, some continuous studies record respondents' television viewing habits and record the grocery products they purchase. It has been found that some respondents watch different programmes, or buy different products, during the first few weeks of such recording, until reverting to their more normal habits.

A study of the demand for taxis in Newcastle Upon Tyne illustrates disguised and undisguised observation and the problem of modified behaviour. This study involved observation of taxi ranks to calculate the average time taxis had to wait before picking up passengers, and the average time that passengers had to wait for a taxi. The taxi drivers knew that research was to be carried out, with the aim of deciding whether to increase the number of taxi licences in the city. Observers were positioned at all the ranks, including the two most popular. Observers at one main rank were positioned openly and were noticeable to anyone in the vicinity (not by design, but as a result of the topography of the area). Although there were several taxis at this rank at the beginning of the first observation period, within minutes there was a mass influx of taxis – far more than arrived at any other similar length of time over the next fortnight. When the results were later analysed it was found that the same number of taxis that arrived at the first rank in the first 15-minute period had departed from the second main rank. The striking difference was that the observers at the second rank were positioned in a hidden location and it was concluded that as soon as the observers were seen by the taxi drivers at the first rank, they contacted their colleagues by radio and called them from the rank which (to the taxi drivers) appeared not to be under observation.

The rationale was that the drivers did not want the number of licences increased and wanted, therefore, to give the appearance of plenty of taxis!

Human or mechanical observation

Various mechanical and electronic devices offer alternatives to a human observer watching an event. It is possible to use closed circuit television cameras for such applications as monitoring a new retail store layout. For monitoring the television viewing habits of respondents in consumer panels, meters attached to their sets have been used for many years and cable television effectively make such meters common to all those households receiving cable output. The set meter records whether the set is on or off at regular intervals and if it is 'on', which channel has been selected.

Another type of continuous research is the retail audit where sales of specific brands are recorded; often this used to be by means of physical stock checks by observers at regular intervals. The replacement of manual stock and shelf counts by laser scanning has been discussed elsewhere in this book, but a dramatic example of how the change in method of data collection towards higher technology is given by the winning, by Gallup, of the contract to compile the record charts (the previous agency, the British Market Research Bureau, used a somewhat slow and cumbersome physical diary system).

A further illustration of observation techniques in continuous research concerns those consumer panels that rely on respondents to place the packaging of relevant products consumed in a special audit bin, for the observer to count during regular visits.

Mechanical observation techniques may use devices like the psychogalvanometer, or lie detector, one version of which records changes in perspiration rates as a result of emotional reaction to stimuli such as test advertisements. Similarly, the tachistoscope allows an object, such an advertisement or a product package, to be illuminated for a fraction of a second to test the advertisement or package for initial impact, legibility, recognition, and so on.

The advantage of observation is objectivity because what actually happens is recorded, compared with the subjectivity of questioning approaches, which, as will be shown shortly, by the very nature of question wording and interviewing can introduce some bias. However, as discussed above, such objectivity is lost if subjects are aware of the observation and modify their behaviour. In practice, the researcher may be unable to even approach the ideal of effective data collection through observation. The fact that the researcher does not have to gain respondent cooperation poses an ethical problem, as exemplified by Crawford.[5] Crawford discusses the use of (unknown to those being observed) one-way mirrors in ladies' changing rooms in American department stores to observe how bras were put on and taken off! This was part of a new product development programme by an American women's underwear manufacturer and was employed because it was thought less provocative than asking women direct questions about this sort of intimate product. It was, of course, a totally unethical research approach, but it does beg the question of where the line should be drawn for *what* to observe – and also it raises the ethical issue of whether respondents' cooperation should be initially gained. If it is, then we return to the problem of modified behaviour. In any case respondent cooperation may be essential, as in the continuous research mentioned earlier.

Indeed, it would be inappropriate to attempt to observe such intimate behaviour as washing, brushing teeth or other personal habits, and some topics themselves are not susceptible to observation – such as attitudes and motivation, which require verbal responses to specialized questions. More mundanely, some simply take too long to be exhibited, so fieldwork would be too time consuming and costly.

It should also be noted that observation requires the design of forms, in much the same way that interview surveys require questionnaires. For example, Figure 8.1 shows the observation form used in the Newcastle taxi observation study discussed earlier.

Observer			Rank	
Date		Time on	Time off	
Taxi			**Passenger**	
Taxi number	Time in	Time out	Time in	Time out

Fifteen minute count: ☐ P/T ☐ P/T ☐ P/T ☐ P/T ☐ P/T

Comments/Weather conditions: _____

_____

Signature _____

Figure 8.1 Newcastle taxi observation form.

8.4 Stage 3: Determining techniques for collecting information

Once it has been determined what information (Stage 1) should be collected and from where it would be found and indeed whether it should be pursued (Stage 2), it then has to be determined how it should be collected. This stage is concerned with the instruments and procedures for data collection; secondary data has to be found, interpreted and summarized, so the main focus of discussion in this stage is on primary data collection.

The following elements of a research design are the major concerns here – though not all of these of course will be part of every research programme:

- the techniques of observation, interview and experimentation
- questionnaire and observation form design
- sample design.

These elements, as with aspects of all other research process stages, are sources of error and bias which may invalidate the whole programme: an inappropriate research instrument, for example asking interview respondents for information they cannot or will not give accurately, or an inappropriate sample asking questions of the wrong people – or too few of the right ones – will seriously affect the utility of research results.

8.5   Interview survey methods

There are, in fact, various types of interview used in research surveys, and typically a distinction is made between personal, telephone and postal interviews Further distinctions can be made between structured and unstructured interviews, and the personal interview can be of a depth or group type. Indeed, new technology provides another kind of interviewing, where the computer provides a vehicle for asking questions and collecting responses, in some cases using the Viewdata facilities of domestic television sets. Each form of interviewing merits a brief outline, as the basis for a choice of methodology.

Postal interviews

Postal questionnaire studies have the obvious advantage over personal interviews of being able to cover a very large geographic area usually with little increase in postal costs. The major characteristic of postal surveys is the absence of an interviewer, which eliminates interviewer bias but at the same time provides little scope for respondents to query the meaning of the questions. The lack of personal contact also means that when a questionnaire is sent to an address, there is no guarantee that the respondent is the addressee, since the questionnaire may be completed by another member of the family, or another member of the organization.

However, on the positive side, where a survey requires the respondent to consult with others, or with filed information, the postal survey provides the necessary time and freedom, and another result of there being no interviewer is that some respondents may be less inhibited about answering certain questions. On the other hand, without an interviewer, misunderstood questions cannot be explained, open questions cannot be probed, and the non-verbal communication of the respondents (facial expressions, intonation and the like) cannot be observed.

However, the single most significant problem usual in postal surveys is a low level of response – it is all too easy for the respondent to ignore a postal questionnaire. Without a carefully constructed covering letter, emphasizing such factors as how useful (and confidential) the respondent's replies will be, or without a reminder, response rates can be as low as single figures. Even with these and the obvious enclosures such as stamped addressed return envelopes, response rates may be so low as to be unrepresentative of the selected sample. The point is, of course, that non-response may not be a random factor – the characteristics of those who do respond may be significantly different from the characteristics of those who do not respond – a factor for which survey results should be tested where possible.

Once such limitations have been identified for a particular study, avoidance may be planned. Despite the important problems, postal surveys are used extensively in practice, perhaps often because it is an acceptable compromise between reliability and validity, and cost considerations.

Telephone interviews

Although not used as much as other interviewing approaches, nor as much in Europe as in the USA, the telephone interview is becoming more important and merits consideration in research design, as long as the sampling can be restricted to those with telephones.

As in the case of postal surveys, there is a geographical advantage although it is less pronounced than with postal questionnaires because of long-distance telephone rates, time-related call charges, and the inability in many cases to make use of cheap rate times (phoning companies at the weekend or in the evenings promises little success).

Telephone interviews are often appropriate for industrial or organizational surveys because most companies have telephones and the chances of contacting someone from the organization during office hours are reasonably good – although it may be more difficult to contact the relevant respondent within the organization.

Once the problems of organizational switchboards are overcome, telephone interviewing can be the quickest of all the interviewing methods because the interview is made from the researcher's desk so no fieldwork travel is involved, and the replies are immediate. This said, there are clearly some questions that cannot be asked over the telephone, such as those asking the respondent to look at something like a product or package, or the type of attitude scales discussed below, and telephone interviews are of necessity restricted to questions which are capable of instant reply. On the other hand, the telephone can sometimes hide the existence of a questionnaire, and the interview can appear more like a conversation to the respondent, and thus more relaxed and less inhibited.

There is certainly increased interest in the form of interviewing, as demonstrated by the coverage received in the marketing research literature, for example by Collins, White and Weitz,[6] who offer additional commentary on the use of the technique.

Telephone interviews and new technology

There have been many calls to use applications of new information technology in marketing research, and Hyett[7] points to the link between telephone interviewing and the use of minicomputers and mainframe computer terminals. He suggests that the computer be used to store the questionnaire and as the interviewer goes through the interview over the telephone, the computer can select and display the appropriate questions for each respondent, and the replies can be keyed directly into the computer store, for immediate analysis.

The more sophisticated cable Viewdata technology, being interactive, will allow questions to be sent down the line to households possessing such a system, and after being displayed on people's television sets, their answers can be keyed in via a Viewdata keypad, or via a home computer keyboard, and sent back along the line to the researcher for analysis, although such systems are as yet in their infancy. However, already tested and used is a compromise between the above approaches, involving the use of a computer visual display unit, presenting the respondent with a self-completion questionnaire. (Such work has been reported by Shugan and Hauser[8]). In The Netherlands, the Telepanel of NIPO/Gallup is an example of using computers in households for answering questionnaires.

Personal interviewing

The distinguishing feature of personal interviewing is, of course, face-to-face communication between respondent and interviewer, which poses problems of bias and error, as well as offering flexibility and control. However, it is the fieldwork cost of interviewing that provides the main disadvantage of this type of data collection. In fact, the sample design employed is of some importance here, because different fieldwork problems occur when using different sampling methods. For example, with a quota sample, the interviewer has to select respondents who possess the required characteristics, while with random sampling, the interviewer must contact a specific name and address.

The presence of an interviewer offers the opportunity for varying degrees of structure. For instance, questions might be open-ended to allow the respondent to answer in his or her own words, without the constraints of pre-determined optional answers in closed questions, and the interviewer can ask the respondent to expand on a point with various probing techniques. In unstructured interviewing, there is more of a conversation because, although certain broad topics are to be explored, there is no set sequence of pre-worded questions. This is sometimes referred to as a depth interview and is an example of qualitative as opposed to quantitative research. The latter would usually contain a number of pre-worded and sequenced questions to which there may only be pre-coded multiple-choice answers.

A variation is the group discussion (or Focus Group) which is generally unstructured and qualitative. With this method several respondents (usually eight in number) are brought together (perhaps in a 'coffee-morning' setting in one of the respondents' homes) and the interviewer guides the discussion through relevant topics, leaving most of the talking to members of the group. This method is widely used to pre-test advertisements. While the costs per respondent may be high with group discussion work as a result of the degree of skill required by the interviewer, and the time that a group discussion takes, if a research programme relied on, say, four groups exclusively, then overall costs would be lower than if a shorter, more structured, questionnaire were used on a sample of, say, 500 respondents.

However, since groups revolve around the sociology of group dynamics, it is not surprising that the interviewer, as group leader, must possess social skills in dealing with such problems as respondents who emerge as group dominators, or adopt the roles de Almeida[9] describes: 'the competing moderator, the choir, the super ego, the compiler, the rationalizer, the conscience, the rebel, the pseudo-specialist and so on'.

A number of important issues have been generated by the assessment of interview survey methods above. First there is the need to clarify the nature of the other survey methods to which reference has been made; second, there is the field of questionnaire design which is implicit in planning interviews and the question of interviewing techniques, before dealing with the major topic of sample design as a constituent of the research plan.

The nature and design of questionnaires vary enormously between projects and involve some considerable skill, but there are a number of general points worth outlining.

8.6   Guidelines for questionnaire design

The data list or information needs drawn up in the first stage of the research process provides the logical basis of the questionnaire. However, caution is needed to avoid writing one question for each discrete item of required information, since it has to be remembered that a questionnaire is going to be used by the interviewer, the respondent, and the programmer and data analyst, who are likely to be different people. In essence, questionnaires have to be designed for the understanding of the various users rather than that of the designer. To illustrate the implications of designing for the several users of the questionnaire, the questionnaire must instruct the interviewer how to use it, since, for example, many interviews require certain questions to be asked of some respondents, while other questions will be relevant to other respondents. Thus the route through a questionnaire varies for different respondents, depending on their characteristics and responses.

For example, a survey was conducted to determine whether people in the broadcasting area of a local commercial radio station would be interested in listening to the station, if it extended its broadcasting hours. The first question was 'Do you listen to the radio?' and the next 'Which station(s) do you listen to?' It is evident that if the answer to Question 1 is 'no', Question 2 is not relevant, so an instruction to the interviewer should be added after Question 1 along the lines of 'if "no" go to Question 6'.

The next issue is how the respondent should be considered when designing questionnaires. One aid could be the use of show cards, so for Question 2 above, providing a complete list of radio stations can help respondents' memories and speed up questions and replies.

In the radio study mentioned, a card was handed to each respondent, at this point in the interview, listing:

> BBC Radio 1
> BBC Radio 2
> BBC Radio 4
> BBC Local Radio
> Local Commercial Radio
> Any Other (please state)

This device is useful for many questions that are likely to have a finite number of responses – that is, closed questions.

The respondent should be the central consideration when wording and phrasing questions, with the aim of ensuring that each question means the same to every respondent, and indeed the same to the researchers. Ambiguous questions are a recurring difficulty. For example, in introducing an interview, if the interviewer asks 'Would you mind answering a few short questions?' some respondents might be positive towards the interview and reply in the affirmative with a 'yes' or nod of the head. However, 'yes' to this question strictly means 'I do mind answering questions' – hence potential confusion. 'Would you answer...' might be a clearer opening.

As well as ambiguities, leading questions are another trap. For instance, questions such as 'You do think that ... don't you?' should not be asked because they suggest the required answer. Another danger concerns the asking of more than one question at a time, such as 'Do you enjoy television and poster advertising?'

Some subdivided questions can act as filters, to ensure that only relevant questions are asked, and in this area flow charts are sometimes useful, since they can highlight groups of questions relevant to some respondents and not to others.

A third wording problem is unclear questions. For example, it is easy for questions including double negatives to be confusing to all concerned, even though they provide subtle and important nuances of meaning. Double negatives should generally be avoided – for instance, consider the problems with the following questions: 'Do you not use non-stick pans?' and 'Is it not uncommon for you to buy unbranded products?'

Questionnaires have typically to include profile questions of some kind, as for example when quota sampling is used, and the interviewer must select those respondents who fit the given quota characteristics. Obvious profile details should not be in question form, for example the sex of the respondent (generally) merely requires noting by the interviewer, although other characteristics need to be in multiple choice form. Age categories, for instance, can be put onto a show card allowing respondents to point to their appropriate category, rather than risking the refusal to answer a direct question on something like age.

There is some debate on whether profile details should be at the beginning or end of a questionnaire – if located at the end, then the respondent's confidence has been gained, and questions answered before any intimate details on age, income, occupation and the like are requested. On the other hand, when quota samples are used, it is necessary to select those who possess appropriate characteristics at the outset, although such questions risk annoying the respondent, who may not proceed with the interview.

Most questionnaires also include reference information. Examples of this would be the identity of the interviewer, and when and where the interview was conducted. This is needed if checks are to be made to ensure that interviewers have been carrying out the given instructions, and to identify those interviewers who have not been following the correct question sequence.

Once designed the questionnaire should be tested or piloted, not merely among fellow researchers or whoever is available at the time, but among the sort of people in the proposed sample. Ideally, a small subsample of the main sample (perhaps 5% or so) should be selected and interviewed, in order that problems of question wording, sequencing and interviewer performance can be noted and subsequently revised.

Let us now examine the main techniques used in motivation and attitude research. For motivation research these are: depth interview, group discussion, projective techniques, third-person test, word association test, sentence and story completion tests, psychodrama, Thematic Apperception Test, and cartoon test.[10] Attitude measures are discussed later and coverage of a variety of scaling techniques is included.

8.7 Motivation research

Depth interview

This interviewing technique has been adapted from the clinical methods of psychoanalysis. It is termed 'depth' interviewing because respondents are encouraged to go deeper and deeper into their level of thought and hence reveal their true opinions, attitudes or motivations on a particular subject. This method needs a trained interviewer, although not necessarily a psychologist.

Because the method requires specialist skill and, because of the extended individual interviews, is so time consuming that it is unusual for more than 15 to 20 depth interviews to be carried out in any particular study, use is often made of recording devices, which are used with the respondent's permission. Tape-recordings or video film is then analysed after the interview is finished. Costs per depth interview vary, depending on the quality and hence the wages of the interviewing staff being used, but a fully completed interview is likely to cost several hundred pounds.

Group discussion

Group discussions are similar to depth interviews except that groups of about 8 to 10 people are used instead of individual respondents. The interviewer takes a more passive role, merely guiding the group discussion and allowing the group members to interact. The objective is that members of the group will stimulate and 'spark off' new ideas and avenues of enquiry amongst themselves.

The cost of a group discussion is currently about £1,500, which would include paying group members and organizing an appropriate venue. For consumer studies, this may be a meeting at a specially equipped room at a market research agency. The group discussion may be observed by the client (sponsor of the research) through a TV circuit or a one-way screen. For professional people a meeting in a hotel could be arranged.

Projective techniques

If persons are relieved of direct responsibility for their expressions, they will tend to answer more freely and truthfully. Projective tests are designed to achieve this end. They are called projective tests because respondents are required to project themselves into someone else's place or into some ambiguous situation. Consider the following examples of projective tests.

Third-person tests

The respondent is encouraged to reply through some third party. The rationale is that there are both 'good' and 'real' reasons for behaviour. 'Good' reasons are socially acceptable, for example to buy environmentally friendly products. 'Real' reasons are sometimes not socially accepted. While 'good' reasons will probably be given in response to a direct questioning approach, such as 'Why did you buy this?', these answers may only be partially true. There may be a 'real' reason for behaviour that the respondent is either unwilling to admit or unable to recognize. An indirect question, for example 'What sort of people buy this?' or 'Why do people buy these?', might be sufficient to reveal 'real' reasons for behaviour.

The widely quoted study of instant coffee usage illustrates this last point.[11] The indirect approach was to ask women what sort of housewife would have compiled the shopping lists shown in Table 2.2. One-half of the sample had the list having instant coffee included. The other list included coffee beans instead. The instant coffee shopping list was seen to have been drawn up by a lazier, less well-organized woman who was described as not being a good housewife. Direct questioning, on the other hand, revealed 'good' reasons for preferring real coffee, which revolved around the product not tasting as good as drip-grind coffee.

Word association test

This type of test, also known as free association, involves firing a series of words at respondents who must state immediately which other words come into their minds. Word association tests can be used to determine consumer attitudes towards products, stores, advertising themes, product features and brand names.

Let us look at some examples. The interviewer says 'soap', to which the respondent might reply 'hygiene', 'lather', 'beauty', and so on. The interviewer says 'margarine', to which the respondent might reply 'health', 'cholesterol', 'convenient', 'butter', 'cost' and so on. The brand name Volkswagen might evoke associations such as 'German', 'durable', 'security', 'common' and 'doesn't rust'.

Sentence completion test

Here the respondent is asked to complete a number of sentences. This test can provide more information than word association. The following are some examples.

In comparing margarine with butter, one might state: 'A housewife using margarine instead of butter is ...'. or 'The healthfulness of margarine is ...' Considering a certain brand of cigars, one might state: 'A man who smokes Manikin cigars is ...'.

Story completion test

This is an extension of the sentence completion technique. Consider the following example: 'A man buys petrol at his regular petrol station which sold a nationally advertised brand. The petrol attendant who knew the man said, "Mr Smith, your battery is now nearly two years old. We have just got in a new product which, when added to the water in your battery, will prolong its life by about a year. It's a bargain at £50." What is the customer's response? Why?'

This technique can provide the seller with data on the images and feelings that people have about a particular product. Another example might be where a group of housewives are asked to complete a story in which the opening sentence is related to supermarket shopping.

Psychodrama

Here, the respondent is asked to play a role and, to do so, he or she is given a complete description of the circumstances. For instance, the role playing of respondents is to depict two alternative pain killers with other respondents playing the role of the pain! And how the pain killer tackles pain. Cooper also describes interesting variations in which respondents are given lumps of clay and are asked to think of the Labour Party, the Conservative Party, and the Liberal Democrats as they mould their clay to reflect their feelings towards these parties. In the clay example the remarks and comments of the participants may be the most illuminating about their true opinions about these political parties.

Thematic Apperception Test

In the TAT test, a series of related pictures as a story is shown to respondents who are then asked to describe what conditions gave rise to the situation, what is happening, and what the outcome will be. The assumption is that in explaining the picture, subjects will tell something about themselves. For example: 'The pictures might show a young housewife looking at a display of "bargain offer" tights, or the same housewife casting her eyes over a merchandising unit offering expensive "branded" tights. The respondent would be asked to comment on the person in the cartoon and the quality of the tights.'

Cartoon test

The cartoon test is a variation of the TAT method and is commonly referred to as a 'balloon test'. Informants are presented with a rough sketch showing two people talking. One of them has just said something represented by words written into a 'speech balloon' as in a comic strip. The other person's balloon is empty and the informant is asked what he or she is replying. Consider the following example: 'Two women are pictured outside Smith's department store and one woman is saying, "What do you think of Smith's department store?"' The respondent is asked to give the reply of the other woman.

Many marketing situations could be usefully tested by this technique. Consider the following examples: 'A chemist is pictured saying "This bottle of Disprin gives you one hundred tablets for seventy-five pence; and this bottle gives you one hundred soluble Aspirin for fifty pence." What is the customer's reply?'

You could show a situation between a shopper returning faulty merchandise and a store assistant. You could picture a husband and wife considering the purchase of an expensive product. Another particular example might be to use a cartoon which shows a conference in progress. One of the delegates says, 'Now this is our present supplier list. We have been with them for quite some time and they have been doing a good job. There is no reason for making any changes. The next subject is ...' Another delegate interrupts to say 'Wait a minute. Loyalty is fine, but there are a lot of other considerations which I think are due for a change.' The respondent is then asked with which delegate he or she is in most agreement and why.

Issues and problems involved in motivation research

It should be noted that motivation research is not without its own special problems and issues. A major problem is the fact that all the above-mentioned techniques require the use of highly skilled interviewers and analysts trained in psychology. This, of course, is a problem which can be overcome, albeit at a cost. Potentially more serious issues and problems relate to the extent to which these techniques are scientific and ethical.

With regard to scientific status, the controversy continues. Critics argue that the techniques are shaky to say the least, with little comparability between various research studies. On the other hand, confirmed advocates of motivation research suggest that the techniques are powerful marketing tools.[12]

With regard to ethical status, critics have long argued that the use of such techniques is tantamount to an invasion of the privacy of the consumer's mind and lays the customer open to manipulation.[13]

No doubt the debate will continue, although it must be said that in recent years the use of these techniques in consumer research has probably declined somewhat. The professional marketer would perhaps be best advised to keep an open mind, picking and choosing from the techniques available, as and where appropriate. And as said before, motivation research and qualitative research in general may be used in an exploratory pilot study to find the relevant aspects and issues of a specific research topic.

8.8   Attitude measurement

Very often marketers try to discover consumer attitudes towards their and their competitors' offerings. This section reviews some of the forms of attitude measurement. Attitude measurements require special consideration because it is far too easy and superficial to ask a respondent questions like: 'What is your attitude towards Smith's Department Store?' only to receive a reply along the lines of 'I like it', or 'It's all right'. While such feelings may be important, it would be of greater use to uncover the reasons for such feelings, and the type of actions in which they are likely to result.

This perspective views an attitude as more than a global evaluation, and considers its structure to be composed of the:

(1) *cognitive component*, which includes what is known, the beliefs about the topic concerned, even if part of this is a misperception;
(2) *affective component*, which is the feelings and evaluations about these beliefs resulting from what is known about the topic;
(3) *conative component,* which includes the behavioural intentions resulting from the cognitive and affective components.

If intentions are based on specific elements of knowledge (beliefs) and evaluations, these beliefs and evaluations need to be discovered, if the results are to be meaningfully used. Furthermore, such attributes are perceived by respondents with varying degrees of strength, so that the concept of degree in measuring attitudes is unavoidable. While some form of scale is required, the straightforward like/dislike continuum would be of only limited value. A more useful approach is to compile a series of scales, each measuring a different attribute of the same attitude. If a department store wishes to identify any scope for improvement on the one hand and perceived strengths to accentuate on the other hand, there are a variety of attitude scaling methods that can be employed and these are outlined below.

Semantic differential

The technique used here is known as the semantic differential, a set of 7-point bipolar scales.[14] The scales are characterized by opposites such as good/bad, active/passive, hot/cold, rough/smooth and strong/weak. One advantage is providing a convenient way of comparing attitudes to different topics, for instance to different stores, on the same scales and on the same pictorial representation (Table 8.2).

Table 8.2 Semantic differential.

	1	2	3	4	5	6	7	
Wide range of goods		S			H	J		Narrow range of goods
Good service		J	S		H			Poor service
High prices	H		J	S				Low prices
Value for money				S	J	H		Poor value for money
Good delivery service	S	J				H		Poor delivery service
Good credit arrangements		S	HJ					Poor credit arrangements
Good shop layout								Poor shop layout
Convenient location	H		H		S			Inconvenient location
Enjoy shopping there								Dislike shopping there
Friendly staff		J	S		H			Unfriendly staff

S = Smith's   J = Jones   H = Henry's

Repertory grid

However, using the semantic differential requires some way of identifying the aspects that are of importance to customers and non-customers, to avoid including irrelevant aspects. Group discussions can be used for this purpose, as could another technique which is called the Repertory Grid.[15] This technique involves asking the respondent how he or she perceives two items of a triad to be similar and different from the third. In Table 8.3 reasons for similarity are shown by a tick and the different item with a cross. While some of the reasons given are likely to be of little use, some might provide bipolar adjectives that the researcher would not otherwise have considered for the semantic differential.

Alternative attitude measurement techniques use statements rather than adjectives, and the scaling is in terms of either the strength of each statement (Thurstone scales) or the strength of the respondent's agreement with each statement (Likert scales).

Likert scales

Respondents may be presented with a series of statements about the topic concerned, and asked to indicate their degree of agreement with each, according to

Table 8.3 Repertory grid.

	Smith's	Jones	Henry's	Longman's	Taylor's	
Friendly staff	✓	✓	✗			Unfriendly staff
Cramped changing rooms		✓	✓	✗		Spacious changing rooms
Attractive decor			✓	✓	✗	Unattractive decor
Has green carpeting	✓	✗			✓	No green carpets

Repertory grid. Each respondent comes up with their own reasons for similarity and difference, so for another respondent presented with Smith's Jones and Henry's, there may be a totally different reason – as there can be for another respondent when presented with Jones, Henry's and Longman's – and so on.

a 5-point scale ranging from 'strongly agree' to 'strongly disagree'.[16] It is important, though difficult in practice, for the range of statements offered to cover the range of cognitive, affective and conative aspects that the topic involves. Table 8.4 shows a version of the Likert scaling technique, where a mixture of positive and negative statements allows respondents' consistency to be checked.

Both the semantic differential and the Likert scale can be used quantitatively by assigning values to each scaling position, and average scores for all respondents' replies can be calculated, either for each scale, or in an overall summation. In Table 8.5, for example, if each scale position is scored from 1 to 6 for each scale (that is, for the first scale, 'S' is scored 2, 'H' is scored 4 and so on), then the positioning of 'S' by all respondents can be averaged and shown pictorially for each scale. Alternatively, the overall average can be calculated for

Table 8.4 Likert scales.

	Strongly agree	Agree	Not sure	Disagree	Strongly disagree
Glogg's has a wide range of goods		✓			
The service at Glogg's is very good			✓		
Glogg's staff are very friendly	✓				
Glogg's shop layout is poor			✓		
I like shopping at Glogg's	✓				
If looking for a pair of jeans I would certainly try Glogg's		✓			

Table 8.5 Scoring scales: Likert analysis.

	SA	A	(%) NS	D	SD
Glogg's has a wide range of goods	5	7	50	36	2
The service at Glogg's is very good	9	34	29	18	10
Glogg's staff are very friendly	20	10	8	37	25
Glogg's shop layout is poor	8	17	20	12	43

all scales. For 'S' here, it would be (2+3+4+3+1+2+3+5+2+3)/10 = 2.8. The latter approach would not be universally applicable, because it assumes equivalence between scales and also implies that every scale is scorable in the same terms, while in fact some scales will be descriptive and not evaluative.

Distance scores

A third way of quantifying the semantic differential is to calculate 'distance' scores. These show how close the topics researched are in terms of the semantic differential scales. Table 8.6 illustrates D-scores for the similarity between 'S' and 'H', and between 'G' and 'J'.

Table 8.6 Distance score calculation.

Dimensions	Scale values for		
	G	H	J
1	2	4	5
2	3	5	2
3	4	1	3
4	3	5	4
5	1	5	2
6	2	3	3
7	3	4	4
8	5	1	3
9	2	6	4
10	3	5	2

Distance score formula $= \sqrt{\Sigma d^2}$

Distance score for G–H =

$$\sqrt{(2-4)^2 + (3-5)^2 + (4-1)^2 + (3-5)^2 + (1-5)^2 + (2-3)^2 + (3-4)^2 + (5-1)^2 + (2-6)^2 + (3-5)^2} = 8.7$$

Distance score for G–J =

$$\sqrt{(2-5)^2 + (3-2)^2 + (4-3)^2 + (3-4)^2 + (1-2)^2 + (2-3)^2 + (3-4)^2 + (5-3)^2 + (2-4)^2 + (3-2)^2} = 4.9$$

Fishbein provided another useful approach by suggesting that respondents might be able to score brands or products along each semantic differential scale (belief) but that they might not regard all bi-polars with equal importance or favourableness. Table 8.7 shows how it is possible to elicit not only a rating along each belief scale, but also a favourableness rating of the scales themselves (favourable/unfavourable). Multiplying the two for each scale and aggregating the scores provides a more meaningful analysis. The attitude is the summation of the weighted belief scores.

The Likert approach could be scored +2 to −2 for the 'strongly agree' to 'strongly disagree' positions for each statement, with the proviso that all positive statements are valued similarly, and negative statements are valued in the reverse order. Thus, statements 1 to 3 would be scored as above, but statement 4 would be −2 for a 'strongly agree' (Likert, 1932) response, through to +2 for a 'strongly disagree' response. As with the semantic differential, an average for all respondents for each statement could be calculated, or the overall summated ratings (which was Likert's original approach). For many marketing research programmes it is more convenient to merely calculate the percentage of respondents who gave each response.

Table 8.7 Fishbein and Ajzen multi-attribute model.[17]

A Good packaging	$\underline{\quad\quad\quad *\quad\quad\quad\quad\quad\quad\quad\quad}$ 1 2 3 4 5	Poor pack
B Good colour	$\underline{\quad\quad\quad *\quad\quad\quad\quad\quad\quad\quad\quad}$ 1 2 3 4 5	Poor colour
A is Important	$\underline{\quad\quad\quad\quad\quad\quad\quad\quad\quad * \quad}$ 1 2 3 4 5	Unimportant
B is Important	$\underline{\quad\quad\quad\quad\quad\quad * \quad\quad\quad\quad}$ 1 2 3 4 5	Unimportant

If the colour and style are promoted as being important, best would be:

$1 \times 1 + 1 \times 1 = 2$

Worst would be:

$5 \times 5 + 5 \times 5 = 50$

In our case, the s core = 24

$\underline{\quad\quad\quad *\quad\quad\quad\quad}$
2   50

Thurstone scales

As an alternative to Likert scales, the Thurstone method of measuring attitudes is worth a brief mention. It presents respondents with a series of statements and requires them to pick out the one statement that most accurately reflects their attitude. The difference between statements should be of a uniform degree to allow the scaling approach to be effective.

The following statements could be presented to respondents:

- 'I think Smith's is the best store in town.'
- 'I think Smith's could be improved.'
- 'I have no feelings one way or the other about Smith's.'
- 'I don't think Smith's is the best store in town.'
- 'I think Smith's should close because it is so bad.'

The scoring here could value the first statement +2, the last statement −2 and the others accordingly. It is often difficult to compile a series of statements that easily facilitate the choice of just one by the respondent, while at the same time maintaining the same distance between them.[18]

8.9   Other survey approaches

Omnibus surveys

Omnibus, or shared, surveys are becoming increasingly popular. The research design of an omnibus survey is constant, but the questions included vary according to which clients 'buy in', thus providing a quick and inexpensive survey approach. As long as the research design and methods are satisfactory, the advantage is that costs are shared among all clients.

Omnibus surveys vary in the specialization of their samples, different operators offering, for example, samples of 4,000 adults nationally, 1,000 motorists nationally or 2,500 managers of small businesses. Clearly the operators do not alter their published designs for a single client, but repeat a survey of the same design at regular intervals. Because the research design is the constant there is a minimum of administration in planning and fieldwork, and it is claimed that the major sources of error and bias will have been removed.

Omnibus surveys can be used in a number of ways. For example, if the same questions are asked in consecutive surveys, the results can either be combined to give a larger sample size, with the aim of reducing sampling error, or analysed to measure change over time. However, this last example should not be equated with continuous research since the same respondents would not be interviewed in consecutive surveys in spite of the same sample design being used.

Most of the opinion polls reported in the national media are omnibus surveys, and the clients are normally paying something between £100 and £600 per question, depending on the operator.

Consumer panels

The panel does not involve group discussions, but is a form of continuous research reporting on the behaviour of the same respondents over time. Households are recruited to the panel and provide information on their buying behaviour in certain specific or general product categories, and on their media habits – such as television, radio and print exposure.

The reporting of behaviour is often by means of a diary, which is completed and either posted to the research agency concerned or collected by a researcher. For example, in a panel for media studies, the radio stations listened to would be noted on a pre-printed chart for each day of the week, and a grocery panel would require the brands, pack sizes, prices paid and stores used to be recorded for the product categories being studied. This often does not involve face-to-face interviewing, but using, for example, a special audit bin, in which the packs of products are placed for a researcher, and the set meter to measure television viewing.

Households are commonly selected on the basis of random sampling (using electoral registers and multi-stage sampling of the type discussed shortly) rather than quota sampling, which provides a further distinction between the methodologies used for continuous as opposed to *ad hoc* research. The major problem with panels is the high mortality rate of panel members, that is, the withdrawal rate due to boredom (and indeed because of members moving home and so on) is high – perhaps up to 40% after the first interview. Clearly, the aim is that replacements should be as representative as possible. However, the problem of recruiting replacements, together with the need to offer members some form of inducement or payments, provides a constant danger of panel composition being unrepresentative. For example, once recruited, new members sometimes change their behaviour, so it might be appropriate to exclude the results from these households for some time until their behaviour reverts to normal.

The basic working of the panel system is that operators compile reports of consumer profiles and other aspects of their buying behaviour, such as stores used, brands preferred, times of purchase and so on, and sell these to their clients. These firms can thus monitor their competitors' marketing, as well as their own, with the additional advantage that a time series of information is built up, allowing the identification of trends and change over time.

Retail audits

The other major form of continuous research is the retail audit, using a representative sample of retail outlets that agree to provide information over a period of time.

The information provided is usually sales of various products. For example, 'Top Twenty' record charts are compiled by the British Market Research Bureau using a retail audit. BMRB collects weekly diaries from their panel members, which contain lists of records sold, and the research agency computes totals for each. The major problem is the representativeness of the retail panel:

it is of course a fairly simple matter to select a list of record shops that is fully representative of the business in Great Britain, by size of shop, area, type of shop and so on. It is quite another matter to persuade all those shops to provide detailed information to BMRB about their sales each week. Fortunately most dealers are willing to carry out this quite onerous task. However, two important multiples, Boots and Smiths, do not at present provide sales information, but there are hopes that both may contribute to the charts in the near future. (BMRB, 1980)

In addition to producing the 'charts', these data are further analysed to give sales by record company, as a service to manufacturers, whose despatches of records to shops frequently bear little relation to sales over the counter in a given week. Manufacturers receive information on sales, market shares and the performance of different types of outlet.

Other agencies – principally Nielsens and Attwoods in grocery and pharmaceuticals, for example – run retail audits covering a range of different products, with some variations in data collection methods. Typically the data are collected by a regular visit by a researcher, who makes a physical stock check of the product categories being studied and compares this with stock levels at the previous visit and with records of what has been bought-in in the meantime. Thus, past stock plus purchases, minus present stock, equals sales (weighted for pilferage, returns and other loss).

8.10 Experimental design

The third form of data collection, having considered observation and interview studies, is experimentation. A simple example demonstrates the nature of marketing experimentation. Suppose a marketer believes sales are low because of inefficient advertising, and wants to establish what will happen if some change is made in advertising. A new advertising campaign is developed and launched, and sales are monitored and compared with sales before the new campaign. In terms of experimentation this would be a simple before–after design, which has been summarized by Boyd *et al.*[19] in the following manner:

Before measure	YES (initial sales = X1)
Experimental variable	YES (new advertising)
After measure	YES (new level of sales = X2)

The difference between the two levels of sales is taken to be the effect of the new campaign. So, if X1 is 5,000 units per month and X2 is 6,000 units per month, the organization might conclude the new campaign to be effective. Clearly, this would not necessarily be valid. If, for example, competitors' distribution systems delayed delivery of competing products to the shops during the time of this new campaign, the customers may be purchasing the test product, not because of an effective advertising campaign, but because of the lack of availability of alternative brands.

It is clearly impossible to control competitors marketing activity when conducting marketing experiments, and there are many other uncontrollable variables to take into account, when designing and analysing experiments. For example, there might be a general trend of increasing sales and, perhaps, sales might have been even higher if the old campaign had continued!

There are dangers of simply comparing sales before and after the introduction of an experimental variable. The effect of time has to be considered, and it might be, as, for example, with poster advertising, that the time delay before achieving any influence might be substantial.

Another problem with the experiment above is that the wrong dependent variable (that is, the actual variable measured to judge the effect of the experimental variable) may be selected. Much depends on what the advertising campaign is trying to do, of course, and it may therefore be more valid to measure changes in attitudes or perceptions rather than sales.

Another way of improving an experimental design like the one above would be to include a control group, that is, to measure the same dependent variables in the control group in the absence of the experimental variable. This allows some degree of assessment of uncontrollable variables. For example, in the illustration above, if for the experimental group (that is, those exposed to the experimental variable), the before–after calculation showed increased sales from 5,000 to 6,000 units per month, but for a control group sales rose from 4,000 to 4,800 per month, then the 20% increase for both groups might mean that there had been little effect of the experimental variable.

This type of design is a before–after with control[20] as shown below:

	Experimental group	Control group
Before measure (initial sales)	X1	Y1
Experimental variable (new advertising)	YES	NO
After measure (new level of sales)	X2	Y2

Therefore, effect of experimental variable $= (X2 - X1) - (Y2 - Y1)$

Marketing experiments can use data from consumer panels or retail audits, with the advantage of being able to demonstrate changes over time more effectively than *ad hoc* research. The test market is the largest marketing experiment because the whole mix is tested, rather than just one variable. Panel data are particularly useful in test markets, because not just sales, but customer profiles, new and repeat buying levels, attitudes, retail preferences, and so on are analysed over a period.

In fact, it is not always necessary to take before measures. For example, the Mason Haire[21] study of coffee usage was an after-only with control design. No before measure was taken, but the sample was divided into experimental and control groups given the different shopping lists. After measures were made for both groups, that is, all were asked to describe the sort of housewife who would have compiled the list.

One reason why a before measure might not be appropriate is that the very existence of one could produce bias. For example, consider the case where a new advertisement for a perfume is being pre-tested, using a research design that involves asking a sample of women which brands of perfume they normally consider purchasing, and then showing a film, which has an advertisement break where the new advertisement is shown. A repeat of the first question could be taken as the after question, and any change in the number of women preferring the test brand of perfume is a crude measure of the effectiveness of the new advertisement. A problem with this sort of design is that people often repeat their first answer in order to appear to be consistent. Others, however, may realize what the test is attempting to do, and this could distort perceptions and responses. This example identifies two further considerations to take into account when planning an experimental design: first, a before measure may bias the after measure (for example, when respondents try to remain consistent); and second, the nature of questioning, especially for before measures, may destroy any attempt to disguise the experimental variable, so that the interaction produces further bias. The aim should be to design an experiment that facilitates the identification and preferably quantification of all variables that can account for differences between before and after measures so that there can be an acceptable isolation of the effects of the experimental variable. Lastly, in operating test markets there is always the problem of experimental discipline, that is, maintaining realistic test conditions rather than 'making' the test work at any cost.

There is an inevitably close relationship between the choice of data collection method and research instrument, and the selection of respondents – or sample design. Actually, the ideal plan would be to include all relevant people in the study, which would make the study a census. Indeed, this is sometimes possible, if the relevant population is small, and perhaps geographically concentrated, as is sometimes the case in industrial markets. It is more usual, however, for populations to be larger, and thus less suitable for a census. In these circumstances, something less than the whole population will be observed or interviewed, and it is necessary to select a sample from the total population.

8.11 Sample design

Probability vs non-probability sampling

Choice in sample design is between those based on the laws of probability (introduced in the section above on sample size) and those based more on subjectivity and referred to as non-probability sampling. The latter includes convenience sampling, which selects those who are easily and readily accessible, and judgement sampling, where those considered relevant and representative are selected, while quota sampling is the most widespread type of non-probability sampling.

Random sampling

When a complete list exists of all individuals or items in the relevant population (that is, a sampling frame), it is possible to design a sample that gives each a calculable chance of each item being selected. This principle provides the basis of random sampling. There is a popular misconception that random is something rather vague and haphazard, like interviewing anyone available in the street, while in fact it is extremely precise.

If a population were composed of 12 items, and each could be listed, then the following are ways of selecting a random sample of, say, 3: (a) the lottery method, where 12 discs (or equivalent) are placed in a receptacle, each disc being labelled to represent one of the 12 items and a blind draw of 3 is made; (b) by reference to mathematical tables of Random Sampling Numbers, three are selected, for example 5, 6, and 8 – items labelled 5, 6 and 8 would then be the sample; (c) with a large sample a more convenient approach would be to divide the population size by the sample size to calculate the sampling interval (n) and every 'nth' item can be selected. In the example above, the sampling interval would be 12/3 = 4. Thus, every 4th item could be taken: 4, 8, 12 or 3, 7, 11 or 2, 6, 10 or 1,5, 9. This is referred to as systematic random sampling and provides a practical method of selecting random sample items.

When there are subdivisions in a population there are four ways of designing a random sample. Take, as a common example for all four, the catchment area of a small store which has been defined as one ward of a parliamentary constituency, where the ward contains 1,000 people divided amongst five Polling Districts, as shown in Figure 8.2.

Assume that a random sample of 100 people is to be taken. The alternative approaches would be as follows. First, select the same number from each Polling District (PD), that is, 20 from each of A, B, C, D and E. Selection could employ the systematic approach described above. This is referred to as stratified random sampling using a uniform sampling fraction.

A second method would be to select that proportion of the sample from each PD that reflects the proportion of the ward that live in each PD. Thus, half of the ward's population live in E (500/1000) so we select 50 people (50% of 100) from E. On this basis, 5 people (50/1000 of 100) would be selected from A, 30 from B, 10 from D and 5 from C. This is again a stratified sample, but this time with a variable sampling fraction.

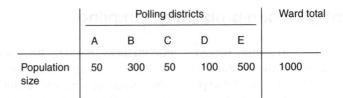

	Polling districts					Ward total
	A	B	C	D	E	
Population size	50	300	50	100	500	1000

Figure 8.2 Population distribution in a selected ward.

Thirdly, it is not always essential to include respondents from each PD, and it may not be convenient if, for example, fieldwork costs of covering all five are high. Then, it is possible to randomly select only some of the PDs and the choice of which to select is itself based on random sampling. It might be decided, for example, to concentrate the fieldwork in just two PDs, where a random selection of 2 from 5 has identified B and D. Then, either 50 people from each would be selected, according to a uniform sampling fraction, or 75 from B and 25 from D, according to a variable sampling fraction. This approach is referred to as multi-stage sampling and there can be many more stages than in this example. In a larger geographic area, for instance, there may be several parliamentary boroughs with only some being selected, and within those selected, only some constituencies chosen, and so on, as illustrated in Figure 8.3.

Fourth, further concentration of fieldwork is possible if only a very few PDs are selected, but the sample includes everyone in these PDs. In the example, if PDs A and C are selected, the sample of 100 would be fulfilled by interviewing everyone in A and C. This is referred to as cluster sampling and can again be implemented through selection at two or more levels, though it is probably better suited to a situation in which the strata are equal in size, since a random selection of just two PDs which, when combined, produce exactly the desired sample size is unlikely to occur.

Geodemographic sampling

ACORN and other geodemographic systems were discussed in the marketing segmentation chapter but it is worth adding to that discussion here because geodemographics are increasingly being used for sampling purposes.

CACI state: 'the selected sample areas can be printed out in terms of constituent postcodes and street addresses eliminating the need for electoral registers'.[22] The Target Group Index sample is selected on this basis, for example.

Quota sampling

With many marketing research programmes no suitable sampling frame exists; for example, there is no complete list of baked beans buyers or buyers of other fast moving consumer goods. Typically, such markets are segmented according to characteristics like age, sex and socio-economic groupings, where there is no accessible sampling frame.

Quota sampling allows for such factors, as the following example demonstrates. Assume that a market is segmented according to age and socio-economic group, producing four segments: (a) 15–34 year-olds in socio-economic group ABC1; (b) 15–34 year-olds in C2DE; (c) 35 years and older in ABC1; and (d) 35 years and older in C2DE. Sufficient data is available for marketing regions (for

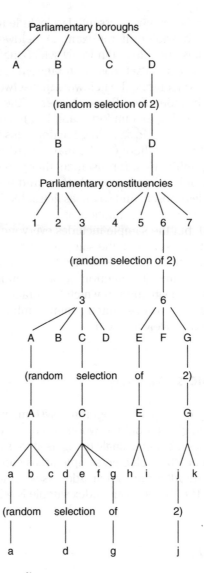

Figure 8.3 Multi-stage sampling.

example, ITV areas) to estimate the incidence of these characteristics in regional populations. For example, 70% of an ITV region might be C2DE, and 67% might be 35 years and older. Assuming that a sample of 500 is required, this type of sample design would produce cells of the relevant sampling characteristics with quotas allocated to each in proportion to their incidence in the population, as shown in Figure 8.4. In this case, because 70% of the population are C2DE and 67% are 35 years or older, the quota of 35 years and older C2DEs is 70% of 67% of 500 (the sample size), and this produces a total of 235.

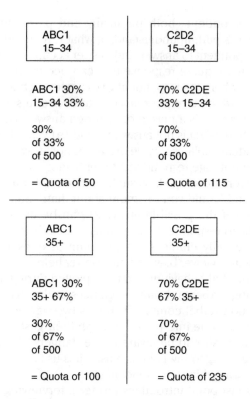

Figure 8.4 Quota sampling.

It is then up to the interviewer to select the correct quotas of respondents with each set of characteristics. This would very often be the basis for street interviewing. Hopefully, the misconception of selecting people at random in the street is now apparent.

8.12 Stage 4: Data collection

In collecting data the main types of error and bias during this 'fieldwork' stage are due to poor interviewing or observation procedures.

Interviewing techniques

The parallel to designing a clear and appropriate questionnaire is the preparation and the development of interviewing skills.

Kahn and Cannell[23] propose three conditions necessary for successful interviewing: accessibility of the interviewer to the respondent, and of the information to the respondent (both physically and psychologically); cognition on the respondent's part, in understanding what is required; and motivation on the part of the respondent to answer, and answer accurately. They also describe five symptoms of inadequate response that can occur during interviewing: (a) partial response, where the respondent gives a relevant but incomplete answer; (b) non-response, which is either refusal to answer or a silent response; (c) inaccurate response, which is a biased or distorted answer; (d) irrelevant response, where the question asked is not answered; and (e) verbalized response problem, where a respondent explains why he or she cannot answer the question.

To encourage respondents to reply more fully and accurately, experienced interviewers develop skills such as using neutral questions, like 'how do you mean?' and 'could you say more about that?'. Sometimes aided recall (indicating some of the possible answers) can be used, as can the explanation of questions to respondents. The danger of explanation, however, is that the interviewer actually changes the meaning of questions, so there is a thin line between interviewer bias and interviewer help.

Non-verbal behaviour can be exploited during interviews, with interviewers employing 'expectant pauses, glances and nods' to elicit more information. Indeed, non-verbal communication is two-way because respondents' intended meanings can be interpreted through their gestures and intonation. However, interviewers should be aware of the dangers of misinterpreting what respondents are trying to say. For this reason it is usual to require interviewers to record verbatim everything a respondent says.

This last point introduces further interviewing problems, since responses have to be recorded as well as questions asked. Open-ended questions, especially, create recording difficulties because each word of sometimes lengthy replies has to be taken down.

Interviewers have to repeat their task with many different respondents, but with the same questionnaire, so the resulting boredom and fatigue should be taken into account when setting the number of interviews, or interviewing time, for each interviewer. The repetition, for example, of asking the same question in the same way over and over again can eventually lead the interviewer to short-cuts by, for example, paraphrasing questions, which provides another source of interviewer bias.

As already stated, interviewers should be given time to become acquainted with the questionnaire before using it, to avoid errors over question sequencing and poor recording of answers.

Interviewers have responsibilities beyond asking questions and recording answers; for example, there is the initial task of making contact with appropriate respondents, and the need to gain sufficient cooperation for the interview to proceed. When quota sampling is used, interviewers are provided with a list of the characteristics they must look for in potential respondents, and errors often occur when interviewers become tired of waiting for the 'right' people to come along. Close supervision can go some way to overcoming this problem, for example by checking that some of those interviewed do indeed possess appropriate characteristics. This encourages interviewers to select more carefully, and, if a quota cell is difficult to complete, to discuss this with a supervisor rather than attempting to cover up. An alternative interviewing point might be decided upon, or merely to try again later. The same could apply in poor weather when no one wants to stop to be interviewed.

When a survey is sampled randomly, interviewers will works from a list of names and addresses. When the named respondent is not at the listed address at the time of call, no one else should normally be interviewed. Instead the threat of checks can discourage such a short-cut. Up to three call-backs are usually made and if there is still no success, another respondent may be randomly selected.

For some surveys, especially those using an electoral register sampling frame, some addresses may be out of date, either because the respondent has moved (or died), or indeed, because the whole street no longer exists. Again, another respondent should be selected from the sampling frame at random (rather than the interviewer choosing the most convenient person).

Often only about a third of the interviewer's time is spent actually interviewing, due to the time needed for travelling to interview points, waiting to contact appropriate people, possibly editing questionnaires at the end of an interviewing period, and certain general administrative functions.

The problem of gaining the cooperation of respondents can be eased by explaining the purpose of the survey and providing evidence of being a bona fide interviewer, which has been made easier for those organizations that have joined the Market Research Society's scheme of allocating identity cards of interviewers. One obstacle that this can overcome is the equation of market researchers with salesmen, which is usually due to the salesmen posing as researchers. If respondents can remain anonymous then this can be emphasized to gain their cooperation, together with encouragement that their replies will be greatly valued and respected.

If interviewers are asked for their opinions on the questionnaire and its design, and on general interview and survey procedures, then because of this extra trust and consultation the interviewer may feel more involved and respected and therefore be more diligent and enthusiastic.

8.13 Stage 5: Data processing

Once the data have been collected they have to be analysed, edited and tested, before communication to the decision maker. It is all too easy for the planning stages of a research programme to revolve around designing samples and questionnaires and little else. When this happens the researcher will be shaken by the problems of data analysis – perhaps hundreds of questionnaires have been returned, how should they be analysed? What should happen to open-ended questions – there appear to be as many different ways of answering these as there are respondents?

The key is to plan in advance – indeed this is another reason for this general division of the whole research process into a series of stages.

A valuable discipline is to list all the data processing requirements in Stage 1, at the time of compiling the data list – it is more likely, then, to be reasonably sure that the data list is accurate.

8.14 Stage 5: Uni- and bivariate analysis

The statistical analysis of the data collected with Osgood, Likert and Thurstone scales (discussed above) may be uni-, bi- or multivariate. Univariate analysis is concerned with the frequency distributions, means and standard deviations of the variables. Testing the significance of differences between means and non-parametric tests are all part of univariate data analysis.

Bivariate analysis is concerned with the relationships between variables in terms of correlations and regression coefficients. These coefficients are measures between variables in terms of correlation of the variables. Correlation coefficients indicate to what degree variables vary in the same or in the opposite direction. For instance, a positive correlation between the level of education and income indicates that people with higher education tend to have higher incomes. If this correlation is 0.60, education explains the variance of income for 36%: $(0.60)^2 = 0.36$. A negative correlation between the level of education and preference for watching football indicates that people with a lower education tend to prefer football more than people with a higher education.

Regression coefficients indicate to what degree a variable is a predictor for another variable: education level may be a predictor for income. With only one predictor, this is called simple regression, but with more than one predictor it is called multiple regression. For instance, apart from education, other variables such as type of job and length of career may be other predictors of income. With more predictor variables it is often possible to explain more variance of the dependent variable (income).

The correlation and regression coefficients are examples of metric coefficients. There are also non-metric coefficients, used with non-metric data; these are called similarity or proximity coefficients and are used as input data for non-metric multidimensional scaling.

8.15 Multivariate analysis

A number of multivariate techniques may be used for market segmentation. The main categorization of these techniques is the distinction of structural and dependence analyses. A second distinction is based on the level of input data: metric or non-metric data.

Structural analysis

In structural analysis the interrelations between variables is explored in order to create a structure that is simpler than the original variables. Typical examples of structural analyses are: factor analysis, cluster analysis, multidimensional scaling and correspondence analysis. With factor analysis a battery of 100 lifestyle statements may be reduced to six or seven underlying factors. This is much easier and relevant to report than the scores on all 100 statements. Structural analysis is used for simplification of complex structures as in lifestyle research, perception and image analysis in categorization and positioning.

Dependence analysis

In dependence analysis a relationship between a dependent or criterion variable and a set of independent or predictor variables is studied, for instance the variables that predict or explain the market share of a brand. Typical examples of dependence analyses are: multiple regression, multiple discriminant analysis, analysis of variance and conjoint analysis. A combination of structural and dependence analysis is LISREL, linear structural relations. LISREL is a combination of factor analysis, multiple regression and other types of multivariate analyses. Dependence analysis is used for explanation and prediction of a dependent variable, such as market share, sales, product or brand evaluation and preference.

Metric and non-metric data

Another important distinction is between the types of data that can be analysed: metric and non-metric data. Metric data are ratio- and interval-level data, often based on correlations and variances. Most multivariate analyses are possible if the data input consists of metric data. Non-metric data are ordinal- and nominal-level data, often based on similarity coefficients and preference ratings. Only non-metric techniques are allowed with non-metric data input. In Table 8.8 the types of multivariate analyses are classified according to these two distinctions.

Table 8.8 Classification of types of multivariate analysis.

	Structural analysis	*Dependence analysis*
Metric data	Factor analysis LISREL	Regression analysis Discriminant analysis LISREL
Non-metric data	Cluster analysis Multidimensional scaling Correspondence analysis	Analysis of variance Conjoint analysis AID, CHAID

In this section the following techniques are mentioned: factor analysis, cluster analysis, multidimensional scaling, correspondence analysis, multiple regression analysis, multiple discriminant analysis, analysis of variance, conjoint analysis and AID/CHAID. A frequently used computer programme package for multivariate analysis is SPSS.[24]

Factor analysis

Factor analysis is a multivariate technique to structure a large array of variables into a smaller set of factors. These factors are underlying constructs that summarize the set of variables. Variables are often highly intercorrelated. These sets of intercorrelated variables are then summarized by one factor. Attitude questionnaires are often factor analysed to reduce the large set of questions to a meaningful small set of factors. This is an exploratory application of factor analysis, called principal components analysis.

Factor analysis may also be applied to test for the number and type of underlying factors in a data set. The researcher may have an idea about how many factors and what type of factors could be expected. This is called confirmatory factor analysis.

Cluster analysis

Cluster analysis provides a set of procedures that seek to separate the data into groups. The goal in such applications is to arrive at clusters of objects, cases or persons that display small within-cluster variation relative to the between-cluster variation. The goal in using cluster analysis is to identify a smaller number of groups such that objects belonging to a given group are, in some sense, more similar to each other than to objects belonging to other groups. Thus, cluster analysis attempts to reduce the information on the whole set of n objects to information about, say, g subgroups where $g < n$.

One of the major problems in strategic marketing consists of the orderly classification of the myriad data that confront the researcher. Clustering techniques look for classification of attributes or subjects on the basis of their estimated resemblance. Cluster analysis is an exploratory method that seeks patterns within data by operating a matrix of independent variables. Usually objects to be clustered are scored on several variables and are grouped on the basis of the similarity of their scores. The primary value of cluster analysis lies in the preclassification of data, as suggested by 'natural' groupings of the data itself. The major disadvantage of these techniques is that the implicit assumptions of the researcher can seriously affect cluster results. Cluster analysis can be applied in strategic marketing for clustering buyers, products, markets, as well as key competitors. It has been found to be a particularly useful aid to market segmentation, experimentation and product positioning.[25]

Several questions need to be answered with respect to a given cluster solution, including:

(1) how the clusters differ,
(2) what is the optimal, that is, correct, number of clusters,
(3) how good is the fit of the solution for a pre-specified level of clusters.

The first question concerns the distinctiveness of cluster profiles. The second question concerns the trade-off between parsimony, in the sense of fewer clusters, and some measure of increase in within-cluster homogeneity resulting from having more clusters in the solution. The third question concerns cluster recovery which can be viewed in terms of the fit between the input data and the resulting solution. This should be high.

Multidimensional scaling

Multidimensional scaling (MDS), unlike other multivariate methods, starts with non-metric data pertaining to perceived similarities or dissimilarities among a set of objects such as brands, buyers, competitors, and so on. The main objective of using the technique is to obtain a configuration showing the relations among the various objects analysed. The attitudinal or perceived similarities (or dissimilarities) among a set of objectives are statistically transformed into distances by placing these objects in a multidimensional space.[26]

Two types of MDS exist: perception and preference scaling. Perception scaling needs similarity data and provides a single space of objects/stimuli. Preference scaling needs preference data of the type: A is preferred to B and B is preferred to C: A > B > C. Preference scaling may be projected into a similarity space to provide a joint space of objects/stimuli and preference vectors or ideal points.

Multidimensional scaling has been applied in strategic marketing in areas such as product positioning, market segmentation, large-scale new product development models, the modelling and evaluation of buying behaviour and the determination of more effective marketing mix combinations. MDS may also be applied in the product development process by finding consumer attitudes towards various product attributes. In such applications the technique can:

(1) construct an object configuration in a product space (perception);
(2) discover the shape of the distribution of consumers' ideal points in this space; this is a joint space of perceptions and preferences;
(3) identify likely opportunities ('market gaps') for new or modified products.

Correspondence analysis

Correspondence analysis is a visual or graphical technique for representing multidimensional tables. It is in fact a 'picture' of a 'table'. It can often be impossible to identify any relationships in a table and very difficult to account for what is happening. Correspondence analysis unravels the table and presents data in an easy-to-understand chart. This technique is particularly useful to identify market segments, track brand image, position a product against its competition and determine who non-respondents in a survey most closely resemble.[27]

Correspondence analysis provides a joint space, that is, a configuration of both objects/stimuli and attributes of these stimuli, whereas multidimensional scaling of similarity data provides a single space with only objects/stimuli.

Multiple regression analysis

Multiple regression is the best known and most frequently used type of dependence analysis. Metric data are needed, both for the dependent and the independent variables. For the independent variables, dummies may be used: variables with only two values, for example the presence or absence of an attribute. With a set of independent or predictor variables a proportion of the variance in the dependent variable may be explained. The dependent variable may be: sales, market share, store traffic, number of visitors to an exhibition and transportation time. Independent variables may be: number of stores, weather, price, distance, number of households in a catchment area, and other factors that may explain or predict the dependent variable.

Regression analysis may be used in an explanatory and predictive sense. Regression may be used to explain variations in a dependent variable, for example to explain the number of visitors to an attraction park with variations in the weather, holidays, distances and prices. It may also be used to predict the number of visitors, if some of these environmental or marketing variables change.

Multiple discriminant analysis

Discriminant analysis is a useful technique to differentiate within groups and predict group membership characteristics. Applications include uncovering characteristics of groups most likely to purchase products and determining the qualities of first-time customers to predict repeat business. Discriminant analysis may be used to validate the clusters obtained from cluster analysis.

Discriminant analysis involves deriving linear combinations of the independent variables that will discriminate between a priori defined groups in such a way that the misclassification error rates are minimized. Discriminant analysis is the appropriate statistical technique when the dependent variable is categorical (nominal, thus non-metric distinction between groups) and the independent variables are metric. Discriminant analysis is very similar to regression, with the only difference that the dependent variable is categorical rather than metric. Discriminant analysis is widely used in market segmentation, studies of the diffusion and adoption of new products, and consumer behaviour analysis, and may also be applied for consumer credit scoring.

Analysis of variance

Analysis of variance (ANOVA) is another well-known type of dependence analysis, related to experimental research designs. In an experimental design, differences between conditions are studied. For instance, in some stores the assortment is changed (group B), in other stores prices are lowered (group C) and in a third group of stores nothing is changed (group A). If the three groups of stores are similar with regard to other factors, ANOVA may be used to test the significance of the sales differences between the three groups of stores. In a more complex, 2×2 design, four types of stores may be distinguished, according to the four groups in Table 8.9. In group D, both the assortment and the prices are changed. In an ANOVA analysis, the significance of the effects of assortment and prices may be tested, as well as the effect of a combination of both effects (interaction effect). In order to study the interaction effect, the inclusion of group D is necessary.

Table 8.9 A 2×2 experimental design.

	Standard assortment	*New assortment*
Standard prices	Group A	Group B
Lower prices	Group C	Group D

Conjoint analysis

Conjoint analysis is concerned with the joint effect of two or more independent variables on the ordering of a dependent variable. It is rooted in traditions of experimentation. A definition of conjoint analysis must proceed from its underlying assumption that a composition rule may be established to predict a response variable from two or more predictor variables. Conjoint analysis, like multidimensional scaling, is concerned with the measurement of psychological judgements, such as consumer preferences.

For conjoint (trade-off) analysis products are essentially bundles of attributes such as price and colour. Conjoint analysis software generates a deck of cards each of which combine levels of these product attributes. Respondents are asked to sort the cards generated into an order of preference. Conjoint analysis then assigns a value to each level and produces a 'ready-reckoner' to calculate the preference for each chosen combination. Conjoint analysis can be used to design packaging, establish price, rank a hypothetical product against existing competitors already in the market and suggest modifications to existing products which would help to strengthen a product's performance.

It seems that various types of marketing planning models and other procedures using judgemental estimates in a formal manner might benefit from the utilization of conjoint models in additive or, more generally, polynomial form. Moreover, buyer preferences for multi-attribute items may also be decomposed into part-worth evaluations in a similar manner. Potential areas of application for conjoint analysis include product design, new product concept descriptions, price–value relationships, attitude measurement, promotional congruence testing and the study of functional versus symbolic product characteristics. The output of conjoint analysis is frequently employed in additional analyses. Since most studies collect full sets of data at the individual respondent level, individual utility functions and importance weights can be computed. This fosters two additional types of analyses:

(1) market segmentation
(2) strategic simulation of new factor-level product combinations.

AID and CHAID

Most types of cluster analysis start with single cases and form clusters by adding similar cases to an existing cluster. These types of cluster analysis are of a 'growth form'. Automatic Interaction Detection (AID) is a type of cluster analysis in which large samples are broken down into homogeneous subsets. AID and Chi AID (CHAID) are cluster techniques with a dependent variable. Based on scores on the dependent variable, clusters are formed that differ maximally between clusters on the dependent variable. The program develops clusters in which the objects or cases differ minimally. At the same time, the differences between the clusters should be large. Large samples are needed to apply AID or CHAID. The clustering stops if the clusters become too small or if the differences between the clusters become too small.

The AID program can only split a group into two subgroups. With CHAID other splits are also possible, based on a Chi-square criterion.

An example of a dependent variable is the usage of a brand in a large sample. In the total sample this usage rate may be 16.5%. With the AID program subgroups are distinguished with significantly lower or higher usage rates.[28] In this example the sample is split according to sociodemographic variables such as geography, age, level of education, income and occupation. The highest rate occurs, for instance, with women, living in North-Central USA, and with an income under $12,000. The lowest usage rate is with men with a low education.

AID and CHAID are techniques for market segmentation.

LISREL

Linear Structural Relations (LISREL) is an overall, both structural and dependence, multivariate technique.[29] All types of metric multivariate analysis may be regarded as specific cases of LISREL. With LISREL the researcher should have an a priori model of how the variables and factors are related. This model or a number of models can be tested with LISREL. The model with the best fit is then assumed to be the 'best' model to represent the data. Usually it is recommended to do single regression and/or factor analysis, whatever is appropriate, before testing the thus developed model with LISREL. An example is a study on consumer expectations.[30] In this study a number of survey questions were reduced to two underlying factors, which is similar to factor analysis. These factors were used to predict the dependent variables: consumption of durables, non-durables, credit, and saving. The latter is similar to regression analysis.

8.16 Stage 6: Communicating results

In the same way that it was suggested in Stage 1 that communication between decision maker and researcher is important for the research program's objectives to be clarified and agreed, so the same applies at the end of the process. Results have to be communicated to the users of research in such a way that their meaning is not distorted and so that they answer the brief as originally agreed.

8.17 Conclusions

Earlier chapters discussed a variety of topics for which specific research techniques are appropriate and this chapter has explored some of these research issues. They include motivation and attitude research (relevant to Chapters 2 and 3, respectively) and segmentation, targeting and positioning research (including mulitivariate approaches) which is relevant to Chapters 6 and 7.

The more general aspects of the consumer research process, such as problem definition, sources of data and data collection methods and techniques, are of great relevance to the study and analysis of consumer behaviour because it is often through these that our knowledge and understanding of such behaviour is provided – whether it be for consumer behaviour in a fairly general sense or related to the purchase of a specific brand (see further reading on p. 230).

This concludes our coverage of the market analysis theme. We now provide some Clippings from the marketing press and Cases which extend some of these issues and can be used for seminar and assignment work. The next and final part of the book moves into the marketing mix elements of product, price, distribution and promotion and discusses these in terms of the relevance of consumer behaviour issues for these elements.

Endnotes

1. G. Zaltman and P.C. Burger, 1975.
2. L. England, 1980.
3. M. Millward, 1987.
4. P. Krauser, 1981.
5. C.M. Crawford, 1970.
6. M. Collins, 1981; G. White, 1982; J. Weitz, 1982.
7. P. Hyett, 1982.
8. S.M. Shugan and J.R. Hauser, 1977.
9. P.M. de Almeida, 1980.
10. E. Dichter, 1964.
11. M. Haire, 1950.
12. E. Dichter, 1964.
13. V. Packard, 1957.
14. C.E. Osgood, G.J. Suci and P.H. Tannenbaum, 1957.
15. This method is adopted from the personality constructs of G.A. Kelly, 1955.
16. R. Likert, 1932.
17. M. Fishbein and I. Ajzen, 1975.
18. L.L. Thurstone, 1929, and L.L. Thurstone and E.J. Chave, 1929. For an overview of attitude scale construction, see A.L. Edwards, 1957.
19. H.W. Boyd, R. Westfall and S.E. Stasch, 1977.
20. H.W. Boyed, et al. 1977.
21. M. Haire, 1950.
22. CACI, 1979.
23. R.L. Kahn and C.F. Cannell, 1968.
24. SPSS for Windows, Release 6.1, *Base System User's Guide, Advanced Statistics, Professional Statistics*, 1995.
25. J.F. Hair, Jr, R.E. Anderson, R.L. Tatham and B.J. Grablowsky, 1984.
26. P.E. Green, F.J. Carmone and S.M. Smith, 1989.
27. M.J. Greenacre, 1984.
28. H. Assael, 1970.
29. A. Diamantopoulos, 1994.
30. W.F. Van Raaij and H.J. Gianotten, 1990.

For further discussion of consumer research, see:

Moutinho L. and Evans M. (1992) *Applied Marketing Research*. Addison-Wesley
Chisnall P. (1994) *Marketing Research*. McGraw-Hill
Crimp M. and Wong V. (1995) *The Marketing Research Process*. Prentice-Hall

Part 3 Clippings from the marketing press and Cases

Case 1   Psychographics – self-concept
Case 2   PRIME Magazine
Clipping 1 Actor slates advertising over stereotyping
Clipping 2 Fear of failure drives yuppies
Clipping 3 Filling in the gaps on Gen X

Case 1 Psychographics –self-concept

There follows a mini-case on the use of self-concept segmentation in fashion markets. (Adapted by the authors from Loudon and Della Bitta: *Consumer Behaviour*, McGraw Hill, 1988.)

The research reported here reflects a self-concept study leading to the creation of a marketing mix for a new perfume based on matching brand image with self-image. The cosmetics company had recently 'taken over' another company and, amongst other products, therefore acquired a perfume. This was to be re-launched on the basis of the following self-concept research.

Respondents were shown three 'advertisements' for perfume. The advertised 'brands' were given three different themes. One used a prestigious, sophisticated theme (the possible brand name here was 'La Vogue'), the second a sensual, slightly naughty theme ('Vamp') and the third a romantic theme (Romano). Each 'advertisement' included appropriate narrative, picture sequences and models.

The results are shown in the tables.

Respondents were asked to position their reactions on each of the scales. In Table 1 we see how respondents perceived the three 'brands'. There was, of course, no difference between the perfumes in a chemical sense – the three advertisements were merely three different ways of marketing the same product.

Table 1 Brand images.

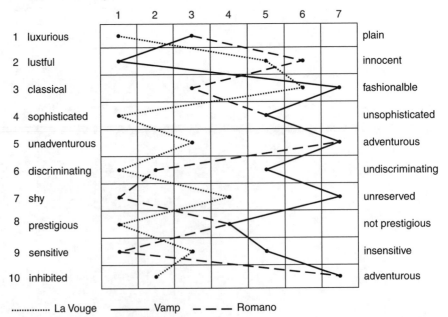

.... La Vouge   ——— Vamp   – – – Romano

Table 1 shows their perceptions of their preferred 'brand'. Table 2 shows how those respondents who preferred each brand saw themselves and Table 3 shows how respondents would want other people to see them – that is, their self-image, but the 'aspirational' self-image in a social context.

Table 2 Self-images.

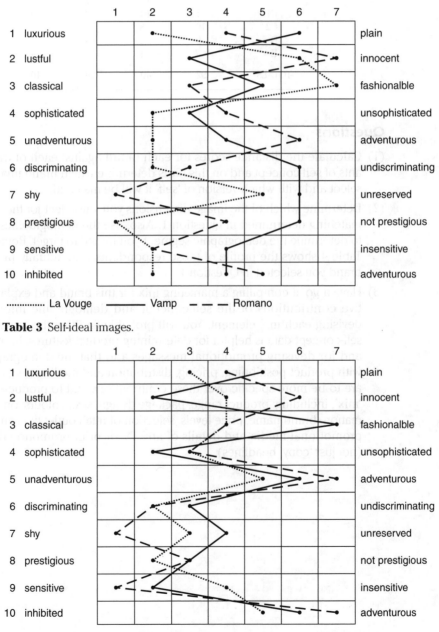

.... La Vouge   ———— Vamp   – – – Romano

Table 3 Self-ideal images.

.... La Vouge   ———— Vamp   – – – Romano

Table 4 Demographic profile of respondents who preferred the brand selected according to the question.

Socio-econs	Age			
	18–25	26–35	36–49	50+
A	14	8	8	5
B	22	11	7	3
C1	21	10	9	2
C2	19	8	5	–
D	9	2	–	–
E	7	1	–	–
TOTALS	92	40	29	10

Questions

(1) Calculate the distance scores for each brand against each of the two variants of self-concept and on this basis determine which brand image you will select and with which version of 'self' it will be matched.

(2) Determine which of the image dimensions you will select for the 'brand-self' matching determined in Question 1. Also, use the demographics in Table 4 to determine the demographic segment you intend to target. Remember that Table 4 shows the profile of those respondents who actually preferred the brand you selected in Question 1.

(3) Have a go at compiling a marketing mix for this brand and explain the relative contributions of the self-concept and demographic information in devising each mix element. You will probably find that the 'psychographic' self-concept data is helpful for determining product features, brand imagery and for devising promotional messages and that the demographics help with product positioning, pricing, distribution and media selection, but you are to be more specific over these contributions and to produce a detailed 'mix', including: product range, package design, size, colours, on pack information, brand name, price levels, selection of retail outlet type and location, promotional media and details of any TV or print promotional messages (not just 'copy' headlines).

Case 2 PRIME Magazine

Introduction

This case introduces a situation related to the launch of a new magazine targeted to readers who are 45–69 years old – the 'Grey market'. The company's strategy relies on a niching approach. The market for PRIME is expected to grow from 11 million to 14 million by the year 2000 and the company is expecting a paid circulation of 50,000 within five years.

The analysis of the case study involves critical issues such as the use of profile segmentation and a concentration targeting strategy, strategic positioning, a direct mail campaign and free sampling.

Case: PRIME Magazine

Between the baby boomers and the senior citizens lies a market in need of its own magazine. That is the feeling of Peter Johnson, managing director of EuroPress Publications, Cardiff, Wales, who plans to issue the first copy of PRIME in September. The national magazine will be targeted to consumers who are 45–69 years old.

Few established consumer magazines concentrate on the 'Grey market', said John F. Morgan, publishing operations officer for Europress. 'We are not going after established magazines claiming we are coming out with a better product', Morgan said. 'We are creating our own new market niche.'

Dubbed the 'Grey' generation, the magazine's audience is active and dynamic, said publisher Johnson. They take care of their health and they are looking for adventure, entertainment and enjoyment. And they have the means to achieve their goals.

The magazine's target audience, Johnson said, possesses 56.3% of the nation's net worth and 51% of all discretionary income. Morgan said nearly 36% of PRIME potential audience have household incomes of £30,000 a year, while 23% have incomes of PRIME'S £37,000 or more.

The median age of readers will probably be 55, Johnson said, just about the time when their children are through college, their houses are paid off and they are at the peak of their earnings curve.

Figure 1 describes the composition of the 'grey market', based on information compiled by Europress Publications, publishers of PRIME. Today's sales depend on the three newly recognized factors listed.

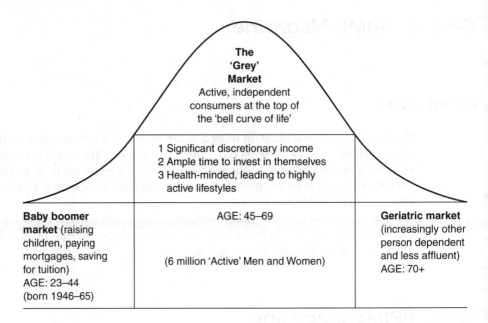

Figure 1 Composition of the 'Grey market'.

This grey generation also spends more liberally than any other group, according to Morgan. He cited a study by Meredith & Co. that showed the group does a lot of brand switching and relies heavily on magazines for information.

The market for PRIME is expected to grow from 11 million to 14 million by the year 2000. The magazine is guaranteeing a circulation of 30,000 at launch, and Morgan said he expects a paid circulation of 50,000 within five years. He also pointed out that the current early-forties generation does not differ that much from the 'grey' generation, 'the market is 25 years long'.

The magazine is not for the retirement crowd, Morgan said, and the editorial content will be 'actively upbeat'. About 30% of the contents will be devoted to 'challenges', with similar proportions covering health and fitness and travel and adventure. The rest is going to be 'pure fun', editor Michael Hurley said.

Challenges can include anything that enriches living, said Hurley. The fitness content will steer readers away from high-intensity exercises that lead to injuries, and highlight those that create well-being with fewer aches and breaks.

The magazine is designed to broaden readers' horizons and help them get involved in new activities. Hurley said articles will cover such topics as trekking in the Australian Outback and registering for a semester at Oxford University.

'It's a magazine for doers, not spectators, for scuba-divers, not couch potatoes', Hurley said.

Prospects selected from upscale mailing lists will receive a letter in August informing them that PRIME is on the way. Two days later, the magazine will arrive with a discount subscription invoice and preview of future contents.

'We will show them what we have to offer', Morgan said, 'they will be hold-ing the actual magazine in their hands, not a fancy mailing piece containing only promises.'

Ten days later they will get a reminder letter. Sixty days later, they will receive the second issue and a second sign-up letter if they have not mailed in their cheque.

Questions

(1) What is the relevance of this segmentation approach to PRIME Magazine?

(2) What are the benefits of a single-segment concentration targeting strategy?

(3) What are the key elements of strategic positioning that should be considered by the PRIME Magazine?

(4) How could PRIME Magazine take an operational approach to product positioning?

(5) What are the key considerations to be taken into account when launching a direct mail campaign?

(6) What concerns should the company have in relation to the policy of giving free samples of the new magazine?

Clipping 1 Actor slates advertisers over stereotyping

Key issues

Marketing to Women

Stereotyping

Marketing to Racial Minorities

Questions

(1)   In 1990 the ASA published the findings of in-depth and lengthy research into the use of female stereotypes in advertising. Do you think 'it is time to treat the consumer with respect'?

(2)   'Most consumer goods are bought by women, so what's wrong with so much advertising being aimed at them ?'

(3)   What are the issues involved with the use of stereotyping in 'sexual'/'sexist' ways ?

(4)   Can any of these aspects of marketing to women hold any general implications for marketing to racial minorities?

Marketing 1 March 1990

Actor slates advertisers over stereotyping

Call for an end to sexism and racism in ad awards ceremony

Flake ad . . . turning an innocent pursuit into an overtly sexual act

By Charlotte Smith

Advertisers take note – yet another high-profile media person has spoken out against the evils of stereotyping in advertising. But this time the challenge struck at the very heart of advertising principles – its "aspirational" quality.

After film maker David Puttnam's elegant plea for social responsibility to the advertising world last year, Art Malik, the prominent actor who starred in Jewel in the Crown, urged advertisers at last week's Golden Break Awards to act responsibly with the images they present. He urged advertisers to look beyond familiar issues of sexism and race to other areas.

His comments presented an implicit challenge to the Advertising Standards Authority (ASA), whose report on women in advertising, three years in the making and published this week, is already being branded as thoroughly predictable.

Was it necessary, asks Rupert Howell, from Howell Henry Chaldecott Lury, to spend £170,000 interviewing more than 2000 people to find out that they object to ads which turn innocent pursuits, such as the eating of a chocolate bar, into an overtly sexual act?

Dave Waters, who made the Flake ad for Gold Greenlees Trott, claims the message is thoroughly "realistic". The ad features a woman in a silk negligèe eating a flake. Waters agrees the ad is overtly sexual, but not sexist.

Seven out of ten women in the ASA report don't agree. More than anything, argues Howell whose agency's Maxell ads won the Golden Break's best campaign award, this type of ad is blatantly unoriginal. "The time has come to treat the consumer with respect."

Howell points to Saatchi's campaign for British Rail which won the Golden Break best commercial award last year as being an "excellent example of originality". The advertisement features people from a range of ethnic groups.

The ASA report has just touched the tip of the stereotypical iceberg.

Part 3, Clipping 1

Clipping 2 Fear of failure drives yuppies

Key Issues

Psychographic segmentation

Questions

(1)   Give examples of some demographic variables that could be used by marketers to measure the potentialities of this typology of seven psychographic subsegments.

(2)   Give examples of some product or service categories that could be usefully matched to this psychographic classification.

(3)   What are some of the limitations associated with the use of lifestyle segmentation?

Marketing April 1987 **(29)**

Fear of failure drives yuppies

Yuppies tend to be driven by a fear of failure and a sence of 'striving conformity', according to a new report. However, the now hackneyed label conceals a raft of different attitudes and lifestyles.

The report from Questel, the qualitative research subsidiary of Audits of Great Britain (AGB), divides the young urban professional group into seven distinct sub-groups.

• The Traditional Striver is cautious and conservative. Ambitions are geared towards a comfortable but hectic home life with lots of dinner parties and when the time is right, children. Tastes are traditional and understated.

• The Blatant Competitor is highly ambitious and a conspicuous consumer of anything which reflects his/her wealth. He/she is a trendsetter and has to have the latest and best of everything.

• The Embarrassed Capitalist is the yuppie with a social conscience, a touch embarrassed by his/her success. Has little interest in dressing fashionably and being seen in the right places, but has a weakness for some traditional yuppie symbols such as fast cars.

• The Hedonist feels his/her wealth is transitory so aims to make the most of the present by doing as little work as possible for as much pay as possible. A highly social creature who spends freely on entertainment and runs up huge credit card debts.

• The Flash Harry is keen to shake off his/her working class origins. Insecure in this new environment he/she accumulates prestige brands, spends heavily on status symbols, and avoids the individualistic purchases.

• The Armchair Materialist is also a product of the working classes. Family life conforms to the stereotype of the male breadwinner and the housewife. He has little interest in fashion and eating out, and is wary of credit. Priorities are a modern, well equipped home and holidays.

• The Sloane Ranger is the seventh and most familiar of the yuppie breeds. He has inherited a wealthy lifestyle and lives in London.

Part 3, Clipping 2

Clipping 3 Filling in the Gaps on Gen X

Key issues

Segmentation of youth markets
Consumer individualism and market fragmentation
Researching youth markets

Questions

(1) What are the implications for consumer behaviour and marketing of the individualism of Generation X?

(2) How can the values and buying behaviour of this segment be properly researched?

Marketing 20 October 1994

Filling in the gaps on Gen X

The youth market is splintering. So, who are your targets? Cathy Bond searches them out

Researchers may replace questionnaires with off-the-wall opinions gleaned from nightclubbers grabbed from the dance floor - "hot data" as ad agencies call it.

Friday night and nowhere to go? Hang around outside a very trendy nightclub. You probably won't get in, but you could amuse yourself by observing the antics of other punter-watchers – a media crew, perhaps, doing another feature on dissipated youth – and maybe a market research team.

They are pursuing a strange hybrid breed known by various names; lately, "slackers". Aged 16 or older, they've opted out of the "loadsamoney" ethos and reputedly spend their time slumped in front of *Beavis and Butt-head* or MTV, seriously nightclubbing or at a rave until morning. Future prospects, we're told, stretch no further than the next CD or video fantasy game.

But they also watch a lot of mainstream TV; eat, drink, shop, and read enough magazines to push the combined circulation of Emap youth titles, such as *Sky* magazine and *Looks*, past the two million mark. Many of them play a sport; some get their kicks joyriding.

Slackers? It reads like a pretty hectic lifestyle. But according to British Market Research Bureau's Youth TGI panel only 16% of 15- to 19-year-olds say they ever go to a rave: lots more watch *Neighbours*, *Red Dwarf* and *Birds of a Feather*, which are hardly subversive material.

There is a jumble of stereotypes here, in fact, and being young, they will mutate much faster than marketers would like. Nonetheless, they represent the future for owners of big brands – companies which need to know their target markets inside out.

Marketers need the data, but does traditional research provide it? It is, after all, structured and formal – not words which readily link with a teenage market. Yet the "Youth 15-19 years Youth TGI" – a mailed questionnaire of up to 60 pages – gets an 86% response. "So much for Generation X," comments BMRB's sales and marketing manager Geoff Wicken.

However, some researchers replace questionnaires and conventional discussion groups with off-the-wall opinions gleaned from nightclubbers grab-bed from the dance floor – "hot data", as ad agencies call it. Tabloids love it and give page spreads to the colourful (if not necessarily accurate) results.

There is a role for on-site research: Saturday night at the disco is a fact of life for drinks marketers, for example. Market re-

Part 3, Clipping 3

searchers can only try to impose some non-intrusive discipline over what generally turns into a fairly boozy session, but as Sue Swalwell, a director of NPD agency Craton Lodge and Knight explains, it is the only way to replicate the consumer's learning curve for a new drink product. "We'll ask first about image, then about taste, and later on in the evening any dissonance between the drink itself and what it's cracked up to be may surface," she says. However, the value of the responce obviously depends on the state of inebriation."

It seems that almost every research technique has been tried out on the multi-faceted youth sector in an effort to pin it down. At school age most children are at least physically in one place, but once they hit 16, the home-orientated unit begins to break down. Within a couple of years there is a disparate group either working, studying or unemployed, at home or independently.

Adam Lury, a partner in Howell Henry Chaldecott Lury, does not accept the popular media concept of "slackers".

"Creating a focus group won't help you to understand it," he says. "Insight comes through watching people in the street, in shops, in the pub – inevitably advertisers will take this one step further. But if you get out the video camera, you stop thinking about these people as real people: they are subjects on TV."

"If you are talking about abstractions like advertising image, a pub, for example, would set up the wrong environment," says Prosper Riley-Smith of market researchers Davis Riley-Smith. "They wouldn't see the TV ads in the pub. Try to set up a sensible discussion, and all you'd get would be a riot – it's all fun and games to them."

Yet a discussion group is an ideal platform for a socially confident young person with views to give and money to spend.

Although Riley-Smith admits that the forum is "desperately artificial", he believes it is a medim that young people understand and thus are no more likely to give false responses than if they are tackled in front of their friends on home ground; maybe less so.

"We don't subscribe to the theory that they lie," he says. "They may be shy, but they are certainly opinionated and are trying to work their way into society, not out of it."

"Let's not call them anarchic," says Graham Hutton, director of research at CIA Media UK. "They are at the leading edge: highly critical of mainstream values and with the confidence to say so. The rebellious bovver boys are another matter. They are followers, not leaders, hiding behind the persona of their peer group."

This could be the teenager who can buy clothes with three-figure price tags, because he steals car radios. Sit him in a room with a two-way mirror and tape recorder, and he will probably

Part 3, Clipping 3

assume that it is a police set-up.

Earlier this year the ad agency Burkitt Bryant Weinreich Clients & Company briefed a market research team to recruit young people who live on the borders of crime, to gather material for a client pitch.

"It was a normal qualitative group discussion," says BBWC&C planning director Simon Silvester, "but we had to use a church hall rather than a house, because of fears that they would be casing the joint. In fact, the vicar insisted on being there to make sure the chairs didn't go missing."

The interviewers were deliberately scruffy, and tapes were banned. "It pays just to listen," says Silvester. "There's a great sense of frustration because they equate social status with money, and the only way they can get that is to steal."

In fact, social research is probably the most difficult topic to handle because respondents can be highly conscious of how their views may affect how others see them. "It's important to give them things to comment on, and ask them why," says Swalwell. "Free discussion leads to self-con-

sciousness and sniggering."

Marketing Direction, which has been analysing the youth sector since 1979, points to two distinct developments. The age when factors such as media consumption, sexual and social awareness start to matter continues to fall, according to director Ricky Baxter, and young people can see quite clearly how they are being manipulated by marketers.

"It's that last element which may account in part for the myth that youth – particularly 16-to 24-year-olds – are beyond communication or recruitment to research by traditional means," says Baxter.

Despite this group's unwillingness to conform, he points out, "they all fall within the obtainable universe from which to draw research. So while it may be quicker to recruit a sub-culture group at an appropriate venue or location, these people do not disappear when not at a rave.

They go home to their parents, flat or squat; they use public transport, they walk and shop in public places".

This age group's behaviour as individual consumers is affected by a rich and varied pattern of lifestyles. The slice-of-life technique, an advertising staple, certainly adds colour.

But for detailed information, say the researchers, you need a formal framework – and don't assume that this will horrify the target group.

"The only sensible way is to hand-pick focus groups," says Ian Zak, joint managing director of Business Development Partnership.

"That done, they won't pull punches. At this age they are prepared to speak out."

Lury has an interesting theory. "The baby-boomers have created 'slackers', because it puts themselves into context, as the focus of power and influence," he says. "Twenty years ago teenagers as a whole were a mystery. Now those teenagers have grown up and they need a new generation gap to give them a sense of identity."

Part 4

Consumer behaviour and the marketing mix

Part 4

Consumer behaviour
and the marketing
mix

9

Product strategy and consumer behaviour

Chapter objectives

(1) To focus on key aspects derived from the interaction between product strategy and consumer behaviour.

(2) To analyse the characteristics of classes of consumer goods and related strategic marketing considerations.

(3) To study critical product policy issues impacting on consumer behaviour: product environment, product attributes, branding, packaging and label information.

(4) To discuss important concepts related to consumer satisfaction, dissatisfaction and the disconfirmation paradigm.

(5) To introduce specific product behaviours, such as product contact and brand loyalty.

9.1   Introduction

The product element of the marketing mix is considered by many to be the most important element. For example, Booz, Allen and Hamilton, a leading US business consulting company, noted a number of years ago, 'if it is accepted that products are the medium of business conduct, then business strategy is fundamentally product planning'.

A major task in product planning concerns the matching of products and services with consumer markets. While products and services may indeed be the medium of business conduct from the producer's viewpoint, the exchange of consumer assets for products is the acid test that determines whether products will succeed or fail. Not only physical products but also services are included in this chapter. Often market transactions involve a combination of products and services; for instance, leasing a car is a combination of a product (car) and a service contract (maintenance and replacement of the car).

A physical product is made in the factory. It is the generic product. Through branding, packaging, image formation and services it becomes an 'augmented product'. The technical and market potential of a product create a 'potential product'. The potential product (or service) includes all future options and capabilities of a product that can be developed through marketing strategy. In this sense, McDonald's is a potential product; a brand and proposition that possesses many future options, for instance business lunches, party service, catering, and breakfast on the route to work.

This chapter focuses on product and service strategy in the context of consumer cognitions, attitudes, behaviours, satisfaction and environmental factors. However, before delving into these issues we provide an overview of the more general marketing strategy context within which these consumer-related dimensions must be viewed by the organization.

9.2 Marketing strategy

Table 9.1 provides a summary of not only the product element, but also price, distribution, promotion and marketing research and some generalized strategy issues relating to consumers and the market. This is a useful framework at this stage because it contributes to the argument that it is the quality of the marketing strategy employed as well as more micro factors associated with each mix element *per se* that has an important bearing on whether or not a product is a success. At the brand level, the image or symbolism a brand carries is often the only competitive advantage that a company has to offer. This frequently happens because in many product classes, the brands offered are relatively homogeneous in their functional utility to the consumer.

In many cases, a favourable image is created through the other elements of the marketing mix. Marketing communication is commonly used to create a favourable image for the brand by pairing it with positively evaluated stimuli, such as attractive settings or scenery. In addition, marketing communication informs consumers as to what attributes they should be looking for in the product class and emphasizes the superiority of the brand in terms of those attributes. It is well known that only a few consumers can tell the difference in taste of various brands of beer in a blind test. Thus, many commercials try to teach consumers that a particular brand tastes great, or at least as good as more expensive beers. Brand image is a key determinant of beer brand choice, although many consumers would likely disavow image and insist that taste is the most important consideration for them.

Price can also create brand images as well as provide a functional relative advantage. In terms of brand images, high prices can connote high quality for

Table 9.1 Marketing strategy elements.[1]

Objective	To get trial	Establish strong brand position with distributors and users	Maintain and strengthen customer loyalty	Seek remaining profit
Product	Few models, high quality	Modular, flexible, more models for segments emerging	Tighten lines not serving good markets; product improvement and differentiation	Reduce line to major profit-producing products
Price	Good value, trade discounts	Long price line from low to premium-priced	Attention to broadening market; promotional pricing to extend brand coverage	Maintain profit levels without regard to share of market
Distribution	Exclusive or selective	Intensive and extensive; quick service to dealers; high dealer inventory	Intensive and extensive; quick service to dealers; low dealer inventory.	Phase out marginal dealers
Promotion	Create awareness, get early trial; fairly heavy advertising and free samples	Create strong brand awareness and preference: maximum use of mass media	Maintain and strengthen customer-dealer relations; continue mass media, sales promotion	Rapid phaseout; sustain enough to sell profitable volume only
Marketing research	Discover weaknesses: identify emerging segments	Market positioning, market gaps: product gaps	Attention to product improvement; search for broader market and new promotion themes	Determine point of product elimination

some products; and it is often stated that consumers perceive a relationship between price and quality. The higher prices of Levi 501 reinforces the advertising and branding imagery to position the line. Price can also be used to position a brand as good value for the money, for example supermarket own labels are often as good as manufacturer brands (and usually made by the same manufacturers) but much cheaper. As a functional relative advantage, through vast economies of scale and large market shares, a company can sometimes sustain a price advantage that no competitor can meet.

Also, a variety of distribution tactics can be used to gain a relative advantage. Good site locations and a large number of outlets are important advantages in the fast-food market and in the markets for other products and services. Also, a variety of in-store stimuli, such as displays, can offer products at least a temporary relative advantage. So we believe it important to include this more general, holistic and strategic mind-set for this Part of the book and in considering the issues we raise for each mix element over the next four chapters.

Table 9.2 shows the main characteristics of classes of consumer goods and some related key marketing considerations.

- Convenience goods are daily used and thus frequently bought goods with a minimum of effort. Examples are sugar, rice, tea, coffee and detergents.
- Shopping goods are usually durable goods for which consumers go shopping, comparing prices, attributes and qualities. Examples are furniture, videorecorders, washing machines and holiday trips.
- Speciality goods are goods with unique technical or image characteristics. Consumers often have a strong brand preference, for instance a Swatch, a Lacoste tennis shirt or a ticket for the U2 concert.

9.3 Product environment

This is concerned with those product-related stimuli that are attended to and comprehended by consumers. In general, the majority of these stimuli are received through the sense of sight, although there are many exceptions. For example, the way a stereo sounds or how a silk shirt feels also influence consumer cognitions, attitudes and behaviours. In this section, we will focus on two types of environmental stimuli: product attributes and packaging.

Product attributes

Products and product attributes are major stimuli that affect consumer cognitions, attitudes and behaviours. These attributes may be physical and concrete or psychosocial and subjective. Psychosocial attributes are, for instance, design and quality. Products are evaluated by consumers in terms of their own values,

Table 9.2 Characteristics of types of consumer goods and some marketing considerations.[2]

Characteristics and marketing considerations	Type of goods		
	Convenience	Shopping	Speciality
Characteristics			
1 Time and effort devoted by consumer to shopping	Very little	Considerable	Cannot generalize: may go to nearby store and exert minimum effort or may have to go to distant store and spend much time
2 Time spent planning the purchase	Very little	Considerable	Considerable
3 How soon want is satisfied after it arises	Immediately	Relatively long time	Relatively long time
4 Are price and quality compared?	No	Yes	No
5 Price	Low	High	High
6 Frequency of purchase	Usually frequent	Infrequent	Infrequent
7 Importance	Unimportant	Often very important	Cannot generalize
Marketing considerations			
1 Length of channel	Long	Short	Short to very short
2 Importance of retailer	Any single store is relatively unimportant	Important	Very important
3 Number of outlets	As many as possible	Few	Few; often only one in a market
4 Stock turnover	High	Lower	Lower
5 Gross margin	Low	High	High
6 Responsibility for advertising	Manufacturer's	Retailer's	Joint responsibility
7 Importance of point-of-purchase display	Very important	Less important	Less important
8 Advertising used	Manufacturer's	Retailer's	Both
9 Brand or store name important	Brand name	Store name	Both
10 Important of package	Very important	Less important	Less important

goals, beliefs and past experiences. Marketing and other information also influence whether purchase and use of the product is likely to be rewarding or not.

As argued before, products and services may be conceptualized in a means–end chain. Physical and psychosocial product attributes give rise to consequences or benefits. These benefits may be functional or psychosocial. For instance, a car can transport four passengers (functional benefit) and rides comfortably (psychosocial benefit). Product benefits have to match consumer values, goals and lifestyle, and may help to create these values and goals (Figure 9.1). For instance the possession of a car helps in realizing the value of being independent and mobile.

It is unlikely that many consumers would purchase a product or service based on the product/service attributes alone. The price of the product or service would likely be important. The store selling the product or service (and the store image) might be considered. In addition, the packaging, brand name and brand identification would likely be factors.

Products are made in factories, but brands are sold in the market. The brand name is thus an important marketing asset. Table 9.3 illustrates some of the characteristics of a good brand name. In fact, for many purchases, the image of the brand created through the non-product variables of price, promotion and channels of distribution may be the most critical determinant of purchase.

The brand name conveys meanings to consumers, even so-called meaningless words.[3] The fictive brand name Whummies probably fits better for breakfast cereals than for laundry detergents. On the other hand, Dehax is probably better for detergents than for cereals. The origin of many brand names may be related to the meaning structure, from attributes via benefits to values (Figure 9.1). Some examples of brand names related to levels of the meaning structure are:

(1) *Physical attribute*: Coca-Cola, dBase, Milka, Nescafé, Nuts and Swatch.
(2) *Psychosocial attribute*: Aquafresh, Crunchy, Dataflex, Fiat Tempra and Lätta (a light margarine).
(3) *Functional benefit*: Becel ('blood cholesterol lowering'), Freedent, Kleenex, Ray Ban, Wash & Go and WordPerfect.

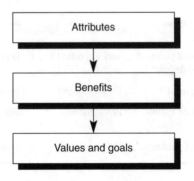

Figure 9.1 Means–end chain of a product or service.

Table 9.3 Characteristics of a good brand name.

Short and simple
Easy to spell and read
Easy to recognize and remember
Pleasing when read or heard, and easy to pronounce
Pronounceable in only one way
Pronounceable in all languages
Always timely (does not go out of date)
Adaptable to packaging or labelling needs
Legally available for use (not used by another firm)
Not offensive, obscene, or negative
Suggestive of product attributes, benefits, values or lifestyle
Adaptable to any advertising medium, especially billboards and television

(4) *Psychosocial benefit*: Easy Rider, Joy and Reliant.
(5) *Value*: Freedom, Lux, Proteq, Safeway and Securicor.
(6) *Lifestyle*: Avant Garde, Elite, Miller High Life, Nomad (tents and rucksacks), Playboy and Society Shop.

Packaging

Packaging is a key element of the product environment. Traditionally, four packaging objectives are considered.

(1) Packaging should protect the product as it moves from the producer through the channel to the consumer.
(2) Packaging should be economical and not add undue cost to the product.
(3) Packaging should allow convenient storage and use of the product by the consumer.
(4) Packaging can be used effectively to provide information to consumers and to promote the product to consumers.

In some cases, packaging has been used as the key to obtaining a relative advantage, for example in the case of Stackers and Pringles potato crisps which are stacked in their tall tube package rather than loose in bags. In other examples, mature products were differentiated on the basis of packaging alone, for example Mars chocolate milk drink, Lucozade and Ribena soft drinks.

Package colours

In addition to the nature of the package itself, it has been argued that package colours have an important impact on consumers' cognitions, attitudes and behaviours. This impact is more than just attracting attention by using eye-catching colours, like Smarties chocolate sweets and Paloma perfume. Rather, it has been argued that package colours connote meaning to consumers and can be used strategically.[4] For instance, the colour of the Ritz cracker box was changed to a deeper red trimmed with a thin gold band. This change was made to appeal to young, affluent consumers. Microsoft Corporation changed its software packages from green to red and royale blue, because consultants argued that green was not eye-catching and connoted frozen vegetables and chewing gum to consumers rather than high-tech software. Canada Dry changed the colour of its cans and bottles of ginger ale from red to green and white when consultants argued that red sent a misleading cola message to consumers. Canada Dry sales were reported to increase 25% after this colour change.

It has also been reported that consumer perceptions of products may change with a change in package colour, for example the new BP 'Supergreen' petrol. Similarly, consumers ascribed a sweeter taste to orange drinks when a darker shade of orange was used on the can or bottle. Philips batteries are sold in black–gold colours; these colours connote 'heaviness' and durability. Batteries with a white colour are perceived as 'cheap' and less durable.

Brand identification and label information

The brand identification and label information on the package, as well as on the product, provide additional stimuli for consideration by the consumer. Brand identification in many cases simplifies purchase for the consumer and makes the loyalty development process possible. For instance, brand names such as Jaguar, Calvin Klein, Chanel or Nina Ricci may well be discriminative stimuli for consumers.

Label information on packages includes: use instructions, contents, recipes, lists of ingredients or raw materials, warnings for use and care of the product, and the like. For some products, this information can strongly influence purchase behaviour. For example, consumers often carefully examine label information on over-the-counter drugs such as cough medicines. Health-conscious consumers often consult package information to determine the nutritional value, sugar content and calories in products such as cereals.

9.4 Product development

Product development is an important tool of marketers to keep present products up to date and to introduce new and hopefully successful products in the market place. A new product should satisfy consumer needs and wants better than existing products do. On the other hand, a new product should fit in the technical and marketing competencies of the firm. The producer should have the expertise to produce the product and should have access to marketing channels (distribution) to sell the product. However, more than one-third of all new products fail at the launch. On the average, sixteen product concepts are needed to retain on successful product.[5]

New product development is not only risky but also costly. More than 50% of the developmental costs are spent on idea generation, screening, and development of test products. if the product is introduced on the market, another 50% of the costs is spent on test marketing and product introduction with sales promotion activities to launch the new or improved product.

New products are needed to defend one's market share and brand name. producers with a large market share need to innovate to keep their product and their brand 'modern' and to stay ahead of the competition. Three criteria are crucial. New products need to be superior on an important attribute or benefit compared with competing products. The success rate of a product is highest if the new product is unique or superior or an important consumer benefit, if a good marketing strategy is employed, and if the technical production of the product is flawless.[6] The success rate was 90% if all three criteria were met (best situation). In the worst situation the success rate was only 7%.

New product development is a lengthy and time-consuming process. Research and development, technical, design and marketing departments are involved, often sequentially. This means that R&D hands the idea to a technical department for further development and testing. Then the design department starts working on the (ergonomic) form and design of the product. Finally, the marketing department develops a marketing plan, including advertising and sales promotion, to bring the product into the marketplace. This is actually not only time consuming but also the wrong sequence of activities.

First, market signals and other information should provide an idea of a consumer 'problem' that can be solved with a new product. Ideas for new products should come from the market and from consumers. However, it is not feasible to simply ask consumers which new products they need. A careful analysis of consumer problems and discomforts should bring the innovative idea of a new product. Further, these departments should not work sequentially, but as a new-product development team. Together with the new product a marketing and communication plan should be developed. An example is the development of the Walkman by Sony. Right from the beginning the price of the Walkman was set at a level most American and Japanese teenagers could afford from their pocket money. Within this price constraint the Walkman was developed. Later a broader range of Walkman products was developed, including more luxurious versions at a higher price. The basic benefit of the Walkman was that people could hear music without carrying a portable radio. This is very important for joggers and cyclists.

With increasing competition, it becomes more and more important to shorten the product development process. Departments should work together and decision making about continuation ('go' or 'no go') should be efficient and based on sound consumer research during the development and testing stages. Too much emphasis on short-term profits should be avoided. A new product often needs time to become accepted in the marketplace.

It is important that not only the technical, 'blind' product is tested, but also the 'augmented product' or the 'product as marketed', including branding, packaging and pricing. The first test is often a laboratory test on taste, smell, texture, handling and functionality. This can be done monadic (only the test product) or paired (test product with competing product(s)). A paired test is also used with testing a product improvement, testing the new against the old product. Analysis of variance and conjoint analysis are frequently used multivariate techniques for the analysis of the results of these tests.

Before introducing the new product in the marketplace, a test market is often selected. This is a city or region in which the product is sold in the stores and advertised in local newspapers. A test market should be a geographical area that is representative for the intended market. In The Netherlands, the cities of Delft or Dordrecht are often chosen for this purpose. Even a whole nation might be selected as a test market. Belgium is a good test market for many American or Japanese products before these products are introduced in the European Union. If the test market is not successful, either the product could be improved, the marketing plan could be adapted, or, in the case of complete failure, the launch of the product in the marketplace could be foregone altogether.

9.5   Services

The first sections of this chapter are about products, although services are also included in the use of this word. In this section, the distinctive characteristics of services will be highlighted. Services become more and more important: more than 60% of all consumer transactions involve services. Most of us work in a service industry and develop and disseminate knowledge (schools, universities, research institutes), check financial information (accountancy firms), give advice to companies (consultancy firms), secure safety and peace (army, police forces and security services), transport people and goods (transportation firms), manage products and brands (marketing and advertising managers), and manage companies and other organizations (general managers). Few of us actually make products or grow agricultural products. In a similar way, most consumers spend more time and money on services than on products. The major differences between products and services are given in Table 9.4.

Table 9.4 Differences between products and services.

	Products	Services
Phenomenon	Tangible	Intangible
Production	In advance, by machines	On the spot, by people
Specification	Mass produced, homogeneous	Tailor-made, heterogeneous differentiation
Cooperation of consumer	Transaction	Production and transaction
Credence	Low, for convenience good High, for speciality good	High

The four Ps of the marketing mix apply to services as well:

■ *Production* of a service is usually on the spot and in cooperation with the client.
■ The *price* of a standard service can be determined beforehand, such as the price of a train ticket. The price of non-standard services can often not be determined beforehand. Both parties may take the risk that the service may take more time and effort than expected. Think of a research agency planning a research project. They may agree to do the research at a negotiated budget, or they may count the hours spent on the project and declare these hours.
■ *Place:* The delivery of services may be at several places. Either the client comes to the service provider, for example the hairdresser's salon, the hairdresser may come to the home of the client. Information services may be handled through the telephone or a computer network such as the Internet.
■ *Promotion* is more important with services than with physical products. A physical product may be shown and demonstrated. The quality of a service has to be believed ('credence'). Marketing communication is thus needed to build up awareness and reputation.

Based on prior experience, on the experiences of others and on advertising, consumers expect a certain quality of a service, for instance a holiday trip. Service providers too (Figure 9.2) have an idea what consumers expect from their services (G1). Hopefully, the ideas of both parties are not too dissimilar. Gap G1 should not be large. The service provider develops guidelines and speci-

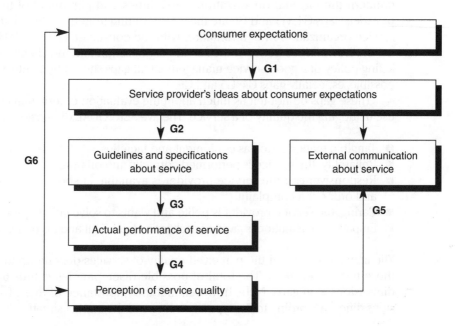

Figure 9.2 Sequence of steps in the provision of a service.

fications about his service based on the perceived consumer expectations (gap G2). Based on these guidelines and specifications the actual service is performed, often by people other than the manager who makes the guidelines and specifications (gap G3). A tour operator's hostesses perform their services based on the guidelines and instructions they receive from the management of the tour operator and on their own judgement. The logical sequence of the service is given in Figure 9.2. This model is very similar to the SERVQUAL model.[7]

Gap G4 is the consumer perception of the quality and other attributes of the actual service. Although the service provider may have done an excellent job, consumers do not always evaluate the quality correctly. A plumber may have done a good repair job, but consumers might evaluate the service quality by his friendliness or cooperativeness. Waiting time for instance, is an important factor for consumers in their quality judgement. Waiting too long in a queue at the post office creates irritation and a lower perception of the service quality.

Gap G5 is the discrepancy that may exist between the external communication (advertising and other communication) about the service and the actual service. The proposition of the advertising campaign should represent the service attributes and quality in a realistic manner, in order not to raise unrealistic expectations.

Gap G6 is the discrepancy between the prior consumer expectations and the perception of the actual service. Note that these prior expectations are not static. These expectations change during the service process, as the consumer gets more experience with the service. Expectations are then lowered or raised accordingly.

It is clear that gaps G1, G2 and G3 are inside the service organization and concern the internal organization, capabilities and personnel of the service provider. Gaps G4, G5 and G6 are the gaps resulting from the internal gaps of the service organization in confrontation with the consumer. Gaps G4, G5, and G6 are on the interface between the service organization and the client. In the marketing policy of a good service management all gaps should be made as small as possible, especially gaps G4, G5 and G6.

These gaps do not tell us much about the evaluation criteria that consumers use in judging the quality of a service. The five SERVQUAL dimensions are:[8]

■ Tangible matters, such as equipment and facilities.
■ Reliability: the service is performed correctly and on time.
■ Responsiveness: the service provider is available at short notice to handle and order or a complaint.
■ Caring: the service provider is polite and wants to solve client's problems.
■ Empathy: the attention is given to each individual client and his or her problems.

The actual quality and the perceived quality of services depend on the gaps on these five dimensions. The total of possible discrepancies is thus 6 gaps × 5 dimensions = 30 gaps. Note, however, that the importance of these five dimensions differs according to the type of service and the market situation.[9]

9.6 Product and service behaviours

From a strategic viewpoint, a major objective of marketing is to increase the probability and frequency of consumers coming into contact with products and services, purchasing and using them, and repurchasing them. We will discuss this objective in terms of three classes of consumer behaviour: product and service contacts and brand loyalty.

Product contact

In the context of a retail store purchase sequence, product contact involves behaviours such as locating the product in the store, examining it and taking it to the checkout counter. Product contacts can occur in other ways besides visits to retail stores, of course. Consumers may come into contact with products and experience them in a variety of other ways. They may receive a free sample in the mail or on their doorstep, or be given a sample in a store; they may borrow a product from a friend and use it. They may also receive a product as a gift, or they may simply see someone else using the product and experience it vicariously. Product contacts are generally more convincing than advertising contacts, because the product can be tried and observed in a realistic situation.

Service contact

A service contact is generally more intensive than a product contact, because the consumer takes an active part in the production of a service. A service contact is a personal contact between the service provider and the client and often better tailored to the needs and wishes of the customer than a product contact.

Brand loyalty

From a marketing strategy viewpoint, brand loyalty is a very important concept. Particularly in today's low-growth and highly competitive marketplace, retaining brand-loyal customers is critical for survival. Keeping customers is often a more efficient strategy than attracting new customers. Indeed, it is estimated that it costs six times more to attract a new customer than it does to hold a current one.[10]

A major problem that has affected the study of brand loyalty is the question of whether it is better to conceptualize this variable as a cognitive, attitudinal or behavioural phenomenon. As a cognitive phenomenon, brand loyalty is thought of as an internal commitment to purchase and repurchase a particular brand. As a attitudinal phenomenon it is a preference for a brand. As a behavioural phenomenon, brand loyalty is simply repeat purchase behaviour. All three approaches (cognitive, attitudinal and behavioural) to studying brand loyalty have their merits and interact with each other. Brand loyalty can be defined as repeat purchase intention and as behaviour. While the major focus of this discussion is on brand loyalty as a behaviour, it should be emphasized that cognitive processes strongly influence the development and maintenance of this behaviour.

In some cases, brand loyalty may be the result of extensive cognitive activity and decision making. A consumer may seriously compare and evaluate many makes and brands of cars, conclude that a Ford Fiesta is the perfect car, and purchase a new one every few years. In other cases, brand-loyal behaviour may occur without the consumer ever comparing alternative brands. A consumer may eat Yoplait yogurt as a child, and purchase and use the product throughout life without ever considering other brands. Yet even in this case, cognitive activity must occur. Decisions have to be made about where and when to purchase the product; some knowledge of the product and its availability must be activated from memory; intentions to purchase it and satisfaction influence the purchase behaviours.

As shown in Table 9.5, brand loyalty can be viewed on a continuum from undivided brand loyalty to brand indifference. The market for a particular brand could be analysed in terms of the number of consumers in each category and strategies could be developed to enhance the brand loyalty of particular groups.

Undivided brand loyalty is, of course, an ideal. In some cases, consumers may purchase only a single brand and forego purchase if it is not available. Brand loyalty with an occasional switch is likely to be more common, though. Consumers may switch occasionally for a variety of reasons: their usual brand may be out of stock; a new brand may come on the market and is tried once; a competitive brand is offered at a special low price; or a different brand is purchased for a special occasion.

Brand loyalty switches are a competitive goal in low-growth or declining markets. As an example, competitors in the blue-jeans market or the distilled-spirits industry must obtain brand switches for long-run growth. However, switching loyalty from one to another of the brands of the same company can be advantageous. For example, Lever Brothers sells both Persil and Radion clothes washing liquid in the UK. A switch from Radion to Persil might be advantageous to Lever Brothers in that Persil is more expensive and may have a higher

Table 9.5 Examples of purchase pattern categories and brand purchase sequences.

Purchase pattern category	Brand purchase sequence
Undivided brand loyalty	A A A A A A A A A A
Brand loyalty/occasional switch	A A A B A A C A A D
Brand loyalty/switch	A A A A A B B B B B
Divided brand loyalty	A A B A B B A A B B
Brand indifference	A B C D E F G H I J

profit margin. For a coffee producer such as Douwe Egberts it is profitable to convince consumers to switch from regular coffee to special coffee such as Mocca or Capucino.

Divided brand loyalty refers to consistent purchase of two or more brands. For example, the shampoo market has a low level of brand loyalty. One reason for this might be that households purchase a variety of shampoos for different family members or for different purposes. Johnson's Baby Shampoo may be used for the youngsters and heavy shampoo users. Other household members may have dandruff problems and use Head and Shoulders. Thus, this household would have loyalty divided between these two brands.

Brand indifference refers to purchases with no apparent repurchase pattern. This is the opposite extreme from undivided brand loyalty. While total brand indifference is not common, some consumers of some products may exhibit this pattern. For example, a consumer may make weekly purchases of whatever bread is on sale, regardless of the brand. Also the purchase of generics may indicate brand indifference.

In many ways these loyalty categories are somewhat arbitrary. The point is that there are varying degrees of brand loyalty. The degree of brand loyalty can be viewed as a continuum and various quantitative indexes can be developed to categorize individuals or households in terms of particular products and services.[11] Developing a high degree of brand loyalty among consumers is an important goal of marketing strategy. Yet the rate of usage by various consumers cannot be ignored. For example, the 18–24 year-old age group uses almost twice as much shampoo as the average user, and families of three or more people make up 78% of the heavy users of shampoo.

Clearly, obtaining brand loyalty among these consumers is preferable to attracting consumers who purchase and use shampoo less frequently, other things being equal.

The relationship between brand loyalty and usage rate is shown in Table 9.6. For simplicity, the dimensions are divided into two categories of consumers rather than considering each dimension as a continuum. The table shows that achieving brand-loyal consumers is most valuable when the consumers are also heavy users. This figure could also be used as a strategic tool by plotting consumers of both the company's brands and competitive brands on the basis of brand loyalty and usage rates. Depending on the location of consumers and whether they are loyal to the company's brand or a competitive one, several strategies might be useful:

Table 9.6 Brand loyalty and usage rate.

	Light users	*Heavy users*
Brand loyalty	Brand-loyal light users	Brand-loyal heavy users
Brand indifference	Brand-indifferent light users	Brand-indifferent heavy users

(1) If the only profitable segment is the brand-loyal heavy user, focus on switching consumer loyalty to the company's brands. For example, comparative advertising such as that used by Avis in the car-rental industry or by Beefeater Gin in the liquor industry may have been appropriate strategies for switching heavy users.

(2) If there is a sufficient number of brand-loyal light users, focus on increasing their usage of the company's brand. For example, the battery market might have been characterized as being composed of brand-loyal light users of Duracell batteries. This brand then demonstrated new uses of the product, such as for toys and torches.

(3) If there is a sufficient number of brand-indifferent heavy users, attempt to make the company's brand name a salient attribute and/or develop a new relative advantage. For example, in the tissue market, Kleenex stresses the brand name in advertising in an attempt to increase the important of the brand name to the consumer. In addition, Kleenex successfully developed the market for paper handkerchiefs by using product-based segmentation on the basis of size of the tissue, for instance men-size tissues.

(4) If there is a sufficient number of brand-indifferent light users, attempt to make the company's brand name a salient attribute and increase usage of the company's brand among consumers, perhaps by finding a sustainable relative advantage. For example, a portion of the market for salt is brand-indifferent consumers. Marvel has just launched a new low-sodium product (Marvel Light) in an attempt to increase market share.

Finally, and as mentioned earlier, it is also important to plot consumers of competitive brands to develop appropriate strategies. For example, if a single competitor dominates the brand-loyal heavy-user market and has too much market power to be overcome, then strategies may have to be focused on other markets.

9.7 Satisfation and dissatisfaction

An area of cognitive research that deserves special consideration in product and service strategy concerns satisfaction and dissatisfaction with products and services and complaints due to dissatisfaction.

Satisfaction

Consumer satisfaction is a critical concept in marketing management and consumer research. It is generally argued that if consumers are satisfied with a product, service or brand, they will be more likely to continue to purchase and use it and to tell others of their favourable experiences with the product or service. If they are dissatisfied, they will be more likely to switch brands and complain to manufacturers, retailers, consumer protection groups and other consumers about the product or service. This negative word-of-mouth communication may be detrimental to the product or the brand.

Given its importance to marketing, then, considerable consumer research has been conducted on satisfaction.[12] While there are a variety of approaches, the most heavily researched approach is the disconfirmation paradigm.[13] This approach views satisfaction with products, services and brands as a result of two cognitive variables, pre-purchase expectations and disconfirmation. Pre-purchase expectations are beliefs about anticipated performance of the product. Disconfirmation refers to the difference or 'gap' between pre-purchase expectations and perceptions of post-purchase (gap G6 in Figure 9.2). Pre-purchase expectations are confirmed when the product or service performs as expected and are disconfirmed when it does not. There are two types of disconfirmation: negative disconfirmation occurs when product performance is less than expected and positive disconfirmation occurs when product performance is better than expected. Satisfaction occurs when performance is at least as good as expected; dissatisfaction occurs when performance is worse than expected.

Based on these ideas satisfaction may be defined as follows:[14] Satisfaction may best be understood as an evaluation of the surprise inherent in a product acquisition and/or consumption experience. In essence, it is the summary psychological state resulting when the emotion surrounding disconfirmed expectations is coupled with the consumer's prior feelings about the consumption experience. Moreover, the surprise or excitement of this evaluation is thought to be of finite duration, so that satisfaction soon decays into, but nevertheless greatly affects, one's overall attitude towards purchasing products and services, particularly with regard to specific retail environments.

An advantage of this approach is that it integrates the concept of satisfaction with consumers' attitudes and purchase intentions. As shown in Figure 9.3, pre-purchase intentions are a function of pre-purchase attitudes, which in turn are a function of pre-purchase expectations. After the product or service is purchased and experienced, it is hypothesized that pre-purchase expectations, if positively disconfirmed or confirmed, will lead to satisfaction. If they are negatively disconfirmed, this will lead to dissatisfaction. Post-purchase attitudes and intentions are then influenced by the degree of satisfaction/dissatisfaction as well as the pre-purchase levels of these cognitions.

Most research on consumer satisfaction using this approach has supported the model.[15/16] This model could be extended to the study of dissatisfaction and complaining behaviour.[17]

A popular model for the assessment of the quality of services is the SERVQUAL model.[18] In this model six 'gaps' are distinguished between expectations, perceptions and instructions on the one hand and actual performance on the other hand (Figure 9.2).

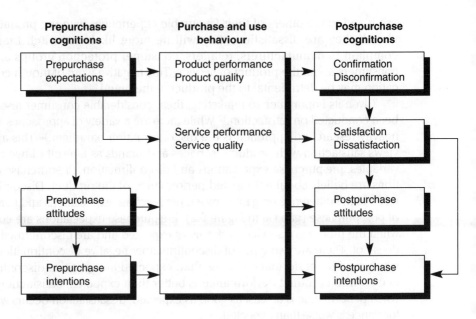

Figure 9.3 Cognitive antecedents and consequences of satisfaction.[19]

Dissatisfaction

As we have noted, dissatisfaction occurs when pre-purchase expectations are negatively disconfirmed, that is the product performs worse than expected or the service quality is lower than expected. Consumers who are dissatisfied with products or services are not likely to purchase these again and may well complain to manufacturers, retailers, consumer protection groups and other consumers. Several generalizations have been offered about consumer dissatisfaction and complaint behaviour:

(1) Those who complain when dissatisfied tend to be members of more up-scale socioeconomic groups (high levels of education and income) than are those who do not complain.

(2) Personality characteristics, including dogmatism and self-confidence, are only weakly related to complaint behaviour, if at all.

(3) The severity of dissatisfaction or problems caused by the dissatisfaction are positively related to complaint behaviour.

(4) The greater the blame for the dissatisfaction placed on someone other than the one dissatisfied, the greater the likelihood of a complaint. People have the tendency to attribute failures to others or to circumstances (and to attribute successes to themselves).

(5) The more positive the perception of retailer responsiveness to consumer complaints, the greater the likelihood of a complaint.[20]

Procter & Gamble receives many telephone calls about its products. The calls fall into three broad categories: requests for information, complaints and testimonials (praise). P&G uses these data to spot problems and correct them early. Because most consumers call with the package in their hand, and because each package has a code printed on it that identifies the plant, the manufacturing date, and sometimes even the shift and line that made it, P&G can trace a problem to the source and correct it.

9.8 Conclusions

The product or service is the most important part of the marketing mix. It is the product or service that provides the benefits that satisfy consumers' needs and wants after the price and the store are forgotten. Products differ largely on their characteristics and marketing considerations. Convenience, shopping and speciality goods are often distinguished as product categories requiring different marketing strategies.

Owing to competition and the faster pace of life there is a strong tendency to shorten product development processes. Research and development, technical, design and marketing departments should work together in an *ad hoc* team in order to develop new products and services faster.

New products and product improvement are needed to maintain the market share and keep the brand 'modern' and to stay ahead of the competition. Two-thirds of new products are, however, a failure in the marketplace so new products should be carefully tested, both in the laboratory and in the test market. New products that do not offer a clear and relevant benefit to consumers are likely to fail.

The quality of products and services is an important means to keep customers loyal and to keep them satisfied. Although expectations with regard to products and services are going up, products and services have to be improved to meet these higher expectations.

Endnotes

1. Adapted from C.R. Wasson, 1978.
2. W.J. Stanton, 1984, p. 138.
3. W.F. Van Raaij and W.M. Schoonderbeek, 1993.
4. R. Alsop, 1984.
5 Based on data of Booz, Allen and Hamilton, 1982.
6. P. Cooper, 1992.
7. A. Parasuraman, V.A. Zeithaml and L.L. Berry, 1985, and V.A. Zeithaml, A. Parasuraman and L.L. Berry, 1990.
8. A. Parasuraman, V.A. Zeithaml and L.L. Berry, 1988, and V.A. Zeithaml, A. Parasuraman and L.L. Berry, 1990.
9. See for service management also: C. Grönroos, 1990.

10. L.J. Rosenberg and J.A. Czepiel, 1983.
11. J.W. Keon and J. Bayer, 1984.
12. Literature reviews are: S.A. Latour and N.C. Peat, 1979, and D.T. Smart, 1982.
13. R.L. Oliver, 1980.
14. R.L. Oliver, 1981.
15. For instance P.A. LaBarbera and D. Mazursky, 1983.
16. An exception is the work by J.R. Churchill, A. Gilbert and C. Suprenant (1982). They found support for the model with a nondurable good but not with a durable good.
17. W.O. Bearden and J.E. Teel, 1983.
18. A. Parasuraman, V.A. Zeithaml and L.L. Berry, 1985.
19. Adapted from R.L. Oliver, 1980, p. 462.
20. M.L. Richens, 1983.

10

Pricing strategy and consumer behaviour

Chapter objectives

(1) To discuss the major considerations derived from pricing strategies and their influence on consumer behaviour and the influence of consumer behaviour on pricing strategy.
(2) To analyse the main cost concepts related to consumer behaviour.
(3) To introduce key issues in pricing such as pricing decisions, analysis of production and marketing costs, pricing objectives, setting prices, price environment and price elasticity.
(4) To study the most important consumer behaviour implications related to pricing such as price cognitions, price sensitivity, perceptions of price and consumer attitudes, processing price information, behaviours connected with price, the price – quality relationship, psychological pricing and price expectations.

10.1 Introduction

Price is perhaps the most unusual element of the marketing mix, partly because it is the only element that generates revenues. All other elements, as well as marketing research, involve expenditures of funds by organizations. Another difference is that although price may seem tangible and concrete, it is perhaps more intangible and abstract than other elements of the marketing mix. For example, in the product area, consumers often have a tangible product to examine, or at least information about a service to evaluate. In the marketing-communication area, consumers read magazine and newspaper ads and get information from salespeople to see, listen to, and evaluate. In the distribution area, consumers have shopping centres and stores to experience. However, the price variable is a rather abstract concept which, while represented as a sign or tag, has relatively little direct sensory experience connected with it. Perhaps because of this, basic research on pricing issues in marketing has been relatively modest compared to work done on the other marketing-mix elements.

These differences should not lead to underestimating the importance of price to marketing and consumer behaviour, however. 'The effects of price changes are more immediate and direct, and appeals based on price are the easiest to communicate to prospective buyers. However, competitors can react more easily to appeals based on price than to those based on product benefits and imagery. It can be argued that the price decision is perhaps the most significant among the decisions of the marketing mix strategy for a branded product.[1]

In this chapter, we focus on some important relationships among consumer cognitions, attitudes, behaviours and the environment, as they relate to the price variable of the marketing mix. We start our discussion by introducing a conceptual view of the role of price in marketing exchanges. Then pricing strategy, the environment and consumer cognitions, attitudes and behaviours are discussed.

10.2   Conceptual issues in pricing

As far as the consumer is concerned, price is usually defined as what the consumer must give up to purchase a product or service. Because price is a pivotal element in the exchange process, a conceptual view of price is introduced that encompasses more than a momentary amount or financial cost to the consumer. Figure 10.1 offers a general model of the nature of marketing exchanges and highlights the role of price in this process. Although we will focus on profit organizations, the model could be developed and analysed in terms of non-profit marketing as well. The major differences in non-profit exchanges are that:

(1) while non-profit organizations may seek money from consumers, they (at least in theory) do not seek surplus funds beyond costs
(2) the value derived by consumers in non-profit exchanges is often less tangible.

Consumer costs

In Figure 10.1 four basic types of consumer costs are identified: money, time, cognitive activity or elaboration, and behavioural effort. Time, cognitive elaboration and effort are also called behavioural costs.[2] These costs, when paired with whatever value or utility the product offers, are a convenient way to consider the meaning of price to the consumer. While it is not argued that consumers finely

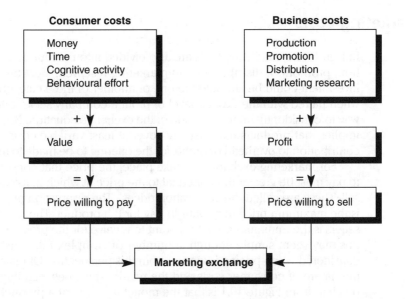

Figure 10.1 The pivotal role of price in marketing exchange.

calculate each of these costs for every purchase, these costs are frequently considered in the purchase of some products.

Consumer budgets

The cost for the consumer is related to the consumer's budget. For consumers with a large monetary budget, the costs are low compared with consumers with small budgets. The cost is the ratio of price and budget: cost = price / budget.[3] As well as monetary budgets, consumers also have time budgets, cognitive elaboration budgets (the maximum of cognitive activity they can expend) and effort budgets (the maximum of effort they can expend).

Most consumers are likely to do some type of planning to create a budget and to access funds and to ensure that sufficient funds are available when they go shopping. Credit-card purchases and payment are not only convenient for the consumer but also may make the purchase seem less expensive. This is because consumers do not see any cash flowing from their pockets or a reduction in their cheque book balances, but merely need to sign their names and not even think about payment until the end of the month. In one sense, if no balance is carried over on the credit card, the purchase is 'free' for the time between the exchange and the payment. Credit cards also facilitate purchasing because little effort is required to access funds. Thus, overall, the use of credit cards may reduce consumers' time, cognitive activity and behavioural effort costs.[4]

Marketing costs

In Figure 10.1, marketing costs are also divided into the four categories of production, promotion, distribution and marketing research. Most business costs and investment could be attributed to one or another of these categories. These costs, when paired with the desired level of profit a company seeks, offer a convenient way to consider the marketing side of the exchange equation. Basically, the model implies that products must usually cover at least variable costs and make some contribution to overhead or profits for the offering to be made to the marketplace.

For marketing exchanges to take place, the price that consumers are willing to pay must be greater than or equal to the price at which marketers are willing to sell. These are called the 'reservation prices'. The reservation price for consumers is the maximum price they want to pay for the product. The reservation price for sellers is the minimum price they want to receive for the product. However, while this may seem simple enough, a number of complex relationships need to be considered when pricing is viewed from this perspective. Of major importance is the nature of consumer costs and the relationships between them. What should be clear from Figure 10.1 is that the monetary price of a product or service may often be only a part of the total price of an exchange for the consumer.

Monetary value

Pricing research has, in the main, focused only on the monetary amount a consumer must spend to purchase a product or service. These research studies have recognized that the same monetary amount may be perceived differently by different individuals and market segments, depending on income levels and other demographic and psychographic variables. However, several important aspects of the monetary cost of offerings are not always considered. One of these concerns the source of funds for a particular purchase. 'Windfall income', for instance money received as a tax refund, interest or as gambling winnings, has a different value to many consumers than does money that is earned through work. With the same price of the product, the costs are perceived as lower by consumers with a large budget compared with consumers with a small budget. Hence, the monetary price of a particular product or service may be perceived differently by the same person, depending on what sources of funds are used to pay for it.

Similarly, the 'actual' price of a credit-card purchase that will be financed at 23% for an extended period is different to the price if cash is used. To consumers who are accustomed to carrying large credit-card balances, this difference may be irrelevant; to others, the difference may forestall or eliminate a purchase.

There are also a number of ways to reduce the monetary amount spent for a particular item, although they often involve increasing other costs. For example, time, cognitive activity and behaviour effort are required to clip and use coupons or mail in for rebates. Shopping around at different stores seeking the lowest price involves not only time, cognitive activity and behavioural effort, but also increases other monetary costs such as transportation or parking.

Time costs

To the consumer, the time necessary to learn about a product or service and to travel to purchase it, as well as time spent in a store, can be important costs. Most consumers are well aware that convenience food stores usually charge higher prices than supermarkets and most consumers purchase from them at least occasionally. Clearly, these consumers often make a trade-off of paying more money to save time, particularly if only a few items are to be purchased. Time savings may result because the convenience outlets are located closer to home and thus require less travel time or because less time is required in the store to locate the product and wait in a queue to pay for it. Given the high cost of operating a car, it might even be cheaper in monetary terms to shop at stores that are closer to home, even if they have higher prices.

However, we should not treat time only as a cost of purchasing. In some situations, the process of seeking product information and purchasing products is a very enjoyable experience rather than a cost for consumers. Some consumers enjoy window-shopping and purchasing on occasion, particularly if the opportunity cost of their time is low. Thus, while in an absolute sense consumers must spend time to shop and make purchases, in some cases this may be perceived as a benefit rather than a cost.

Cognitive activity

There is a cost of making purchases in terms of the cognitive activity or elaboration involved and this is often overlooked. Thinking and deciding what to buy can be hard work. When a consumer is trying to decide which product to purchase, a number of stores could be visited, a number of advertisements could be seen and heard. Consumers, after some time spent on deliberation, narrow the choice to a few alternative brands. They have also to take into account and assess the different varieties, combinations and optional accessories which are associated with the product. Many consumers would never make all of these comparisons, but consider the cognitive activity that would be required to make even a small fraction of them. Clearly, it would not only take a lot of time, but would be very taxing in terms of cognitive work.[5] Yet, if even only a few comparisons are made, some cognitive effort must be expended.

In addition to all of the cognitive work involved in comparing purchase alternatives, the process can also be quite stressful. Some consumers find it difficult and dislike making purchase or other types of decisions. To some, finding parking spaces, shopping in crowded stores, waiting in long checkout queues and viewing anxiety-producing advertisements can be a very unpleasant emotional experience. Thus, the cognitive activity involved in purchasing can be a very important cost.

The cost involved in decision making is often the easiest one for consumers to reduce or eliminate. Simple decision rules or heuristics, for example the affect referral rule, can reduce this cost considerably (see Section 5.5). The affect referral rule is a type of synthesized decision rule which can be used by the consumer to select the brand with the highest perceived overall rating. By repeatedly purchasing the same brand and being brand loyal, consumers can practically eliminate any decision making within a product class, for example, other heuristics might be to purchase the most expensive brand, the brand on sale or display, the brand that the consumer's parents used to buy, the brand a knowledgeable friend recommends, the brand a selected store carries, or the brand a selected salesperson recommends.

On the other hand, there are some situations in which consumers actively seek some form of cognitive involvement. While consumers may enjoy periods in which they are not challenged to use much cognitive energy or ability, they may also seek purchasing problems to solve as a form of entertainment.

Behavioural effort

It is clear then that buying things involves behavioural effort, and thus costs. Many consumers are not physically comfortable with this behavioural effort, and some avoid large shopping centres or shop in only a small number of the stores available. As with time and cognitive elaboration, behavioural effort can also be a benefit rather than a cost. For example, walking around in shopping centres and stores is sometimes done as a source of relaxation.

Perhaps the most interesting aspects of behavioural effort is the willingness of consumers to take on some marketing costs in order to reduce the amount of money they spend and to make trade-offs among various types of costs. In some cases, consumers will perform part of the production process to get a lower price. For example, consumers may forgo the cost of product assembly for pieces of furniture and even computers and do it themselves to save money.

There are also cases in which consumers will take on at least part of the cost of distribution to lower the price. Catalogue purchases require the consumer to pay the cost of delivery directly, yet may be less expensive than store purchase. If they are not, the consumer at least saves shopping time and effort in order to have the product delivered to the home. Consumers will also perform promotion, for instance, through word-of-mouth and referrals to friends. They also perform market research by comparing prices and qualities. They participate in marketing research, for companies for instance by filling out questionnaires and taking part in consumer panels, in order to receive lower prices or other merchandise 'free'.

A final trade-off of interest in terms of pricing concerns the degree to which consumers participate in purchase/ownership. Consumers have several options with regard to purchase:

(1) They can buy the product and enjoy its benefits as well as incur costs such as inventory and maintenance.
(2) They can rent or lease the product and enjoy its benefits but forgo ownership and often reduce some of the other costs, such as maintenance.

(3) They can hire someone else to perform whatever service the product is designed to perform and forgo ownership and other post-purchase costs.
(4) They can purchase the product and hire someone else to use and maintain it for them.

For many durable goods, such as cars, furniture, lawn mowers and garden tools, at least several of these options are available. Clearly, price is a lot more than just money.

Value to the consumer

Up to now, we have discussed four aspects of price from the consumer's point of view. We have suggested that consumers can sometimes reduce one or more of these costs, but this usually requires an increase in at least one of the other costs. Purchases can be viewed in terms of which of the elements is considered a cost or a benefit and which is considered most critical for particular purchases. However, regardless of what cost trade-offs are made, it seems that whatever is being purchased must be perceived to be of greater value to the consumer than merely the sum of the costs. In other words, the consumer perceives that the purchase offers benefits greater than the costs, and is willing to exchange to receive these benefits.

While this view of price is useful, consumers seldom finely calculate each of these costs and benefits in making brand-level decisions. Rather, for many types and brands of consumer packaged goods, the amounts of money, time, cognitive activity or elaboration and behavioural effort required for a purchase are very similar. For these goods, choices between brands may be made on the basis of particular brands, benefits or imagery, although price deals may be important.

For some purchases, all of these costs and trade-offs may be considered by consumers. Yet, the major importance of this view of price is not the degree to which consumers actively analyse and compare each of the costs of a particular exchange. Instead, this view is important because it has direct implications for the design of marketing strategies.

10.3 Pricing strategy

Pricing strategy is of concern in three general situations:

(1) when a price is being set for a new product;
(2) when a long-term price change is being considered for an established product;
(3) when a short-term price change is being considered.

Marketers may change prices for a variety of reasons, such as an increase in production costs, a change in the price of competitive products, or a change in distribution channels.

Many models have been offered to guide marketers in designing pricing strategies. Most of these models contain similar recommendations and differ primarily in terms of how detailed the assumptions are, how many steps the pricing process is divided into and in what sequence pricing tasks are recommended. A six-stage model is developed:[6]

(1) Analyse consumer/product relationships.
(2) Analyse the environmental situation, for example positioning and competing products.
(3) Determine the role of price in marketing strategy.
(4) Estimate relevant production and marketing costs.
(5) Set pricing objectives.
(6) Develop pricing strategy and set prices.

This six-stage model differs from traditional approaches primarily in that greater emphasis is placed on consumer analysis and greater attention is given to the four types of consumer costs in developing pricing and marketing strategies. The six stages are discussed below. Although consumer analysis is not the major focus in all of them, this strategic approach is intended to clarify the role of consumer analysis in pricing and to offer a useful overview of the pricing process.

Analyse consumer/product relationships

Pricing strategy for a new product generally starts with at least one aspect given: the company has a product concept or several variations of a product concept in mind. When a price change for an existing product is being considered, typically much more information is available, including sales and cost data.

Whether the pricing strategy is being developed for a new or existing product, a useful first stage in the process is to analyse the consumer/product relationships. Answers must be found for questions such as: How does the product benefit consumers? What does the product mean to them? In what situations do they use it? Does it have any special psychological or social significance to them? Of course, the answers to these questions depend on which current or potential target markets are under consideration.

A question that must be answered honestly is whether the product itself has a clear differential advantage that consumers would be willing to pay for, or whether a differential advantage must be created on the basis of other marketing-mix variables. This question has important implications for determining which of the four areas of consumer costs (money, time, cognitive activity or behavioural effort) can be appealed to most effectively.

Suppose the company Welsh Cakes Limited is considering marketing traditional Welsh cakes for home consumption and is analysing consumer/product relationships. The company is considering three forms of Welsh cakes and, after considerable research, has developed the consumer behaviour assumptions shown in Table 10.1. This type of analysis illustrates several important concepts. First, it is clear that consumers of the three types of Welsh cakes make trade-offs in the costs they are willing to incur. Consumers of Welsh cakes made from a mix are willing to spend a greater amount of time, cognitive activity and behavioural effort to save money, and may get a poorer tasting Welsh cake. Consumers of confectionery store Welsh cakes, on the other hand, are willing to pay a higher price to reduce these other costs and may get a better tasting Welsh cake.

Second, this analysis has clear implications for market segmentation. It is important to determine the size of the markets for the different product forms, their geodemographic profiles, their consumption and buying habits, as well as the degree of market overlap. That is, are these different consumer groups or are they the same consumers who eat different types of Welsh cakes in different situations?

Third, while this analysis has a number of implications for all facets of marketing strategy, our focus is on the implications for pricing. Clearly, the question of what Welsh cake means to consumers is critical for determining appropriate pricing strategies. For example, the Welsh cake-mix market is apparently very price sensitive. Thus, while a reduction of the other types of consumer costs or an increase in value (taste) may offer market opportunities, the price of the mix would likely have to remain low.

The frozen Welsh cake consumer apparently values having the product on hand, and while willing to make some trade-offs, wants a better tasting Welsh cake. This market is not as price sensitive as the Welsh cake-mix market and likely considers preparation effort an important cost. Thus, within the frozen Welsh cake market, consumers may pay a higher price for better tasting Welsh cakes or cakes that can be prepared more quickly and easily. Perhaps the consumer/product relationship could be summarized as 'Welsh cakes are a traditional quick and relatively tasty snack or dessert'. The consumer of confectionery store Welsh cake likely focuses strongly on product quality assurance and taste, and is not highly price sensitive. Thus, taste, ingredients and quality assurance are worth a higher price.

Table 10.1 Relative consumer costs for various Welsh cake product forms.

	Welsh cake mix	Frozen Welsh cake	Confectionery store Welsh cake
Cost			
Money	Low	Middle	High
Time	High	Middle	High
Cognitive activity	High	Middle	Low
Behaviour effort	High	Middle	Middle
Value			
Taste	Worst	Middle	Best

This brief example illustrates an approach to evaluating the relationships between consumers and products. One of the important outcomes of this analysis is an estimate of how sensitive consumers are to various prices, other costs being about the same. In economics, this is called price elasticity, which is a measure of the relative change in demand for a product or service for a given change in price. Once the company has a clear idea of these relationships and opportunities, it can then focus attention on other aspects of the market environment.

Analyse the environmental situation

As we have already discussed (Chapter 1 in particular) organizations must consider elements of their environment: economic trends, political views, social changes, legal constraints, changes in technology, 'green' issues and other forces of influence, when developing pricing strategies. These elements should be considered early in the process of formulating any part of the marketing strategy and should be monitored continually. By the time a company is making pricing decisions, many of these issues have already been considered. While this may also be true for competitive analysis, consideration of competition at this point is critical for developing pricing strategies.

In setting or changing prices, the company must consider its competition and how that competition will react to the price of the product or service. Initially, consideration should be given to such factors as:

(1) Number of competitors
(2) Market share of competitors
(3) Location of competitors
(4) Conditions of entry into the industry
(5) Degree of vertical integration of competitors
(6) Financial strength of competitors
(7) Number of products and brands sold by each competitor
(8) Cost structure of competitors
(9) Historical reaction of competitors to price changes.

Analysis of these factors help determine whether the price should be at, below, or above competitors' prices. However, this analysis should also consider other consumer costs relative to competitive offerings. Consumers often pay higher prices to save time and effort.

Role of price in marketing strategy

This is concerned with determining whether the price is to be a key aspect of positioning the product/service or whether it is to play a different role. If a company is attempting to position a brand as a bargain product or service, for example as in the case of the motel chain Forte Travelodge, setting a lower price is clearly an important part of this strategy. Amstrad video cassette recorders (VCRs) positions itself as just as good as (and even emphasizes simplicity of use as a key differential advantage) but with a lower price than the other brands, for example. Similarly, if a company is attempting to position a brand as a prestige, top-of-the-line product or service, then a higher price is a common cue to indicate this position. Suntory whisky, a Japanese brand, has long used this approach, for example. Of course, the success of these types of strategies also depends on analysing the trade-offs with other elements of consumer costs.

In many situations, price may not play a particularly important positioning role other than in terms of pricing competitively. If consumers enjoy convenience in purchasing (for example free delivery), or if the product has a clear differential advantage, the price may be set at or above that of the competition but not highlighted in the positioning strategy. In other cases, when the price of a product or service is higher than that of the competition, but there is no clear differential advantage, the price may not be explicitly used in positioning. For example, premium-priced wines do not highlight price as part of their appeal.

Production and marketing costs

The costs of producing and marketing a product effectively provide a very useful benchmark for making pricing decisions. The variable costs of production and marketing usually provide the lowest price a company must charge to make an offering in the market. However, there are some exceptions to this rule. These exceptions typically involve interrelationships among products. For example, a company like Sega or Nintendo may sell its computer games hardware below cost to sell a greater volume of software. Or supermarkets may sell a number of items below cost, that is, loss leaders, to build store traffic and increase sales of other products.

Set pricing objectives

At the beginning of this Part of the book we introduced the more general and strategic issues of marketing planning and here we remind the reader that as with the other mix elements, pricing objectives should be derived from overall marketing objectives, which in turn should be derived from corporate objectives. In practice, the most common objective is to achieve a target return on investment. This objective has the advantage of being quantifiable. It also offers a useful basis for making not only pricing decisions but also decisions on whether to enter or remain in specific markets. For example, if a company demands a 25% return on investment, and the best estimates of sales at various prices indicate that a product would have to be priced too high to generate demand, then the decision may be to forgo market entry. Other types of pricing objectives are listed in below.[7]

(1) Increase sales.
(2) Target market share.
(3) Maximum long-run profits.
(4) Maximum short-run profits.
(5) Growth.
(6) Stabilize market.
(7) Desensitize customers to price.
(8) Maintain price-leadership arrangement.
(9) Discourage entrants.
(10) Speed exit of marginal firms.
(11) Avoid government investigation and control.
(12) Maintain loyalty of middlemen and get their sales support.
(13) Avoid demand for 'more' from suppliers, labour, in particular.
(14) Enhance image of firm and its offerings.
(15) Be regarded as 'fair' by ultimate customers.
(16) Create interest and excitement about the item.
(17) Be considered trustworthy and reliable by rivals.
(18) Help in the sale of weak items in the line.
(19) Discourage others from cutting prices.
(20) Make a product 'visible'.
(21) 'Spoil market' to obtain high price for sale of business.
(22) Build store traffic ('loss leaders').
(23) Maximum profits on product line.
(24) Recover investment quickly.
(25) Decrease demand in periods of supply shortages.

Develop pricing strategy and set prices

The preceding stages, if worked through effectively, should provide the information necessary to develop pricing strategies and set prices. Basically, the meaning of the product or service to the consumer and consumer costs and values have been analysed. The environment has been analysed, particularly competition. The role of price in the marketing strategy has been determined. Production and marketing costs have been estimated. Pricing objectives have been set. The pricing task now is to determine a pricing strategy and specific prices that are:

(1) sufficiently above costs to generate the desired level of profit and achieve stated objectives;
(2) related to competitive prices in a manner consistent with the overall marketing and positioning strategy;
(3) designed to generate consumer demand based on consumer cost trade-offs and values.

In some cases, prices may be developed with a long-run strategy in mind. For example, a *penetration price policy* may include a long-run plan to sequentially raise prices after product introduction at a relatively low price. A *skimming price policy* may include a long-run plan to systematically lower prices after a high-price introduction and selling the product to innovators and early adopters. An intermediate price policy, somewhere between penetration and skimming, may also be used.

However, most price changes occur as a result of a change in consumers, the environment, competition, costs, strategies and objectives. Examples of the relationships among these variables can be found in the pricing of air fares, holidays and cars. For example, major airlines attempt to compete with low-price airlines by lowering the fares on competitive routes and raising the price on routes the low-price airlines do not serve. In addition, the major airlines have engaged in efforts to cut costs to try to be more competitive with the low-price airlines. Consumers have a basic choice between attempting to minimize travel costs by spending more time shopping for low prices, foregoing some flexibility in departure times and dates and giving up some additional services versus paying full fare and receiving these benefits. Often, business travellers may pay the higher full-fare price, while leisure travellers spend the time and effort necessary to get cheaper fares.

This example illustrates how a change in the environment (market deregulation) led to a change in competitors (entrance of low-price airlines), which led to a change in pricing strategies (price cuts for some seats but overall attempts to maximize revenues per flight) and cost-cutting efforts. Many consumers also changed as they became more involved in the purchase of airline tickets and perhaps even travelled more by plane as prices fell, at least in the short run.

10.4 Price perception

As we said at the beginning of this chapter, price is perhaps the most intangible element of the marketing mix. From an environmental perspective, this means that the price variable typically offers very little for the consumer to experience at the sensory level, although it may generate considerable cognitive activity, time and behavioural effort. In the environment price is usually a tag, a few symbols on a package, or a few written on a list, or spoken on TV or radio or by a salesperson in a store or on the phone. The price variable also includes purchase contracts and credit-terms information.

One area that has been the subject of consumer research on price information in the environment is *unit pricing*. Unit pricing is common for grocery products and involves a shelf tag that indicates the price per unit (kg or litre) for a specific good. This information is designed to help shoppers make more informed purchases in comparing various brands and package sizes. Displaying unit price information in a table format in the store leads to switching to lower-priced brands, for example private labels.[8]

How price information is communicated also has an effect. For example, the advent of scanner checkout systems has reduced price information in the environment for many products, because prices are no longer stamped on each package. Having each item marked increases consumers' certainty of price recall and decreases errors in both exact price and unit-price recall.[9] Some differences were found in the effects of shelf price tags, supporting the idea that not only the price itself but also the method by which price information is communicated, affects consumer cognitions and behaviours.

Price cognitions

As already mentioned, there is typically little sensory experience connected with the price variable. Yet information about prices is often attended to and comprehended, and the resulting meanings influence consumer behaviour. For some purchases, consumers may make a variety of price comparisons among brands and evaluate trade-offs among the various types of consumer costs and values.

There have been several attempts to summarize the research on the effects of price on consumer cognitions, choice processes and behaviour, but these reviews have found few generalizations to offer.[10] For example, it has long been believed that consumers perceive a strong relationship between price and the quality of products and services. Experiments typically find this relationship when consumers are given no other information about the product or service except price. However, when consumers are given additional information about products (which is more consistent with marketplace situations), the price – quality relationship is diminished.

Price perceptions and attitudes

We discussed the concept of perception in Chapter 3 and in the current context price perceptions are concerned with how price information is comprehended by consumers and made meaningful to them. One approach to understanding price perceptions is information processing.[11] An adaptation of this approach is outlined in Figure 10.2.[12]

This model illustrates an approach to describing price effects for a high-involvement product or purchase situation. Basically, it suggests that price information is received through the senses of sight and hearing. The information is then comprehended, which means that it is interpreted and made meaningful, that is consumers understand the meaning of price symbols through previous learning and experience.

The stated price for a particular brand may be considered a product attribute. This knowledge may then be compared with the prices of other brands in a product class, other attributes of the brand and other brands, and other consumer costs. Finally, an attitude is formed towards the various brand alternatives.

For a low-involvement product or purchase situation, price may have little or no impact on consumer cognitions or behaviours. For many products, con-

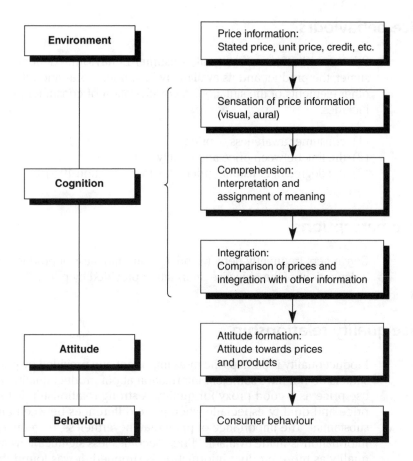

Figure 10.2 Conceptual model of cognitive processing of price information.

sumers may have an implicit price range. As long as prices fall within this range, price is not even evaluated as a purchase criterion. Similarly, some products and services are simply purchased without ever inquiring as to the price but simply paying whatever is asked for at the point of purchase. Impulse products located in the checkout area of supermarkets and drugstores may frequently be purchased this way, as might other products for which the consumer is highly brand loyal. In the latter cases, consumers may well make purchases on the single attribute of brand name without comparing price, other consumer costs, or other factors.

In other cases, price information may not be carefully analysed because consumers have a particular price image for the store they are shopping in. Discount stores such as Superdrug, Toys Я Us or PC World may be generally considered low-priced outlets, and consumers may forgo comparing prices at these outlets with those at other stores.

Price behaviours

Price could affect a variety of consumer behaviours, depending on the consumer, the product and its availability in various stores and other channels, and other elements of the situation. A consideration of consumer pricing behaviour includes:

(1) consumer awareness of prices;
(2) the link between price and quality;
(3) the degree of consumer price sensitivity (Section 10.5).

Price perceptions

Consumers frequently perceive price as an indicator of product or store image, independent of the objective information provided by price.

Price-quality relationship

Product quality is perhaps the most important cue provided by price. When consumers do not have sufficient information about product quality, they frequently use price as a good proxy for quality. A strong relationship is found between price and quality, especially when price differences between alternatives are substantial. The importance of price may, nevertheless, be reduced when other information is made available. Price becomes less significant as an indicator of quality as more product information is supplied. It was found that in the purchase of carpeting, the intrinsic characteristics of the product were much more important than extrinsic cues such as price in influencing quality perceptions.[13] The fact that consumers use price as a quality indicator in some cases and not in others prompted several researchers to investigate under what conditions price dominates as a cue for product quality. Their findings showed that consumers will use price as a surrogate for quality when:

■ they have strong beliefs that quality differences exist between product alternatives;
■ they have little experience or information concerning the product.[14]

Thus, a consumer who believes that there are significant quality differences between brands of cordless telephones and has little knowledge, experience or information with regard to the product will tend to use high price as an indicator of high quality. Further, if the price information is linked to a well-known brand, a price – quality association is even more likely.[15] These studies confirm that price tends to be discounted as an indicator of quality when consumers have experience and information to rely on. In such cases, product quality is likely to be evaluated on a multi-attribute basis.

10.5 Psychological pricing

Perception of price is relevant in another context here, namely the sensitivity to certain price points. For example, consumers appear to be more sensitive to prices ending with an odd number of just under a round number (odd – even pricing). Or they may find products priced in multiples, such as five for £1.90, preferable to single-item prices. These pricing policies are referred to as psychological pricing because they rely on consumers' perceptual sensitivity to certain price points.

Odd–even pricing is used by retailers in the belief that an item priced at £3.99 is seen by the consumer as less expensive than an item provided at £4.00. It is felt that the consumer would associate a £3.99 price with £3.00 rather than £4.00. This example demonstrates the concept of perceptual price zones. Most consumers perceive odd prices as being lower than even prices. When consumers were asked to recall odd and even prices seen two days earlier, they were more likely to understate the odd prices.[16] Further, increasing odd prices was less noticeable to consumers than increasing even prices. These results provide economic justification for setting prices at odd rather than even levels.

Multiple pricing also conveys an image of economy to the consumer. Obtaining a product at five for £1.90 implies a small saving over five single units purchased at 40 pence each. Consumers are likely to buy in multiples as long as it is a frequently purchased product and the consumer recognizes a clear saving. But if multiple pricing becomes too complicated, consumers are likely to reject multiple purchases.

Price sensitivity

Consumer sensitivity to price changes is another key factor that directly influences retailer and manufacturer pricing strategies. The measure of price sensitivity used most often is a consumer's price elasticity or response to changes in price. Price elasticity is measured by the percentage change in quantity purchased compared to a percentage change in price. If the percentage decrease in quantity is more than the percentage increase in price, demand is elastic. If the percentage decrease in quantity is less than the percentage increase in price, demand is inelastic.

Price elasticity

Price elasticity can provide a way of segmenting markets, by classifying consumers by their price sensitivities. If price-sensitive consumers have particular demographic or regional characteristics, deals, coupons or other sales promotion strategies can be directed to these consumers. Some attempt has been made to define consumers more responsive to deals and coupons by postal area code and use direct mail to send coupons to these consumers. Price promotions could also be directed to postal code areas with consumers demonstrating greater price sensitivity.

We can also make the distinction between upside elasticity (sensitivity to price increases) and downside elasticity (sensitivity to price decreases). In a study of three products, it was found that consumers were more elastic on the downside than on the upside. That is, they were more likely to increase consumption with a decrease in price than to decrease consumption with an increase in price. Small price increases may increase profits since they are likely to produce insignificant changes in response.[17]

Other studies of consumer price sensitivity have focused on factors that may change such sensitivity. For example, one study found that the consumer's price elasticity decreases when the consumer is accompanied by a friend,[18] and another found less price sensitivity when the salesperson is viewed as an expert.[19] Consumers are more likely to be price elastic when they are shopping alone and when they are confident in their own appraisal of the product.

Price expectations

Consumers' expectations regarding a standard price level and price range are important determinants of their sensitivity to prices. Consumers develop a standard price for most products, what they regard as a fair price. The standard price serves as a basis or anchor for judging other prices. There is a range around the standard price that is not likely to produce a change in quantity consumed or a switch in brands. But outside this range, significant changes may occur, producing greater price elasticity. For example, a consumer may expect to pay 75 pence for a one-litre container of fresh fruit juice. A variation of five pence either way would not be noticed. But, more than a five-pence increase in price may cause the consumer to look for another brand, and more than a five-pence decrease may cause the consumer to purchase two containers. A five-pence change is therefore the point where some price sensitivity comes into play. This threshold is called the 'just noticeable difference' (JND).

Price expectations also refer to an acceptable price range across brands in a product category. The consumer buying fresh fruit juice for 65 pence may be sceptical of a one-litre container selling for less than 50 pence, thinking something must be wrong with a brand priced that low. On the other hand, if the consumer is in a petrol station convenience shop on Sunday and needs fresh fruit juice, the upper price limit he or she sets may be £1.10. Therefore, the acceptable price range for fresh fruit juice (for a one-litre container) based on this consumer's price expectations is between 50 pence and £1.10. An acceptable range of prices is determined by an upper limit above which the product or service would be judged too expensive and a lower limit below which the quality of the product or service would be suspect.

Greater price sensitivity

Greater consumer price sensitivity has resulted in:

(1) manufacturers putting more emphasis on pricing strategies;
(2) discount retailers gaining in market share;
(3) increased sales of distributor and private label brands.

The switch from manufacturers' brands to private labels or retailers' brands has been particularly evident. Private brands sell from 15% to 30% below manufacturers' brands. Manufacturers of national brands have reacted to this shift by cutting prices. Leading companies such as Procter & Gamble, Kellogg, Coca-Cola and Lever have begun to put more emphasis on outright price cuts than on coupons and deals as price incentives. Procter & Gamble has also begun to introduce product lines on a price basis ('every day low prices') and decreased the emphasis and the amount of expenditures allocated to trade sales promotions.

The emphasis on price does not mean less emphasis on quality. As consumers become more price conscious, they are also becoming more value conscious. Some consumers are actually spending more on products that last longer with a view to saving money in the long run.[20] The greatest emphasis is on better quality at the same price. Further, price sensitivity and the emphasis on value are expected to be here to stay.

Nevertheless, and despite consumers' greater price sensitivity and emphasis on value, in times of recession some companies use specific methods of increasing consumer prices. Among these methods are: increase price for same quantity and quality; maintain price for less quantity; maintain price for less quality or auxiliary services; reduce or eliminate price deals; and increase interest rate and charges.

Some pricing strategies should not be pursued by companies either because they are considered illegal or because they are perceived as unfair by customers and can seriously affect the long-term performance of an organization. These include:

(1) Price fixing: Conspiring with competitors to fix prices (cartel).
(2) Deceptive pricing: Pricing practices that mislead consumers, such as marketing items with a fictitious price, crossing this price out and then putting on the normal price as though it were a bargain.
(3) Predatory pricing: Setting prices low to drive out competitors, then raising prices (penetration pricing policy).
(4) Price discrimination: Charging similar, competing distribution channel members different prices, which lessens competition or tends to create a monopoly.

10.6 Conclusions

Consumers exchange much more than simply money for goods and services. They also exchange their time, cognitive activity or elaboration and behavioural effort, not only to earn money, but also to shop and make purchases. Thus, analysis of these elements, and of the value consumers receive in purchase and consumption, may provide better insights into the effects of price on consumer behaviour. The relationship between consumer behaviour on the one hand and marketing strategy (beyond each discrete mix element) is the key not only to the pricing element of the mix but also each of the other elements.

Endnotes

1. V.R. Rao, 1984.
2. T.M.M. Verhallen and W.F. Van Raaij, 1986.
3. T.M.M. Verhallen and R.G.M. Pieters, 1984.
4. G. Garcia, 1980.
5. S.M. Shugan, 1980.
6. J.P. Peter and J.C. Olson, 1987.
7. Adapted from A.R. Oxenfeldt, 1973.
8. J.E. Russo, 1977.
9. V.A. Zeithaml, 1982.
10. For instance V.R. Rao, 1984; V.A. Zeithaml, 1984; K.B. Monroe and R. Krishhan, 1983.
11. J.C. Olson, 1980.
12. J.P. Peter and J.C. Olson, 1987.
13. J.J. Wheatley, J.S.Y. Chiu and A. Goldman, 1981.
14. C. Obermiller and J.J. Whitley, 1985.
15. W.B. Dodds and K.B. Monroe, 1985.
16. R. M. Schindler, 1984.
17. K.B. Monroe, 1976.
18. A.G. Woodside and J.T. Sims, 1976.
19. A.G. Woodside and J.W. Davenport, Jr, 1976.
20. W.F. Van Raaij and G. Eilander, 1983.

Distribution strategy and consumer behaviour

Chapter objectives

(1) To study the impact of channel strategy on consumer behaviour.
(2) To introduce key issues related to store recognitions, store behaviours and store environment.
(3) To analyse a number of relevant factors and managerial criteria that need to be considered when designing channel strategies.
(4) To discuss many important elements which are derived from the interaction between store retailing and consumer behaviour, ranging from store location and store layout to in-store stimuli and store image.

11.1   Introduction

Channels of distribution, in economic terms, provide form, time, place and possession utilities for consumers. Form utility means that channels convert raw materials into finished goods and services in forms the consumer seeks to purchase. Time utility means that channels make goods and services available when the consumer wants to purchase them. Place utility means that goods and services are made available at places where the consumer wants to purchase them. Possession utility means that channels facilitate the transfer of ownership of goods to the consumer.

Distribution channels have a very important impact on consumer cognitions, attitudes and behaviour. The locations of shopping centres and stores, as well as specific products and other stimuli within these environments strongly, influence what consumers think and feel and what behaviours they perform, such as store contacts, product contacts and transactions. In return, consumer actions at the retail level determine the success or failure of marketing strategies and have an important impact on the selection of future strategies. Thus, it is important to focus and analyse the relationships among consumer cognitions, attitudes, behaviours and environments at the retail level.

Figure 11.1 provides a model of the basic relationships among cognition, attitudes, behaviour and the environment at the retail level and the role of channel strategy. Marketing managers have many decisions to make in designing effective channels of distribution. For example, decisions must be made as to whether to use store retailing or non-store retailing or some combination of the two. Decisions must be made concerning who will perform what marketing functions within the channel.

Manufacturers are concerned with developing consumer brand loyalty, that is, that consumers repeatedly purchase their brand. Retailers are concerned with developing consumer store loyalty, that is, that consumers repeatedly visit their stores. Different members of a distribution channel may be primarily concerned with influencing different consumer behaviours. Retailers affect consumers most directly, and perhaps most influentially, for many types of products and most services.

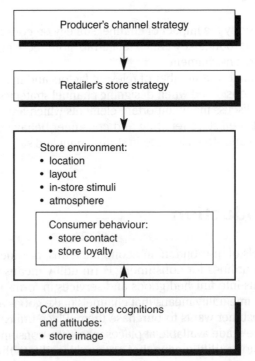

Figure 11.1 Channel strategy and consumer behaviour.

11.2 Consumer/product relations

The starting point for designing effective channels, as it is with the other mix elements, is an analysis of consumer/product relationships. At least six basic questions must be considered:

(1) What is the potential annual market demand? That is, given a particular marketing strategy, how many consumers are likely to purchase the product and how often?
(2) What is the long-run growth potential of the market?
(3) What is the geographic dispersion of the market?
(4) What are the most promising geographic markets to enter?
(5) Where and how do consumers purchase this and similar types of products?
(6) What is the likely impact of a particular channel system on consumers? That is, will the system influence consumer cognitions and behaviours sufficiently to achieve the marketing (sales) objectives?

While these questions emphasize that consumers are the focal point in channel design, the answers require an analysis of a variety of factors. Consumer-related questions in considering the *nature of the product or service* are crucial:

(1) What consequences or values does the product or service provide the target market?
(2) How much time and effort are target-market consumers willing to expend to shop for, locate and purchase the product?
(3) How often do target-market consumers purchase the product? Thus, it is the relationships among consumers, the product and the channel that are critical, rather than the analysis of these factors in isolation.

Other factors are the environmental conditions, degree of competition, distribution costs, channel coverage, the company's competence to administer the channels, degree of control, and characteristics of middlemen. These factors must be analysed both in terms of their relationships with and impact on the consumer, and in terms of their relationships with the other variables.

1 Environmental conditions

We have often returned to one of the themes of Chapter 1, namely the current and expected changes in the economic, social, political and legal environments in which the company operates. This information is critical in channel design, because channels typically involve long-term commitments by the company that may be difficult to change. Thus, situational analysis of the macro environment is critical in channel design in order to respond to potential problems and to exploit opportunities.

2 Competition

The size, financial and marketing strengths, and market share of a company's competitors are major concerns in designing effective marketing strategies. For channel decisions, a key issue concerns how major competitors distribute products and how their distribution system affects consumers.

3 Costs

While channel strategies seek to provide form, time, place and possession utilities for the consumer in order to affect consumer cognitions, attitudes and behaviour, these strategies are constrained by the cost of distribution. In general, a basic goal is to design a distribution system that facilitates exchanges between the company and consumers but does so in a cost-efficient manner. Thus, costs can be viewed as a constraint on the company's ability to distribute products and services and to serve and influence consumers. In general, companies seek distribution systems that minimize total distribution costs at a particular level of customer service.

4 Coverage

There are two meanings of the term coverage in channel strategy. First, there is the idea that seldom can every member of a selected target market receive sufficient marketing coverage to bring about an exchange. Second, coverage also refers to the number of outlets in a particular geographic area in which the product or service will be sold. Distribution coverage can be viewed along a continuum ranging from intensive, through selective, to exclusive distribution. Exclusive distribution has the connotations of a rare product or brand with an exclusive high quality.

5 Competence

A frequently overlooked criteria in designing channels is the company's competence to administer the channels and to perform channel tasks at all levels to ensure effective distribution to the consumer. Both financial strength and marketing skills are crucial.

6 Degree of control

An important managerial criterion in designing channels is the degree of control desired for effective marketing of the product to the consumer.

7 Characteristics of middlemen

A final but extremely important consideration in designing channels concerns the characteristics of the intermediaries that are available and willing to handle the manufacturer's product. If no acceptable middlemen are available, then the company must either market direct, encourage the development of intermediaries or forgo entering a particular market.

In addition to such factors as the size, financial strength, and marketing skills of intermediaries, consumer perceptions of intermediaries can be crucial in channel strategy. Thus, manufacturers and retailers must consider the consumer/store relationships, that is, the relationships between the store environment, consumer cognitions, attitudes and behaviours.

11.3 Store location

Retail stores are relatively closed environments that can exert a significant impact on consumer cognitions, attitudes and behaviour. In this section, we will consider three major decision areas in designing effective store environments: store location, store layout (Section 11.6) and in-store stimuli (Section 11.7).

Store location

Store location is a critical aspect of channel strategy. Good locations allow ready access, can attract large numbers of consumers, and can significantly alter consumer shopping and purchasing patterns. Even slight differences in location can have a significant impact on market share and profitability. Research on retail location has been dominated by a regional urban economics, rather than a behavioural approach, though this is changing in significant ways. Thus, it is not surprising that many of the assumptions upon which the models are based offer poor descriptions of consumer behaviour. Recent research has begun to integrate behavioural variables such as store image and perceived distance into location models. However, most models still place primary emphasis on economic variables and assumptions, and on predicting rather than describing consumer behaviour. Consumers are considered primarily in terms of demographic and socioeconomic variables, and in terms of traffic patterns and distances to various locations. Three general approaches to store location include the checklist method, the analogue approach, and regression models.

Site selection and evaluation

The foundation of site selection research is to provide a forecast of the sales volume of the proposed site.[1] This requires extensive analysis both in terms of the general location (region, town, area) and the specific sites contained within those areas. Site selection is as crucial as the choice of a retail area, especially for stores relying on customer traffic patterns to generate business.[2] Many consumers visit the store because it is conveniently located or because they incidentally see the store when walking through a shopping centre or high street. Apart from store-loyal customers, stores rely on consumers that incidentally see the store during their shopping trip. It is obvious that these consumers may become loyal customers afterwards, if they are satisfied with the store's assortment and service.

Existing models

Comprehensive discussions have already been presented on this area.[3] However, a brief overview of these models will assist in understanding the potential applications of more behaviourally based database marketing and the use of geodemographics in particular. Approaches to modelling site location may be separated into two main groups.[4] One approach is to forecast store turnover, either based on the location and characteristics of the outlet *or* on an analogous group of competing stores. The second approach is based on finding an appropriate general location with a suitable socioeconomic structure.

1 Checklist method

The checklist method can be used in either of the above approaches to modelling site location. It involves the systematic consideration of a number of factors, thereby attempting to remove the subjectivity of selecting between sites.[5] It is a very unsophisticated approach to site location research, but is valuable as an input to the more advanced models detailed below.

2 Analogue approach

The analogue approach is the simplest and most popular one.[6] Potential sales are estimated on the basis of existing store revenues at similar sites, the competition at the proposed site, expected market shares at that site, and the size and density of the site's primary trading area. The reliability of the analogue approach is contingent upon similarities between the analogue and the proposed store, including the similarities in the physical, sociodemographic and competitive aspects of the two trade areas.

3 Regression model

Regression models were first applied to retail location analysis in the 1960s, and were necessary because of the increasingly complex array of data available to the retail analyst. The regression model develops a series of regression equations showing the association between potential sales and a variety of independent variables at each location under consideration. The impact of such independent variables as population size, average income, the number of households, nearby competition, transportation barriers and traffic barriers are studied.

Problems with existing models

On a macro level, models may be criticized 'because they are simplifications of reality, models by definition are never comprehensive and involve a lot of subjective retail experience. Judgement is still essential in successful site selection'.[7] The success of these models is largely dependent upon the quality of the initial data, the proper application of statistical procedures and the analyst's intuitive understanding of the problem.[8]

On a more specific level, existing site location models may be criticized on the basis that they do not quantitatively consider the impacts of other retailers, nor how that success might vary as a function of a competitor's potential action of adding or decreasing the number of outlets within the trade area.[9]

Improvements in information technology have allowed retailers not only to store all of this data, but also to manipulate and merge several sources of data to reduce the risk in their site location decision making. The growing area, for retailers at least, is the development of Geographic Information Systems which combine commercial, syndicated and retailers' own data. The development of database marketing has been central in this.

Trade area analysis

Trade area survey and analysis provides a method for defining the spatial extension of retail trading performance on a map and constitutes an important facet of store assessment research.[10] Trade area surveys obtain information about the names, expenditure patterns and shopping habits for retail outlets visited by samples of consumers. Using these data, customer spotting techniques designate the samples as customers for a certain retail outlet and then spot them as dots on a map. This map is called a 'customer spotting map' and is used as a base map for trade area analysis.[11] Customer spotting leads easily into the delineation of the primary trade area, and the evaluation of penetration rates within it.[12] Trade area boundaries are determined by the point at which competitive advantage is lost to an alternative shopping destination.[13]

Once the trade area has been delineated, the focus shifts onto the market potential of that area, that is, the buying power, both now and in the future. The next step is to identify the number and income level of households within that area in order that the actual and potential level of sales can be ascertained. To project the level of sales into the future requires a projection of the number and type of households.[14]

Effective location management inherently involves the monitoring of the organization's trade area and adapting to any changes that occur within it. Trade area analysis may be used to determine the effects that other stores within an outlet's trade area might have. For example, once a store has delineated its trade area, it can then study other outlets that impact on the same catchment area. Each of these other stores could then be classified under one of four main categories: competitors, generators, cannibals and neutrals.

1 Competitors

Competitors are those stores which would have a possible negative effect on an outlet's sales within its trade area.

2 Generators

Generators are those retailers that positively impact on the sales of a given outlet through their spatial interaction. That is, they will attract customers to the area in their own right who would not have necessarily come to the area and thus may not have shopped at the initial outlet. A retailer should identify those stores that are sales generative and decide whether or not they would be allies in attracting customers.[15]

3 Cannibals

Cannibals are those outlets belonging to the same chain which have been introduced to the trade area due to exceeded sales expectations or expansion, and which draw customers away from the original store to the new location.

4 Neutrals

The proximity of neutrals neither adds nor detracts from a retailer's sales. Nevertheless it is important for the retailer to identify them in order for the trade area to be monitored sufficiently.

For an existing store, it can be determined if the current retail strategy still matches the needs of consumers. Using trade area analysis, the British supermarket chain Tesco has the ability to advise not only on new store potential but on the past and future performance of existing branches, the purchasing behaviour and preferences of their catchments and the trading strength of other retailer's branches.[16] The focus of promotional activities can thus be ascertained.

11.4 Calculation of trade areas

Spatial monopoly

The spatial monopoly model assumes that a retailing centre serves the needs of people in its area, and that the characteristics of the market can be associated with the characteristics of the retailing in the centre. Spatial monopoly models assume that:[17]

(1) each retail unit sells an undifferentiated product;
(2) consumers will use the closest facility;
(3) no physical or psychological barriers exist.

One of the best examples of this approach are the five- and ten-minute isochrones which assumed that a retail unit's trade area consisted of those regions contained within ten minutes' driving time of the unit. These types of studies are still used for shopping centres, particularly at neighbourhood level.[18] However, it has been empirically proven that many customers of a retail unit come from an extensive territory on a regular basis, often by-passing similar facilities. More sophisticated location studies would modify these patterns to take account of the penetration rates of competitors.

When dealing with more complex systems, this approach can be further enhanced through the use of Thiessen polygons, a geometric procedure for delineating the trade areas of a number of similar facilities in space.[19] It is still, however, a very crude rule of thumb and is probably most widely used in the absence of systematic data.

While spatial monopoly models may be somewhat appropriate for use with facilities such as ATMs[20], they are by no means sophisticated enough for highly differentiated retailers with geographically, demographically and psychologically diverse customer groups.

Market penetration

The method of market penetration seeks not only to delineate the confines of a unit's trade area, but also to identify the penetration rate which the unit has managed to secure within that space. This requires two types of data:[21]

(1) a list of customers that can be assigned to residential areas;
(2) information as to the number of potential households or customers within that area.

One of the most effective methods of acquiring this information is to employ a customer survey.[22] Alternatively, the retail unit may possess quite extensive customer information through the use of scanning (EPOS system) and this may provide the basis of a trade area map.[23] Many companies have developed their own address-based management information systems for billing and maintenance purposes, and postcoded customer files can be used directly to describe the current customer base.[24]

Surveys can:

(1) provide estimates of trade area density;
(2) show the effects of competition within an area;
(3) provide valuable inputs into promotional strategy;
(4) evaluate store performance.

However, there are a number of problems in basing trade area definitions on the results of customer surveys.[25] Results can be distorted, if they are based on visits to a store rather than on individual customers. A primary trade area drawn on the basis of visits will tend to be smaller than one that relies on individual customers. The same problem may occur in the use of EPOS generated data.

Dispersed markets

Delineating trade areas for dispersed markets can be a far more complex task. One method that is used is to define the customer profile of the store and then use geodemographic information to help locate those customers. Dispersed markets have also benefited tremendously from the use of regression modelling.[26]

Forms of analysis

There are several forms of analysis of trade areas: subdivisions, market penetration ratio, and demand surface.

1 Subdivision of the trade area

In the subdivision of the trade area, per capita sales and total sales are calculated for each unit area. A trade area is subdivided into three parts, according to total sales. The primary trade area has the geographic core from which a store generates most of its business. It is defined by grouping together the unit areas with the highest per capita sales until an area accounting for 60% to 70% of the stores total sales has been reached. The secondary trade area is the area adjoining the primary trade area and contributes 15% to 20% of total sales. The tertiary or fringe trade area is composed of the residual districts from which the store draws all its remaining customers.[27]

2 Calculation of the market penetration ratio

The market penetration ratio is another measure of demand density. It may be calculated by dividing a store's per capita sales by its per capita sales potential. This ratio is the most popular measure for representing demand density.

3 Quantitative analysis of the demand surface

Besides the two previous traditional methods, quantitative analysis has recently been used to describe the demand surface. The typical techniques used are spatial filtering and trend surface analysis, but these are techniques beyond the scope of this book.

11.5   Geodemographics

Origins and applications in retail area analysis

We have already discussed the development and nature of geodemographics in earlier chapters, notably Chapter 6. It is relevant to return to the topic here because the early origins of geodemographics and one of the main applications of the various geodemographic systems revolve around the question of how to analyse 'catchment areas'. The origin was based in local government in order to determine where and how to target community and social facilities. Commercially, there are now several systems, including ACORN, MOSAIC, PIN-POINT and SUPERPROFILES.[28] Table 11.1 shows how the area around a luxury car dealership can be analysed by ACORN.

There are various ways in which such analysis could be used in building retail customer typologies. Zones and small 'grid square' areas could be produced, for example. If such classifications are considered relevant, each zone in the catchment area of each store in the analogue group can be allocated to a typology.

CACI, and others, can provide a profile of a catchment area, as already shown (SITE analysis) together with the 'index of usage' (based on TGI data[29])

Table 11.1 ACORN application on car dealership (1991 categories). This table shows how the area around a car dealership can be analysed by ACORN.

Catchment area analysis

ACORN group	% of area	×	Model X index	=	Area sales potential
A1	30.6	×	186	=	56.9
A2	2.3	×	101	=	2.3
A3	3.2	×	112	=	3.6
B4	24.9	×	128	=	31.9
B5	5.8	×	73	=	4.2
C6	3.5	×	152	=	5.3
C7	5.8	×	258	=	15.0
D9	13.7	×	95	=	13.0
E12	4.6	×	113	=	5.2
F14	4.7	×	47	=	2.2
F17	0.8	×	63	=	0.5 +
Total					140.1

If model X would be bought by 5% of the national population and the catchment area is 10,000, a sales potential of 10,000 × 5% = 500 would be expected. But the index here is 140.1, so for this catchment area the sales potential is 500 × 1.401 = 700.

Source: Adapted by the authors from © CACI Limited, 1995 (OPCS and GRO(S) © Crown Copyright 1991). All rights reserved. ACORN is a registered trademark of CACI Limited.

for each geodemographic group in the catchment, in terms of their usage of the products or services sold by the retailer concerned. This overall index can be the weighting factor for the more generalized regional statistic of product/service usage, perhaps based on family expenditure data.

Because there has been a full ACORN analysis of the Target Group Index[30], it is easy to determine each ACORN category's interest in the product concerned. In fact the TGI sample design is now based on ACORN categories. In addition, the National Readership Survey is similarly analysed by ACORN and this can provide readership profiles for media selection purposes.

Retailers can conduct their own geodemographic profiling. Customer addresses can be easily geocoded by having OS Grid references appended to each postcode. The result can be a scatter map showing the boundaries of the catchment area and the areas within this of greater customer density.[31]

Geodemographics and other databases

There is an increase in the desire to obtain even more detailed information about customers and trading areas as segments become better defined and understood for competitive advantage. There have been technological developments since the early 1980s in this respect. Consumer panels, retail audits and EPOS systems provide the retailer with a potential plethora of information. But in addition consumer panels allow marketing research to be conducted at 'household level' through the use of bar code scanners. Panel members are supposed to scan the bar codes of the products, even for the weekly groceries, they have purchased and a code on a card for which store they were from. Bar codes can also be scanned to indicate which newspapers they have read and to which radio stations they have listened.

For retailers the resulting information can be very useful. It is possible to analyse the type of household that buys what from where. Their responses to advertising can be to some extent measured. In some cases such as in the HTV region, which is a split region (HTV Wales and HTV West), marketing experiments can be conducted with different versions of an advertisement going out to the two halves of the region. Panel members' shopping patterns with respect to the brand concerned can then be determined. The now defunct StatsScan project by Nielsen in South Wales was another example.[32]

This data can be linked with data from bar code readers in retail outlets. Bar codes on products can be matched with customers via credit and debit (switch) cards. The next phase of these developments is about to be unleashed. That is the use of 'smart' cards on which can be stored a vast amount of information on the owner, from age and date of birth to previous purchases and even medical records.

Retail checkouts will be able to read some of this information and match special offers with individual customers. For example, as can be seen in Figure 11.2, special offers relevant to a shopper's child's birthday can be made at the right time and the shopper's new purchases can be added to the bank of information

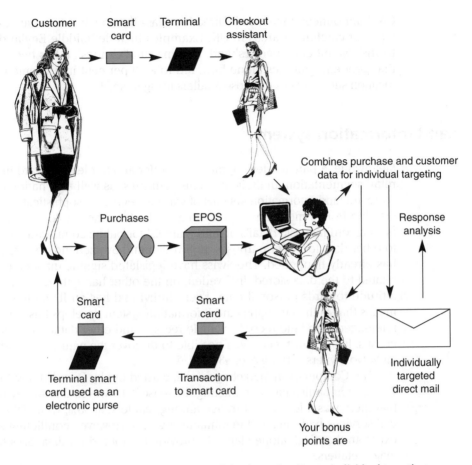

Figure 11.2 Smart card and EPOS based databases leading to individual targeting.

on his or her previous purchases. Hence the amount and quality of information grows, and so does the 'relationship' with individual customers.[33] The information collected via bar code scanners can be fed into custom-designed databases.

It is known that mailing lists are being sold extensively and every time we sign our name on something related to purchasing behaviour, there is a chance that we go into someone's database somewhere, and then get passed on to other interested marketers. By merging databases fairly detailed profiles of customers and potential customers in catchment areas can be developed. The resulting information has the ability to help retailers not only to select site branches in the most appropriate locations but also to target their customers, once there. As mentioned in Chapter 6, though, this is raising obvious ethical concerns.

Something of a merger takes place between geodemographic databases and psychographic databases. CACI now offer their 'ACORN Lifestyle'. The TGI now contains a number of lifestyle questions and these can be analysed by traditional geodemographic clusters to enrich the original geodemographics. In 1994

CACI announced their Retail Direction Classification System which defines 39 types of catchment areas in UK. Examples include 'middle England, market towns', 'slumbering centres' and 'nestling rural centres'. It has been recorded that geodemographics alone have led to a 30 per cent improvement in retail location success rates for those retailers using them.[34]

Land information system

Meanwhile, a parallel development may offer another leap forward in terms of retail segmentation analysis. In some countries, as well as a national census, there are land information systems of various degrees of sophistication. The progression from a mere land registry to a land information system means moving from recording basic details of land 'parcels' for public administration purposes to other data for other purposes. In Sweden and Switzerland, for example, this has already happened. The Swiss have legislated significant secrecy clauses related to the data stored. In Sweden, on the other hand, there is a more open attitude towards personal data. Every individual has an ID number and this means that as the emerging land information system develops this can be cross-referenced with land records, vehicle records and other databases, such as the census. It is, for instance, even possible to discover the names and addresses of all Volvo owners earning over £30,000.[35]

The Computers in Marketing Survey, carried out by DunnHumby, found that 72% of companies had a marketing database.[36] However, this survey indicated that there was a lower occurrence among retailers, at 55%, while 69% of financial services had one, and manufacturing 75%. However, conflicting evidence exists, in that CACI alone claims to provide computerized databases to 75% of major retailers.[37]

Geodemographic data would appear to be particularly useful for retailers, because they tend to have sufficient data on customer numbers, but personal data on these consumers is likely to be deficient.[38] More detailed consumer information can now be obtained either in selecting a specific site, or in searching for appropriate general locations with a suitable socio-economic structure. Information on the retail geography of specific locations can also be obtained either through the development of the retailer's own in-house database, or by buying commercial databases such as Shopping Centre Planner. The latter will provide relative proportions of floorspace. Drive time estimates for any site in the UK can also be estimated based on CACI's computerized isochrone system.

It may be pointed out that typologies such as ACORN are very general and may not be best fitted to a specific type of store.[39] 'A major concern to the retail location analyst is that, given the assertive marketing of such companies, it is more difficult critically to evaluate the bases and appropriateness of the packages offered.'[40]

What is clear, however, is that retailers are increasingly turning to such sophistication and as technology allows for easier and quicker analysis of ever increasingly large and diverse databases, the creation of tailored in-house systems is likely to continue.

11.6   Store layout

Store layout can have important effects on consumers. At a basic level, the layout influences such factors as how long the consumer stays in the store, how many products the consumer comes into visual contact with and what routes the consumer travels within the store. Such factors may affect what and how many purchases are made. A basic question of store layout is the grouping of complementary product classes. In a do-it-yourself store, the paint brushes will be close to the section with paints. In a clothing store, the blouses are close to the skirts. There are many types and variations of store layouts; two basic types are the grid and free-flow layouts.

Grid layout

In a grid layout, all counters and fixtures are at right angles to each other and resemble a maze, with merchandise counters acting as barriers to traffic flow. Such a layout is designed to increase the number of products a consumer comes into visual contact with, thus increasing the probability of purchase. The grid design can help channel consumers towards store sections with more profitable products. Grid layout techniques may increase the probability of consumers returning to the store and following similar 'traffic patterns' on repeat visits.

Free-flow layout

In a free-flow layout, the merchandise and fixtures are grouped into patterns that allow unstructured flow of customer traffic. Merchandise is divided on the basis of fixtures and signs, and customers can come into visual contact with all departments from any point in the store. A free-flow arrangement is particularly useful for encouraging relaxed shopping and impulse purchases.

Shelf position

In supermarkets and do-it-yourself stores shelf positions are important for the turnover of the products. Often, breadth and height are distinguished. The breadth is the horizontal number of package facings on a shelf, next to each other. The height is the vertical number of facings. Articles at eye level attract most attention from shoppers, especially if these articles are at the right side of the aisle, in the normal walking direction. Each shelf position has its own turnover index. In Table 11.2 these indexes are given, based on a study in American A&P supermarkets.[41] The turnover of an article moved from the fifth to the first shelf will decrease by 41.6%.[42]

Table 11.2 Turnover indexes at different shelf levels.

Fifth shelf (eye level)	137
Fourth shelf	102
Third shelf (middle level)	100
Second shelf	90
First shelf (floor level)	57

Information on the turnover levels at different shelf positions leads to the following advice:[43]

■ Products with a high turnover and margin should be placed at eye level, on the right side of the aisle.

■ Private labels are often placed at eye level, with the higher priced national brands at a lower level.

■ Heavy articles such as large packages of detergents are placed on the floor.

■ Small and costly articles, such as cigarettes, are placed at the fourth or fifth shelf, and often close to the checkout counter.

■ Articles that are needed, such as sugar, may be placed at less attractive spots. Consumers will find these anyway.

■ Consumers should be able to compare products and prices within a category from one position. This is especially important in a busy situation. A vertical positioning is then better than a horizontal positioning of products.

■ Packages with similar colours should not be placed next to each other. Otherwise consumers could easily confuse these brands and select the 'wrong' brand.

■ Filled shelves are more attractive than half-empty shelves. The shelves should be well maintained, cleaned and filled. Damaged products should be removed.

11.7 In-store stimuli

In most environments there is an endless number of stimuli that could affect cognitions, attitudes and behaviour. A store is no exception. Stores have many stimuli that affect consumers: the characteristics of other shoppers and salespeople, lighting, noises, smells, temperature, shelf space and displays, signs, colours and merchandise, to name a few. In-store signs are useful for directing consumers to particular merchandise and for offering product benefit and price information. Signs affect consumer cognitions (consumers apparently process different sign information) and consumer behaviour at the point of decision and sale. Sales increase with the use of certain types of signs.

Colour has been shown to have a variety of physical and psychological effects on consumer perceptions of retail store environments. Colour can have customer drawing power as well as image-creating potential. For example, warm-colour environments are appropriate for buying situations associated with unplanned impulse purchases. Cool colours may be appropriate where customer deliberations over the purchase decision are necessary.

Research generally supports the idea that more shelf space and in-store displays increase sales and that the presentation of merchandise in the store has an important effect on consumer behaviour.

Considerable research supports the idea that music played in the background while other activities are being performed affects attitudes and behaviour. Music is played in many retail stores and banks, but relatively little basic research has been conducted on its effects on consumer behaviour. The tempo of background music affects consumer behaviour.[44] The slow-beat musical selections led to higher sales volumes, as consumers spent more time and money, though it seems likely that music affected their behaviour without their being totally conscious of it.

Store-related cognitions

A variety of cognitive and affective processes could be discussed in relation to retail stores. However, two major mental variables of managerial concern at the retail level are store image and store atmosphere. Both deal with the influence of store attributes on consumers' cognitions and attitudes rather than how marketing managers perceive the stores.

Store image

Store image should be treated on the basis of what consumers think about a particular store. This includes perceptions and attitudes based on sensations of store-related stimuli received through the senses. Operationally, store image is commonly assessed by asking consumers how favourable or important various aspects of a retail store's operation are. Scaling techniques, such as the semantic differential, are widely used for this purpose.

Store image research involves surveying consumers concerning their perceptions of and attitudes about particular store dimensions. Often the same attributes will be studied for competitive stores to compare the strengths and weaknesses of a particular store's image with that of its closest competitors. Developing a consistent store image is a common goal of retailers. This involves coordinating the various aspects of store image to appeal to a specific market segment.

Store atmosphere

Store atmosphere primarily involves in-store emotional states that consumers may not be fully conscious of when shopping. These emotional states are difficult for consumers to verbalize, are rather transient and affect in-store behaviour in ways consumers may not be aware of. Environmental stimuli affect consumers' emotional states, which in turn affect approach or avoidance behaviours.[45]

Approach behaviours refer to moving towards and avoidance behaviours refer to moving away from various environments and stimuli.

Store-related behaviours

Throughout this section we have discussed a number of cognitive and environmental variables designed to affect consumers' store-related behaviours. There are many such behaviours that marketing managers want to encourage in the retail environment. Two basic types of behaviour are store contact and store loyalty.

Store contact

Store contact involves the consumer locating, travelling to and entering a store. Store coupons, rebates and local advertising are commonly used tactics to increase these behaviours. Store location decisions are strongly influenced by heavy traffic and pedestrian patterns, which facilitate store contact. Also, the visibility of the store and its distance from consumers are variables used to select locations that can increase store contact.

Store loyalty

Repeat patronage is usually desired by retailers. Store loyalty, repeat patronage intentions and behaviours can be strongly influenced by the arrangement of the environment, particularly the reinforcing properties of the retail store. For example, in-store stimuli and the attributes associated with store image are the primary variables used to influence store loyalty. Thus, reinforcing tactics and positive attributes of the store are used to develop store loyalty.

Store loyalty is a major objective of retail channel strategy and it has an important financial impact. Thus, the analysis of the store environment, and consumers' store cognitions, attitudes and store behaviours are critical for successful retailing.

11.8 Conclusions

This chapter has presented an overview of channel strategy and the relationships between store environment, cognitions, attitudes and behaviour. It is the consumer and the relationships between the consumer and the other criteria that should determine the appropriate channel strategy. Current trends in analysing customers in catchment areas have been discussed and, as with our discussion of individualism and database marketing in Chapter 6, it is clear that in the retail environment, retailers are increasingly being able to understand and cater for their consumers on an ever more individual basis, with ever greater depth of knowledge of their behaviour as consumers.

Endnotes

1. A.C. Lea, 1989.
2. B. Berman and J. Evans, 1992.
3. C.S. Craig, A. Ghosh and S. McLafferty, 1984; A.C. Lea 1989; A.C. Lea and G.L. Menger 1990; A.C. Lea and G.L. Menger 1991.
4. M.J. Breheny, 1988.
5. Initially developed by R.L Nelson, 1958.
6. B. Berman and J. Evans, 1992.
7. D. Rogers, 1992, p. 11.
8. K.G. Jones and D.R. Mock, 1984.
9. P.J. Kelly *et al.*, 1993.
10. R.L. Davies and D.S. Rogers, 1984.
11. H. Kohsaka, 1992.
12. K. Jones and J. Simmons, 1990.
13. S. Anderson, 1987.
14. K. Jones and J. Simmons, 1990.
15. B. Berman and J. Evans, 1992.
16. S. Moore and G. Attewell, 1992.
17. K. Jones and J. Simmons, 1990.
18. K. Jones and J. Simmons, 1990.
19. K. Jones and J. Simmons, 1990.
20. Automatic Teller Machines.
21. K. Jones and J. Simmons, 1990.
22. W. Applebaum, 1968.
23. EPOS means: Electronic Point of Sale.
24. J.R. Beaumont and K. Inglis, 1989, p. 596.
25. C. Blair, 1983.
26. C. Blair, 1983.
27. S.B. Cohen and W. Applebaum, 1960.
28. See also Chapter 6 on market segmentation.
29. TGI is Target Group Index.
30. Reported in 34 volumes of buyer profiles in most product-markets and based on samples of over 20,000 annually.
31. P. Sleight, 1993.
32. P. Ody, 1989.
33. J. Foenander, 1992.
34. M. Johnson, 1989.
35. L. Kreitzman, 1987.
36. D. Reed, 1993.
37. P. McGoldrick, 1990.
38. D. Reed, 1993.
39. S. Bowlby *et al.*, 1984.
40. P. McGoldrick, 1990.
41. Study of *The Progressive Grocer* and A&P supermarkets in 1982. These results are reported by J.R. Rossiter and L. Percy, 1987, p. 316.
42. (57/137)100 = 41.6%.
43. J.M.G. Floor and W.F. Van Raaij, 1993, chapter 22.
44. R.E. Milliman, 1982.
45. R.J. Donovan and J.R. Rossiter, 1982.

The discussion of store location is based on work by L. O'Malley, M. Patterson and M. Evans, including the paper 'The Application of Geodemographics in Retail Site Location and Trade Area Analysis: A Preliminary Investigation' in *Marketing Intelligence and Planning*, Vol. 13 No. 2, pages 29–35, 1995, ISSN 0263-4503.

12

Marketing-communication strategy and consumer behaviour

Chapter objectives

(1) To analyse the impact of promotion strategies on consumer behaviour.
(2) To provide an overview of the promotion mix and the advantages and disadvantages of each type of promotion strategy.
(3) To discuss key factors related to the management of promotion strategies, including advertising and personal selling.
(4) To introduce an analytical view of relevant areas such as copy strategy and cognitions derived from promotion, advertising and consumer attitudes, persuasion processes, overt behaviour derived from promotion and information contact effects.

12.1 Marketing-communication mix

Marketers communicate information about their products or services and try to persuade consumers to buy these. Marketing communication results in environmental stimuli created to influence consumers' cognitions, attitudes and behaviours. The major marketing-communication instruments are advertising, sales promotion, personal selling, and publicity (marketing-PR). Further marketing-communication instruments are sponsorship, in-store communication, direct-marketing communication, trade shows and exhibitions.[1] The combination of some of these instruments is the *marketing-communication mix*. Most successful products and brands require marketing communication to create a sustainable differential advantage over their competitors. Through the use of marketing-communication campaigns companies are able to inform consumers about product attributes, prices and places where products are available. This information may save consumers both time and money by reducing the costs of search.

Advertising

Advertising is any paid, non-personal presentation of information in mass media about a product, brand, company or store. It usually has an identified sponsor. Much advertising is intended to influence consumers' images, beliefs, and attitudes towards products and brands, and to influence their behaviours. In fact, advertising has been characterized as image management, creating and maintaining images and meanings in consumers' minds.[2] Advertisements may be conveyed via a variety of media: television, radio, print (magazines, newspapers), billboards, signs, and miscellaneous media such as hot-air balloons and T-shirt decals. Although the typical consumer is exposed to literally hundreds of advertisements daily, the vast majority of these messages receive low levels of attention and comprehension. Thus, it is a major challenge for marketers to develop advertising messages and select media that expose consumers, capture their attention and generate the appropriate comprehension processes and attitude change.

Sales promotion

Sales promotions are direct inducements to the consumer to make a purchase. This is done by either a temporary price discount or giving away additional value (premium) with the purchase of a product. Although TV advertising may be more glamorous, more money is spent on sales promotion techniques. Sales promotion may be defined as a temporary improvement of the price–value ratio, in order to increase sales. The key aspect of sales promotions is to move the product today, not tomorrow. In sum, most sales promotions are oriented at changing consumers' short-run purchase behaviours. The exception are thematic promotions, in which premiums are given away, even if no product has been bought, for instance giving away small gifts to children.

Personal selling

Personal selling involves direct interactions between a salesperson and a potential buyer. Personal selling can be a powerful communication method, although it is an expensive one. Because two-way communication is possible, situation involvement tends to be fairly high and salespeople can adapt their sales presentations to influence consumers effectively. Certain products are heavily promoted through personal selling. Life insurance, cars, computers and houses are examples. As the costs of direct, face-to-face selling increase, personal selling by telephone, called telemarketing, has become increasingly popular.

Publicity

Publicity is any unpaid form of communication about the marketers' company, products or brands. For instance, an article in *PC World* comparing various brands of laptop portable computers provides useful product information to consumers, at no cost to the marketers of the computers. Similarly, descriptions of new products or brands, brand comparisons in trade journals, newspapers or news magazines, or discussions on radio and TV provide product information to consumers. Marketing-PR is the instrument to create to contact journalists. Free publicity can be either positive or negative, of course.

Another type of publicity reached through marketing-PR is a thematic contest or other happening around the brand for instance organizing the Camel Trophy, an international contest with Landrovers in a rough terrain. This creates free publicity in newspapers. It comes close to sponsorship of a sports or other event.

Publicity may be more effective than advertising, because consumers may not screen out the messages so readily. In addition, publicity communications may be considered more credible, because they are not being presented by the marketing organization. Publicity is difficult to manage, however. Marketers sometimes stage 'media events' in the hope of generating free publicity. They hope that the media will report the event and perhaps show a picture of the product. Companies have little control over what type of publicity (if any) would result, however.

In sum, marketers can choose from among many different marketing-communication strategies. They often combine several different instruments into an overall strategy called the *marketing-communication mix*. Table 12.1 summarizes advantages and disadvantages of each type of marketing-communication strategy.

12.2 General communication model

The various marketing-communication methods described above are the most direct ways that marketers-communicate with consumers. Developing a successful marketing-communication strategy, then, is largely a communication problem. Figure 12.1 presents a simple model that accounts for how a message is communicated from a source to a receiver. The source of the communication, the manufacturer of products, service provider or propagator of ideas, determines which information is to be conveyed. The message is encoded, that is, translated into appropriate symbols, and transmitted (through a medium) to a receiver (consumer). The receiver must decode the message, that is, interpret the symbols/comprehend the message, and take appropriate action, such as purchase.

Table 12.1 Some advantages and disadvantages of major marketing-communication instruments.

Advertising

Advantages

Can reach many consumers simultaneously.
Relatively low cost per exposure.
Excellent for creating brand images.
High degree of flexibility.
Variety of media to choose from.
Can accomplish many different types of
marketing communication objectives.

Disadvantages

Many consumers reached are not potential buyers
(waste of marketing communication money).
High visibility makes advertising a major target
for marketing critics.
Advertising exposure time is usually brief.
Advertisements are often quickly and easily
screened out by consumers.

Personal selling

Advantages

Can be the most persuasive promotion tool.
Salespeople can directly influence
purchase behaviours.
Allows two-way communication.
Often necessary for technically
complex products.
Allows direct one-on-one targeting
of marketing-communications effort.

Disadvantages

High cost per contact.
Sales training and motivation can be expensive
and difficult.
Personal selling often has a poor image, making
sales force recruitment difficult.
Poorly done sales presentations can hurt sales
as well as company, product and brand image.

Sales promotion

Advantages

Excellent approach for short-term
price reductions for stimulating demand.
A large variety of sales promotion tools.
Can be effective for changing a variety
of consumer behaviours.
Can be easily tied in with other promotion
tools.

Disadvantages

May influence primarily brand loyal customers to
stock up at a lower price but attract few new
customers.
May have only short-term impact.
Overuse of price-related sales promotion tools
may hurt brand image and profits.
Effective sales promotions are easily copied
by competitors.

Publicity (marketing-PR)

Advantages

As 'free advertising', publicity can be
positive and stimulate demand at no cost.
May be perceived by consumers as more
credible, because it is not paid for by the seller.
Consumers may pay more attention to these
messages, because they are not
quickly screened out as are many
advertisements.

Disadvantages

Company cannot completely control the
content of publicity messages.
Publicity is not always available.
Limited repetition of publicity messages.
Seldom a long-term marketing communication
tool for brands.
Publicity can be negative and hurt sales as well as
company, product and brand images.

Figure 12.1 also shows the relevant agents and stimuli involved in each of these stages and the major activities that occur at each stage. Although each stage is important to the success of marketing-communication strategies, two are

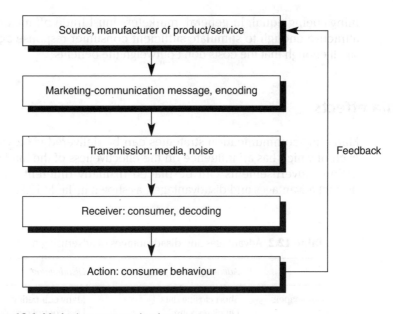

Figure 12.1 Marketing-communication process.

especially critical. The first occurs when the marketer/source creates (encodes) the marketing-communication message to convey a particular meaning. The second critical stage occurs when consumers are exposed to the marketing-communication message and interpret (decode or comprehend) it. A huge amount of research has addressed each of these stages and activities in the communication process.

Source effects

The source of a marketing-communication message influences its effectiveness.[3] For instance, salespersons whom customers perceive as credible, trustworthy, expert, and similar to themselves are often more effective than other salespersons. Celebrity spokespersons are often hired to appear in TV and radio advertisements where they serve as the source for messages about the product, for example Robbie Coltrane for Persil and Billy Connolly for Kaliber.

Message effects

The actual informational content of the message influences its effectiveness. The larger the print advertisement, the higher the coupon value, the bigger the sweepstakes or contest prize, the more attractive the package premium, the more effective the marketing-communication strategy is likely to be, all other things being equal. In general, marketers must trade off making the message attractive enough to stimulate sufficient consumer response against making it small enough that the costs don't outweigh the benefits.

Media effects

Marketing-communication strategies can be delivered via a variety of media, each of which has an influence on the effectiveness of the marketing communication. Advertisements can be placed in many different media, each with distinct advantages and disadvantages, as shown in Table 12.2.

Table 12.2 Advantages and disadvantages of advertising media.[4]

	Advantages	*Disadvantages*
Newspapers	Short closing data Quick response Geographical segmentation	Many competing ads Less control over page position Poor reproduction quality
Magazines	High reproduction quality Prestige of medium	Long closing date Delayed response
Television	Sight and sound Product demonstration One message at a time	TV clutter No complex information Intrusiveness
Radio	Intimacy, humour Relatively inexpensive	No visual component Easily avoided by consumers Less attentive listening
Direct mail	Personalized High reproduction quality Measurable	Government regulation
Posters	Colour, large size High reproduction quality	No complex information No audience research
Point of sale	Immediacy at point of purchase Three-dimensional display	Retailer cooperation needed Difficult pinpointing audience

Receiver characteristics

The success of a marketing-communication campaign will be affected by the characteristics of the consumers who receive it. Foremost among these factors are the consumers' knowledge about and enduring involvement with the product or brand being promoted. Another important receiver characteristic is consumers' deal proneness, their general inclination to use promotional deals such as buying on sale or using coupons. Some consumers are much more likely to respond favourably to sales promotions than others who consider them a waste of time.

Actions

Although the key consumer action of interest to marketers is purchase of the promoted product or brand, other behaviours may also be the targets of marketing-communication strategy. For instance, some marketing communications are intended to generate store contact or to build store traffic. Other campaigns may attempt to stimulate word-of-mouth communications between consumers.

Managing marketing-communication strategy

Developing and implementing an effective marketing-communication strategy is a complex, difficult task. Although no single approach or 'magic formula' can guarantee an effective marketing-communication mix, the following steps identify the key activities in managing marketing-communication strategy:

(1) Analyse consumer/product relationships (Section 12.3).
(2) Determine marketing-communication objectives and budget (Section 12.4).
(3) Design and implement the marketing-communication strategy (Section 12.5).
(4) Evaluate effects of the marketing-communication strategy (Section 12.6).

12.3 Analysing consumer/product relationships

Developing an effective marketing-communication strategy begins with an analysis of the relationships between consumers and the products or brands of interest. This requires identifying the appropriate target markets for the product or service. Then, marketers must identify consumer needs, goals and values, their levels of product and brand knowledge and involvement, and their current attitudes and behaviour patterns. In short, marketers must strive to understand the relationship between their target consumers and the product or brand of interest.

When dealing with a new product or brand, marketers may have to conduct considerable marketing research to learn about the consumer/product relationship. This research could include interviews to identify the dominant means–end chains that reveal how consumers perceive the relationships between the product or brand and their own self-concepts and values. Other methods might include group discussion interviews, concept tests, attitude and use surveys, and even test marketing. For existing products and brands, marketers may already know a great deal about consumer/product relationships. Perhaps only follow-up research might be necessary here.

FCB Grid

Table 12.3 presents a simple grid model used by Foote, Cone and Belding, a major advertising agency, to analyse consumer/product relationships. The Grid also shows the typical locations of several different products. The FCB Grid is based on two concepts: consumers' involvement and their salient knowledge, meanings and beliefs about the product.

Consumers have varying degrees of felt involvement (enduring plus situation involvement) with a product or brand, denoted as lower or higher involvement in the grid model. Moreover, various types of knowledge, meanings and beliefs may be activated when consumers evaluate and choose among alternative products or brands. Some products are considered primarily in terms of rational factors, such as the functional benefits of using the product. These are termed 'think' products in the grid model. Included in this category are such products as investments, cameras and car batteries, all products purchased primarily for their functional consequences.

In contrast, 'feel' products are considered by consumers primarily in terms of non-verbal images (visual or other types of images) and emotional factors, such as psychosocial benefits and values. For instance, products purchased primarily for their sensory qualities, such as ice cream, soft drinks, cologne, as well as products for which emotional consequences are dominant, flowers or jewellery, are feel products in the FCB Grid. An example of the practical application of this concept can be seen in the use of scent strips for perfume products which allow consumers to experience 'feel' products. Marketing research shows that consumers are more likely to buy products that they have sampled. Scent strips can be placed on advertisements that can be seen (and smelled) by millions of consumers. Scent strips appear to be a very effective marketing communication device. Scented strips make sampling easier and a lot less expensive.

Because the consumer/product relationships are quite different in the four quadrants of the grid, the FCB Grid also has implications for developing marketing-communication strategy, including developing creative advertising, measuring advertising effects and selecting media in which to place advertisements.

Table 12.3 FCB Grid for analysing consumer/product relationships.[5]

Involvement	'Think' products	'Feel' products
High	Individual retirement account 35 mm camera Refrigerator Car battery	Car Wallpaper Perfume
Low	Insecticide Clothes pins	Greeting card Rum Ice-cream bar

The appropriate marketing-communication strategy depends on the product's position in the grid. Sometimes, a product can be 'moved' within the grid. In general, FCB has found that traditional *'think'* products often can be marketed successfully using *feel* advertising marketing-communication strategies. In sum, the FCB Grid model illustrates how a careful analysis of the consumer/product relationship can help in the development of effective marketing-communications.

12.4 Marketing-communication objectives

Marketing-communication strategies can have behavioural, attitudinal and cognitive effects on consumers. Thus, marketing-communication may be designed to meet one or more of the following eight objectives.[6] Category need, awareness, knowledge, facilitation, intention, and post-purchase knowledge structuring are cognitive objectives. Attitude and satisfaction are affective objectives. Behaviour is obviously a behavioural or conative objective.

1 Category need

Consumers' perception of a need that can be satisfied with the product. Category need is often an objective during the first stage of the product life cycle. During this stage consumers have to be informed about the benefits of the product, for example an interactive CD-player, rather than the brands. Collective campaigns, for instance for cheese, potatoes or travel insurance, have a category need objective.

2 Brand awareness

Brand awareness is consumer association of a brand with a product category, for example the Nissan 300ZX as a sports car. This may be new knowledge or a reminder. If consumers actively remember a brand, it is called active brand awareness. If consumers only recognize a brand in a choice situation, it is called passive brand awareness. Active brand awareness is needed, if consumers have to remember the brand themselves in a choice situation. Passive brand awareness is needed, if the brand names are available in the choice situation, for example self-service stores.

3 Brand knowledge

Brand knowledge and beliefs are more extensive than brand awareness. It is the knowledge of brand characteristics, benefits and meanings. In later stages of the product life cycle, brands will often be differentiated and this differentiation has to be communicated to target groups.

4 Brand attitude

Brand attitude is an evaluation of the brand in terms of favourableness. Brand attitude may be a global affect ('I like this brand') or an articulated evaluation of beliefs.

5 Behavioural/purchase facilitation

Purchase facilitation is information of how and where to purchase the brand, including location of the store and methods of payment. It is actually not information about the product or brand, but about the other relevant marketing-mix elements (price and distribution).

6 Behavioural/purchase intention

Intention is close to behaviour. It is a consumer plan to visit a specific store or to buy a specific product or brand in the future or a plan to engage in another specific behaviour.

7 Behaviour, purchase

Store traffic, store patronage, purchase of the brand or other specific behaviour, such as returning a response card or calling a telephone number with a request for more information. The communication objective may be to change or to reinforce the behaviour.

8 Post-purchase satisfaction

Increasing the user satisfaction with the brand is a major objective. For fast-moving consumer goods it may be the most important communication objective to keep customers. Another post-purchase objective is to structure the brand knowledge of users in order to increase their satisfaction and commitment. Many consumers tend to read advertising of the brand they just purchased in order to decrease their cognitive dissonance and to find arguments supporting their choice.[7]

Before designing a marketing-communication strategy, marketers should determine their specific marketing-communication objectives and the budget available to support it. The long-run objective of most marketing-communication strategies is to influence consumer behaviour, especially store patronage and brand purchase. Many marketing communications are designed to directly and quickly affect consumer purchases of a particular brand. For example, the rebate programmes and low-interest financing offered by car manufacturers are intended to stimulate short-run sales of certain makes and models. Finally, many marketing communications have multiple objectives. For example, some food companies frequently use a sales promotion strategy of placing coupons on the package. This promotion is designed to stimulate immediate sales and to encourage repeat sales, with the long-run goal of creating more brand-loyal consumers.

Some marketing-communication campaigns are designed to first influence consumers' cognitions and attitudes in anticipation of a later influence on their overt behaviours. When a new product or brand is introduced, a primary objective for advertising marketing communications may be to create awareness of the product and some simple beliefs about it. Marketers also try to generate publicity for new products for these reasons, as well as to create a favourable brand image. These cognitions are intended to influence sales behaviours at some later time.

12.5 Designing and implementing marketing-communication strategy

Designing alternative marketing-communication strategies and selecting one to meet the marketing-communication objectives is based largely on the consumer/product relationships that have been identified through marketing research. Implementing the marketing-communication strategy may include creating advertisements and running them in various media, designing and distributing coupons, putting salespeople to work and developing publicity events. Many of these tasks may be done with the aid of an advertising agency or a marketing-communication consultant.

Designing marketing-communication strategies

Consider the various consumer segments portrayed in Table 12.4. These groups are defined by consumers' purchase behaviour and attitudes towards a brand. Consumers who dislike the brand and never buy it are not likely to be persuaded by any marketing communications and can be ignored. On the other hand, consumers who never buy the brand but have a favourable (or at least neutral) attitude towards it are vulnerable to the company's marketing communications. Free samples, premiums, contests or coupons may encourage these consumers to try the brand and move them to an occasional user segment. Occasional purchasers of the brand are vulnerable to the marketing-communication strategies

Table 12.4 Consumer segments and vulnerability.[8]

Purchase pattern	Attitude toward our brand		
	Like	*Neutral*	*Dislike*
Buy regularly	Brand loyal	Regular customers vulnerable to competition	
Buy occasionally	Occasional customers to our brand, vulnerable to competition		
Never buy	Loyal to other brands, vulnerable to our brand		Forget it!

for competing brands. In that situation, a marketing-communication objective might be to encourage repeat purchases of the brand.

Finally, brand-loyal consumers who like a company's brand and purchase it consistently can be influenced by marketing communications designed to keep them happy customers. The airlines have used a phenomenally successful marketing communication, commonly called 'frequent flyer programmes', to reinforce the attitudes and purchase behaviour of their frequent customers. Consumers rack up mileage on flights taken with the airline and receive free trips when sufficient mileage has been accumulated. The programmes are supposed to be limited to frequent flyers, usually defined as those taking 12 or more plane trips per year. In any case, these incentive programmes have seemed so successful that they are being copied by other types of companies. Now an increasing number of companies from banks to retailers to car rental agencies are trying to mimic the airlines' success with frequent-buyer programmes of their own by giving 'airmiles'.[9] Under these plans, customers accumulate points, usually based on money spent, that can be cashed in for prizes, discounts or indeed free airline tickets.

Phone calls by salespeople to 'check up on how things are going' may reinforce customers' attitudes, satisfaction and intentions to rebuy when the need arises. Finally, marketing communications can inform current consumers of new uses for existing products.

Three important points must be kept in mind. First, appropriate marketing-communications depend on the type of relationship consumers have with the product or brand, especially their level of enduring involvement. Second, marketing-communication methods vary in their effectiveness for achieving certain objectives. Personal selling, for example, is usually more effective for closing sales. Advertising is more effective for increasing brand awareness among large groups of consumers. Third, marketing-communication objectives will change over a product's or brand's life cycle as changes occur in consumers' relationships with the product and the competitive environment. At the introduction stage, category need and brand awareness are important; at later stages brand knowledge, attitudes, intentions and satisfaction are important. A marketing-communication strategy that worked well when the product was introduced is not likely to be effective at the growth, maturity or decline stages of the life cycle.

In the remainder of this section, advertising and personal selling strategies are further discussed.

Developing advertising strategy

A number of factors must be considered in developing advertising strategy. One model of advertising strategy identifies five key elements[10], presented below:

- *Driving force*: The value orientation of the advertising strategy; the end goal or value on which the advertising is focused.
- *Consumer benefits*: The key positive consequences for the consumer that are to be communicated in the advertisement, either visually or verbally.

- *Message elements*: The concrete or abstract product attributes or features that are to be communicated in the advertisement, either verbally or visually.
- *Leverage point*: The specific way in which the value or end goal is linked to the specific features of the advertisement; the 'hook' that activates or taps into the driving force.
- *Executional framework*: All the details of the advertising execution: models, clothes used, setting, as well as the overall scenario or action plot, the advertisement's overall theme or style, the vehicle for communicating the means–end message.

Each of these advertising strategy factors requires many decisions by marketing and advertising agency personnel. As we have seen, the first step in developing an advertising strategy is to analyse the consumer/product relationship. Means–end measures of consumers' knowledge structures are useful for this purpose. From a means–end perspective, the end goals or values that consumers seek to achieve are the key to developing effective advertising strategies. The marketer must select the key value, end state, goal or benefit to be communicated in the advertisement. Then, the marketer must communicate that the product attributes can achieve or satisfy this end goal or value.[11]

The attribute, consequence, and value levels of product knowledge in a means–end chain are directly related to three of the major decision elements of advertising strategy. Knowing consumers' salient product attributes help marketers decide which *message elements* to include in an advertisement. Should ads for Walkers' crisps emphasize their flavour or crunchiness? Data about the important functional consequences consumers perceive can help identify the key *consumer benefits* to be communicated. Are Golden Wonder crisps for snacking or an accompaniment for sandwiches? Values or end goals are directly related to the *driving force* of the advertising strategy.

Finally, developing the *executional framework* and the *leverage point* requires selecting and putting together the specific executional aspects of an advertisement: the product attributes mentioned or shown, the models used, the camera angles, the plot, the various cuts to different scenes, and soon, to effectively communicate the connection between the product and the basic needs, goals and values the consumer is seeking. These decisions require creative imagination that can be guided by means–end data. This is a convenient framework that organizes and gives focus to the many decisions. Generally, it should produce more coherent and effective advertising that communicates complete means–end meanings.

Developing personal selling strategies

The process of developing a personal selling strategy is illustrated in Figure 12.2. The model is referred to as ISTEA, which stands for impression, strategy, transmission, evaluation and adjustment.[12] This model suggests that salespeople's influence depends on their skills at performing five basic activities:

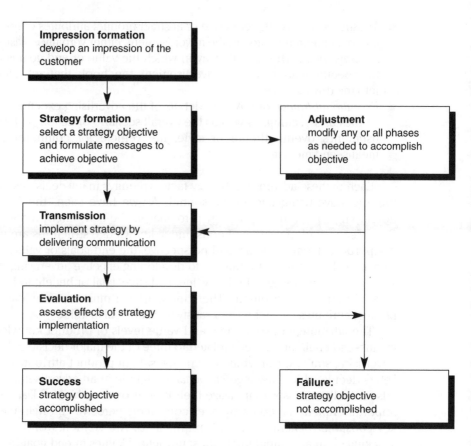

Figure 12.2 A model of the personal selling process.[13]

(1) Developing useful *impressions* of the customer.
(2) Formulating selling *strategies* based on these impressions.
(3) *Transmitting* appropriate messages.
(4) *Evaluating* customer reactions to the messages.
(5) Making appropriate *adjustments* in presentation should the initial approach fail.

According to this model, the personal selling process works as follows. In the first activity, the salesperson combines information gained through past experience with information relevant to the specific interaction to develop an impression of the customer. Salespersons can derive information about their target customers by examining past experiences with this and other customers, by observing the target customer during an interaction, and by projecting themselves into the target customer's decision-making situation.

In the second activity, the salesperson analyses his/her impression of the customer and develops a communication strategy which includes an objective for the strategy, a method for implementing the strategy and specific message formats.

Having formulated the strategy, the salesperson transmits the messages to the customer. As the salesperson delivers the messages, he or she evaluates their effects by observing the customer's reactions and soliciting opinions. On the basis of these evaluations, the salesperson can make adjustments by either reformulating the impression of the customer, selecting a new strategic objective or changing the method for achieving the strategic objective or the salesperson can continue to implement the same strategy.[14]

Although this model was developed for industrial (business-to-business) marketing situations, it is consistent with the communication approach to consumer marketing communication discussed above.[15] The model emphasizes analysis of the customer as the starting point for strategy development. Research confirms that impression formation (consumer analysis) and strategy formulation by salespeople improved their sales performance.[16]

12.6 Evaluating effects of marketing-communication strategy

Evaluating the effects of a marketing-communication strategy involves comparing its results with the objectives. For example, clearly stated cognitive objectives such as 'increase brand awareness by 25 per cent' are relatively easily evaluated, although different methods of measuring awareness may give different results. Moreover, it is often difficult to determine whether a change in brand awareness resulted from the marketing-communication strategy or from something else, such as word-of-mouth communications. Similarly, marketing-communication objectives stated in behavioural terms, such as 'increase the overall sales of the brand by 10 per cent', are often hard to evaluate. It is often difficult to determine what factors caused a sales increase. Increases in competitors' prices, opening new sales territories and outlets, and various other factors may be responsible for the increase in sales. Likewise, if sales decrease or remain the same during the campaign period, it is difficult to determine whether the communication strategy was ineffective or whether other factors were responsible for the effect.

Sales promotion tools such as coupons are used to stimulate short-term sales, and coupon redemption rates can give a good idea of the effectiveness of the sales promotion campaign. The sales revenue and gross contribution achieved by salespeople can also be compared to determine their relative effectiveness. Experimental approaches and other research (surveying target consumers' recall and recognition of advertisements and brands) can also be used to examine the effects of advertising. In sum, while measuring the effectiveness of marketing-communication strategies may be difficult, marketers do have methods for estimating these effects.

Measuring advertising effects

Because the major impact of advertising tends to be on consumers' cognitions, measuring its effects is often difficult. Given that the costs of advertising are very high, marketers have tried to develop measures of the communication effectiveness of advertisements. This is usually called copy testing. Two types of measures are most common: recall and persuasion (belief and attitude change). Advertising recall measures have been attacked for not really measuring the important impacts of advertisements.[17] For certain types of advertisements (reminder or image ads) recall may be an important objective, but note that brand recall is more relevant than advertisement recall. Some advertisements are intended to create high levels of brand or product awareness, and a measure of top-of-mind awareness (TOMA) such as brand name recall may be quite appropriate. Advertising research methods include concept tests, pre-tests, post-tests, and campaign evaluation or tracking research.

Concept test

The concept is the 'creative translation' of the advertising proposition or message into consumer language and interests. In a concept test, the advertising concept is tested, including comprehension, thoughts, feelings, and spontaneous associations with the concept. Often a story board is used to give an impression of the concept of a commercial. Is the concept attractive, convincing, credible, persuasive, and understandable even with a brief exposure?

Pre-test

Pre-test research is normally done when the advertisement or commercial is almost finished, but before the ad is placed in the media. It is a last check whether the ad will deliver the message to the audience. Barriers in the communication and misperceptions may be detected and can be 'repaired'. Advertisements with very favourable pre-test outcomes may be placed more frequently in the media, whereas advertisements with less favourable results may get a lower frequency or may not be placed at all. Sometimes physiological methods, such as galvanic skin response, are used to assess affective reactions to the advertisement.

Post-test

A post-test is a measure after the advertisement or commercial has been placed in the media. Recall and recognition are post-test measures. Post-tests are used to assess whether the ad delivers the message in a realistic broadcast situation. It might be even a measure of the reach of the campaign.

Campaign evaluation

Campaign evaluation is broader than a post-test, because it concerns the effects of a campaign with many ads and not of a specific advertisement or commercial. For campaign evaluation, pre- and post-measures are needed to assess the changes caused by the campaign, for example changes in brand awareness, TOMA, attitude, knowledge and intention. This is also called monitoring or tracking research, if the advertiser polls consumers regularly about these effect measures.

Marketing-communication environment

The marketing-communication environment includes all marketing-communication instruments marketers use to influence consumer cognitions and behaviours: advertising, sales promotions, personal selling and publicity. The marketing-communication environment also includes the physical and social environment in which the campaigns are experienced. Many of these factors can affect the success of a campaign. In this section, we discuss three environmental factors that can influence advertising and sales promotion strategies: clutter, level of competition and types of advertising executions.

1 Communication clutter

A key marketing-communication objective is to increase the probability that consumers come into contact with, attend to and comprehend the message. In recent years, however, competition has so increased that the effectiveness of any given marketing-communication strategy may be impaired by clutter, the growing number of competitive messages in the environment. Advertisers have long been worried that the clutter created by multiple advertisements during commercial breaks and between television programmes will reduce the communication effectiveness of each advertisement. Clutter also affects other types of marketing-communication strategies, especially sales promotions. Over the past decade, marketers have dramatically increased their spending on sales promotions.

2 Level of competition

The level of competition is a key aspect of the marketing communication environment for a product category. As competition heats up, marketers' use of sales promotions usually increases. Moreover, the types of marketing-communication strategy change as competitive pressures increase. Comparative advertising, featuring direct comparisons with competitive brands, may become more common. In fiercely competitive environments, marketing communication often becomes the key element in the marketer's competitive arsenal. Marketers may develop complex marketing-communication mixes that include couponing, premiums, advertisements, price reductions, publicity and other marketing communicational tools.

3 Advertising content

Marketers have studied a great many content characteristics of advertisements. These include such factors as fear, humour, sexual content, one- and two-sided arguments, size of print ads, length of broadcast ads, strong visual images, specific claims, celebrity spokespersons, multiple repetitions, subliminal stimuli and many others. Few generalizations have been gained from this research, however. Partly this is because the effects of any advertisement are a function of the knowledge and involvement of the consumer audience and the environment in which exposure takes place. Thus, it is likely that fear appeals or humour or sex might be effective in one situation but not in another.

One content characteristic of current interest concerns the dominant theme or type of information in the advertisement. Different types of advertising have different impacts on consumers' knowledge, meanings, beliefs and attitudes about a product, including their moods, emotions and image meanings. Most frequently, informational, factual or reason-why advertisements are contrasted with transformational, emotional or image advertisements. If attended to and comprehended at a deep, elaborate level, informational advertisements are thought to create new semantic knowledge or beliefs about the product, its attributes and consequences.[18] On the other hand, emotional and image advertisements are thought to create different types of meanings.[19] They make consumers feel differently about themselves and perhaps about their relationship with the product. Such meanings may affect product purchase, especially for 'feel' products.

A particularly interesting issue concerns the ability of so-called transformational advertisements to influence consumers' interpretations of their product use experiences.[20] Transformational advertisements create images, feelings, meanings and beliefs about the product that may be activated when consumers use it. These meanings then 'transform' consumers' interpretations of product usage. Consumers then experience the product differently than if they had not been exposed to the advertisement. This is more common than you might think. The effects of transformational advertisements have not been heavily researched as yet, but their likely impacts on consumers' product-use experiences are consistent with our view of consumer cognition.

12.7 Mental and behavioural effects

Mental effects concern the cognitive processes, knowledge, meanings, beliefs and attitudes. Interpretation processes (attention and comprehension) and integration processes (especially attitude formation) are of critical importance. Consumers' comprehension processes vary in depth and elaboration, depending on their levels of knowledge and involvement. Thus, exposure to a stimulus, whether an advertisement, a coupon or a sales presentation, may produce meanings that vary in number (elaboration), level of abstraction (semantic versus sensory) and interconnectedness. Consumers also may form inferences about product attributes or consequences, or the marketer's motivation. In this section, we will examine several mental and behavioural effects that are relevant to understanding the effects of advertising. They include consumers' attitudes towards advertisements and persuasion processes.

Attitude towards the advertisement

Advertisers have long been interested in measuring consumers' evaluations of advertisements. Recently, researchers have become interested in the affective and evaluative meanings associated with the advertisement itself: consumers' attitude towards the advertisement. Research suggests that consumers' attitudes towards the advertisement can influence their attitudes towards the advertised product or brand.[21] That is, advertisements that consumers like tend to create more positive brand attitudes and intentions than advertisements they don't like.

Persuasion processes

Persuasion refers to changes in consumers' beliefs and attitudes caused by marketing communication. Current research suggests that there are two 'routes' or types of cognitive processes by which advertising persuades: central and peripheral routes.[22]

Central route

The central route to persuasion involves the deep, elaborate comprehension processing, under conditions of high involvement of the consumer. In the central route, consumers focus on the key product message communicated in the advertisement. Central processing forms semantic beliefs about the attributes and consequences of a product or brand. If these beliefs are activated and used in integration processes, they may affect consumers' brand attitudes and purchase intentions. In sum, in central cognitive processes, consumers:

(1) interpret the advertisement message and form beliefs about product attributes and consequences;
(2) integrate these meanings to form brand attitudes and intentions.

Peripheral route

The peripheral route to persuasion is quite different. Here consumers are low involved and not motivated to process the advertisement message about the product. But they may still pay attention to the advertisement, perhaps for its entertainment value. Soft-drink advertisements featuring pop singers seem to encourage this type of processing. In peripheral processing, non-product features of the advertisement are given greater attention. Based on their meanings and beliefs about the advertisement, consumers may form attitudes towards the advertisement, but not towards the product. Interestingly, though, evidence is mounting that attitude towards the advertisement may influence attitudes towards the brand, thus causing some indirect persuasion.[23]

Whether consumers engage in central or peripheral processing depends largely on their goals during exposure to the advertisement. If exposure occurs while the consumer is actively considering purchase of the product, central processing is likely. If exposure occurs when the consumer is uninterested in the product (low enduring and situation involvement), peripheral processing is more likely.

Marketing-communication behaviours

Ultimately, marketing communication must affect not only consumers' cognitions and attitudes, but also their behaviours. A company's sales, profits and market share objectives can be accomplished only if consumers perform a variety of behaviours, including purchase of its product. Different types of marketing communication can be used to influence the various behaviours in the purchase/consumption sequence. Because we have already discussed purchase behaviour in this chapter, we focus here on two behaviours that are critical to the success of marketing-communication strategies: information contact and word-of-mouth communication with other consumers.

Information contact

Consumer contact with marketing communication information is critical to the success of a marketing-communication strategy. Information contact with marketing communications may be intentional, as when consumers search the newspapers for coupons (purposeful learning). But probably it is most often incidental, as when the consumer just happens to come into contact with a marketing communication when engaging in some other behaviour (incidental learning). Sometimes, marketing-communication contact can even trigger the purchase decision process, as might occur in coming across a sale or an incentive promotion. As a practical matter, the marketer must place the marketing-communication message in the target consumer's physical environment to maximize chances for exposure, and design the marketing communication so that it will be noticed (attended to). This requires knowledge of the media habits of the target market.

Placing information in consumers' environments may be easy when target consumers can be identified accurately. For example, catalogue marketers can buy lists of consumers who have made mail-order purchases in the past year. Then they can send promotion materials directly to these target consumers. Of course, sending coupons or a prize contest promotion through the mail does not guarantee that consumers will open the envelope and read its contents.

Contact for personal selling marketing communications can be achieved through 'cold calls' on consumers. But referrals and leads (or consumers contacting salespeople during their search process) are likely to be more successful. Marketers sometimes encourage referrals by offering gifts in return for the names of potential customers. Telephone contact or telemarketing is an increasingly popular method of personal selling, not only in a business-to-business context.

Exposure to marketing-communication messages is not enough, however. Consumers must also attend to the marketing-communication messages. Marketing communications that generate high levels of situation involvement (large discounts, big prizes) are likely to be noticed and receive higher levels of attention. How well the marketing communication interacts with such consumer characteristics as enduring involvement and existing knowledge also affects the level of attention. For instance, the effectiveness of price-reduction promotions depends largely on consumers' price sensitivity.

Word-of-mouth communication

Word-of-mouth or social communication can be a powerful influence on consumer behaviour. Marketers may want to encourage consumers' word-of-mouth communication about a marketing communication. This helps to spread awareness beyond those consumers who come into direct contact with the campaign. Consumers may share information with friends about good deals on particular products, a valuable coupon in the newspaper, or a sale at a retail store. For example, a consumer may phone a friend who is looking for tyres to say that ATS is having a great sale. Consumers sometimes recommend that their friends see a particular salesperson who is especially pleasant or well informed, or who offers good deals on merchandise. Consumers often pass on impressions of a new restaurant or retail store to their friends. As these examples illustrate, simply by placing information in consumers' environments, marketers can increase the probability that the information will be communicated to other consumers. And because personal communication from friends and relevant others is a powerful form of communication, marketers may try to design marketing communications that encourage word-of-mouth communication.

12.8 Conclusions

This chapter has focused on the analysis of the impact of promotion strategies on consumer behaviour. The major promotion methods (promotion mix) used by marketers have been discussed, as well as the advantages and disadvantages of each type of promotion strategy. A general communication model has also been presented. The chapter introduced key aspects related to the management of promotion strategies and the analysis of consumer/product relationships. Aspects of promotion objectives and budgeting as well as the design and decision making related to promotion strategies have also been covered. Key factors determining effective advertising strategies are analysed, as well as the development of personal selling strategies. The discussion then evolved to the analysis of important aspects related to the evaluation of the effects of promotion strategy, covering topics such as the promotional environment, promotion clutter, competitive intensity, copy strategy and cognitions derived from promotion. The last section of the chapter covered a number of issues related to advertising and consumer attitudes, persuasion processes, overt behaviour derived from promotion and information contact effects. There are clear links between much of this chapter and Chapter 3 in which we discussed an approach to understanding how consumers respond to marketing-communications activity.

Endnotes

1. J.M.G. Floor and W.F. Van Raaij, 1993, 2nd edition.
2. T.J. Reynolds and J. Gutman, 1984.
3. B. Sternthal, R. Dholakia and C. Leavitt, 1978.
4. Adapted from S. Baker, 1979.
5. D. Berger, 1986, p. 35.
6. J.R. Rossiter and L. Percy, 1987; J.M.G. Floor and W.F. Van Raaij, 1993, 2nd edition.
7. D. Ehrlich, L. Guttman, P. Schonbach and J. Mills, 1957.
8. Adapted from Y. Wind, 1977, pp. 313–20.
9. A sales promotion programme in The Netherlands of retailers (Albert Heijn, Vroom & Dreesmann), Shell and other companies.
10. J.C. Olson and T.J. Reynolds, 1983.
11. See Section 9.3 for the means–end chain. T.J. Reynolds and J. Gutman, 1984.
12. B.W. Weitz, 1978, p. 502.
13. Adapted from B.W. Weitz, 1978, p. 502.
14. B.W. Weitz, 1981.
15. R.W. Olshavsky, 1975.
16. H. Sujan, 1986.
17. L.D. Gibson, 1983.
18. M.B. Holbrook, 1978.
19. J.A. Edell and R. Staelin, 1983.
20. C.P. Puto and W.D. Wells, 1984.
21. A.A. Mitchell and J.C. Olson, 1981; M.P. Gardner, 1985.
22. R.E. Petty, J.T. Cacioppo and D. Schumann, 1983.
23. J.A. Edell and M.C. Burke, 1984.

13

Trends and developments in consumer behaviour

Chapter objectives

(1) To explore some of the most relevant changes and pressures affecting marketing.
(2) To analyse some key trends impacting on consumer behaviour.
(3) To discuss specific trends influencing consumer behaviour in the areas of marketing research, segmentation, branding, packaging, marketing communication and retailing.[1]

13.1 Introduction

Chapter 1 introduced the notion of the marketing environment and the importance of monitoring the economic, social, technological and other environments in order to spot emerging trends in the marketplace and among consumers.

As was pointed out, the marketer of today faces rapid changes and in addition to those discussed in Chapter 1 there are: social and economic polarization; the rise of the retailer; the saturation of markets; the growing concentration of power in a handful of multinationals; and new technology. Technology is transforming what companies do, how they do it and how they communicate. The marketing environment is changing, as are the ingredients of success, for example the changing relationship between distributors and suppliers. Distributors are becoming new 'virtual manufacturers' (for example, in electrical goods, music, leisure, holidays, DIY, computers, motor oils, and so on). The sheer speed of change, growing economic turbulence and intense global competition make the marketer's task as difficult as it is increasingly important.

Amongst the many pressures for marketing change, two are most salient in terms of consumer behaviour: (1) the changing marketplace with most product markets being saturated and (2) the changing consumer giving rise to market fragmentation. Even the legitimacy of the brand is in question. Much of the current crisis of legitimacy of brands has got something to do with the attempt to have a lowest common denominator appeal.

Marketing as a management function is becoming more ethically responsible, value oriented, broadened, conservation oriented, flexible and anticipatory. The marketing concept will be broadened to include the social responsibility of organizations – a belief that an organization has an obligation to society to preserve and protect the environment and to contribute to a better quality of life for all citizens. Also, because consumers are more quality-conscious, value-creating marketing and value-added marketing will become the predominant approaches. These approaches represent an entire system that includes speed, convenience, follow-up and an obsessive pursuit of consumer satisfaction. The new neo-marketing philosophy is essentially customer-centric.

13.2 The evolving consumer

Two trends are happening simultaneously: everything is becoming the same, differences are becoming greater! ... This appears to be contradictory. And it is, to some extent. On the other hand, the same trends are evident round the world. There are more working women in every country. There is a similar demand for convenience, for products that are healthy and nutritious, for fast food. And the same brand names are appearing in more and more countries. On the other hand, we find that the fastest-growing products are not aimed at the mass market but at particular segments, not based on demographics but on lifestyle. Consumers are struggling to find and express their unique identity. Consumers are demanding greater variety with products tailored to their individual, local needs. Consumers are showing more concern for local identity. In the 1990s, many people do not want to see exactly the same store and exactly the same merchandise wherever they go. Brands that reflect local or national attributes and identity could become even more powerful in a globalizing world. Consumers may begin to see global brands as indiscriminate, boring, standardized, undistinguished. But this fact does not gel with the underlying social trends. There is an increasing homogenization of tastes and demands as well as convergence of lifestyles, in international markets. Global marketing – and the trend 'look ma, no borders' – is here to stay. The global market is becoming a melting pot, not just with people, but with products and services. National markets will become more accessible and identical.

Marketers are indeed beginning to realize that they have to look at social trends or they could get caught out. Marketers need to find out how changing consumer values will affect their products and services. There is a new 'socioquake' taking place which is set to transform the mainstream society, and is based on some key important trends:

- The importance of the 'video game generation'.
- Cocooning (the stay-at-home syndrome), also meaning that consumers want self-preservation and protection.
- The trend towards food combined with drugs ('foodacenticals').
- Fantasy adventure: consumers need emotional escapism (for example, virtual reality and sensavision television).
- Small indulgences: consumers feel that they deserve something special.
- Egonomics: 'No one is quite like me, so I want customability'. Customization or 'I want to be me'.
- Down-ageing: older (in people terms) is becoming better.
- The vigilante consumer: Consumers want companies to act more responsibly and admit mistakes.
- SOS (Save Our Society): doing good is now a must.
- Possible deconsumption: during recessions consumers normally cut down quality expectations, moving back up the scale as better times return. In the last recession, however, quality expectations have stayed in place while consumers have cut down on volume. For some markets, it could be the start of a new phenomenon – deconsumption – caused by feelings of being almost choked-up by too much consumption.
- Middle-age culture: society will increasingly be led by a middle-age culture (the children of the sixties) ... and they also have money.
- 'Home is hot': home delivery, home offices, home decor, home furniture, home safety – anything to do with 'la maison' or making people feel at home – will find a huge market (for example, McDonald's has just launched a new restaurant chain creating imitation home cooking). The late 1990s will be the age of the home user, with companies targeting a new market known as SOHO (small office, home user).

Consumers today are more interested in 'transactional convenience' than in location and accessibility. There is also another paradigm shift: consumers are on the brink of moving into a 'consciousness paradigm' based on several converging trends and the focusing on individual development. Furthermore, the trend towards mind-over-matter is becoming visible. The mind is far more powerful than we have accepted. Consumers begin to feel there is more to life than just the physical, material world. In the future, companies will increasingly be judged on how they treat the environment and consumers may be more concerned than at present, with experiences rather than possessing things.

In a world of exponential choice, the consumer is no longer a grateful and passive recipient. He or she is an expert and active participant. The consumer market's demand is for speed, innovation and responsiveness ... and there is already 'a surplus of everything' ... (product proliferation). Market saturation is a crucial issue needing a structural change. For example, the European car market has an over-capacity of seven million vehicles per year. Chronic over-capacity is also the driving force behind major changes occurring in the UK banking institutions, building societies and insurance companies. Even 'new' markets like the personal computer sector face a shake-out. Market saturation is not just a short-term recessionary phenomenon, it is true saturation. Economic turbulence is a fact of life, although inflation has been brought under control in most countries.

As a result of the reduction in trade barriers worldwide, there will be further reductions in price to consumers. The increased competition will force producers to pay much more attention to activities such as servicing and quality.

The new consumer word is cautious, sceptical and worried, something that will not end with the recession. Consumers have been scarred by the rollercoaster to boom and recession. And yes, there is a reaction against image-led marketing. Those who 'buy' the marketing may well go a step forward, and become 'prosumers' – people who actively and deliberately take part in the process of design, shaping or even producing a product or service, knowing it's 'for them'. Virtual reality will be pervasive, enabling the modelling of products and permitting experience of production machinery by companies.

Consumers are feeling bored by the 1990s yearn for finer things in life. They expect more value for their money, and value does not necessarily mean inexpensive. Not everyone is buying into the back-to-basics movement. It may be true that the attitude of greed and avarice is over but consumers are going for value. This does not mean consumers want the 1980s attitude back. In terms of quality, consumers still want the best. They buy less of it, but what they do buy is still the best. The consumer has been facing so many social pressures: 'You can't drink, and you can't have fun.' A possible marketing strategy is to position product and services as the alternative to boredom in the 1990s! Despite the recession, the up-market segment is growing and it will continue to grow. Consumers are not necessarily going for luxury so much as conspicuous consumption or status buying. They are seeking a redefinition of luxury goods and services. People are still pretty much concentrating on family, traditional values and inconspicuous consumption but the tide could turn if the economy picks up. The good-life mind-set will in time come back.

13.3　The shift from matter to mind

Today consumers think increasingly in terms of qualities rather than quantities. Consumers do not want more of the same, but different and better. This represents a shift from matter to mind. The companies and marketers who succeed will be those who stay in tune with the shift from quantity to quality and from matter to mind, but who also realize that it is not a choice of one or the other, but the unique and skilful handling of the interaction of both that counts. Increasingly, products and services are consumed by the mind as experiences and more and more companies are incorporating desires for features. For instance, the Japanese are working on the notion of sensuous cars. Basically, the car itself gives the consumer a kind of delight and surprise, bursting open the door, hearing the sound, smelling the scent of leather, pressing the accelerator – everything is being thought through now almost emotionally! This can also be seen in the trend towards atmospherics and corporate identity aromas. Smell impregnation can influence consumer purchase. Many companies are already using it, ranging from department stores to menswear shops and from shoe stores to airlines. Retail stores and other consumer environments when impregnated with several fragrances can 'provoke' specific reactions in people and enhance the likelihood of purchase and/or consumer satisfaction.

Traditional consumer life-stages are fragmenting. Today, fractured career paths, redundancy and self-employment, rising divorce and the increase in the SSWD group (Singles, Separated, Widowers and Divorcees) – all of it disrupts that pattern. And all of it fosters a 'contingency mentality'. The single-person market accounts for about one-third of all the households in the UK. Markets need to be understood in terms of occasions. Market fragmentation is taking place in individuals' lives. They eat both health food and junk food and have a repertoire of brands, depending on the occasion. We may see some new coalitions of consumers *per se*, not now based on demographics or psychographics but based on cognition.

Consumers will change their preferences considerably. People will change residences, jobs and even occupations more frequently, especially in industrialized countries. A host of new medical technologies will make life longer and more comfortable in the industrialized world. Better nutrition and the 'wellness' movement will raise life expectancies. In developed countries, children born in the 1980s will live to an average of 70 for males and 77 for females.

New gender roles, role-reversal, the rise of the 'new man' and the increasing emancipation of women are all visible in our society. A good example of the latter is the message used by Triumph International in its recent advertising campaign for ladies' lingerie – 'New hair, new look, new bra. And if he doesn't like it, new boyfriend'.

Market fragmentation is accelerating. A few years ago, washing yourself was something you did with soap. Now you can choose from cleansing bars, shower gel, facial wash cream, scrubs for face and body show moisturizing, exfoliating, anti-bacterial, deep-cleansing. There were already 105 new ways to wash, condition or style hair in Europe in 1994.

Today, in many markets, product or service quality is uniformly high and price differences between competitors worldwide – there are no 'relevant differences' between rival brands (perceived product parity). They are largely right. Many products and services are at parity on the important attributes, and it is the less important attributes that often determine product or service choice. Consumers are also increasingly aware of the alternatives on offer and rising standards of quality and service, and so their expectations of service and quality are elevated. They are increasingly critical of the quality of the product or service they experienced. Consumers have smaller zones of tolerance, the difference between desired and adequate expectations.

Consumers are being very hard on 'hard' product attributes (functional attributes of the brand) and soft on the 'soft' product attributes (image aspects). They are saying: 'I want that product positioning but get it right, company brand! And I don't want to pay more for it!' Some are even casting doubts about contemporary marketing. For example, doubts about the value of ever more costly brand advertising, which often dwells on seemingly irrelevant points of difference. Consumers used to pay more to get more features or better quality. Now, lean marketing means marketers must deliver more for less. Consumers are testing the quality/price trade-off to the point of destruction.

We are becoming a society that is trained in price sensitivity. Customer sophistication and price sensitivity are rising. There is also a strong downward price pressure. Consumers also become sophisticated in understanding marketing. Customer expectations of services will rise. Some experts are saying that service, not price, will be the differentiating factor of the 1990s. Consumers may be willing pay a little more for excellent service and convenience. One of the best ways to differentiate a company in a parity environment is by helping the customer understand the company behind the product.

Research areas to be addressed for the future, concern such issues as product/service quality gaps, value for money (value analysis), and the link between perceived product/service quality, customer satisfaction and customer retention. Product/service quality and customer care will remain key components, subject to the constraints of controlling cost ratios and remaining price-competitive. It is increasingly important for companies to analyse the cost of quality, which can be expressed as follows:

COQ = COC + CONC + CDA

where:
COQ = Cost of quality
COC = Cost of conformity (with industry standards)
CONC = Cost of non-conformity (when the company is planning to go beyond the required quality standard levels of the industry). The company here is trying to approach zero defects, zero-risks and zero-breakdowns.
CDA = Cost of differential advantage (when quality is seen as a competitive weapon).

Total quality management (TQM) is about reducing TGWs (things gone wrong). That is essential, but in a crowded market, increasing TGRs, or things gone right, is the real trick! Cutting TGWs is mechanical, but increasing TGRs requires creativity. These days, quality as measured by the numbers is merely a pass to the playing field. You score by making your customers glow!

There is also an emphasis on customer retention and customer loyalty. Professional marketers regard increasing customer loyalty as the single most important issue. It is critical to encourage long-term loyalty. And this must be based on meaningful, long-term preference! There is also the anticipated increase in expenditure behind 'loyalty programmes'.

Product or service recovery has its economic value, can increase customer loyalty and customer retention. Marketing managers should take into account the additional costs of replacing customers over those of trying to retain customers who may be dissatisfied. There is a relationship between customer retention and profitability and success. Also, customer retention enhances corporate image and possible insulation from price competition.

Customer loyalty and building long-term relationships is vital. The more saturated the market, the more difficult and expensive it is to win new customers, and the more valuable existing customers are. Marketing is focusing more on retention of existing customers and less on attracting new ones.

Recent research findings revealed that shoppers have less product loyalty. Therefore, marketers are concentrating their efforts on the 3R approach – Relationships, Retention and Recovery. The stability of relationships between buyers and sellers can be derived from the bonds, which are outcomes of adaptations and investments made by the interacting partners aiming at higher efficiency and more cost-effective exchanges. These bonds range from knowledge and social bonds to legal and economic bonds. It's time to think of customers as assets!

A recent survey suggests that businesses lose between 15% and 20% of customers a year. A retention rate of 80% means that customers, on average, remain loyal for five years. Improving retention to 90% leads to the average life of a customer doubling to ten years. Brand loyalty share has an important role in defining brand equity and brand valuation. Satisfied customers can become part-time marketers of the brand.

13.4 Marketing information systems

As introduced in Chapter 6 we are now living in a period of data explosion. Today's customer information systems differ in the scale of the database, the depth and amount of information about individuals and the degree of use for information. Database marketing is directly linked with the maximization of the value of long-term, loyal customers. Many companies are building databases in order to 'own' the customer, to 'own' a market niche and to form long-term relationships with customers.

Computerised Marketing Technologies (CMT) has launched the UK's most comprehensive consumer database – CONSUMER BANK contains data on over 40 million individuals, selectable by 240 different variables. It has been developed by overlaying the electoral register with data from many other sources including lifestyle, mail responsive, geodemographic, shareholder and the National Shoppers Survey. CONSUMER BANK is growing constantly. CMT offers a profiling service with CONSUMER BANK using CHAID, the company's high-speed analysis tool.

Customer information technologies are changing the nature of competition. Today there are too many products, too many advertisements, and the daily torrent of data has made customer information systems more important than ever. Customer databases are needed to make relationship marketing really work.

Many other trends are taking place in the area of marketing research. For example, a new research device called SONAR takes a sounding of subconscious buying decisions. This new technique attempts to delve into consumers' subconscious minds – not with psychoanalysis, but with computer games. 'Emotional

Sonar' developed by Emotion Mining Co. from Wellesley, Mass., USA, works by getting at consumers' subconscious emotions with a simple eye – hand game on the computer in order to quantify emotions. Companies like Campbell Soup, Coca-Cola, Lipton and CBS are already using it. The technique is designed to measure respondents' emotions without surveys or questionnaires and yields results that are bias-free. The inventors of the device say that it is important to be able to gauge subconscious responses to measure not only what the consumer is aware of, but where the subconscious is poised to move. The key is not to dig too deep to find out, and to still have recognizable information that is under the surface of conscious awareness. A typical session using SONAR takes one hour and a half, covers four topics and includes a test session. No questions are ever asked on the computer itself. The moderator drops a topic, and respondents are left to free-associate on their own with descriptive words or drawings on the computer. They can also consult a thesaurus. Respondents draw spontaneous pictures (15 minutes per topic) or type in emotional words or phrases that track intensities. Data is ranked from unpleasant to pleasant in different categories of emotions.

A new marketing research methodology is available for new product testing which combines video technology with panel research techniques. It is called screen-test and makes use of consumers' VCRs to test products, concepts, advertisements, and so on. Participants receive videotapes to view in their homes, which is the same environment where they receive product information and form opinions. The versatility of video allows better control over the presentation of research stimuli than product demonstrations. Lighting, visual perspectives, elapsed time, presentation sequence and sales can be predetermined and controlled on a videocassette.

13.5 Segmentation, targeting and positioning

In terms of market segmentation, targeting and positioning, the greatest influence in the demand for most products and services is not just market growth but demographics. There will be a metamorphosis in marketing, meaning that the economic polarization by the end of the century will stretch income distribution so that any given slice will be smaller while the average 'core' will shrink. More niches will develop, especially in high income bands. An 'economic fallback' will happen that will result in the mass market of middle-class consumers being replaced by a market of haves and have-nots!

Marketers are focusing their efforts on a process called demassification. The demassification of marketing is the corporate response to living in the age of diversity. The 1990s is the decade of microsegmentation and narrower niches. Companies have been snitching their market segmentation strategy from a 'shotgun' approach to a 'rifle' approach or even, to 'laser-gun' marketing. In the next century, 'one-to-one' marketing will also become an effective segmentation policy. Still, 'neighbourhood marketing' is already being applied by supermarkets, discount stores, banks and other retail outlets. For example, in the US these stores and branches are using a Message Memory Module (MMM) as a new point-of-purchase advertising medium which customizes in-store advertising. The device is based on a microprocessor installed at each store through a direct broadcast satellite system which plays customized advertisements at regular intervals. It reaches customers three to four times and is targeted to the specific outlet and its patrons, by even containing a greeting by the store or bank manager. Retailers have found that in-store audio advertising, at regular intervals, has increased sales as much as 150%. On some items, this is really a good example of what is called 'marketing with memory', instead of marketing to a 'nameless, faceless' target!

Positioning issues are in. But a much clearer positioning (not overpositioning/confused positioning) of premium and discount brands is needed. The four major positioning errors incurred by companies need to be rectified:

(1) Underpositioning – some companies discover that buyers have only a vague idea of the brand. Buyers do not really know anything special about it;
(2) Overpositioning – buyers may have too narrow a picture of the brand. Thus a consumer might think that a company makes only fine glass in the range of £1,000 and up, when in fact it makes affordable fine glass starting at around £50;
(3) Confused positioning – buyers could have a confused image of the brand. This confusion might result from making too many claims or changing the brand's positioning too frequently;
(4) Doubtful positioning – buyers may find it hard to believe the brand claims in view of the product's features, price or manufacturer.

What is needed is a 'solutions' positioning! The pressure to be 'different' and smart enough to attract and retain customers is increasing and it is much harder to maintain positive, long-term product differentiation. Also, product positioning is moving into 'competitive frameworking' which is based not only on the perceptual similarities and differences between products or brands, but also on the study of comparative use patterns by consumers and target market contrasts.

13.6 Branding and packaging

The role of the 'corporate brand' is growing in importance. The company brand will be the main marketing mode of the future, providing the total brand experience. Today's consumer is not only more aware but also more knowledgeable of the company behind the brand, and is able (and prepared) to use that knowledge to help differentiate competitive offers.

'Half-hearted' brand strategies are one of the reasons why some manufacturers have been pushed to the edge. The real brand split today is between real brands like Mars, Kellogg, Sainsbury and Marks and Spencer and pseudo-brand products which fail to provide real product benefits or value for money, or fail to get the production, research and development or promotional support they need. They are not brands, they fall into the category of 'manufacturer label'!

Some brand marketers thought they could do it without real product quality. They thought they could do it all with glitz and packaging. That has given retailers and even tertiary brands the opportunity to 'nibble away at the myth of quality'. The most critical ingredient is not the brand name, but what lies behind it! Pretty pictures and lofty slogans will not help. Buyers want to know what the company stands for!

Brands like Marks and Spencer and McDonald's which over-arch social differences could flourish in a fragmenting society. The threat from own-label products will get tougher. Retailers are turning own-labels into brands in their own right.

The issue of brand equity or brand valuation is of great importance nowadays. Brand equity research needs to identify all the consumer relationships with the brand. Researching consumer relationships with a brand can ascertain unrecognized product benefits, failure of the brand to incorporate into consumers' lifestyles, a blurred image or elusive personality. Companies need to find out the consumers' mind-set orientation, where the product category or brand fall on a logical or emotional continuum. Companies can build brand loyalty by strengthening current brand assets, refining obstacles, creating more memorable product personalities or positions and adjusting 'out-of-sync' brand assets. It is important to convert marketing liabilities into assets. A possible conversion technique assesses the commitment of consumers to their current brand choices and their potential for change. Familiar brands will give consumers the security they need. There is a trend towards the use of mixed and endorsed brands, gaining the benefits of corporate identity and the strength of individual brands. Super brands are becoming more prominent and brand comprehension and identity are vital issues to be considered when implementing future branding strategies.

What about trends in packaging? Are we going to see a talking package in the near future? Yes, 'chatty' packages, self-destructing packages and packages that simply ooze with personality will soon be a reality. The Selame Design Company from Newton, Boston, Mass. in the US is currently researching and testing all sorts of technological wonders, including advanced holograms with 3-D images. Holograms will be specially popular for packaging cosmetics, coffee and liquor products. We will see the incorporation of voice chips into packaging. For example, different spots on a food package would describe vitamin content, fat content and cooking directions. Pharmaceutical companies will probably be the first to use the 'chatty' packages as they look for ways to protect themselves from lawsuits. With more companies marketing their goods globally, packaging will have fewer words and rely on symbols and universally understood pictures. Also, because of the environmental concerns in our society, we will see the appearance of self-destructing packages, made from time-programmed polymers that turn the containers into a harmless powder (this is taking a little longer to happen). In order to reduce space in recycling storage areas, companies may turn to the incredible shrinking package. For example, a bottle could be built with a bellows-type construction that would allow it to decrease in size as its contents are consumed.

A tremendous improvement in scanning technology is also expected. Universal Product Codes (UPC) will be reduced to the size of a pinhead. Packaging will be more visually interesting in the next decade. Emphasis will be on package personality and identity. The physical dimensions of packages will change. Instead of packages being the same old square box, the package shape will have to be so unique that the consumer will instantly identify what product it is. Companies will continue to leverage brand image. Of course, technology will also play a pivotal role in the packaging of the future. For example, soon we will see the use of smart packages (for example, microwavable foods would come in packages that the oven could 'read' the hungry consumer would not have to do a thing except pop it in).

Because of environmental concerns, we will see alternative materials being used for packages. Companies will cut back on inks with metallic elements and use more recycled materials. It will be more difficult to achieve the brilliant colours and clean looks that have the most shelf impact. The recession has not put the brakes on new product development!

13.7 Marketing communication

As Chapter 6 demonstrated, companies are looking to create a more personal understanding of the customer base and communicate with customers on a more immediate and personal level. Is this the creation of the 'mass of individuals market'? The shape of marketing communication is expected to acquire a more 'corporate dimension'; a more holistic approach to promoting a company and its brands is emerging. Within the trend towards customer-focused Integrated Marketing Communications (IMC), one important goal is to maximize 'brand contacts', or all the ways the customer or prospect comes in contact with the organization. Also, companies need to empathize with customers. As for advertising agencies, account planners are increasingly becoming suppliers of consumer premise and unambiguously demonstrate its effectiveness. 'Through the line' marketing will continue, but there is an increased recognition of the value of the less 'tangible' communication media.

The fragmentation of marketing communications is already taking place. Mass advertising will continue to grow less cost-effective due to the fragmentation of audiences and audience time. The trend now is moving towards the growth of narrowcasting, the presentation of specialized programming to a specific audience. Due to the utilization of digital compression technology, soon there will be available 180 television channels in Europe, and even up to 500 channels by the year 2000. Digitalization, satellite and cable will all help to reach the forecasted development. Other important trends like video on demand, active, participative and interactive television will change the face of television in years to come.

Simplistically, the increased supply of advertising airtime from the new satellite channels will mean that airtime rates will fall. But because the number of viewers reached is lower, the cost-per-thousand (CPM/CPT) viewers will be relatively higher. Satellite television will see advertising revenue rise steeply to £775 billion by the year 2003 (38% of total revenue). This will be facilitated by an increase in television viewing share to the satellite channels of 21% of total viewing by 2003.

There will be more 'time-compressed TV commercials' and an increase in the use of place-based advertising (for example checkout media in schools, in medical surgeries, train and underground stations and so on), the latter providing advertisers with almost captive audiences. Place-based advertising reaches some huge, highly targeted 'waste-free' market audiences, when they are most attentive, so that messages will be noticed and in some cases, in some trusted and credible environments. As a viewing environment, some of these are virtually distraction-free and with no 'zapping' (changing TV channels). For example, in the US, Healthlink delivers 140 million highly targeted viewers, 13,250 paediatric and family practice offices, with recall sources that are comparable to prime-time television and with waste-free delivery.

Before any marketing mix can 'act upon' a consumer, the consumer must first want to engage the mix. Consumers interact with traditional mass media advertising less than any other element of the marketing mix. This is where interactive promotion and advertising will play an important role in the future. The media objectives of reach and frequency do not reflect interactivity. This is a natural consequence of a mass media orientation, because consumers can do nothing to alter the content of an advertisement sent out to them whether they want it or not. Consumers do not really possess advertising, and their lives are not affected by the bulk of advertisements that they passively receive. With the advent of advertising on demand through the Internet and CD-ROM as well as voluntary and individualized advertising, the future of advertising is set to change and consumer interactivity with companies is going to increase. Some advertising agencies in this brave new world of advertising interactivity are already changing their names and calling themselves communication agencies.

Marketers will continue to use traditional media to present a broad view of the brand and tap into the interactive marketing to provide consumers with more details or allow them to ask questions. Direct Response Television (DRTV) is a direct route to brand-building as well as sales.

Customized multimedia systems which can be integrated with existing systems will be the norm. Computers will make it possible to read a newspaper, journal or magazine aimed at the particular interests of an individual – a mass medium tailored to the individual. For example, readers can already access different sections of a newspaper while on-line by clicking on various parts of the menu. Multimedia technology will be the basis for the appearance of electronic newspapers.

Already present is the trend towards the concept of 'grazing' on television, that is, to watch two or more TV channels at the same time. Technology has allowed this to occur and it is already in use in the United States. Its implications and consequences for advertisers in terms of consumer behaviour are:

(1) even less consumer attention span;
(2) less attitudinal change;

(3) less consumer involvement;

(4) less comprehension in the content of the message;

(5) less consumer commitment in the final purchase or decision-making.

This is a worrying trend for advertisers. In the United States, the average viewer changes TV channels (he or she does what is called 'zapping') every three minutes. The image of an essentially passive TV viewer does not exist. Television viewers are very active. The idea that viewers are 'glued' to their TV sets is a myth.

Advertising is increasingly being perceived by consumers as a kind of show-business and entertainment activity. Increased surrealism as well as more visual and verbal puzzles will be used in advertising copy in the future. This trend can produce different levels of consumer involvement, ranging from a temporary frustration to immediate enjoyment. The cross-advertising phenomenon (with budgets shared by different organizations), incidental advertising such as product placements and broadcast sponsorship will increase in scope in the near future. There is an opportunity for advertisers to cooperate and place their products or services in an advertisement for another product. And this is an interesting way of funding commercials. There are already 'product placement advertising agencies' in existence, like the New Media Group in England. The increase in sponsored programmes and the advent of satellite broadcasting could offer product placements and incidental advertising even more scope.

'Infomercials' (a commercial presentation using a chat-show format) are already widely used in the US and will soon appear in Europe.

Investment in direct marketing (including direct mail) is forecasted to reach 75 billion pounds within the European Union by the year 2000. This amount will represent half of all advertising expenses. A new generation of 'smart' direct mail techniques that use highly qualified names from super-accurate relational databases will be predominant.

One of the fastest growing direct marketing media is the direct response billboard, which features direct response advertisements with free phone numbers. Many well-known companies, like Procter and Gamble are using this type of billboards.

In terms of key trends in sales promotion, we will see the appearance of more novel sales promotion tools via new media vehicles and the blurring of sales promotion and advertising (brand 'velocity'). Brand 'velocity', not image, is one of the elements of the new marketing order. Brand velocity is the right mix of image advertising and sales promotion that produces sales volume and market share increases without borrowing from future sales. To achieve short- and long-term brand velocity, the right mix of sales promotion and image advertising must be sustained and blended so as not to be distinct from one another.

More of the advertising budgets is being diverted to promotions.

More and more companies are launching customer cards as a promotional device, which are functional cards containing a magnetic strip that holds key credit and demographic information.

New, state-of-the-art Point-Of-Purchase (POP) and Point-Of-Sale (POS) tools are also appearing. The shelves may soon be talking: Ladd Electronics from Aanoga Park, California in the US introduced 'Soundtron', an electronic audio announcement device designed for selling and advertising in self-service retail stores. The unit is about the size of a book. Announcements are triggered by a built-in infrared sensor which detects a potential customer approaching from up to 35 feet away. Stores can record messages of up to 32 seconds for a single message or four segments of 16 seconds. The sound level will not interfere with background music systems or other store announcements.

Promotions can also be integrated with electronic fund transfer systems.

In the 21st century non-manipulative selling techniques will be the key to survival, because increasingly sophisticated customers will not fall for gimmicks or deception. In the future, sales will become almost incidental – a natural outgrowth of a long-term relationship between customers and suppliers. Still, it is important to examine the purpose of the relationship and examine costs and revenues associated with every relationship. Companies need to establish and maintain relationships with customers in accordance with the costs and revenues attached to the relationships. Some companies are already determining activity-based costs (ABC) associated with the overall profitability of the existing customer base. With the help of long-term relationships, the costs of marketing can be decreased at the same time that it can be more selective.

13.8 New retailing trends and the consumer

We are in the midst of a retailing revolution. Changes in the retail food trends are considerable. There are fewer stores: 1.6 per 1,000 people is now the world average. There is an increasing structural concentration: 10% of stores typically account for 70% of turnover. Hypermarkets and chains are taking a large share of food store turnover: an average of 68%. There is greater use of private labels: between 13% and 40% across European countries; and also greater use of optical scanning technology. Home shopping could soon be known as home scanning. There are already scanning services targeting in-home users. For example, in the US, Scanfone is a bar-code scanner, a telephone and a bill paying system. Scanfone is an electronic home shopping system that allows users to whip out a scanning wand and order items from specially bar-coded catalogues. For US $9.95/month, home shoppers receive a special touch-tone phone, a light-pen bar-code scanner, a magnetic stripe credit card reader and a catalogue of grocery items. The order and payment system works much like the credit authorization networks consumers see whenever they use a credit card in stores. Safeway has 6,500 items listed in its catalogue. Shoppers can specify desired delivery times. Scanfone subscribers are given what appears to be 'an alphabetized dictionary' of bar codes next to a list of the companies that they pay bills to on a regular basis. Funds are electronically transferred the same way they would if a cheque had been written.

The mass retailing of branded products by 'category killers' like Toys Я Us and PC World, offering consumers convenience, good locations, services, wide choice and low prices, are here to stay.

There is a proliferation of suburban and out-of-town shopping centres and a trend towards a suburban lifestyle. There is the danger of town centres declining to the level of a combination of niche shopping and discount shopping. But, the end of the century could see the conclusion of the trend towards suburbanization – an American rather than a European trend. The number of superstores is increasing. These superstores are dominated by multiple chains, with an increasingly European base, and are diversifying from food into everyday products. This will lead to growing uniformity and concentration in the retail sector which will ultimately restrict consumer choice. There will be an increasing sameness of names and type of shops in the high streets and shopping malls across Europe. Calle Serrano in Madrid will bear a remarkable resemblance to Oxford Street in London. We will be in the age of the Euro-retailer.

Some of the most important trends in retailing affecting consumers are electronic retailing, in-home shopping and teleshopping, more price competition, more and better information (for example, from scanner data), more chains and franchises. More terminal smart cards will be used as an 'electronic purse' as well as automated checkout machines. Supermarkets will be providing customers with do-it-yourself scanners in order to allow them to calculate their own bills. There is also the 'off-the-grid' trend which represents the whole notion of shopping outside of the parameters of retail as currently defined. For example, for teenagers to buy jeans in a shopping mall is not 'cool' anymore; the trend is for them to buy 'small brands' and go to flea-markets.

A qualitatively new type of distribution channel is emerging – instead of marketplaces determined by where goods physically sit, 'marketspaces' are developing, where the crucial issue is access to information about these goods (for example, electronic motor auctions). Distribution is now essentially an information system in this 'high tech/high touch' society.

For example the high-tech superstore will be using the following innovations:

- video trolleys – in which an infrared beam triggers advertisements as the trolley passes through different parts of the store;
- aromatics – distinctive aromas are circulated to whet consumer appetites;
- talkback devices – a flat box contains pre-recorded messages that is triggered when a shopper's hand breaks the electric field;
- the checkout saver – tailors discount coupons to encourage customers to buy competitor's products or higher-value foods next time;
- pedestrian monitor – counts people in and out of stores to optimize staff numbers and measure effect of store promotions;
- infrared shelf beams – these count the number of times a product is picked up, showing which are the most eye-catching parts of the store.

Some experts are saying that shopping will be increasingly seen as an adventure by consumers. Perhaps this is an appropriate note on which to conclude the text part of this book!

13.9 Conclusions

Vision is the art of seeing things invisible. Vision is not forecasting the future. It is creating the future by taking purposeful, urgent action in the present. Marketing managers need to realize that it is not enough to react to future trends but that what they need is to be able to anticipate the future; even better, they need to be able to influence the future!

This chapter discussed some of the most relevant changes affecting the practice of marketing today, the many pressures requiring marketing change as well as the key trends impacting on consumer behaviour. The evolving consumer was analysed in terms of many trends and society developments such as: global markets, specific trends ranging from cocooning and 'home is hot' to SOS (Save Our Society) and egonomics, the 'conscientious' paradigm, product and market parity, market saturation, 'prosumers', the shift from matter to mind, the 'contingency mentality' and market fragmentation.

An overview of trends in the area of marketing information systems and marketing research was introduced as well as key developments in market segmentation, targeting and positioning. Trends in branding and packaging were also discussed. Finally, emerging issues and future trends in marketing communication and retailing were analysed in terms of their major implications, from a consumer behaviour perspective.

Note

1. Some of the trends proposed throughout this chapter have been derived from ideas presented in *Marketing Business* and *Marketing News* during the 1990s.

Part 4 Clippings and Problems

Clipping 1 Has the DM medium finally come of age?
Clipping 2 Benetton drops its shock tactic
Problem 1 Brand switching
Problem 2 Targeting the Euro-consumer

Clipping 1 Has the DM medium finally come of age?

Key issues

Increase in use of database and direct marketing
Consumer reactions to being individually targeted
Likely future of direct marketing

Questions

(1)   Why has direct marketing expanded so rapidly?

(2)   How might consumer attitudes affect direct marketing?

(3)   What are the implications for direct marketing of current trends in consumer behaviour?

(4)   What are the implications for consumer behaviour of the increased use of direct marketing?

Marketing 1 June 1995

Has the DM medium finally come of age?

By Neill Denny

After years of gung-ho predictions by direct marketers, it seems that the widespread use of the medium by fmcg companies is at last becoming a reality.

The best evidence produced yet suggests that almost one third (29%) of fmcg companies are engaged in direct marketing, with another third (32%) investigating and experimenting.

These are the findings of joint ISBA/Royal Mail research, based on interviews with 50 large packaged goods companies with a combined annual sales of £24bn.

Currently 40% of the £1bn a year these firms spend on marketing goes below the line. Sales promotion takes the biggest slice (23%), followed by point of sale (6%), and direct mail (4%).

Converted brand owners

Brand owners already converted to direct marketing typically have several brands, high-priced and specialist products with a high consumption per household.

The path blazed by pioneers, such as Nestlé's Buitoni, Procter and Gamble's Pampers and Heinz's 57 varieties, is now being trod by names such as Oxo, Guinness, Brooke Bond, McVitie's and Kimberly-Clark.

High-value brands have been initially more receptive to direct marketing because a higher unit price makes the cost of direct contact proportionally lower.

But they are also often brands which have the potential to be supplied direct to the consumer.

Chris Gater, chief executive at Brann, which numbers Unilever Grants and Guinness among its clients, says the growth of card loyalty programmes has alarmed brand owners.

"They see the retailers owning the customer contact, giving them excessive power. They want part of that, because if you allow

Part 4, Clipping 1

the retailer to continue they are increasing their power at the expense of the brand owner. It's about owning the customer relationship," he says.

The third, and still the largest group (39%), are the rejectors, who can see no benefit in using direct marketing. They generally produce a single brand with a low price which is consumed occasionally. Here, building direct relationships is unlikely to be economic. Gater says:

"There will always be a group who will think for the wrong reasons it won't work, and another where the maths don't work."

A typical comment in the report from one food marketer is: "I cannot just go to the board and say I'm moving £2m of the spend into direct marketing and have no idea of the return we'll get." While one soft drinks client comments: "We are in the business of selling products – not getting PR for our use of technology. I've yet to be convinced that this is the route for mass-market consumer products."

Despite these negative views, other indicators point to continuing fmcg interest in direct marketing not least from the consumer.

Henley Centre findings confirm what direct marketers long suspected: relevant communications are received favourably, and not seen as junk mail. Of 1000 people polled this spring, 64% viewed the post as "a good way of getting more information about products you are interested in".

Confidential information

Another 58% were happy to provide personal details to companies "if they can provide a better service, but only if the information remains confidential".

The costs of holding and interpreting data are falling fast, and desktop PC platforms allow marketers to access data without involving the IT department.

Simon Hall, managing director of Barraclough Hall Woolston Gray, says the union between fmcg and direct marketing is permanent. "It's staggering the return you can get – it's a very up-beat message."

As Heinz marketing director Lawrence Balfe says: "We need a rapid and efficient means of speaking to our key consumers. We see the direct link with our loyal consumers as essential to develop our consumer franchise."

For years, pundits have predicted that one day direct marketing would be taken up seriously. Many mistook the conversion of Heinz as evidence enough. A year later, news that a third of fmcg companies are using direct marketing shows that Heinz was just the beginning.

Clipping 2 Benetton drops its shock tactic

Key issues

Effects of different types of advertising appeal on consumers
Effects of consumer attitudes and behaviour on advertising appeals

Questions

(1)   Benetton has long employed shock tactics – why and what has the effect been on consumers?

(2)   What concepts from the study of consumer behaviour can you use to explain

(a) Benetton's approach and

(b) the effects on consumers?

(3)   Discuss different advertising appeals that could be employed by clothing companies and compare and contrast them with Benetton's previous approach and present approaches.

Marketing 20 April 1995

Benetton drops its shock tactic

Benetton ad: no longer using controversial advertising

By Conor Dignan

Benetton is to axe its controversial shock tactics advertising for a new creative drive, Luciano Benetton has revealed in an exclusive interview with *Marketing*.

The president of the Benetton Group, which has 7000 stores around the world, said: "It is now the moment for something new," signalling an end to the campaign which has featured dying Aids-sufferers, riot scenes and the blood-stained clothes of a dead soldier.

But Benetton denied that the decision to drop controversial advertising was influenced by court cases in Germany brought by franchise holders who sell Benetton clothing.

They are refusing to pay money owed to Benetton and cite the advertising as a major cause of declining sales.

Benetton's latest ads featured barbed-wire images and no new work is expected to appear until late this year. The new ads will centre on a new design school, Fabrica, being opened by Benetton in North-east Italy.

The shift in ad strategy follows a difficult year for Benetton, which has been forced to slash prices by 20% to retain market share and turnover.

In the UK, the group's 240 outlets have undergone a major facelift.

But the UK market has fared better than other European markets including Germany, where around 50 Benetton stores have closed.

Despite the change, Benetton continue to originate advertising from Italy under creative director Oliviero Toscani.

Problem 1   Brand-switching

Introductory comments

The use of brand-switching models can be seen as a suitable method of analysing brand performance.

To build brand-switching model, it is necessary to have detailed consumer-panel data. The following information is required:

- which brand was brought in the current period
- which brand was brought in the last period
- the frequency of purhcase
- the quantity bought
- the multi-product purchase picture

From the data available, an analysis is carried out to discover the loyalty to a particular brand, how consumers are behaving in terms of switching from one brand to another, and the quantity bought per buyer.

It is important that only one unit of purchase is made on each buying occasion and that there is no overlapping or multi-product purchase at this time. If these conditions are not met, brand-switching analysis cannot be carried out satisfactorily.

Problem

Consider a market in which there are three products and purchasing behaviour is available over three time periods. In period one, the shares held by the three products were 45%, 30%, and 25%, respectively. In period two, the shares changed to 45%, 28% and 27%. As as shown in Figure 1 buyers have switched from one product to another. For example, of the 45% who bought product A in period one 36% have remained loyal, 5% have switched to product B and 4% to product C. A similar pattern emerged between periods two and three.

Questions

(1) From this set of data draw up a matrix in which the product bought in the last period is represented by the columns and the product bought in this period is represented by the rows.

(2) Build up equations from the matrix to reflect the patterns in the product switching.

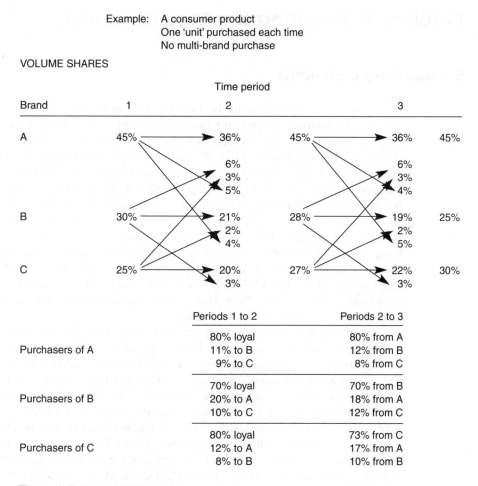

Example: A consumer product
           One 'unit' purchased each time
           No multi-brand purchase

VOLUME SHARES

Brand	Time period			
	1	2	3	
A	45%	36%	45%	36%	45%

	Periods 1 to 2	Periods 2 to 3
Purchasers of A	80% loyal	80% from A
	11% to B	12% from B
	9% to C	8% from C
Purchasers of B	70% loyal	70% from B
	20% to A	18% from A
	10% to C	12% from C
Purchasers of C	80% loyal	73% from C
	12% to A	17% from A
	8% to B	10% from B

Figure 1 Product switching pattern.

Problem 2 Targeting the Euro-consumer

Introductory comments

Much has been written about the new challenges of marketing to Euro-consumers. Discussions abound on whether the 'Euro-consumer' actually exists or may be expected to materialize sometime in the near future. Arguments have developed against depicting the 340 million people of the European Union as Euro-clones, drinking Euro-beer, eating Euro-wurst and watching Euro-soaps on Euro-satellite TV. If it is not realistic to visualize a global European market, can we still identify some large segments that would allow economies of scale in marketing? At least two large segments appear to stand apart: the concentration of urbanites living mainly within a 250-mile radius of Cologne and the 'new wave' segment of fashion-conscious European teenagers. Thus, one might assume that social demographic and psychological segmentation methods will be more useful for marketers in the new Europe than older methods based on geography, language or culture. However, this assumption is not shared by all competitors eyeing the European market.

Two recent attempts have been made to extend established US lifestyle segmentation methods to new markets. First, Rena Bartos' well-known categorization of women into four groups has been extended to nine markets outside the US. The groups include housewives who plan to work in the future, housewives who plan to stay at home, working women who are career-minded. These are further subdivided into four life-cycle groups: married women with children at home, married women with no children at home, unmarried women with no children at home, and unmarried women with children. Bartos finds that her typologies are valid across countries and cultures, including the United Kingdom, Italy, Germany, Australia and Japan. The similarities between countries reveal larger between-segment differences than between-country differences. These results underline the impact of values and lifestyle on segment formation, rather than culture or ethnicity.

Second, the well-known VALS analysis is echoed in a new approach to the Australian market, based on 10 segments. These groups are named 'basic needs', 'fairer deal' 'conventional family life', 'look-at-me', 'something better', 'real conservatism', 'young optimism', 'visible achievement', 'traditional family life' and 'socially aware'. Creators of the Australian typologies believe that it can be applied to all countries in varying degrees. For example, the US, Canada and Japan contain high proportions off 'visible achievers', whereas the 'fairer deal' category is notable in Britain, and the 'look-at-me' lifestyle is well represented in Germany.

It may be, however, that this search for macro lifestyle segments is a moot issue. Japanese manufacturers appear to be moving more in the direction of micro-marketing. Changing trends in lifestyles and values in Japan mean that consumers there attach increasing importance to fashion and fun. For example, cars are seen as fashion items or adult toys rather than as a means of getting around. One way that Japanese automobile manufacturers are responding to this trend is by narrowly segmenting the market and catering to a wide range of wants, needs and fantasies. Not only is flamboyant automobile design an issue, but so is the creation of a unique interior environment for each of the new models of the up-scale fashion cars. Small niches mean small production runs and flexible production capabilities – an ominous development for competitors abroad. Computerized order entry, model changes every two to four years, ever lower inventories and shorter delivery times: all combine to make these innovative manufacturers into redoubtable competitors.

It does not take a great leap of imagination to visualize Japanese automobile companies entering the European market and carving out exciting new small niches, where slight differences in consumer lifestyles and values can be easily accommodated and fashion becomes the name of the game. Fast-changing, experiential consumption may replace predictable old brand loyalties. In this case, the much talked about monolithic segments of European consumers may prove to be irrelevant. In their place, micro-markets, with their own lifestyles and value systems, may flourish in response to highly tailored product offerings. Then, only the most nimble and innovative companies will survive in the super-segmented European Market.

Problem

Mykado Foods Limited is one of the new market leaders in the growing market segment of healthy and diet foods. The most important marketing strategy for the next three years is to penetrate the European market with a selected line of Euro-brands. John McWilliams, the company's marketing manager, was pondering about the key strategic considerations and effectiveness of such a strategy.

Questions

(1) Comment on the barriers to developing standardized pan-European brands.

(2) Comment on this statement: 'there is no such thing as a true European'.

(3) Analyse some key consumer trends which have implications for standardizing pan-European brands.

References

Amine, Lyn S. (1990). Entering the 1990s: Targeting the 1992 Euro-Consumer. *Academy of Marketing Science News*, **11** (1), January.

The *Economist*, November 4 1989, p. 79.

References

Aaker, D.A. (1991), *Managing Brand Equity*. New York: The Free Press.

Aaker, D.A. and Shansby, J.G. (1982), Positioning your product. *Business Horizons*, (May/June), 56–62.

Achenbaum, A.A. (1964), The purpose of test marketing. In: Kaplan, R.M. (Ed), *The Marketing Concept in Action*. American Marketing Association.

Advertising Standards Authority (1990), Herself Reappraised. London: ASA.

Aguilar, F.J. (1967), *Scanning the Business Environment*. London: Macmillan.

Alderfer, C.P. (1972), *Existence, Relatedness*, and Growth. New York: The Free Press.

Alsop, R. (1984), Color grows more important in catching consumers' eyes. *The Wall Street Journal*, 29 November, 37.

Anderson, J.R. (1983), *The Architecture of Cognition*. Cambridge, MA: Harvard University Press.

Anderson, S. (1987), The Swedish land data bank. *International Journal of Geographic Information Systems*, **1**(3).

Antonides, G. (1989), An attempt at integration of economic and psychological theories of consumption. *Journal of Economic Psychology*, **10**, 77–99.

Antonides, G. (1991), *Psychology in Economics and Business. An Introduction to Economic Psychology*. Dordrecht, The Netherlands: Kluwer Academic Publishers.

Antonides, G., Arts, W. and Van Raaij, W.F. (1991), *The Consumption of Time and the Timing of Consumption*. Amsterdam: North-Holland.

Applebaum, W. (1968), *Store Location Strategies*. Reading MA: Addison-Wesley.

Arbeit, S.P. (1984), Confronting the crisis in mass marketing. In: Kotler, P. and Cox, K. (Eds), *Marketing Management and Strategy. A Reader*. Englewood Cliffs, NJ: Prentice-Hall, 3rd edition.

Asch, S.E. (1946), Forming impressions of personality, *Journal of Abnormal and Social Psychology*, **41**, 258–90.

Assael, H. (1970), Segmenting markets by group purchasing behavior: An application of the AID technique. *Journal of Marketing Research*, **7**, 153–8.

Assael, H. (1984), *Consumer Behaviour and Marketing Action*. Boston, MA: Kent Publishing Company, 2nd edition.

Assael, H. (1987), *Consumer Behaviour and Marketing Action*. Boston, MA: Kent Publishing Company, 3rd edition.

Avlonitis, G. and Kouramenos, A.G. (1995), The changing consumer in Greece. *International Journal of Research in Marketing*, **12**.

Ayer, N.W. (1969) (see Claychamp and Liddy, 1969).

Baker, S. (1979), *Systematic Approach to Advertising Creativity*. New York: McGraw-Hill.

BBC (1984a), Not By Jeans Alone. Commercial Breaks.

BBC (1984), Moneybox, Radio 4.

Beal, G. and Rogers, E. (1951) Informal sources in the adoption process of new fabrics. *Journal of Home Economics*. October, **49**, 630–34.

Bearden, W.O. and Teel, J.E (1983), Selected determinants of consumer satisfaction and complaint reports. *Journal of Marketing Research*, 20 February, 21–8.

Beatty, S.E. and Smith, S.M. (1987), External search effort: An investigation across several product categories, *Journal of Consumer Research*, **14**, 83–95.

Beaumont, J.R. and Inglis, K. (1989), Geodemographics in practice: development in Britain and Europe. *Environment and Planning*, **21**, 587–604.

Beik, L.L. and Buzby, S.L. (1984), Profitability analysis by market segments. In: Kotler, P., and Cox, K. (Eds), *Marketing Management and Strategy*. A Reader. Englewood Cliffs, NJ: Prentice-Hall, 3rd edition.

Bellizzi, J.A., Crowley, A.E. and Hasty, R.W., (1983), The effects of colour in store design. *Journal of Retailing*, (Spring), 21–45.

Berger, D. (1986), Theory into practice: The FCB Grid. *European Research*, January, 35–46.

Berlyne, D.E. (1963), 'Motivational problems raised by exploratory and epistemic behavior. In: Koch, S. (Ed), *Psychology: A Study of a Science*, **5**, New York: McGraw-Hill, 284–364.

Berman, B. and Evans J. (1992), *Marketing*. New York: Macmillan 5th edition.

Bernstein, D. (1974), *Creative Advertising*. Harlow: Longman.

Bettman, J.R. (1979), *An Information Processing Theory of Consumer Choice. Reading*, MA: Addison-Wesley.

Bettman, J.R. and Sujan, M. (1987), Effects of framing on evaluation of comparable and noncomparable alternatives by expert and novice consumers. *Journal of Consumer Research*, **14**, 141–54.

Biehal, G. and Chakravarti, D. (1983), Information accessibility as a moderator of consumer choice. *Journal of Consumer Research*, **10**, 1–14.

Biehal, G. and Chakravarti, D. (1986), Consumers' use of memory and external information in choice: Macro and micro perspectives. *Journal of Consumer Research*, **12**, 382–405.

Binsted, D. (1986), Learning to cope with change. *Management Decision*, **24**(3).

Bird, D. (1992), EC tunes in to direct marketing. *Marketing*, 14 May.

Birdwell, A. (1968), Influence of image congruence on consumer choice. *Journal of Business*, January.

Birnbaum, M.H. (1983), Thinking and feeling: A skeptical review. *American Psychologist*, **36**, 99–101.

Blair, C. (1983), Sampling issues in trade area maps drawn from shopper survey. *Journal of Marketing*, **14**, 98–106.

Blattberg, R. and Golanty, J. (1978), Tracker: An early test market forecasting and diagnostic model for new product planning. *Journal of Marketing Research*, **15**, 192–202.

Block, R. (1992), Sales talk, BBC Radio 4, January.

BMRB (1980), *The Charts*. British Market Research Bureau. London.

Bonoma, T.V. and Shapiro, B.P. (1983), *Segmenting the Industrial Market*. Lexington, MA: Lexington Books.

Book, A. (1981), Presentation at Newcastle Upon Tyne Polytechnic on behalf of American Express.

Boote, A.S. (1984), Interactions in psychographics segmentation: Implications for advertising. *Journal of Advertising Research*, February, 29–35.

Borcherding, K. (1983), Entscheidungstheorie und Entscheidungshilfeverfahren für komplexe Entscheidungssituationen. In: Irle, M. (Ed), *Methoden und Anwendungen in der Marktpsychologie*. Göttingen, FRG: Verlag für Psychologie, Dr. C.J. Hogrefe, 64–173.

Boring, E.G. (1930). *American Journal of Psychology*, **42**, 444–5.

Bowlby, S., Brehany, M. and Frost, J. (1984), Store location: Problems and methods expanding into new geographical areas. *Retail and Distribution Management*, **12**(6), 41–6.

Boyd, H. W., Westfall, R. and Stasch, S. F. (1977), *Marketing Research*: Text and cases. Georgeon Ontario: Irwin 4th edition.

Bradley, M.F. and Lambkin, M. (1995), Ireland. *International Journal of Research in Marketing*, **12**.

Bradley, U. (1982), *Applied Market and Social Research*. Van Nostrand Reinhold.

Breheny, M.J.(1988), Practical methods of retail location analysis: A review. In: Wrighting, N. (Ed), *Store Choice, Store Location and Market Analysis*. London; Routledge.

British Market Research Bureau (BMRB) (1988), The Target Group Index.

Broadbent, D.E. (1977), The hidden pre-attentive processes. *American Psychologist*, **32**, 109–18.

Brucks, M. (1985), The effects of product class knowledge on information search behavior. *Journal of Consumer Research*, **12**, 1–16.

Bruner, J.S. and Tagiuri, R. (1954), Person perception. In: Lindzey, G. (Ed), *Handbook of Social Psychology*, **2**, Reading, MA: Addison-Wesley.

Bruner, J.S., Goodnow, J.J. and Austin, G.A(1956), *A Study of Thinking*. New York: John Wiley.

CACI (1979), *ACORN- A new approach to Market Analysis*. London: CACI Market Analysis Group.

CACI (1981), *ACORN: A New Approach to Market Analysis*. London: CACI Ltd.

CACI (1993), *The Acorn Targeting Classification*. London: CACI Ltd.

Cacioppo, J. T and Petty, R. E (1982), The need for cognition, *Journal of Personality and Social Psychology*, **42**, 116–31.

Capon, N. and Davis, R. (1984), Basic cognitive ability measures as predictors of consumer information processing strategies. *Journal of Consumer Research*, **11**, 551–63.

Channel 4 (1990), Direct Marketing. Equinox Series.

Churchill, J.R., Gilbert, A. and Suprenant, C. (1982), An investigation into the determinants of customer satisfaction. *Journal of Marketing Research*, **19**, November, 491–504.

Claycamp, H. and Liddy, L. (1969), Prediction of new product performance: An analytical approach. *Journal of Marketing Research*, **6**, 414–20.

Coad, T. (1992), Distinguishing marks. *Marketing Business*, **14**, October, 12–15.

Cohen, S.B. and Applebaum, W. (1960), Evaluating stores sites and determining store rent. *Economic Geography*, **36**, 1–35.

Cohen, J.B. and Basu, K. (1987), Alternative models of categorization: Toward a contingent processing framework. *Journal of Consumer Research*, **13**, 455–72.

Collins, M. (1981), Telephone interviewing: A solution or a new set of problems? *Market Research Society Newsletter*, 180, 5.

Cooper, P. and Tower, R. (1992), Inside the consumer mind. *Journal of the Market Research Society*, **34**(4), 299–311.

Cosmas, S.C. (1982), Life styles and consumption patterns. *Journal of Consumer Research*, March, 453–5.

Cox, D.F. (1967), *Risk Taking and Information Handling in Consumer Behavior*. Boston, MA: Harvard Business School.

Craig, C.S., Ghosh, A. and McLafferty, S. (1984), Models of the retail location process: A review. *Journal of Retailing* (Spring), 5–36.

Craik, F.I.M. and Tulving, E. (1975), Depth of processing and the retention of words in episodic memory. *Journal of Experimental Psychology: General*, **104**, 268–94.

Cravens, D.W. (1982), *Strategic Marketing*. Homewood, IL: Irwin.

Cravens, D.W., Hills, G.E. and Woodruff, R.B. (1980), *Marketing Decision Making. Concepts and Strategy*. Homewood, IL: Irwin.

Crawford, C. M. (1970), Attitudes of marketing executives toward ethics in market research. *Journal of Marketing*, **34**(2), 46–52.

Cunningham, S.M. (1967), Perceived risk and brand loyalty. In: Cox, D.F. (Ed), *Risk Taking and Information Handling in Consumer Behavior*. Boston, MA: Harvard Business School, 507–23.

Dalrymple, D.J. and Parsons, L.J. (1986), *Marketing Management Strategy and Cases*. New York: John Wiley, 4th edition.

Darden, W.R. and Perreault, W.D. Jr. (1977), Classification for market segmentation: An improved linear model for solving problems of arbitary origin. *Marketing Science*, **24** November, 259–271.

Davidson, H. (1975), *Offensive Marketing*. Harmondsworth: Penguin.

Davidson, H. (1987), *Offensive Marketing or How To Make Your Competitors Followers*. Harmondsworth: Penguin, 2nd edition.

Davies, G.J. and Brooks, J.M. (1989), *Positioning Strategy in Retailing*. London: Paul Chapman Publishing.

Davies, R.L. and Rogers, D.S. (Eds) (1984), *Store Location and Store Assessment Research*. Chichester: John Wiley.

Davis, H. and Rigaux, B. (1974), Perception of marital roles in decision processes. *Journal of Consumer Research*, **1**, 51–61.

Davis, L.A. (1982), Market positioning considerations. In: Bailey, E.L. (Ed), *Product-Line Strategies*. New York: The Conference Board, 37–9.

Dawes, R.M. (1975), The mind, the model, and the task. In: Castellon, H.L. and Restle, F. (Eds), *Proceedings of the 7th Annual Indiana Theoretical and Cognitive Psychology Conference*, 119–29.

Day, G.S., Shocker, A.D. and Srivastava, R.K. (1979), Customer-oriented approaches to identifying product markets. *Journal of Marketing*, **43**(4), 8–19.

de Almeida, P. M. (1980), A review of group discussion methodology. *European Research*, **3**(8),114–20.

Delozier, W. (1976), *The Marketing Communications Process*. New York: McGraw-Hill.

Diamantopoulos, A. (1994), Modelling with LISREL: A guide for the uninitiated. In: Hooley, G.J. and Hussey, M.K. (Eds), *Quantitative Methods in Marketing*. London: Academic Press / Harcourt Brace, 105–36.

Dichter, E. (1964), *Handbook of Consumer Motivations*. New York: McGraw-Hill.

Dickson, P.R. (1982), Person-situation: Segmentation's missing link. *Journal of Marketing*. **46**(4), 56–64.

Dickson, P.R. and Ginter, J.L. (1987), Market segmentation, product differentiation, and marketing strategy. *Journal of Marketing*, **51**(2), 1–10.

Dodds, W.B. and Monroe, K.B. (1985), The effect of brand and price information on subjective product evaluations. *Advances in Consumer Research*, **12**, 85–90.

Donovan, R.J. and Rossiter, J.R. (1982), Store atmosphere: An environmental psychology approach. *Journal of Retailing*, **58** (Spring), 34–57.

Doyle, P. and Saunders, J. (1985), Market segmentation and positioning in specialized industrial markets. *Journal of Marketing*, **49**(2), 24–32.

Dublow, J. (1992), Occasion used benefit segmentation. *Journal of Advertising Research*, March/April, 11–18.

Dwek, R. (1992), Direct marketing: A vote of confidence. *Marketing*, 19 March.

Edell, J.A. and Staelin, R. (1983), The information processing of pictures in print advertisements, *Journal of Consumer Research*, **10**, 45–61.

Edell, J.A. and Burke, M.C. (1984), The moderating effect of attitude toward an ad on ad effectiveness under different processing conditions. *Advances in Consumer Research*, 11, 644–9.

Edmonson, R. (1993), reported in 'Levi Zips into Youth Market with Hip Ads', *Marketing*, 17 June.

Edwards, A.L. (1957), *Techniques of Attitude Scale Construction*. New York: Appleton Century Crofts.

Ehrlich, D., Guttman, L., Schonback, P. and Mills, J. (1957), Postdecision exposure to relevant information. *Journal of Personality and Social Psychology*, **54**, 98–102.

Einhorn, H.J. and Hogarth, R.M. (1985), Ambiguity and uncertainty in probabilistic inference. *Psychological Bulletin*, **92**, 433–61.

Elrod, T. and Winer, R.S. (1982), An empirical evaluation of aggregation approaches for developing marketing segments. *Journal of Marketing*, **6**(4), 65–74.

Employment Census (1984), London: HMSO, Department of Employment.

Engel, J.F., Fiorillo, H.F. and Cayley, M.A. (1972), *Market Segmentation. Concepts and Applications*. New York: Holt, Rinehart & Winston.

Engel, J.F., Blackwell, R.D. and Miniard, P. W. (1995), *Consumer Behavior*. Chicago, IL: The Dryden Press.

England, L. (1980), Is research a waste of time? *Marketing*, 16 April, 5–7.

Etzioni, A. (1986), Rationality is anti-entropic. *Journal of Economic Psychology*, **7**, 17–36.

Etzioni, A. (1988), Normative–affective factors: Toward a new decision-making model. *Journal of Economic Psychology*, **9**, 125–50.

Evans, B. (1959), Psychological and objective factors in the prediction of brand choice: Ford versus Chevrolet. *Journal of Business*, October.

Evans, J. and Berman, B. (1985), *Marketing*. New York: Macmillan, 2nd edition.

Evans, M.J. (1989), Consumer behaviour toward fashion. *European Journal of Marketing*, **23**(7), 7–16.

Evans, M.J. (1981), So who's a dedicated follower of fashion? A perspective of the behaviour of fashion consumers. SSRC/MEG presentation, University of Strathclyde.

Evans, M.J. (1994) Domesday Marketing? *Journal of Marketing Management*, **10**(5).

Evans, M.J. and Moutinho, L. (1992), *Applied Marketing Research*. Wokingham: Addison-Wesley.

Evans, M.J., O'Malley, L. and Patterson, M. (1995). Direct marketing; rise and rise or rise and fall? *Marketing Intelligence and Planning*, **13** (2).

Fahey, L. and Narajanan, V.K. (1986), *Macroenvironmnetal Analysis for Strategic Management*. New York: West Publishing.

Farhangmehr, M. and Veiga, P. (1995), The changing consumer in Portugal. *International Journal of Research in Marketing*, **12**.

Festinger, L. (1957), *A Theory of Cognitive Dissonance*. Evanston, IL: Row, Peterson.

Filser, M. (1996), The changing French consumer. *International Journal of Research in Marketing*, **13**.

Fishbein, M. and Ajzen, I. (1975), *Belief, Attitude, Intention, and Behavior*. Reading, MA: Addison-Wesley.

Floor, J.M.G. and Van Raaij, W.F. (1993), *Marketing-Communicatie Strategie* [Marketing-Communication Strategy]. Houten, The Netherlands: Stenfert Kroese.

Foenander, J. (1992), The use of smart card technology for target marketing in the retail sector. *Journal of Targeting, Measurement and Analysis for Marketing*, **1**(1).

Ford, G.T. and Smith, R.A. (1987), Inferential beliefs in consumer evaluations: An assessment of alternative processing strategies. *Journal of Consumer Research*, **14**, 363–71.

Fourt, L.A. and Woodlock, J.W. (1960), Early prediction of market success for new grocery products. *Journal of Marketing*, **25**, 31–8.

Foxall, G.R. (1980), *Consumer Behaviour: A Practical Guide*. London: Routledge.

Foxall, G.R. (1983), *Consumer Choice*. London: Macmillan.

Foxall, G.R. and Goldsmith, R.E. (1994), *Consumer Psychology for Marketing*. London: Routledge.

Frank, R.E., Massy, W.F. and Wind, Y. (1972), *Market Segmentation*. Englewood Cliffs, NJ: Prentice-Hall.

Fraser, A. (1989), How a better targeted database could rule out junk mail but invade privacy. *Campaign*, 1 December.

Freud, S. (1901), *Psychology of Everyday Life*. London: Hogarth Press.

Furse, D.H., Punj, G.N. and Stewart D.W. (1984), A typology of individual search strategies among purchasers of new automobiles. *Journal of Consumer Research*, **10**, 417–31.

Gabor, A. and Granger, C.W.J. (1966), Price as an indicator of quality. *Economica*, **33**, 43–70.

Galbraith, J R. (1979), *Organizational Design*. Reading, MA: Addison-Wesley.

Gallup (1982), A comparison between American, European and Japanese Values. World Association for Public Opinion Research Annual Meeting, 21 May , Maryland, USA.

Garcia, G. (1980), Credit cards: An interdisciplinary survey. *Journal of Consumer Research*, **7**, 327–37.

Gardner, M.P. (1985), Does attitude toward the ad affect brand attitude under a brand evaluation set? *Journal of Marketing Research*, **22**, 192–8.

Gaskill, S. and Cooke, K. (1992), Significant issues in data protection: Lifestyle profiling and data matching. *Journal of Targeting, Measurement and Analysis for Marketing*. **1**(1).

Gatignon, H. and Robertson, T.S.(1985), A propositional inventory for new diffusion research. *Journal of Consumer Research*, **11**, March, 849–67.

Gensch, D.H. and Javalgi, R.G. (1987), The influence of involvement on disaggregate attribute choice models. *Journal of Consumer Research*, **14**, 71–82.

Gibson, L.D. (1983), Not recall. *Journal of Advertising Research*, **23** (February/March), 39–46.

Gijsbrechts, E., Swinnen, G. and Van Waterschoot, W. (1995), The changing consumer in Belgium: Recent changes in environmental variables and their consequences for future consumption and marketing. *International Journal of Research in Marketing*, **12**.

Glaser, S. (1985), The marketing system and the environment. *European Journal of Marketing*, **19**(4).

Goldman, A.E. (1982), Market segmentation analysis tells what to say to whom. *Marketing News*, **15**, January, 10–11.

Gorn, G.J. (1982), The effects of music in advertising on choice behavior: A classical conditioning approach. *Journal of Marketing*, **46**, 94–101.

Gredal, K. (1966), Purchasing behavior in households. In: Kjaer-Hansen, M. (Ed), *Readings in Danish Theory of Marketing*. Copenhagen, Denmark: Einar Harcks Forlag, 84–100.

Green, P.E. (1977), A new approach to market segmentation. *Business Horizons*, **20** February, 61–73.

Green, P.E. and DeSarbo, W.S.(1979), Componential segmentation in the analysis of consumer trade-offs. *Journal of Marketing*, **43**(4), 83–90.

Green, P.E. and Srinivasan, V. (1978), Conjoint analysis in consumer research: Issues and outlook. *Journal of Consumer Research*, **5**, 103–23.

Green, P.E., Carmone, F.J. Jr and Smith, S.M. (1989), *Multidimensional Scaling. Concepts and Applications*. Boston, MA: Allyn & Bacon.

Greenacre, M.J. (1984), *Correspondence Analysis in Practice*. London: Academic Press.

Greenley, G.E. (1986), *The Strategic and Operational Planning of Marketing*. Maidenhead: McGraw-Hill.

Grönroos, C. (1990), *Service Management and Marketing*. Lexington, MA: Heath, Lexington Books.

Grunert, K.G., Grunert, S.C., Glatzer, W. and Imkamp, H. (1995), The changing consumer in Germany, *International Journal of Research in Marketing*, **12**.

Hair, J.F., Jr, Anderson, R.E. Tatham, R.L. and Grablowsky, B.J. (1984), *Multivariate Data Analysis*. New York: Macmillan.

Haire, M. (1950), Projective techniques in marketing research. *Journal of Marketing*, **14**, 649–56.

Haley, R.I. (1968), Benefit segmentation: A decision oriented research tool. *Journal of Marketing*, July, 30–5.

Haley, R.I. (1983), Benefit segmentation. 20 Years later. *Journal of Consumer Marketing*, **2**, 5–13.

Hall, W.K. (1980), Survival strategies in a hostile environment. *Harvard Business Review*, September–October.

Hamilton, R., Haworth, B. and Sadar, N. (1982), Adman and Eve. Department of Marketing, Lancaster University.

Hammond, K., Ehrenberg, A. and Goodhart, G. (1993), Brand segmentation: A systematic study. In: Saunders, J. *et al.* (Eds), *Marketing Education Group Conference Proceedings*. Loughborough.

Hansen, F. (1972), *Consumer Choice Behavior. A Cognitive Theory*. New York: The Free Press.

Heckett, P.M.W., Foxall, G.R. and Van Raaij, W.F. (1993), Consumers in retail environments. Chapter 15 in: Gärling, T. and Golledge, R.G. (Eds), *Behavior and Environment: Psychological and Geographical Approaches*. Amsterdam, The Netherlands: Elsevier, 378–99.

Henley Centre for Forecasting (1978), Planning Consumer Markets and Leisure Futures.

Henley Centre for Forecasting (1984), Leisure Futures, Summer Institute for Fiscal Policy Studies (1986).

Henley Centre for Forecasting (1992), Presentation to Market Research Society, 5th March, Bristol.

Hirschman, E.C. (1980), Innovativeness, novelty seeking, and consumer creativity. *Journal of Consumer Research*, **7**, December, 283–95.

Hirschman, E.C. and Holbrook, M.B. (1992), *Postmodern Consumer Research*. Newbury Park, CA: Sage.

Hogg, M., Long, G., Hartley, M. and Angold, S. (1993), Touch me, hold me, squeeze me, freeze me: Privacy – The emerging issue for relationship marketing in the 1990s. In: Saunders, S. *et al.* (Eds), *Marketing Education Group Conference Proceedings*. Loughborough.

Holbrook, M.B. (1978), Beyond attitude structure: Toward the informational determinants of attitude. *Journal of Marketing Research*, **15**, November, 545–56.

Holbrook, M.B. and Hirschman, E.C. (1982), The experiential aspects of consumption: Consumer fantasies, feelings, and fun. *Journal of Consumer Research*, **9**, 132–40.

Holbrook, M.B., Chestnut, R.B., Oliva, T.A. and Greenleaf, E.A. (1984), Play as a consumption experience: The roles of emotions, performance, and personality in the enjoyment of games. *Journal of Consumer Research*, **11**, 728–39.

Holt-Hansen, K. (1978), The taste of music. *Perceptual and Motor Skills*, **33**(3), 1023.

Howard, J.A. and Sheth, J.N. (1969), *The Theory of Buyer Behavior*. New York: John Wiley.

Howe, E. (1992), as reported by Dwek, R., DMA warned of High Tech's Threat to Privacy. *Marketing*, 23 July.

Humby, C. (1989), New developments in demographic targeting. *Journal of Market Research Society*, **31**(1).

Hyett, P. (1982), Should we be having more of IT? *Market Research Society Newsletter*, **3**, 196.

Institute for Fiscal Studies (1986).

Institute of Marketing (1975), Moor Hall, Cookham.

Jacoby, J., Speller, D.E. and Kohn, C.A. (1974a), Brand choice behavior as a function of information load, *Journal of Marketing Research*, **11**, 63–9.

Jacoby, J., Speller, D.E. and Kohn, C.A. (1974b), Brand choice behavior as a function of information load: Replication and extension, *Journal of Consumer Research*, **1**, 33–42.

Jain, S.C. (1981), *Marketing Planning and Strategy*. Cincinnati, OH: South Western Publishing.

Johnson, E. and Russo, J.E. (1984), Product familiarity and learning new information. *Journal of Consumer Research*, **11**, 542–50.

Johnson, G. and Scholes, K. (1984), *Exploring Corporate Strategy*. Englewood Cliffs, NJ: Prentice-Hall.

Johnson, M.(1989), The application of geodemographics to retailing – meeting the needs of the catchment. *Journal of Marketing Research Society*, **31** (1), 7–36.

Johnson, R.D. and Levin, I.P. (1985), More than meets the eye: The effect of missing information on purchase evaluations. *Journal of Consumer Research*, **12**, 169–77.

Johnson, R.M. (1984), Market segmentation: A strategic management tool. In: Kotler, P. and Cox, K. (Eds), *Marketing Management and Strategy*. A Reader. Englewood Cliffs, NJ: Prentice-Hall, 3rd edition.

Jones K. and Simmons, J. (1990), *The Retail Environment*. London: Routledge, 284–376.

Jones, K.G. and Mock, D.R. (1984), Evaluating retail trading performances. In: R.L. Davies and D.S. Rogers (Eds) *Store Location and Store Assessment Research*. Chichester: John Wiley, 333–60.

Kahn, R. L. and Cannell, C. F. (1968), Interviewing. *International Encyclopedia of the Social Sciences*, **2**(2), 118–35.

Kahneman, D. and Tversky, A. (1979), Prospect theory: An analysis of decision under risk. *Econometrica*, **47**, 263–91.

Kahneman, D. and Tversky, A. (1984), Choices, values, and frames. *American Psychologist*, **39**, 341–50.

Kapferer, J. N. (1992) *Strategic Brand Management*. London: Kogan Page.

Kassarjian, H.H. (1971), Personality and consumer behaviour. *Journal of Marketing Research*, November.

Kassarjian, H.H. and Robertson, T.S. (1991), *Perspectives in Consumer Behavior*. Englewood Cliffs, NJ: Prentice-Hall, 4th edition.

Katona, G. and Mueller, E. (1955), A study of purchase decisions. In: Clark, L.H. (Ed), *Consumer Behavior. The Dynamics of Consumer Reaction*. New York: New York University Press, 30–87.

Katz, E. and Lazarsfeld, P.F. (1955), *Personal Influence*. New York: The Free Press.

Keller, K.L. and Staelin, R. (1987), Effects of quality and quantity of information on decision effectiveness, *Journal of Consumer Research*, **14**, 200–13.

Kelley, H.H. (1967), Attribution theory in social psychology. In: Levine, D. (Ed), *Nebraska Symposium on Motivation*. Lincoln: University of Nebraska Press.

Kelly, G.A. (1955), *The Psychology of Personal Constructs*. New York: W.W. Norton.

Kelly, P.J., Freeman C.D. and Emlen, J. (1993), Competitive impact model for site selection: The impact of competition, sales generators and own store cannibalisation. The *International Review of Retail, Distribution and Consumer Research*, **3**(3), 237–59.

Keng, K.A. and Ehrenberg, A.S.C. (1984), Patterns of store choice. *Journal of Marketing Research*, 21 November, 399–409.

Keon, J.W. and Bayer, J. (1984), Analyzing scanner panel households to determine the demographic characteristics of brand loyal and variety seeking households using a new brand switching measure. In: Belk, R.W. *et al* (Eds), *AMA Educators' Proceedings*. Chicago, IL: American Marketing Association, 416–20.

Key, W.B. (1973), *Subliminal Seduction*. Englewood Cliffs, NJ: Signet.

Klein, N.M. and Bither, S.W. (1987), An investigation of utility-directed cutoff selection. *Journal of Consumer Research*, **14**, 240–56.

Kohsaka, H. (1992), Three-dimensional representation and estimation of retail store demand by bicubic splines. *Journal of Retailing*, **68**(2), 221–37.

Kotler, P. (1984), *Marketing Management, Planning, Control and Evaluation*. Englewood Cliffs, NJ: Prentice-Hall.

Kotler, P. (1991a), *Marketing Management. Analysis, Planning, Implementation, and Control*. Englewood Cliffs, NJ: Prentice-Hall, 7th edition.

Kotler, P. (1991b), Philip Kotler explores the new marketing paradigm. Marketing Science Institute, Spring.

Kouremenos, A. and Avlonitis, G.J. (1995), Greece. *International Journal of Research in Marketing*, **12**.

Krauser, P. (1981), Research: A safe bet for the light against product failure. *Campaign*, **31**, July, 33–5.

Kreitzman, L. (1987), Census of opinions. *Marketing*, 18 August.

LaBarbera, P.A. and Mazursky, D. (1983), A longitudinal assessment of consumer satisfaction/dissatisfaction: The dynamic aspect of the cognitive process. *Journal of Market Research*, November, 393–404.

Latour, S.A. and Peat, N.C. (1979), Conceptual and methodological issues in consumer satisfaction research. *Advances in Consumer Research*, **6**, 431–37.

Lawson, R.W. (1988), The family life cycle: A demographic analysis. *Journal of Marketing Management*, **4**(1), 13–32.

Lazarsfeld, P.F. and Kate, E.(1955), *Personal Influence*. New York: Free Press.

Lazarus, R.S. (1984), On the primacy of cognition. *American Psychologist*, **39**, 124–29.

Lazer, W. (1981), Lucrative marketing opportunities will abound in the upbeat 1980s. In: McCarthy, E.J. *et al.* (Eds), *Readings in Basic Marketing*. Homewood, IL: Irwin.

Lazer, W. and Culley, J.D. (1983), *Marketing Management. Foundations and Practices*. Boston, MA: Houghton Mifflin.

Lea, A.C. (1989), An overview of formal methods for retail site evaluation and sales forecasting: Part 1. *The Operational Geographer*, **17**, 8–17.

Lea, A.C. and Menger, G.L. (1990), An overview of formal methods for retail site evaluation and sales forecasting: Part 2. *The Operational Geographer*, **7**, 17–23.

Lea, A.C. and Menger, G.L. (1991), An overview of formal methods for retail site evaluation and sales forecasting: Part 3. *The Operational Geographer*, **7**, 17–26.

Leeflang, P.S.H. and Van Raaij, W.F. (1993), The changing consumer in The Netherlands. *International Journal of Research in Marketing*, **10**, 345–63.

Lehtinen, U. (1974), A brand choice model. Theoretical framework and empirical results. *European Research*, **2**, 51–68, 83.

Levitt, T. (1964), Marketing myopia. In: Bursk E.C. and Chapman, J.F. (Eds), *Modern Marketing Strategy*. Cambridge, MA: Harvard University Press.

Lewin, K. (1936), *Principles of Topological Psychology*. New York: McGraw-Hill.

Likert, R. (1932), A technique for the measurement of attitudes. *Arch. Psychology*, No. 140.

Littman, R.A. and Manning, H.M. (1954), A methodological study of cigarette brand discrimination. *Journal of Applied Psychology*, **38**, 185–90.

Long, G., Angold, S. and Hogg, M. (1992), Who am I? In: *Marketing in the New Europe and Beyond*. MEG Conference Proceedings, Salford, July.

Luck, D.J. and Ferrell, O.C. (1985), *Marketing Strategy and Plans*. Englewood Cliffs, NJ: Prentice-Hall, 2nd edition.

Lusch, R.F. and Lusch, V.N. (1987), *Principles of Marketing*. Boston, MA: Kent Publishing Company.

McCarthy, E.J. (1977), *Basic Marketing Learning Aid*. Homewood, IL: Irwin.

McCormick-Publicis (1985), Mantrack study, conducted by Research Bureau Ltd.

McDonald, M. (1984), *Marketing Plans: How to Prepare Them, How to Use Them*. London: Heinemann.

McGoldrick, P. (1990), *Retail Marketing*. New York: McGraw-Hill.

McNulty, C. and McNulty, R. of Taylor Nelson (1987).

Mahajan, V. and Jain, A.K. (1978), An approach to normative segmentation. *Journal of Marketing Research*, **15**, 338–45.

Malhotra, N.K. (1982), Information load and consumer decision making. *Journal of Consumer Research*, **8**, 419–430.

Maloney, J.C. (1962), Curiosity versus disbelief in advertising. *Journal of Advertising Research*, **2**, 2–8.

Mancuso, J.R. (1969), Why not create opinion leaders for new product introductions? *Journal of Marketing*, **33**, 20–5.

Market Research Society (1981), Working party report on social grade.

Market Research Society (1989), *Journal of the Market Research Society*, Special Issue on Geodemographics, **31**(1).

Market Research Society (1992), *Newsletter,* June.

Marsh, C. (1991), Microdata from the 1991 Census of population in Britain. *Journal of the Market Research Society*, **33**(4).

Martin, J. (1988), Problem segmentation. *International Journal of Bank Marketing*, **4**(2), 35–57.

Maslow, A. (1954), *Motivation and Personality*. New York: Harper & Row.

Massey, A. (1992), Reaching a census on the marketing. *Marketing*, 15 October.

Merrill, J.R. and Weeks, W.A. (1983), Predicting and identifying benefit segments in the elderly market. In: Murphy, P. *et al* (Eds), *AMA Educator's Proceedings*. Chicago, IL: American Marketing Association, 399–403.

Midgely, D. and Wills, G. (1979), *Fashion Marketing Lateral Marketing Thoughts*. Bradford: MCB Prem, 131.

Milliman, R.E. (1982), Using background music to affect the behaviour of supermarket shoppers, *Journal of Marketing*, **46** (Summer), 86–91.

Millward, M. (1987), How to get better value from your research budget. *AMSO Handbook and Guide to Buying Market Research in the UK*, 6–10.

MINTEL (1988), Regional Lifestyles.

MINTEL (1981), Market Intelligence Special Report on the Teenage Market.

MINTEL (1990), Drinks Market.

Mitchell, A.A. (1988), The big gap. *Marketing*, 18 August, 29–31.

Mitchell, A.A. and Olson, J.C. (1981), Are product attribute beliefs the only mediator of advertising effects on brand attitude? *Journal of Marketing Research*, 18(August), 318–32.

Mitchell, A. and Littlewood, S. (1992), Marketing's smart transformation. *Marketing*, 21 May.

Monroe, K.B. (1976), The influence of differences and brand familiarity on brand preferences. *Journal of Consumer Research*, **3**, 42–9.

Monroe, K.B. and Krishnan, R. (1983), A procedure for integrating outcomes across studies. *Advances in Consumer Research*, **10**, 503–8.

Moore, S. and Attewell, G. (1992), To be and where, not to be: The Tesco approach to location analysis. *OR Insight*, **4**(1), January–March, 21–4.

Moore, W.L. and Lehmann, D.R. (1980), Individual differences in search behavior for a nondurable. *Journal of Consumer Research*, **7**, 296–307.

Murray, H. (1979), So you know how advertising works? *Management Decision*, **17**, 369–90.

Mushkat, M. and Roberts, E. (1986), Environmental adaptation in Hong Kong public enterprise. *European Management Journal*, Spring.

Nelson, R.L (1958), *The Selection of Retail Locations*. New York: McGraw-Hill.

Newport, J.P., Jr. (1985), Frequent-flyer clones. *Fortune*, 29 April, 201.

Nilsson, O.S. and Solgaard, H.S. (1995), Denmark. *International Journal of Research in Marketing*, **12**.

Nueño, J.L. and Bennett, H. (1996), The changing Spanish consumer. *International Journal of Research in Marketing*, **13**.

Nye, D. (1981), *Three Psychologies: Perspectives from Freud, Skinner and Rogers*. Monterey, CA: Brooks/Cole.

O'Brien, S. and Ford R. (1988), Can we at last say goodbye to social class? *Journal of the Market Research Society*, **30**, 289–332.

O'Malley L., Patterson M. and Evans, M. (1995), The Application of Geodemographics in Retail Site Location and Trade Area Analysis: A Preliminary Investigation. *Marketing Intelligence and Planning*, **13**(2), 29–35.

Obermiller, C. and Wheatley, J.J. (1985), Beliefs in quality differences and brand choice. *Advances in Consumer Research*, **12**, 75–8.

Ody, P. (1989), Getting to know your customers. *Retail and Distribution Management*, July/August.

Ogilvie, D. (1983), *Ogilvy on Advertising*. London: Multimedia Publications.

Oliver, R.L. (1980), A cognitive model of the antecedents and consequences of satisfaction decisions. *Journal of Marketing Research*, 17 (November), 460–9.

Oliver, R.L. (1981), Measurement and evaluation of satisfaction processes in retail settings. *Journal of Retailing*, (Fall), 27.

Olshavsky, R.W. (1975), Customer–salesman interaction in appliance retailing. *Journal of Marketing Research*, **12,** May, 208–12.

Olshavsky, R.W. and Granbois, D.H. (1979), Consumer decision making – fact or fiction? *Journal of Consumer Research*, **6**, 93–100.

Olson, J.C. (1980), Implications of an information processing approach to pricing research. In: Lamb, C.W. Jr, and Dunne, P.M. (Eds), *Theoretical Developments in Marketing*. Chicago, IL: American Marketing Association, 13–16.

Olson, J.C. and Reynolds, T.J. (1983), Understanding consumers' cognitive structures: Implications for advertising strategies. In: Percy, L. and Woodside, A. (Eds), *Advertising and Consumer Psychology*. Lexington, MA: Lexington Books.

Osgood, C.E., Suci,G.J. and Tannenbaum, P.H. (1957), *The Measurement of Meaning*. Urbana, IL: University of Illinois Press.

Oskamp, S. (1965), Overconfidence in case-study judgments. *Journal of Consulting Psychology*, **29**, 261–265.

Oxenfeldt, A.R. (1973), A decision-making structure for price decisions. *Journal of Marketing*, **37** January, 48–53.

Packard, V. (1957), *The Hidden Persuaders*. New York: McKay.

Parasuraman, A., Zeithaml, V.A. and Berry, L.L. (1985), A conceptual model of service quality and its implications for future research. *Journal of Marketing*, **49** (Fall), 41–50.

Parasuraman, A., Zeithaml, V.A. and Berry, L.L. (1988), SERVQUAL: A multiple item scale for measuring customer perceptions of service quality. *Journal of Retailing*, **14** (Spring), 12–40.

Parfitt, J.H. and Collins, B.J.K. (1968), The use of consumer panels for brand-share prediction. *Journal Marketing Research*, **5**, 131–45.

Payton, T.H. (1988), The electric car – Some problems of driver attitudes and product fit. *Journal of the Market Research Society*, **30**(1), 73–85.

PDMS (1993), Reported in *Marketing*, 22 April.

Perry, M. (1988), Conceptual overview and applications of international marketing positioning. *European Management Journal*, **6**(4), 420–4.

Peter, J.P. and Olson, J.C. (1987), *Consumer Behavior. Marketing Strategy Perspectives.* Homewood, IL: Irwin.

Petty, R.E., Cacioppo, J.T. and Schumann, D. (1983), Central and peripheral routes to advertising effectiveness: The moderating role of involvement. *Journal of Consumer Research*, **10**, 135–45.

Petty, R.E. and Cacioppo, J.T. (1986), The elaboration likelihood model of persuasion. In: Berkowitz, L. (Ed), *Advances in Experimental Social Psychology*, **19**, New York: Academic Press, 123–205.

Petty, R.E., Brock, T.C. and Ostrom, T.M. (Eds) (1981), *Cognitive Responses in Persuasion.* Hillsdale, NJ: Lawrence Erlbaum.

Piercy, N.F. (1985), The corporate environment for marketing management: An information– structure–power theory of marketing. *Marketing Planning and Intelligence.* **3**.

Piercy, N. and Morgan, N. (1993), Strategic and operational market segmentation: A managerial analysis. *Journal of Strategic Marketing*, 123–40.

Pieters, R.G.M. and Van Raaij, W.F. (1992), *Reclamewerking* [How Advertising Works]. Houten, The Netherlands: Stenfert Kroese.

Pieters, R.G.M. and Verplanken, B. (1991), Changing our mind about behavior. In: Antonides, G. Arts, W. and Van Raaij, W.F. *The Consumption of Time and the Timing of Consumption.* Amsterdam: North-Holland, 49–65.

Piper, J. (1977), Britain's ethnic markets. *Marketing*, January.

Piper, J. (1978), The teeming teenage market place, *Marketing*, February.

Polhemus, E. and Randall, H. (1994), *The Rituals of Love.* London: Picador.

Porter, M.E. (1979), How competitive forces shape strategy. *Harvard Business Review*, **57**(2), 137–45.

Pras, B. and Summers, J.(1975), A comparison of linear and nonlinear evaluation process models. *Journal of Marketing Research*, **12**, 276–81.

Pride, W.M. and Ferrell, O. C. (1987), *Marketing. Basic Concepts and Decisions.* Boston, MA: Houghton Mifflin, 5th edition.

Pringle, L.G., Wilson, R.D. and Brody, E.(1982), News: A decision-oriented model for new product analysis and precasting. *Marketing Science*, **1**, 1–29.

Punj, G. and Stewart, D.W. (1983), Cluster analysis in marketing research: Review and suggestions for application. *Journal of Marketing Research*, **20**, 134–48.

Puto, C.P. (1987), The framing of buying decisions. *Journal of Consumer Research*, **14**, 301–15.

Puto, C.P. and Wells, W.D. (1984), Informational and transformational advertising: The differential effects of time. *Advances in Consumer Research*, **11**, 638–43.

Raju, P.S. (1980), Optimum stimulation level: Its relationship to personality, demographics, and exploratory behavior. *Journal of Consumer Research*, **7**, 272–82.

Rao, V.R. (1984), Pricing research in marketing: The state of the art. *Journal of Business*, (January), S39.

Rawlins, M. (1984), Doctors and Drug Makers, *The Lancet*, 4 August, 276–8.

Ray, M.L. (1977), When does consumer information processing research actually have anything to do with consumer information processing? *Advances in Consumer Research*, **4**, 372–5.

Reed, D. (1993), Base relief. *Marketing Week*, 15 October, 20–1.

Regional Trends (annually), London: Central Office of Information.

Research Services Ltd. (1981), SAGACITY.

Reynolds, T.J. and Gutman, J. (1984), Advertising is image management. *Journal of Advertising Research*, (February/March), 27–37.

Richards, E.A. and Rachman, D. (Eds) (1978), *Market Information and Research in Fashion Management.* Chicago, IL: AMA.

Richens, M.L. (1983), Negative word-of-mouth by dissatisfied consumers: A pilot study. Journal of Marketing, **47** (Winter), 69.

Ries, A. and Trout, J. (1986), *Positioning: The Battle for your Mind*. New York: McGraw-Hill, revised 1st edition.

Ritson, M. (1995), *Marketing to Generation X: Strategies for the Measurement and Targeting of 'Advertising's Lost Generation'*, Second Annual Henry Stewart Conference on Advances in Targeting Measurement and Analysis for Marketing, 7 June, London.

Robertson, T.S. and Kassarjian, H.H. (1991), *Handbook of Consumer Behavior*. Englewood Cliffs, NJ: Prentice-Hall.

Robinson, P., Faris, C. and Wind, Y. (1967), *Industrial Buying and Creative Marketing*. Allyn and Bacon.

Roedder John, D. and Cole, C.A. (1986), Age differences in information processing: Understanding deficits in young and elderly consumers. *Journal of Consumer Research*, **13**, 297–315.

Rogers, D. (1992), A review of sales forecasting models most commonly applied to retail site evaluation. *International Journal of Retail and Distribution Management.* **20**(4), 3–11.

Rogers, E.M. (1983), *Diffusion of Innovations*. New York: The Free Press.

Rogers, T.B., Kuiper, N.A. and Kirker, W.S. (1977), Self-reference and the encoding of personal information. *Journal of Personality and Social Psychology*, **35**, 677–88.

Roselius, T. (1971), Consumer rankings of risk reduction methods. *Journal of Marketing*, **35**, 56–61.

Rosenberg, L.J. and Czepiel, J.A. (1983), A marketing approach to customer retention. *Journal of Consumer Marketing*, **2**, 45–51.

Rokeach, M. (1973), *The Nature of Human Values*. New York: The Free Press.

Rossiter, J.R. and Percy, L. (1983), Visual communication in advertising, In: Harris, R.J. (Ed), *Information Processing Research in Advertising*. Hillsdale, NJ: Lawrence Erlbaum, 83–125.

Rossiter, J.R. and Percy, L. (1987), *Advertising and Promotion Management*. New York: McGraw-Hill.

Rudd, J. and Kohout, F.J. (1983), Individual and group consumer information acquisition in brand choice situations. *Journal of Consumer Research*, **10**, 303–9.

Rudolph, H.J. (1947), *Attention and Interest Factors in Advertising*. New York: Funke Wagnalls.

Russo, J.E. (1977), The value of unit price information. *Journal of Marketing Research*, **14**, 193–201.

Samuelson, P. (1948) Consumption theory in terms of revealed preference. *Economica*, 15 November.

Saunders, J. and Saker, J. (1994), The changing consumer in the UK. *International Journal of Research in Marketing*, **11**, 477–89.

Schiffman, L.G. and Kanuk, L.L. (1987), *Consumer Behavior*. Englewood Cliffs, NJ: Prentice-Hall, 3rd edition.

Schindler, R.M. (1984), Consumer recognition of increases in odd and even prices. *Advances in Consumer Research*, **11**, 459–62.

Schoenfeld, G. (1990), Welcome to the age of 'unpositioning'. *Marketing News*, **24**(8), 16 April, 11.

Schramm, W. and Roberts, D. (Eds)(1971) *The Process and Effects of Mass Communication*. Urbana,IL: University of Illinois Press.

Scitovsky, T. (1976), *The Joyless Economy*. New York: Oxford University Press.

Scott, R. (1978), *The Female Consumer*. Associated Business Programmes.

Seger, E. (1977), How to use environmental analysis in strategy making. *Management Review*, March.

Shay, P.A. (1978), Consumer revolution is coming. *Marketing*, September.

Shaw, R. and Stone, M. (1988), *Database Marketing*. Gower Press.

Shugan, S. M. and Hauser, J.R. (1977), P.A.R.I.S.–An interactive market research information system. *Discussion paper 292*. Northwestern University: Center for Mathematical Studies in Economics and Management Science.

Shugan, S.M. (1980), The cost of thinking. *Journal of Consumer Research*, **7**, 99–111.

Simon, H.A. (1955), A behavioural model of rational choice. *Quarterly Journal of Economics*, **69**, 99–118.

Simon, H.A. (1976), From substantial to procedural rationality. In: Latsis, S.J. (Ed), *Method and Appraisal in Economics*. Cambridge, UK: Cambridge University Press, 129–48.

Simon, V. (1991), When is outbound effective? *Target Marketing*, **14**, 11, November, 65–8.

Sleight, P. (1993), *Targeting customers: How to use geodemographic and lifestyle data in your business*. NTC Publications, 75–86.

Smart, D.T. (1982), Consumer satisfaction research: A review. In: McNeal, J.D. and McDaniel, S.W. (Eds), *Consumer Behaviour: Classical and Contemporary Dimensions*. Boston, MA: Little, Brown, 286–306.

Smith, W.R. (1956), Product differentiation and market segmentation as alternative marketing strategies. *Journal of Marketing*, **21**, July, 3–8.

Snyder, M. and DeBono, K.G. (1985), Appeals to image and claims about quality: Understanding the psychology of advertising. *Journal of Personality and Social Psychology*, **49**, 586–97.

Social Trends (annually), London: Central Office of Information.

Solgaard, H.S. and Nilsson, O.S. (1995), The changing consumer in Denmark. *International Journal of Research in Marketing*, **12**.

Solomon, M.R. (1983), The role of products as social stimuli: A symbolic interactionism perspective. *Journal of Consumer Research*, **10**, 319–29.

Stanton, W.J. (1984), *Fundamentals of Marketing*. New York: McGraw-Hill.

Sternthal, B., Dholakia, R. and Leavitt, C. (1978), The persuasive effect of source credibility: Tests of cognitive response. *Journal of Consumer Research*, **5** March, 252–60.

Stout, R., Guk, R., Greenberg, M. and Dublow, J. (1977), Usage incidents as a basis for segmentation. In: Wind, Y. and Greenberg, M. (Eds), *Moving Ahead with Attitude Research*, American Marketing Association.

Sujan, H. (1986), Smarter versus harder: An exploratory attributional analysis of salespeople's motivations. *Journal of Marketing Research*, **23** February, 41–9.

Sujan, M. (1985), Consumer knowledge: Effects on evaluation strategies mediating consumer judgments. *Journal of Consumer Research*, **12**, 31–46.

Sujan, M. and Dekleva, C. (1987), Product categorization and inference making: Some implications for comparative advertising. *Journal of Consumer Research*, **14**, 372–78.

Sunday Times/MORI (1992), Portrait of the Electorate, 12 April.

Svenson, O. (1983), Decision rules and information processing in decision making. In: Sjöberg, L. Tyszka, T. and Wise, J.A. (Eds), *Human Decision Making*. Bodafors, Sweden: Doxa, 131–62.

Taylor Nelson, C. and McNulty, R. (1987), *Applied Futures*, Social Value Groups.

Thomas, H. (1992), Is the map to be redrawn? *Marketing*, 20 February.

Thomas, M. (1980), Market segmentation. *Quarterly Review of Marketing*, **6**(1) (Autumn), 25–7.

Thorpe, R.H. (1975), *The External Environment of Organisations*. Management Bibliographies, MCB University Press, Bradford.

Thurstone, L.L. (1929), Theory of attitude measurement. *Psychological Review*, **36**, 222–41.

Thurstone, L.L. and Chave, E.J. (1929), *The Measurement of Attitude*. Chicago, IL: University of Chicago Press.

Toffler, A. (1970), *Future Shock*. London: Bodley Head.

Tversky, A. (1972), Elimination by aspects: A theory of choice. *Psychological Review*, **79**, 281–99.

Tversky, A. and Kahneman, D. (1974), Judgment under uncertainty: Heuristics and biases. *Science*, **185**, 1124–31.

Twedt, D.W. (1964), How important to marketing strategy is the heavy user? *Journal of Marketing*, **28**(1), 71–2.

Unger, L. (1981), Consumer marketing trends in the 1980s when growth slows. *European Research*, April.

Van Raaij, W.F. (1977), Consumer information processing for different information structures and formats. *Advances in Consumer Research*, **4**, 176–84.

Van Raaij, W.F. (1988), Information processing and decision making. Cognitive aspects of economic behavior. In: Van Raaij, W.F., Van Veldhoven, G.M. and Wärneryd, K.-E. (Eds) (1988), *Handbook of Economic Psychology*. Dordrecht, The Netherlands: Kluwer Academic Publishers, 74–106.

Van Raaij, W.F. (1989), Affective and cognitive reactions to advertising. *International Journal of Advertising*, **8**(3), 261–73.

Van Raaij, W.F. (1993), Postmodern consumption. *Journal of Economic Psychology*, **14**, 541–63.

Van Raaij, W.F. and Antonides, G. (1994), *Consumentengedrag. Een Sociaal-Wetenschappelijke Benadering* [Consumer Behaviour. A Social-Science Approach]. Utrecht, The Netherlands: Lemma.

Van Raaij, W.F. and Eilander, G. (1983), Consumer economizing tactics for ten product categories. *Advances in Consumer Research*, **10**, 169–74.

Van Raaij, W.F. and Gianotten, H.J. (1990), Consumer confidence, expenditure, saving, and credit. *Journal of Economic Psychology*, **11**, 269–90.

Van Raaij, W.F and Schoonderbeek, W.M. (1993), Meaning structure of brand names and extensions. *European Advances in Consumer Research*, **1**, 479–84.

Van Raaij, W.F., Van Veldhoven, G.M. and Wärneryd, K.-E. (Eds) (1988), *Handbook of Economic Psychology*. Dordrecht, The Netherlands: Kluwer Academic Publishers.

Van Raaij, W.F. and Verhallen, T.M.M. (1994), Domain-specific market segmentation. *European Journal of Marketing*, **28**(10), 49–66.

Van Raaij, W.F. and Wandwossen, K. (1978), Motivation-need theories and consumer behavior, *Advances in Consumer Research*, **5**, 590–5.

Varaldo, R. and Marbach, G. (1995), The changing consumer in Italy. *International Journal of Research in Marketing*, **12**.

Verhallen, T.M.M. and R.G.M. Pieters (1984), Attitude theory and behavioral costs. *Journal of Economic Psychology*, **5**, 223–49.

Verhallen, T.M.M. and Van Raaij, W.F. (1986), How consumers trade-off behavioural costs and benefits. *European Journal of Marketing*, **20**(3/4), 19–34.

Vollering, J.B. (1984), Interaction based market segmentation. *Industrial Marketing Management*. **13**, 65–70.

Wahba, M.A. and L.G. Bridwell (1976), Maslow reconsidered: A review of research on the need hierarchy thoery. *Organizational Behaviour and Human Performance*, **15**, 212–40.

Wasson, C.R. (1978), *Dynamic Competitive Strategy and Product Life Cycles*. Austin, TX: Austin Press.

Webber, R. (1992), Making sense of the Census. *Marketing*, 3 September.

Webster, F.E., Jr (1992). The changing role of marketing in the corporation. *Journal of Marketing*, **56**, October, 1–17.

Weitz, B.W. (1978), Relationship between salesperson performance and understanding customer decision making. *Journal of Marketing Research*, **15**, November, 502.

Weitz, B.W. (1981), Effectiveness in sales interactions: A contingency framework. *Journal of Marketing*, (Winter), 85–103.

Weitz, J. (1982), Getting our lines crossed. *Market Research Society Newsletter*, (197), 3.

Wells, W.D. and Gubar, G. (1966), The lifecycle concept in marketing research. *Journal of Marketing Research*, November, 335–65.

Wheatley, J.J., Chiu, J.S.Y. and Goldman, A. (1981), Physical quality, price and perceptions of product quality: Implications for retailers. *Journal of Retailing*, **2** (Summer), 100–116.

White, G. (1982), Telephone research without tears. *Market Research Society*.

Whitehead, J. (1992), The case for a simple, standard postcode sector classification. *Journal of Targeting, Measurement and Analysis for Marketing*, **1**(1).

Wilson, R.M.S., Gilligan, C. and Person, D.J. (1992), *Strategic Marketing Management. Planning, Implementation and Control*. Oxford: Butterworth-Heinemann.

Wind, Y. (1977), Brand loyalty and vulnerability. In: Woodside, A.G., Sheth, J.N. and Bennett, P.D.(Eds), *Consumer and Industrial Buying Behaviour*. New York: North Holland.

Wind, Y. (1978), Issues and advances in segmentation research. *Journal of Marketing*. **42**(3), 317–37.

Wind, Y. (1980), Going to market: New twists for some old tricks. *Wharton Magazine*, **4**(3).

Wind, Y. and Cardozo, R. (1984), Industrial market segmentation. In: Kotler, P. and Cox, K. (Eds), *Marketing Management and Strategy. A Reader*. Englewood Cliffs, NJ: Prentice-Hall, 3rd edition.

Wind, Y. and Robertson, T.S. (1983), Marketing strategy: New direction for theory and research. *Journal of Marketing*, **47**(2), 12–25.

Winter, F.W. (1979), A cost-benefit approach to market segmentation. *Journal of Marketing*, **43**(4), 103–11.

Winter, F.W. and Thomas, H. (1985), An extension of market segmentation: Strategic segmentation. In: Thomas, H. and Gardner, D. (Eds), *Strategic Marketing and Management*. Chichester, England: John Wiley, 256.

Wittink, D.R. and Leeflang, P.S.H. (1995), Marketing in ontwikkeling [Marketing in development]. *Maandblad voor Accountancy en Bedrijfseconomie*, **69**, 387–99.

Women in Media (1981), *Women in Advertising*. London: WIM Video.

Woodside, A.G. and Sims, J.T. (1976), Retail sales transactions and customer 'Purchase pal' effects on buying behaviour. *Journal of Retailing*, **52** (Fall), 57–64.

Woodside, A.G. and Davenport, J.W. Jr. (1976), Effects of price and salesman expertise on customer purchasing behaviour. *Journal of Business*, **49** January, 51–9.

Wright, P. (1974), The harassed decision maker: Time pressures, distractions, and the use of evidence, *Journal of Applied Psychology*, **59**, 555–61.

Wright, P. (1975), Consumer choice strategies: Simplifying vs optimizing. *Journal of Marketing Research*, **12**, 60–7.

Wright, P. (1980), Message-evoked thoughts: Persuasion research using thought verbalizations. *Journal of Consumer Research*, **7**, 151–75.

Wright, P. and Weitz, B. (1977), Time horizon effects on product evaluation strategies. *Journal of Marketing Research*, **14**, 429–43.

Yalch, R.F. and Elmore-Yalch, R. (1984), The effect of numbers on the route to persuasion. *Journal of Consumer Research*, **11**, 522–7.

Young, S., Ott, L. and Feigin, B. (1978), Some practical considerations in market segmentation. *Journal of Marketing Research*, **15** (August), 405.

Zajonc, R.B. (1984), On the primacy of affect. *American Psychologist*, **39**, 117–23.

Zaltman, G. and Burger, P.C. (1975), *Marketing research*. Illinois: Dryden Press.

Zeigarnik, B. (1927), Über das Behalten von erledigten und unerledigten Handlungen [About the persistence of completed and incompleted behaviours]. *Psychologische Forschungen*, **9**, 1–85.

Zeithaml, V.A. (1982), Consumer response to in-store price information environments. *Journal of Consumer Research*, **9**, 357–68.

Zeithaml, V.A. (1984), Issues in conceptualizing and measuring consumer response to price. *Advances in Consumer Research*, **11**, 612–16.

Zeithaml, V.A., Parasuraman, A. and Berry, L.L. (1990), *Delivering Quality Service. Balancing Customer Perceptions and Expectations*. New York: The Free Press.

Zoltners, A.A. and Dodson, J.A. (1983), A market selection model for multiple end-use products. *Journal of Marketing*, **47**(2), 76–88.

Index